The
Process of
Language Understanding

The Process of Language Understanding

Edited by

G. B. FLORES D'ARCAIS

University of Leiden
and
Max Planck Institut für Psycholinguistik
Nijmegen

and

R. J. JARVELLA

Max Planck Institut für Psycholinguistik
Nijmegen
and
Netherlands Institute of
Advanced Studies
Wassenaar

JOHN WILEY & SONS

Chichester · New York · Brisbane · Toronto · Singapore

Library of Congress Cataloging in Publication Data:

Main entry under title:

The Process of language understanding.

   Includes indexes.
   1. Psycholinguistics.   2. Comprehension.   I. Flores
D'Arcais, Giovanni B.   II. Jarvella, R. J.
P37.P73   1983   401'.9   82-23754
ISBN 0 471 90129 6

British Library Cataloguing in Publication Data:

The Process of language understanding.
   1. Psycholinguistics   2. Comprehension
   3. Thought and thinking
   I. Flores d'Arcais, G. B.   II. Jarvella, R. J.
   401'.9   BF455

   ISBN 0 471 90129 6

Typeset by Preface Ltd, Salisbury, Wilts
Printed by Page Bros. (Norwich) Ltd.

List of Contributors

Manfred Bierwisch

Akademie der Wissenschaften, der D.D.R., Berlin, D.D.R.

Lisa Bohn

Kent State University, Kent, Ohio, USA

Herbert H. Clark

Stanford University, USA

Anne Cutler

M.R.C. Applied Psychology Unit, Cambridge, UK

Joseph H. Danks

Kent State University, Kent, Ohio, USA

Johannes Engelkamp

Universität des Saarlandes, Saarbrücken, German Federal Republic

Ramona Fears

Kent State University, Kent, Ohio, USA

Giovanni B. Flores d'Arcais

University of Leiden, Netherlands, and Max Planck Institut für Psycholinguistics, Nijmegen

Donald J. Foss

University of Texas at Austin, USA

Simon Garrod

University of Glasgow, UK

Robert J. Jarvella

*Max Planck Institut für Psycholinguistics, Nijmegen, and N.I.A.S., Wassenaar, Netherlands
(now at the University of Umeå, Sweden)*

Guust Meijers

University of Tilburg, Netherlands

James R. Ross   *University of Texas at Austin, USA*

Anthony Sanford   *University of Glasgow, UK*

Robert Schreuder   *University of Leiden, Netherlands*

Contents

List of Contributors   v
Preface   ix
Introduction   xi

1   The Process of Language Understanding: A Few Issues in
    Contemporary Psycholinguistics   1
    G. B. Flores d'Arcais and R. Schreuder

2   Lexical Complexity and Sentence Processing   43
    A. Cutler

3   Recognizing Morphemes in Spoken Words: Some Evidence for a
    Stem-organized Mental Lexicon   81
    R. J. Jarvella and G. Meijers

4   How On-line is Language Processing?   113
    M. Bierwisch

5   Great Expectations: Context Effects During Sentence Processing   169
    D. J. Foss and J. R. Ross

6   Comprehension Processes in Oral Reading   193
    J. H. Danks, L. Bohn, and R. Fears

7   Pragmatic Influences in Producing and Perceiving Language: A
    Critical and Historical Perspective   225
    R. J. Jarvella and J. Engelkamp

8   Topic Dependent Effects in Language Processing   271
    S. Garrod and A. Sanford

9   Making Sense of Nonce Sense   297
    H. H. Clark

Subject Index   333

Preface

Determining how language is ordinarily produced and understood may be considered basic to explaining much about how people communicate with one another. The present volume appears at a time when it seems sensible to take some account of the successes of recent approaches to the study of language processes, and identify further problems for research. The nine original contributions making up this book cover a range of psycholinguistic topics and phenomena related specifically to the question of how normal language understanding occurs. Based partly on symposium papers delivered at the most recent international congress of psychology, and consisting in about equal part of invited further contributions, the book takes a frank and often quite critical stand on both issues and evidence. Taken as a whole, the collection serves to bind current lines of development in psycholinguistics with theoretical ideas emerging from work done at the end of the 1970s. The book thus should provide a useful point of departure for viewing the kinds of problems which will be faced in the decade now begun.

Wassenaar 1982

G. B. Flores d'Arcais

R. J. Jarvella

Introduction

Psychology and linguistics have come to be rather interesting scientific bedfellows. Although writers have entertained thoughts about language and the mind since antiquity, only in about the last century have such issues been raised largely in an interdisciplinary context. Before disposing of a recognized field of study, psychologists of language tended to be formally associated with faculties of philosophy, medicine, or history. When psychology in general achieved some standing as an independent discipline, one of the first treatises written by a psychologist about language was Wilhelm Wundt's *Die Sprache* (1900). For his linguistic ideas, Wundt clearly had let himself be inspired by work emanating from the Leipzig School, or the so-called German *Junggrammatiker*. To a significant extent, *Die Sprache* amounts to a compendium on, and psychological interpretation of, theories and evidence which Wundt's contemporaries and colleagues in and about Leipzig had assembled and put forward.

In the late 1950s and early 1960s in Cambridge, Massachusetts, history came relatively close to repeating itself. George Miller, himself already recognized as a new pioneer in the study of language and communication, seized the opportunity provided by the revolutionary approach being taken by Noam Chomsky in linguistics to bring about the modern birth of psycholinguistics. In doing so, he helped bring an end to the epoch of radical behaviorism which had dominated much of psychology after Wundt. Since Miller's initiative, cognitive psychologists have become aware of the nature of human language as perhaps never before. But that is not to say that either linguistics in general, or psycholinguistics in particular, has had an especially easy time the last 20 years. In fact, it might be argued that at least language psychologists have too often been tempted to propose elegant solutions to problems at the cost not only of realistic description, but also their own metatheoretical goals. In some sense, the kind of linguistics which has contributed most to this development, namely various versions of transformational generative grammar, may have been too abstract and removed from ordinary language use to expect something different (see Flores d'Arcais and Schreuder, Chapter 1).

In the last few years, however, the formula for doing work in psycholinguistics seems to have changed somewhat. Probably for the better, the underlying processes of most interest seem on the way to becoming ones which are more easily subject to empirical investigation. On the one hand, linguistics together with the philosophy of language seems to be moving in a direction more useful to describing linguistic communication and language use as they are. In such work, there is increasing recognition of these as being dynamic processes embedded in transitory human activities, and they are less often regarded as timeless and largely impersonal idealizations. On the other hand, spurred on by relevant research from other neighbouring disciplines, psychologists primarily interested in language seem in a more favourable position to strike out on their own, and free themselves from linguistic metaphors which have already served their purpose. In general, the study of language seems increasingly directed to the description of the intentions, actions, processes, and consequences of ordinary linguistic exchange. In psycholinguistics, this trend may be expected to lead to more observations being gathered, and experiments held, outside the traditional bastion of the laboratory.

Books which bring together chapters written by a number of different authors run the risk of appearing like special issues of trade journals, as simple collections of papers devoted to some major topic within a field of research. The present volume is not immune to this danger. On the other hand, the contributors have been requested to deliver something more substantial than a journal paper, and provide both a broader theoretical perspective and the presentation of a topic more detailed than might be given within that limited format. Moreover, as editors we have tried to address representatives of different 'schools' or orientations, with the aim of being able to offer a more reliable general picture of developments in language understanding research at the start of the 1980s. No book, of course, can present every theoretical idea or topic for investigation which characterizes a period, and this one is no exception. But the topics that are covered and the views presented in this volume do provide insight into a respectable cross-section of recent work taking place.

As the title suggests, the collection as a whole is intended to contribute to our understanding of what happens during language comprehension, as speech or writing is perceived and interpreted. This focus reflects an orientation common to much current research in the field, placing emphasis on the cognitive processes which underlie comprehension above the representation of linguistic input alone.

PSYCHOLINGUISTICS AT THE END OF THE 1970s

By mentioning some features which are characteristic of recent psycholinguistic work, the book can be better placed in context. The special features standing behind and helping identify this period are outlined in the opening chapter. That paper, by Flores d'Arcais and Schreuder, should serve as a further and more extended introduction. On the other hand, it may be useful here, especially for the less specialized reader, to point to a few recent developments as they are reflected in the choice of material for this volume.

One aspect of language which until recently has been all but ignored by psychologists is morphology, or the internal structure of words. There are probably several reasons for this neglect. One is undoubtedly the dominant role which syntax and sentence structure has occupied in linguistics itself. This interest has spilled over, making syntax a chief protagonist of psycholinguistic research for nearly a quarter of a century. But factors such as clearly renewed interest in the word as a psychological as well as linguistic 'unit', and in languages with richer inflectional processes than English, are now serving to promote the development of studies on word structure. The second and third chapters of this book give, and are, examples representing this trend, and provide a valid basis for entering into this area. These two papers, but especially that of Anne Cutler, also reflect developments in research on lexical access, an important focus of recent research.

A second subject treated here, and one which has fuelled much debate in the last few years, is the question of the immediacy and continuity of mental computations made during language comprehension, stimulated by work which emphasizes moment-to-moment considerations in speech perception. In contrast to earlier models of language understanding which emphasized perceptual decisions at the level of constituents or full clauses without great concern for 'microprocessing' during the identification of linguistic input, today theories of 'on-line' processing entertain the notion of continuity of perception as information becomes jointly available from speech and from higher-level knowledge sources. To what extent such a point-by-point type of analysis will actually serve to elucidate the processes underlying language comprehension is still unknown, but, at least methodologically, it seems to represent an additional step forward. Theoretically, the issue is dealt with here in a series of strong formal arguments by Manfred Bierwisch, whose chapter seems likely to become a basic reference point for future theorizing on sentence comprehension.

A further feature characterizing contemporary approaches to language understanding—and, more generally, models in cognitive psychology as a whole—is their concern with mutual influences between hypothesized processing components. In psycholinguistics, interaction in this sense is now often taken to occur between processing of 'top-down' (or conceptual) and 'bottom-up' (or stimulus) information, and also between different sublevels of computation. The contributions here by Joseph Danks, Lisa Bohn, and Ramona Fears, and by Donald Foss and James Ross, highlight this kind of general approach.

Another recent area of rapid growth, but one which has until now developed largely apart from other psycholinguistic studies, is research in the field of discourse representation. We have not included a specific treatment within this increasingly important domain, but the present chapter by Simon Garrod and Anthony Sanford is more than tangentially related to it, as well as representing a contribution to the study of comprehension processes beyond the sentence.

Following the earlier absence of much attention to the role of pragmatic factors in language use, in recent psycholinguistics, work in pragmatics has become increasingly central in models of both language production and understanding. In this book two contributions, by Herbert Clark and by Robert Jarvella and Johannes Engelkamp, exemplify these types of consideration.

THE SPECIFIC CONTRIBUTIONS

When first being planned, this volume was intended to serve as a kind of 'state of the art' description of research on language understanding at the beginning of the 1980s. The purpose it ultimately fulfils may be something in addition to this. In today's world of psycholinguistics, it would be too encouraging to proclaim that while much remains to be learned, what currently can be said about psychology and language has the properties of a well-rounded and coherent whole. For that, things are moving too fast; research which just a few years ago was regarded as ground-breaking may, in fact, have signalled only the beginning of more wide-ranging revision. In this context, the most useful function the present volume might serve may be to stress problems above solutions, and suggest what remains to be done rather than simply summarizing what has been. To the extent that the questions asked, but not yet fully answered here, are the right questions, or closer to being right, the book may help serve as a stimulus for further research and theory.

The contents are roughly divisible into three parts. Further background to the main issues raised, and other questions of contemporary interest in language understanding, is, as mentioned, provided in the first chapter. There, Flores d'Arcais and Schreuder largely set the stage for what follows. Chapters 2 and 3 are then both concerned with access and representation in the internal lexicon. These two papers, by Cutler and by Jarvella and Meijers, take contrasting though not mutually exclusive positions on the issue of linguistic complexity and word processing. Reviewing evidence from a variety of new and recent studies, Cutler arrives at the conclusion that lexical complexity in any major linguistic sense, unlike for example word frequency, has no direct effects on the time needed to retrieve mental representation of words. Cutler thus suggests that all meanings, forms, or syntactic features of a word become available for use in parallel. The work reported by Jarvella and Meijers, secondly, concerns morphological factors in the recognition and comparison of spoken word forms. Their research clearly demonstrates that both inflectional and lexical prefixes in such word tokens retard decisions made about them. As these authors further propose, a model of lexical access, for spoken or written language, should probably recognize the perceptual salience of words' roots or stems; internal morphological processes, whether of a reconstructive or retrieval nature, might account for differences in the recognition of lexical form *per se*.

The middle section of the book is primarily concerned with sentence processing. A stimulus to some of the work presented here is a debate which raged especially in the late 1970s between proponents of autonomous and interactive component theories of speech and language processing. The book's fourth chapter, by Bierwisch and entitled 'How on-line is language processing?', raises the hope that a less radical and more rational perspective on the power and limits of such approaches can help generate the kind of experimental research which is still badly needed. While recognizing that human language processing may be both rather flexible and interactive, Bierwisch carefully tries to spell out what the assumptions and claims of current theory actually imply, and the conditions which would need to be met for them to be fully warranted. He then demonstrates that the determination of scope relations is one of a number of cases for which full on-line interpretation of speech is formally excluded.

Chapters 5 and 6 present experimental data relevant for the question of on-line processing during oral reading, and the nature of context effects in the processing in heard discourse of words which are semantically related to prior information perceived. Here, Danks, Bohn, and Fears first chart the temporal course of disruptions in oral reading occasioned by the presence of syntactic, semantic, and more clearly non-linguistic inconsistencies in otherwise understandable text. On the basis of their data, they argue for specific types of process interactions in lexical access and in the understanding of sentences and discourse. Secondly, Foss and Ross present a set of studies aimed at disentangling several possible explanations of semantic facilitation in language processing. The evidence which they report argues against a general local effect as well as rapid decay of facilitation in natural speech contexts, and is consistent with the effect reflecting more rapid integration of information into higher-level cognitive representations.

The final third of the book is concerned principally with discourse and conversation, and the pragmatic factors which can effect understanding in them. Chapter 7, by Jarvella and Engelkamp, begins with a discussion of utterance properties which are often interpreted as bearing on the flow of ideas in discourse and reflecting intended informativeness, such as definiteness of articles used, word order, and phonetic prominence. The present authors arrive at the conclusion that such interpretations often fail to recognize the actual function of the linguistic means used by speakers, that more and finer distinctions need to be drawn than usually have been, and that, to study their interrelation, research in specifically more distinct languages and with more regard for naturalness is called for. In Chapter 8, Garrod and Sanford then take up the role which topic-oriented knowledge may play in discourse understanding. The force of their conclusions, based on the speed of reading and integrating sentences in written text, is that the immediate inferential capacities of a language understander extend well beyond purely local constraints in discourse. From their work, making connections to a text base in the assignment of reference appears to require additional time primarily when the information domain needing access falls partly outside the general topic of discussion.

Finally, in the last contribution to the present collection, Clark points to the striking difficulty which expressions most easily interpreted in the context of speaking pose for models of language understanding which proceed by reconstructing the meaning of utterances from the meanings of their parts. As Clark succinctly points out, what a listener often appears to do is not actually to construe linguistic meaning *per se*, but rather to form a set of inferences about what a speaker wants, and thus why he says what he does.

The Process of Language Understanding
Edited by G. B. Flores d'Arcais and R. J. Jarvella
© 1983 John Wiley & Sons Ltd.

1

The Process of Language Understanding: A Few Issues in Contemporary Psycholinguistics

GIOVANNI B. FLORES D'ARCAIS and
ROBERT SCHREUDER

*University of Leiden; Max Planck Institut für Psycholinguistik, Nijmegen, and
University of Leiden, Netherlands*

INTRODUCTION

This chapter is like a prime in a lexical decision paradigm, with the following chapters of the book as its targets. Our purpose is to preactivate the reader's attention to the issues discussed there. While we have tried to summarize a certain amount of background information, we have not attempted to provide a full or even a very extensive view of psycholinguistic literature. Recent surveys (Levelt, 1978; Danks and Glucksberg, 1980) adequately serve that purpose. Instead, we have tried to point to directions in which empirical research and theoretical work has been moving. We briefly marshal evidence available for different positions, identify problems which are still controversial or unresolved, and highlight strong points and weaknesses of current models and theories.

Most work on language comprehension has been aimed at one of three levels: *word recognition*, *sentence understanding*, or *discourse interpretation*. Of these topics, the first two represent central problems in contemporary cognitive psychology. Word recognition was studied at one time mainly within a general human information processing framework. More recently it has been connected more directly with other work on the psychology of language. Sentence comprehension experiments, on the other hand, have provided the empirical core for psycholinguistic theory for many years. Discourse processing has only recently become a major focus of attention, though studies of word and sentence processing *in a discourse context* go back some ten years or

1

more. We will give central attention to the first two topics, and consequently treat the third more superficially. As to the first topic, we limit our discussion to word understanding in linguistic context, leaving aside the large literature dealing with recognition of words in isolation.

It will be our intention to emphasize the processes which take place and can be measured as language comprehension occurs rather than the states reached in understanding as estimated retrospectively. A strong interest in 'real-time' processes underlies recent research on language understanding, and differentiates it from work done prior to the mid 1970s. We will try to ask whether this shift reflects only a change in perspective and research methodology, or also in theory.

The chapter is organized as follows. We first sketch some of the characteristics of present day approaches to language processing. We examine the main psychological positions concerning autonomy of syntax, discuss the interactive approach to sentence comprehension, and consider the properties of real-time approaches to sentence processing. We then discuss the clausal hypothesis for sentence perception and discuss the notion of perceptual strategies in language comprehension. The next topics taken up are the issue of a multiple versus a single-stage computation in language understanding, lexical access during sentence comprehension, and the effects of lexical ambiguities. Finally, context effects on sentence comprehension are discussed, and the last section summarizes the main features of a few models of discourse comprehension.

Contemporary approaches to language understanding

The last twenty years roughly constitute the modern history of psycholinguistics. It is not difficult to pick out a few general ideas which characterize the research carried out during this period.

As most elementary textbooks on cognitive psychology describe, 'classic' psycholinguistic research done in the 1960s attempted to explore the *psychological reality* of linguistic constructs such as phrase structure rules and grammatical transformations. One hypothesis tested in several well known experiments was that the perceptual complexity of a sentence will be related to its derivational complexity, as described in generative grammar. This *derivational theory of complexity* (DTC) did not survive the critical theoretical assaults eventually mounted on it. On the other hand, just those authors most critical of the idea of psychological reality of linguistic rules, namely Fodor, Bever, and Garrett (1974), interpreted results from their study as favouring of the psychological reality of levels of linguistic representation (especially of *deep* and of *surface structure*). Other investigators (e.g. Bransford and Franks, 1971, and their colleagues) however, argued that the representation assigned to sentences during comprehension is *not* a linguistic structure, but the product of constructive, inferential processes in which linguistic context, non-linguistic context, general knowledge shared by speaker and listener, and the sentence itself all play a role. Gradually, more attention had also been paid to the importance of pragmatic factors on sentence understanding (see, e.g. Clark and Clark, 1977). More recent models of sentence comprehension (e.g. Marslen-Wilson and Tyler, 1980) propose that the processing of stimulus information interacts with other knowledge on a moment-by-moment basis during language understanding.

Among the more important developments in language understanding research from the beginning of the modern period of psycholinguistics to the present, one can point to the following. First, there has been a gradual and clear shift from linguistically based models to more psychologically based ones. Whereas in the 1960s psycholinguists frequently used linguistic constructs as a source of inspiration, in the 1970s models were produced which more typically incorporated general psychological principles. Occasionally these succeeded in placing constraints on linguistic theory itself. Second, related to the change in perspective from linguistics to psychology, there was a change from models characterized by well defined *algorithms*, such as the use of grammatical transformations in the construction of a structural description of a sentence, to models characterized by *heuristics* such as perceptual strategies for segmenting and interpreting the words in an incoming speech signal. Third, a number of *artificial intelligence* models of language comprehension have been introduced, with apparent evolution towards models intended to reflect psychological processes taking place during language processing, and to account for the errors a listener makes in understanding. Fourth, the general consequences on perception of background knowledge and of linguistic and non-linguistic context, and of the communicative context of language use have been increasingly recognized. Fifth, there has been a transition in methods used, from predominantly *off-line* (retrospective) data collection procedures to predominantly *on-line* (immediate automatic processing).

AUTONOMOUS PROCESSING OF SYNTAX

One long-standing issue in psycholinguistics has been whether syntactic analysis of sentences constitutes a separate and autonomous stage in their perception. This question is one of several useful in contrasting an autonomous versus an interactive view of language processing. Still often debated, it remains an open question. Whether syntactic processing is done independently of, or is continuously interrelated with, other subprocesses in understanding has never been decisively answered (see Forster, 1979; Holmes, 1979, for some further recent discussion).

During the early years of modern psycholinguistic research, syntax was a central concern. Computing the structural description of a sentence was taken to be vital and necessary to understanding it. Semantics was taken by linguistics to be *interpretative*, to be added onto, or computed using, a syntactic representation. As interest in the nature of underlying grammatical representations and their relation to meaning structures increased, there was a corresponding shift of attention in psychology. Models of sentence processing based on direct inference of meaning became popular; ultimately, semantics and pragmatics came to serve as a new source of theoretical insight, and syntax to be treated as rather marginal.

We will discuss the following three issues. First, is there a stage of perceptual processing which is autonomous and independent, and corresponds to syntax? Second, is computation at this stage obligatory for comprehension to occur? Third, if full syntactic computation occurs automatically as a sentence is processed, are the results of this computation invariably used, or do they serve as a kind of 'emergency' back-up system, to supplement, when necessary, the results of other analyses performed? The available evidence does not always permit a clear answer to one of these questions irrespective of the others, but we will still consider them each in turn. One point, however, should first be made clear. Discussion of the autonomy of syntax has become somewhat polarized around the necessity of syntactic computation in language comprehension. But this is not the central issue. There is little doubt that syntax allows for the construction of a small set of interpretations, and often a unique one, for a given sentence. As Forster points out, 'the whole point of a language having a syntax is to provide a clear and unmistakable indication of the correct interpretation of the sentence' (1979, p. 55). The question rather has to be put differently. We need to ask whether there is a stage of syntactic computation in the process of language comprehension which functions *without* the assistance of semantic and pragmatic cues. Specifically, this can be reduced to the question of whether the listener *normally* does his syntactic computations unaided by such cues.

Of the three principal questions raised about autonomy, the first has received the most attention. It can be formulated as follows: is it possible that syntactic processing is based exclusively on syntactic cues? In that case, decisions about syntactic analysis would be made without reference to the possible meaning of a sentence. Forster and Olbrei (1973) call this *autonomous* position the *constancy hypothesis*, and claim that in sentence understanding the total processing time directly attributable to syntactic computation for different sentences of the same type should remain constant despite variations in meaning. An alternative, *interactive* view would hold that semantic information or pragmatic cues play a significant role in syntactic decision-making: the analysis of sentence structure begins directly with consideration of the potential meaning of an utterance. Unlike the constancy hypothesis, such a position implies that the syntactic component of the total processing time will be affected by semantic properties.

The issue already has a respectable history. In early experiments comparing understanding of active with passive sentences (e.g. Slobin, 1966; Herriot, 1969), syntactic differences were found to be reflected in response time *only* when semantic or pragmatic constraints did not bias a single interpretation. Thus, Slobin found that passive sentences took longer to verify when they were *reversible*, such as in (1) below:

(1) The girl was hit by the boy.

In such sentences, the decisive cues available to the listener or reader to decide the participant roles are structural. With *non*-reversible sentences such as (2):

(2) The flowers were watered by the girl

on the other hand, there was no difference in verification time between the passive and the corresponding active: in (2) semantic and pragmatic considerations block a possible interpretation of the flowers doing the watering.

These early results, as well as Herriot's (1969), were replicated in an experiment by Quinn (quoted by Steedman and Johnson-Laird, 1978) using sentences with preposed indirect objects such as (3) and (4):

(3) The man took the girl the boy
(4) The man took the girl the coat.

As compared to the corresponding forms without 'dative movement' such as (5), 'reversible' sentences like (3) turned out to be more difficult.

(5) The man took the boy to the girl

Again this may be because in the absence of semantic or pragmatic cues, a syntactic analysis is needed to decide among alternative interpretations.

The clearest evidence for an autonomous stage of syntactic processing in sentence understanding is perhaps to be found in work by Forster and his associates (Forster and Ryder, 1971; Forster and Olbrei, 1973). Forster and Ryder tested subjects with sentences presumably differing in syntactic complexity and which were at the same time either normal, bizarre, or anomalous. Across semantic conditions, the different syntactic structures resulted in similar relative difficulty. Of course, such 'negative' evidence is not unambiguous, nor does it mean direct support for the independence of the computation stages. However, the results found at least suggest that syntactic processing may be carried out for a given sentence in the same way, independently of strong differences in meaningfulness. Forster and Ryder argue that semantic processing is probably delayed until a syntactic representation has been computed.

Somewhat more convincing are results by Forster and Olbrei (1973), which also indicate that the time required to analyse a particular syntactic structure may be approximately constant, and that the potential reversibility of a sentence's subject and object has little relevance for this processing. The conclusion seems simple here: there is a syntactic level of processing which is independent of semantic effects. According to Forster, then, the hypotheses a listener makes about syntactic structure are based on syntactic cues alone. Semantic processing is carried out only after the relevant syntactic analysis has been performed. Further evidence for this view comes from another experiment by Forster (1979). In rapid serial visual presentation of sentences with distorted word order, recognition was equally disrupted for meaningful and anomalous stimulus material, such as in (6) and (7);

(6) The was speech written carefully
(7) The was dream added relatively.

Apparently items of both kinds were analysed syntactically in the same way.

Holmes's (1979) experiments, which further elaborate on the work of Forster and Olbrei (1973), suggest that the situation is not so simple, however. According to Holmes, semantic processing is not delayed until a clause's deep structure becomes available. Rather, sentence processing is taken to begin with a superficial analysis in which an initial structural representation is computed. This surface representation has an effect on semantic processing, which in turn influences the assignment of a definitive structure. The process then ends with a second reading of the input and checking of hypotheses made about underlying structure. Thus, Holmes's model has three stages: a surface structure is constructed, followed by a semantic analysis, and finally by a checking of the output of the previous two stages. This kind of *mixed* model brings us closer to an interactive theory, in which syntactic and semantic processing are taken to influence each other mutually as the meaning of a sentence being perceived is reconstructed.

There are many pieces of evidence against the 'pure' autonomous viewpoint, such as studies by Greene (1970) and Engelkamp (1976), to quote almost at random. Work from our own laboratory with Dutch sentences varying in semantic integration and pragmatic plausibility (Flores d'Arcais, 1978b, 1982; v.d. Steen, unpublished) has shown that sentence comprehension is less affected by differences between syntactic constructions than by semantic complexity and pragmatic plausibility.

An interactive perspective of language processing is already implicit in the work of Slobin (1966) and Herriot (1969). Put forward in its most explicit and general form by Marslen-Wilson and Tyler (Marslen-Wilson, 1973, 1975, 1976; Marslen-Wilson and Tyler, 1980), it assumes a flexible processing system in which different levels—phonological, syntactic, semantic and pragmatic—actively communicate with one another; the results developed using any knowledge source are made available to affect the operations using any other available source (Marslen-Wilson and Tyler, 1980). The evidence obtained by Marslen-Wilson and Tyler comes from experiments using a variety of on-line techniques, ranging from sentence shadowing to target monitoring with several types of targets. This approach will be discussed in the next section.

Forster (1979), while acknowledging that the evidence for the fully autonomous view is limited, and for semantic and pragmatic effects in sentence processing rather abundant, still argues that autonomy of syntax remains plausible, since, though linguistic, the site of operation of other factors might fall outside (and beyond) the syntactic processor *per se*. According to Forster, such factors affect *message processing*, *not syntactic processing*. This position seems to us equivalent to discarding the autonomous point of view in its 'strong' form.

It is questionable whether a strong autonomous position is viable at all. Even in Forster and Olbrei's (1973) model, syntactic computation is preceded by a stage of word identification, which presumably includes extraction of the meaning of words, and it is difficult to envisage a post-lexical mechanism or procedure capable of completely neutralizing this semantic information.

Let us now consider our second question, namely whether syntactic computation is 'obligatory' or 'optional'. Forster (1974) and Garrett (1976) argue that the syntactic structure of a sentence is computed even when the listener would be able to grasp the meaning of the sentence without it. That syntactic computation is *not* a required stage in sentence processing, on the other hand, is a characteristic of approaches such as Bever's (1970) and, more recently, of work in artificial intelligence (AI) (e.g. Riesbeck and Schank, 1978). Bever argues that the listener will use deep syntactic analysis only when sufficient semantic cues are not available; whenever possible, he will extract sentence meaning on the basis of relations directly available from lexical semantic constraints and surface structure. Within the model of sentence understanding proposed by Riesbeck and Schank (1978), semantic and conceptual operations precede syntactic processing, and this is more optional than obligatory. Still within AI, some language understanding models, such as Wilks's (1978) translation program, manage *without* any syntax at all: the input is translated directly into meaning structures, often quite successfully.

Empirical evidence relevant to this question is scarce and difficult to obtain. The fact that language may sometimes be understood without syntactic analysis is insufficient grounds for maintaining that computation of this kind is an 'optional' phase in sentence processing. However, a partial answer to the question might be given by experiments showing that syntactic computation takes place automatically even when it is not instrumental in comprehension. The evidence on this point is itself quite meager. By way of example, we will cite some work done in our own laboratory (Flores d'Arcais, 1982), in which the effect of syntactic violations on sentence processing was compared with the effect of semantic and pragmatic violations.

In one of these experiments, subjects' eye fixations were recorded as they read sentences which could contain a syntactic, a semantic, or a spelling error. The primary task requirements were to comprehend the sentences and report the errors noticed. The eye fixation measurements showed that readers looked longer and more frequently at syntactic errors even in cases in which they did not report noticing the errors. These results suggest that even when the reader may apparently not be consciously aware of syntactic violations, nor his comprehension appear disturbed, at some level he probably does process and detect these distortions, as indicated by the fact that he looks longer and more frequently at the locus of such violations in the written sentences. Thus, these results suggest a level of automatic syntactic computation taking place alongside other processing and interacting with it only for the minimum necessary to produce a meaningful interpretation of the output. It is interesting in this connection that Jarvella and Nelson (1982) recently reported that there seems to be a syntactic residue in perception, especially for sentences which listeners have failed to understand using pragmatic constraints. Results of the two kinds mentioned do not of course imply that syntactic information is processed only at a *shallow* level: local and non-local syntactic cues are likely to be used continuously in constructing a representation of an incoming signal. Depending on the demands of the linguistic task, both in the outside world and in the laboratory (e.g. when confronted with easy or difficult sentences, pragmatically plausible vs. unexpected information, etc.), the processor may depend in greater or lesser degree on information from the results of automatic syntactic computations.

Our third question was whether the output of syntactic computations is always used, or used only when stronger evidence is not available, as a kind of fall-back system. Direct evidence on this point is also difficult to obtain. Data on the development of understanding for complex sentences (Flores d'Arcais, 1978b) show that children may not make much use of syntactic information if sentences are semantically well integrated and pragmatically plausible, but do so with semantically and pragmatically odd material.

In two other experiments (reported in Flores d'Arcais, 1982) subjects were presented with sentences and requested, in an incidental task, to detect syntactic anomalies. The primary task was to answer questions about sentence content. The main result was that comprehension in the face of syntactic violations seemed to occur relatively undisturbed, whereas semantic and pragmatic anomalies were clearly more disruptive. This suggests that the most relevant cues for constructing a representation of the meaning of a sentence may be semantic and pragmatic, when analysis on these levels leaves room for uncertainty, syntactic cues take on increasing importance. As a whole, this study indicates that while syntactic processing may be carried out automatically, the results of these computations are not necessarily used. The amount and the depth of such use is likely to be related to the difficulty of the linguistic task. When faced with a pragmatically plausible and syntactically canonical sentence, a listener often will be able to extract a correct interpretation by using cues such as word order and semantic plausibility. However, when faced with more complex structures or content diverging from pragmatic expectations, the listener has to rely on several sources of information, and in this case syntactic cues become essential in uniquely specifying the correct interpretation. Syntactic information is therefore always available as a result of an automatic computation, but is used more or less depending on the presence or absence of other evidence which might be of easier access, or as a control on the output of other computations which have taken place simultaneously.

LANGUAGE COMPREHENSION AS AN INTERACTIVE PROCESS

The autonomy of syntax position is one aspect of a more general view in which language comprehension is seen as consisting of a series of autonomous processing stages each of which is entirely or largely unaffected by the processes taking place at other levels. An alternative position and more interactive view has widely gained ground in psycholinguistic theories of the past decade. That conceptual knowledge and stimulus information interact to produce a meaningful representation of a message heard or read, is a rather general assumption underlying most models of understanding. To state that the perception of language implies such knowledge is almost trivial, as it is to claim that context affects word recognition or sentence perception.

Almost all theories of language processing recognize a contribution of both *top-down* and *bottom-up* information to perception: the difference between them lies mainly in the emphasis put on the amount and the form of the contribution of one or another knowledge source, or on the form and type of the processes which underly the interaction. The problem then becomes to determine *what kind* of interaction takes place, at *what* levels and *when*.

Available models emphasize one or both of the following two types of interaction, which conceptually are important to distinguish. One is the interaction between stimulus information and conceptual information, both knowledge-based and obtained from linguistic and non-linguistic context. The other is the interaction among levels of processing and of organization, for example between aspects of syntactic and semantic processing.

Interactive models proposed within psycholinguistics share a series of properties, the most important of which are perhaps the following:

(a) Processing proceeds in parallel *at all levels*. This means that work at one level does not wait until processing has been completed at other levels.

(b) Results from one processing level are available at all other levels. This means that a central processor might rely on computation from one level for making decisions at some other level. One may think of the interaction among levels in two ways: one in which they are organized hierarchically, such that information from non-adjacent levels has to pass through intermediate levels, and another, a 'cross-talk' model in which all levels communicate with each other directly.

(c) The processor is free at any moment to use evidence available from any level to continue its work. This is a direct consequence of (a), but also means that the processor may choose to use whatever information is more useful, be it phonological, syntactic, semantic, or pragmatic.

One of the most explicit interactive theories of language understanding is that proposed by Marslen-Wilson and Tyler (Marslen-Wilson, 1975; Marslen-Wilson and Tyler, 1980). According to these authors, three sources of knowledge—lexical, syntactic, and interpretative—interact with the sensory input. Following this approach, the listener is taken to attempt to interpret any utterance word by word from its very beginning. The model has been worked out most explicitly to account for word recognition in sentence and discourse context, as a major point of convergence between stimulus information and the available knowledge. In Marslen-Wilson and Welsh (1978), human speech recognition is viewed as a mixed 'top-down' and 'bottom-up' process, in which higher-order constraints directly affect lexical interpretation once an initial phonetic analysis has been started. In this view, the top-down/bottom-up interaction itself is taken to produce the listener's conscious percept of a word.

Another problem concerns the point at which interaction begins, or, put in other terms, the amount of stimulus information which is necessary to drive the top-down mechanism. Some findings suggest that the recognition system can select, or perhaps guess, a correct entry in the lexicon soon after the beginning of a word and at a point where stimulus information alone would be insufficient to provide a unique candidate. For example, experiments in which subjects monitor sentences for word-targets specified in advance show that words in normal sentential context could be correctly identified with response latencies of 250–275 msec (Marslen-Wilson, 1975; Marslen-Wilson and Tyler, 1980). This suggests that subjects began to prepare their responses 150–200 msec after the onsets of the words in question and well before their complete acoustic form was complete. Essentially the same type of results have been obtained in speech-shadowing experiments (Marslen-Wilson, 1975; Marslen-Wilson and Tyler, 1980). These results, whatever their robustness, is support of an interactive point of view.

Evidence for top-down effects on word recognition and interaction between stimulus information and knowledge based on linguistic context is abundant in a variety of interesting and ingenious experimental studies. One of the most dramatic demonstrations on context effect in word recognition is the phenomenon of *phoneme restoration* (Warren, 1970). In a number of experiments, Warren replaced one phoneme from a word in a spoken sentence with a noise of the same intensity. Presenting the word in an appropriate context, he found that subjects (a) perceived the word 'normally', thus *restoring* the missing phoneme; and (b) were not able to accurately locate the 'coughing' sound, which was heard as background noise. Thus, contextual constraints seemed to be used by the perceiver to supply appropriate information not present in the speech signal. Words which are highly predictable in context are also recognized faster than unpredictable words. For example, Morton and Long (1976) found shorter monitoring latencies for initial phoneme targets in words which were highly predictable in context, than for targets in low conditional probability words. Listeners also are faster at detecting mispronunciations in words easily predictable from context (Cole and Jakimik, 1978): in this task, apparently, high transitional probability words are retrieved faster, and the mispronounciation which occurs in the word to be recognized is also discovered earlier.

Similarly, the subjects tested by Marslen-Wilson and Welsh (1978) were requested to shadow sentences which, unknown to them, contained a mispronounced word. Fluent restorations of the disturbed speech sound during shadowing were more frequent for highly predictable words than for words which in context were unpredictable.

Top-down effects seem particularly evident when stimulus information is incomplete or ambiguous. A useful demonstration of differential effects of context according to stimulus quality has been given by Garnes and Bond (1976). These authors used sets of words whose initial phoneme was either unambiguous or at the phonetic boundary between two English phonemes. For example, for the word *bait*, *date* or *gate* the initial speech sound was either a clear instance of the phoneme [b], [d] or [g] or a sound at the boundary between [b] and [d] or [d] and [g]. The words of interest were presented at the end of a neutral or a 'biasing' sentence. The results were quite clear: when the stimulus information was unambiguous, the sentence context did not affect identification of the critical word: subjects would perceive and accept sentences such as 'Check the time and the bait'. However, for acoustically less well defined words, the context biased word identification, and the same acoustic token was reported as *date* in 'Check the time and the date', but as *gate* in 'Paint the fence and the gate'.

The results above, as well as many others, support a point of view according to which contextual information interacts with stimulus information in the development of linguistic percepts. In the process of recognizing a word, there is probably some trade-off between stimulus information and context: when the input signal is undistorted and unambiguous, contextual effects may be of limited importance, but when the signal is impoverished or indeterminate, context exercises a much stronger influence.

PROCESSING DURING LANGUAGE UNDERSTANDING

As we have pointed out, a defining characteristic of recent psycholinguistic research on language comprehension is its reliance upon on-line experimental techniques. In contrast, the best known and most widely cited studies from the 1960s were off-line experiments, involving retrospective tasks executed *after* test sentences were read or heard. Typical examples are memory experiments by Savin and Perchonok (1965) and Mehler (1963), and the early 'click' studies (Fodor and Bever, 1965; Garrett, Bever, and Fodor, 1966).

Theories from this period were intended to explain the process of sentence *comprehension* as well as the nature of memory for language. The idea that comprehending sentences implies recovering their deep structure through a process of 'undoing' the transformations in its derivation, for example, received its main support from studies of memory. Similarly, the insight that language comprehension occurs via reconstruction of constituent structures was also derived from responses given after whole sentences had been processed. And, in general, hypotheses about processes during language understanding were tested off-line. Of course, theoretical proposals based on such distant indices of processing need not be wrong. But to the extent that the results obtained do not directly reflect immediate perceptual processes, relating them to understanding required making a sizable inferential step.

Research done during the last decade has been increasingly characterized by response elicitation techniques applied *during* the presentation of verbal material. A few such are mentioned briefly below.

A typical on-line task calls for experimental subjects to monitor spoken sentences for targets. These might be linguistic (phonemes, words, mispronunciations, etc.) or non linguistic, for example an extraneous noise superimposed on the acoustic signal. In the well known 'click' studies (for reviews see Fodor, Bever and Garrett, 1974; Levelt, 1978), a brief noise was superimposed at different points in sentences, for example at or near a main constituent boundary. In the first such experiments, the subjects wrote down the sentences heard and marked the position where they believed that the clicks heard had occurred. This procedure clearly involved sentence recall, and several investigators criticized it, arguing that the results could to a large extent be explained by response bias (see Ladefoged, 1967; Reber, 1973; Levelt, 1978). In more recent studies this task usually has been modified, for example by having the subject press a button as soon as he hears the click. In this way the technique became a direct, on-line type of procedure. Perhaps the most widely used on-line method in the 1970s was the phoneme monitoring task first developed by Foss and his associates (Foss, 1969, 1970;

Foss and Jenkins, 1973; etc.). Detecting target phonemes in sentences has been shown to be sensitive to a number of linguistic variables. For example, listeners usually take relatively longer to respond to a phoneme target beginning a word following an ambiguity.

The logic underlying the use of all such tasks is rather straightforward. A basic assumption is that the language processor has only a limited capacity. The amount of processing capacity or attention available at any given moment being constant, it becomes divided between analysis of the stimulus material and the target. When the primary stimulus material requires relatively much attention, less capacity or attention is available for the task of detecting the target. Given a specific target, then, the more complex is the task of language processing, the more difficult it should be to react to this additional signal. For example, if a listener is engaged in understanding a difficult sentence, he should be less apt to quickly and/or correctly detect clicks or target phoneme. This should be reflected in a larger number of errors, longer latencies and the like in such a task.

Such targets might also be made more subtle. In one experiment in our laboratory (Flores d'Arcais, 1978a) we used as a target shift in *localization* of a binaural speech signal. Subjects were presented with sentences with a difference in intensity of a few decibels between the two ears. With such presentation, listeners subjectively localized the sound as being heard within their head, slightly to the left or to the right of the mid-sagittal plane. The relative intensities presented to the two ears were shifted at some point, and the task of the subject (who was listening for understanding) was to react as soon as he noticed the shift.

Another on-line task recently being exploited is speech shadowing (Marslen-Wilson, 1973, 1975, 1976). Some of Marslen-Wilson's trained 'close shadowers' were able to repeat back phonetic input at delays of the order of 300 msec, so that they could start saying words in sentences of which they had heard only a small segment. An interesting consequence of this behaviour in shadowing tests was the occurrence of 'error repairs': a shadower sometimes substituted a semantically or pragmatically appropriate word for one intentionally mispronounced or distorted when the speech was recorded. This phenomenon is highly interesting for several reasons. In the first place it suggests that speech perception is sensitive to contextual effects very early in word recognition. Second, the phenomenon is evidence for the interactive view of word recognition: the distorted words began correctly, and were also contextually appropriate. Third, the fact that shadowers are capable of monitoring at very short delays, and seem able to effectively use phonetic and contextual constraints at the same time suggests that listeners normally may wait no longer than necessary before taking perceptual decisions, and that they construct an interpretation as soon as they can.

THE CLAUSAL HYPOTHESIS

In the process of internally representing a spoken utterance, a listener needs to make perceptual decisions as to whether, for example, a sequence of connected acoustic events constitutes a token of a certain linguistic category (e.g., Did the speaker intend to say *night rate* or *nitrate*?) Connected speech consists of a complex and nearly continuous flow of acoustic energy, which a listener needs to recode mentally. From the sequence of physical information, he will construct linguistic structures. It is important to know what these structures are, how they are organized and what is the eventual result of the organization process.

Two questions are relevant here: (a) At what points in the speech sound are internal divisions made and what are the perceptual units which result from this segmentation? (b) Are these units also the ones relevant for higher-level processing, or is further recoding and segmentation required?

Perceptual units have been sought at different levels, ranging from sounds and syllables, to words and constituents, to full clauses. In this section we will mainly discuss evidence- on the clause being a significant coding unit in perceiving language, and point to some recent qualifications of this hypothesis.

Until recently, psycholinguists had assumed that segmentation at some level takes place, and that the material between perceptual boundaries is treated psychologically as a coherent structure; once divisions have occurred to define such units, the information obtained would be recoded for processing at a higher level. The perceptual elements proposed as processing units have mostly been defined in purely structural terms; typically, as constituents or clauses, on a surface or deep structure level. To summarily review this approach, early evidence that the constituent is a relevant unit of processing came from the work of, among others, Johnson (1968), who showed how transitional error probabilities in short-term recall of sentences were relatively high at the boundaries between sentences' main constituents, and Garrett, Bever, and Fodor (1966), who showed that brief noises heard in sentences tend to be perceptually localized into such boundaries. As more evidence using variations of the latter technique was acquired, arguments were raised about whether the perceptual units obtained correspond to deep 'sentoids' (Bever, Lackner, and Kirk, 1969; see also Fodor, Bever, and Garrett, 1974) or surface structures (e.g. Chapin, Smith, and Abrahamson, 1972).

Further evidence for perceptual segmentation at the level of clauses comes from a variety of experiments using different methods, including reaction time to clicks heard in sentences. These experiments are obviously less vulnerable to the main criticism raised against the first click studies, namely that displacement may not be a perceptual effect, but a result of memory or response bias. Clicks imposed on or near major clause boundaries appear to be more perceptually salient than clicks within major constituents (Holmes and Forster, 1970). Clicks located towards the end of clauses tend to elicit longer reaction times than clicks located at their beginning (Abrams and Bever, 1969). Processing load seems therefore to increase towards the end of the clause, while at its beginning the language processor is more free to dedicate its efforts to the events extraneous to the sentence.

In a study by Wingfield and Klein (1971), localization of the source of the signal was used as the dependent variable in an ear switching paradigm. A sentence began monaurally at one ear and was switched to the other, with subjects required to indicate where the switching had occurred. Source localization was found to be more accurate at syntactic boundaries between clauses than elsewhere.

Other evidence that speech is segmented naturally at the level of the clause comes from studies using 'probe' techniques such as Suci, Ammon, and Gamlin (1967) and experiments on immediate recall of discourse (Jarvella, 1970, 1971). The latter show that verbatim recall is highest for words within the last clause presented before the signal is interrupted, and much lower for all segments presented before the last clause. Such results suggest that each sentence in discourse is processed and organized clause by clause. In another probe paradigm, Caplan (1972) presented subjects with sentences made up of two clauses and asked them to decide as quickly as possible whether a target word presented afterwards had occurred in the sentence. Reaction time to probe words heard in the last clause was shorter than from the first clause, even when the two words were identical and equidistant from the sentence end. For example, the probe word in sentences (8a) and (8b) was in both cases *oil*:

    (8a) Now that artists are working in *oil*, prints are rare.
    (8b) Now that artists are working fewer hours, *oil* prints are rare.

In (8b), reaction time was shorter than in (8a) for this word. Quite similar evidence comes from other studies (e.g. Kornfeld, 1973; Flores d'Arcais, 1978a).

The above studies speak for of a view of sentence comprehension sometimes called the 'clausal hypothesis' (Fodor, Bever and Garrett, 1974; Carroll and Bever, 1976; Marslen-Wilson, Tyler, and Seidenberg, 1978). This hypothesis is characterized by two major features. First, clauses are taken to be the primary units of normal speech perception. Incoming material is organized in immediate memory clause by clause; the listener or reader accumulates evidence until the end of a clause. Second, at the end of a clause, working memory is cleared of surface grammatical information and the content of the clause is represented in a more abstract form. Note that these two major properties are logically independent.

Let us consider some important features of this view. First, in its early form, the clausal hypothesis is still formulated in structural terms: processing units are defined by grammatical categories. Second, as Marslen-Wilson, Tyler, and Seidenberg (1978) point out, the hypothesis can be formulated in different versions, from a *strong* form according to which a clause's interpretation would be delayed until its end, to a *weak* form suggesting that some partial and preliminary hypotheses about clausal meaning might be produced quite readily but that a definitive decision would be taken only once it is fully perceived. Third, the view of clausal processing, even in its weakest form, implies some discontinuity in the construction of sentence interpretations. This notion may prove intractable in light of evidence of uninterrupted semantic processing from on-line research in sentence perception. Fourth, the hypothesis implies that incoming speech is organized and processed clause by clause without making allowance for possible effects of clause internal structure, verb type, number and form agreement, and so on. There are obvious differences between a clause of the length of the present one and a short imperative like 'Get out'. Finally, the clausal hypothesis assumes that working memory is cleared as each clause is completed, without specifying whether this release is independent of the type of relation of the clause to the rest of the sentence.

Evidence and arguments bearing on these characteristics arise from a variety of sources, and suggest rather substantial modification of the clausal hypothesis suggested originally. The notion of the clause as a *structural* unit in language perception has been challenged by Carroll and Tanenhaus (1975) and Carroll and Bever (1976). These authors argue that listeners, rather than constructing well formed syntactic units of the size of clauses, try to isolate complete and coherent sets of grammatical relations. For example, sequences which allow the listener to isolate an intact subject-verb-object relation may represent optimal perceptual units. Accordingly, it is not the structural clause, but the *functional* clause which is the basic unit in terms of which listeners segment speech. Complete clauses often serve as good segmentation units, but so do smaller segments. Segmentation will be affected by a variety of factors, such as grammatical completeness, surface marking, length and complexity, and a functional clause may or may not coincide with a structural one, depending on these factors. Tanenhaus and Carroll (1975) propose a hierarchy of functional clauses, ranging from simple sentences to nominalizations, and argue that more complete clauses serve as better segmentation units. Main clauses make better functional clauses than adverbial subordinate clauses, and these in turn are better than relative clauses, etc. Some experimental evidence seems to support this view. Carroll and Tanenhaus (1975) for example, found that listeners tend to mislocate brief tones superimposed on sentences towards clause boundaries more often with functionally complete clauses than with functionally incomplete clauses.

According to the clausal hypothesis, when processing within a clause is completed, the result is recoded for storage in long-term memory and working memory is cleared. Data from Jarvella (1971), Caplan (1972), and others seem to speak in favour of this hypothesis. An alternative position is that this clearing operation done at the end of a clause might not be all-or-none, and that more residual surface information from some clauses might be retained in subsequent processing than for others. This might be the case, for example, when the full interpretation of a prior clause requires understanding of a later clause, as in example (9):

(9) Although he was tired, John continued his work.

We might expect differences in processing at the end of clauses depending on their degree of 'completeness', and this view is not consistent with the clausal hypothesis in its purest form.

Some evidence pointing to this alternative has been provided by Flores d'Arcais (1978a). In this study, already mentioned, subjects were asked to detect changes in relative amplitude in a speech message presented binaurally with a small difference in intensity across the two ears. It was found that detection latencies were generally longer when the 'ear shift' took place during presentation of subordinate clauses than during main clause. However, ear shift for subordinate clauses was *relatively* faster to detect than for main clauses in sentence-final position. These results for perception are consistent with similar evidence for short term memory (Jarvella and Herman, 1972), and were interpreted as follows. When a subordinate clause precedes, in order to process a following main clause, the listener has to 'carry forward' some additional load. This does not manifest itself, however, with the reverse clause order, namely with the subordinate in second position. That is, there may be residual differences in surface representation when clauses of different kinds are heard. Main clauses may usually be processed without reference to a following subordinate but not vice versa. How much this residual is depends on the type of clause and on its relation to what follows.

Results reported by Marslen-Wilson, Tyler and Seidenberg (1978) are also consistent with this position. These authors obtained indications of differences in processing for sentences of 'high' and 'low' completeness using rhyme and category monitoring latency techniques: the subject was requested to press a button as soon as he noticed a word rhyme with a given target, or when he noticed a word belonging to a given semantic category. The results show an increase in monitoring latency across the boundary between clauses in 'high completeness' sentences, as compared to 'low completeness' items. The results of Tanenhaus and Carroll (1975) and Carroll and Bever (1976) manifest the same trend.

Given this evidence, the clausal hypothesis might be modified by assuming that after a clause's structure is completed, its continued presence in working memory depends on what type of clause it is; when no surface information is needed for further processing, it may be cleared from the short-term store. Thus only as much information as is necessary may be retained in working memory for further processing. On this view, the initial clause's interpretation should provide the processor with the information necessary for deciding to what extent the memory store can be released of surface information.

Finally, let us consider the apparent inconsistency of the clausal hypothesis with on-line measures of processing obtained by Marslen-Wilson and Tyler (e.g. Marslen-Wilson, 1973; Marslen-Wilson and Tyler, 1980; Marslen-Wilson, Tyler, and Seidenberg, 1978). In the last study mentioned, the authors concede that a mechanism capable of segmenting clause-like structures is not incompatible in principle with the notion of maximally fast interpretation of speech. On the other hand, their results do not provide evidence for the clausal hypothesis. With a rhyme and category monitoring task, the speeds of judgements in the immediate vicinity of clause boundaries do not exhibit striking differences before and after a clause is completed. Semantic facilitation effects were obtained early in sentences before a clause was concluded, and suggest that lexical information introduced at the beginning of sentences is used in predicting the sequence which follows.

A strong version of the clausal processing hypotheses seems ruled out by on-line evidence of this kind. Weaker forms need not be. Experimental results supporting the notion of clause-by-clause processing are rather strong, just as data favouring high speed contextual effects. A weak version of the clausal hypothesis, claiming that the end of the clause is marked by perceptual closure and by concomitant freeing of working memory, can logically be combined with the notion that from the beginning of processing, a listener is occupied with information of all sorts needed to construct an interpretation. To specify more precisely how these two points of view can be melted together into a consistent theory, capable of accounting for more than part of the experimental evidence available, and able to make new, testable predictions, should be a goal of future research.

The evidence reported in the second part of this section, as well as the theoretical proposals made by Tanenhaus, Carroll, and Bever on the notion of functional clauses (Carroll and Tanenhaus, 1975; Tanenhaus and Carroll, 1975; Carroll and Bever, 1976; Carroll, Tanenhaus, and Bever, 1978) suggest that the clausal hypothesis should be modified along the following lines. First, it is likely that the listener constructs an interpretation of the sentence from the very beginning; the end of the clause marks only a point of definitive perceptual closure. Second, the processing unit is probably not a structural unit defined in linguistic terms. We would like to call this a *propositional structure*, which may or may not correspond structurally to a clause. It is this propositional unit which is probably sent to long-term memory in an abstract form when a consistent and stable semantic interpretation is reached. Third, unlike the original clausal hypothesis, surface information within each clause—or within each propositional unit—is not necessarily cleared from working memory without leaving a residue, but undergoes a process of decay which is dependent on the completeness of the clause: whenever within a propositional unit some indication is present that the sentence is functionally incomplete, surface information might be kept for some 'looking back' function. Finally, clausal processing will be affected by features such as clause length and syntactic complexity.

With the proposed modifications, a strong clausal hypothesis does not survive. A weaker form, however, seems consistent with the evidence available and not incompatible with the notion of an on-line, continuous processing of a sentence starting with the onset of the speech signal received. Work still ahead within a clausal hypothesis framework will need to determine better the relation between semantic and pragmatic factors and clause structure in sentence and discourse comprehension.

PERCEPTUAL STRATEGIES IN SENTENCE UNDERSTANDING

A basic notion in the clausal view of language perception is that the listener tries to make perceptual decisions about incoming speech as soon as it is possible to construct complete linguistic units. This position has been developed explicitly by Fodor, Bever and Garrett (1974). In principle, perceptual segmentation of the speech signal could be accomplished by parsers using different procedures. On the one hand perceived structure could be the result of systematic application of linguistic rules to the speech input; on the other extreme, such structures might be the outcome of simple perceptual heuristics which enable the listener to identify linguistic units and major grammatical relations, signal the end and the beginning of a clause, etc. Of course, any parser can be misled into a 'garden path' interpretation of a sentence which eventually fails and has to be corrected. Consider sentence (10), one such example discussed by Bever (1970).

(10) The horse raced past the barn fell.

Most listeners/readers tend to interpret the first six words of (10) as a full sentence, ending with the word *barn*. This solution, however, cannot explain the word *fell* once this has to be integrated into the sentence. An analogy with the visual perception of 'impossible' figures or of scenes such as those represented in Escher's drawings is here very tempting. In discussing such examples, Bever (1970) proposed the idea that linguistic structure results from the application of perceptual strategies, which are based on more general perceptual and cognitive principles of organization, and which are very likely to be very similar, or identical to, principles which also underly non-linguistic behaviour.

The introduction of this notion marked an interesting break with psycholinguistic theories based on transformational grammar, and prompted the development of models characterized by 'psychological' rather than linguistic mechanisms. The idea of perceptual strategies has even influenced linguistic theories, as we shall briefly see. Several authors have further elaborated on this notion. For example, Clark and Clark (1977) have presented an extensive list of perceptual strategies by which they attempt to account for the segmentation of several types of sentence structure.

Within linguistics there have recently been several attempts to produce sentence parsers which operated much like human listeners or readers, namely from left-to-right, which are characterized by the same kind of difficulties humans have, for example, in processing multiple embeddings, and which have limited working memory capacity. Parsers of this type are Kimball's (1973) model and Frazier and Fodor's (1978) *'sausage machine'*. Both these parsers are characterized by two levels of operation in the analysis of spoken or written material.

Kimball's model (1973) includes a first stage parser which works from left-to-right and connects each lexical unit it encounters to a phrase marker. New phrasal units which are completed are then 'snipped off' from the left and sent to a second-stage parser which reassembles them and performs further processing. An utterance is then divided into constituents to which syntactic categories are assigned.

The parser operates left-to-right, and decides when each constituent begins and ends. It does this using seven principles which are much like Bever's (1970) perceptual heuristics, capable of joining units into a phrase. For example, Kimball's *closure* principle reads as follows: 'A phrase is closed as soon as possible, unless the next node parsed is an immediate constituent of that phrase'.

Frazier and Fodor's (1978) paper represents another attempt to produce a psychologically plausible sentence parsing device. This parser also performs the syntactic analysis of a sentence in two steps. The first step, carried out by the *preliminary phrase packager* (PPP, or the 'sausage machine') assigns lexical and phrasal nodes to groups of few words. The second step is performed by a device called *sentence structure supervisor* (SSS); in it the phrases produced by the PPP component are joined into complete phrase markers which constitute the definitive structure of the sentence analysed. Thus, the parsing process consists of two phases, one low level and one high level. At the low level the PPP works essentially as a heuristic device moving through an input sentence with a window of limited width and accommodating no more than half a dozen words at a time. This component searches for local structure, using syntactic cues such as determiners, conjunctions and the like, and operates on the basis of principles such as *minimal attachment.* Each lexical item thus should be attached into the phrase marker with the fewest possible number of terminal nodes, linked with the nodes already present, etc. The units linked in this first stage may constitute clauses, combination of clauses, or simply phrases. The units produced by PPP are therefore not necessarily well defined in structural terms. Some similarity with the notion of 'functional clause' proposed by Carroll and Tanenhaus (1975) is evident here. Higher-level monitoring and integration of the results of this preliminary analysis is thus performed in the second stage by the sentence structure supervisor.

Other models which attempt to incorporate psychological limitations of human sentence understanding are Bresnan's (1978) parser, and Fodor's (1979) 'superstrategy'.

Another approach to parsing is offered by models inspired by the augmented transition networks (ATN) (Wood, 1970; Kaplan, 1972. See the discussion of ATN models in psycholinguistics in Levelt, 1978.) ATN parsers have considerable potential. However, only a relatively small effort has been made to develop a psychologically realistic parser along these lines (see, e.g. Wanner and Maratsos, 1975; Kaplan and Bresnan, 1980). Contemporary working artificial intelligence has also produced models characterized by devices having features much like the perceptual strategies proposed by psycholinguists. One example is Riesbeck's parser (Riesbeck and Schank, 1978) which operates on the basis of heuristics such as we have been discussing here.

The postulation of perceptual strategies as a feature of models of language comprehension represents an attempt to consider linguistic structures as outcomes of psychological processes. However, this approach is not without problems. For one thing, the choice of strategies tends to be *ad hoc*, depending on the particular structure the psycholinguist happens to be dealing with. As a consequence, such strategies are difficult to formalize, and remain largely at the intuitive and descriptive level, much as did the principles of perceptual organization proposed by Gestalt psychologists. The only attempt to incorporate the notion of perceptual strategies in a *formal* system until now has been within the framework of ATN grammars. Furthermore, perceptual strategies can hardly be used in the same form in a theory of production. If the construction of a theory of language comprehension compatible with a theory of production is attempted, difficulties can then arise. A perceptual theory need not hypothesize the same mechanisms and components of a theory of production, of course, but reality does call for processing devices which exploit largely similar information in the two cases.

In his discussion of perceptual strategies in 1970, Bever made strong analogies between certain such psycholinguistic principles, for example that the same word cannot have two functions at the same time, with principles underlying visual perception such as the double function of the margin in a Rubin figure. It is easy and suggestive to go on with this kind of analogy. A question of interest is whether visual examples and the description of perceptual segmentation of language in terms of principles of visual perception have any explanatory power, or whether they are only attractive metaphors. We believe that to the extent to which principles of perceptual grouping tell us something about the way visual perception is organized, within the limits of the basically descriptive and phenomenological approach on which these principles are based, the same should hold for language processing. The integration of these principles into strong models represents, however, work still to be done. It is also for future work to produce reasonable ideas about the way these principles may be implemented in submechanisms or procedures in the process of comprehension. One obvious way is to incorporate them within parsers such as those mentioned in this section.

LANGUAGE COMPREHENSION AND NON-LITERAL MEANING

Theories of comprehension have been aimed principally at explaining understanding of direct, literal meaning. An attempt to account for comprehension of idiomatic expressions, metaphor, jokes and the like until recently attracted little attention, probably on the basis of a principle that one should not take up difficult questions before answering simpler ones. However, specific attention now also began to be given to comprehension of 'non-direct' meaning in conversation, such as meaning conveyed, the interpretation of figures of speech and idioms, and in general the process of understanding what a speaker intends. Any theory of language comprehension ultimately has to explain how such expressions are used and understood. Moreover, no small part of the linguistic messages used in face to face communication consists of metaphorical expressions, indirect requests, rhetorical and other socially relevant devices. In the context of the present book, it is appropriate to consider the extent to which studies of the comprehension of non-literal meaning contribute to, and can be interpreted within, a general theory of language understanding. In this section we try to summarize some of the main evidence bearing on literal vs. non-literal meaning and the understanding process.

To date, most studies in this domain have focused on the direct-indirect meaning opposition. The basic question asked has been in what order we compute interpretations of utterances. In the case of metaphorical expressions, for example, do we first compute a *literal* interpretation and then a figurative one, do we compute both or several meanings at the same time, or can we even ignore literal meaning? The evidence we consider here comes from two types of experiments: studies of *literal* and *indirect* or *conveyed meaning*, and studies of *metaphor*.

Indirect requests

We will first take up studies which have examined how a listener may compute the different interpretations an utterance may receive in a typical communication situation (e.g. Clark and Lucy, 1975). Consider, for example, the following sentence produced by a speaker in a room with the windows open:

(11) It's cold in here.

Usually, this is more than an observation about the inside temperature; it will be intended to get the listener to close the windows, to shut the door behind him, to put on a jacket, and so on.

The subjects in Clark and Lucy's study were requested to draw simple deductions from pairs of conversationally conveyed requests such as 'Can you open the door' vs. 'Must you open the door?' It took longer for them to make these inferences from indirect than from direct requests. The evidence obtained suggested to Clark and Lucy that listeners construct the literal meaning of utterances before their indirect meaning. They thus proposed the following two-stage model to account for the results. First the literal meaning M_1 is computed and checked against the context. If this does not fit the context, an intended meaning M_2 is computed. The second step requires the extra time observed.

It remains to be seen whether the longer latencies for indirect requests depend on these two computation steps: the listener first would have to compute a *literal* interpretation and only after this step has been completed, would go on to interpret the *indirect request* implicit in the statement. An alternative explanation of Clark and Lucy's (1975) results is that both interpretations of a sentence, the literal and the indirect, are computed in parallel; the literal one terminates earlier. On the basis of results from a series of clever and amusing experiments on the comprehension of indirect speech acts, recently, Clark (1979) has abandoned his earlier serial model and has maintained that both M_1 and M_2 are computed as parts of a single 'package', and that different sources of information are used in computing them. Whether the listener makes use of one meaning only or both together, he argues, depends on several factors. Thus, Schweller (reported in Clark, 1979) compared the time it took people to understand sentences in two contexts: contexts which would induce M_1 alone and contexts which would induce M_1 *and* M_2. Highly stylized sentences for making requests were understood more quickly when presented as *requests*, while sentences less conventionally used for making requests were understood more quickly literally.

Up till now, we have considered the hypothesis that only the literal vs. both the literal and intended meaning of an utterance are computed. In the case of idiomatic expressions, however, it is possible that no literal meaning is computed at all, or that it is computed in parallel with, and more slowly than, the more idiomatic one. This conjecture underlies the experiments of Clark and Schunk (1980) on indirect speech acts, and of Swinney and Cutler (1979) on *idiomatic* expressions. Swinney and Cutler tried to determine whether people would compute literal analysis of word strings before entering an *idiom* mode of processing, or whether both the *literal* and the *idiomatic* meaning of idiomatic expressions would be processed simultaneously. In their study, phrasal idioms were judged to be acceptable English as quickly as matched control phrases, thus supporting the latter hypothesis. At least the literal meaning does not seem to be first: either the idiomatic meaning is computed alone, or the two meanings are processed in parallel. Unlike certain uses of metaphorical expressions, idiomatic expressions and 'freezes', however, are probably highly lexicalized. This hypotheses is supported by experiments by Kemper (1981) who showed that in naturalistic contexts figurative interpretation of proverbs is more rapid than literal interpretation. More detailed evidence is presented by Cutler in Chapter 2 of this book.

Metaphorical expressions

In rhetoric and philosophy, metaphorical use of language had been an object of observations and study for centuries, and recently has also attracted the attention of linguists and psycholinguists. In this section, we summarize a few points from recent theoretical and empirical work with metaphor, bearing on the question of processing for non-literal meaning in language in general. Among several reviews available, a recent chapter by Green (1980) offers an interesting and relevant discussion. As in the case of indirectly conveyed meaning, a serial stage model for understanding metaphor might at first seem the most intuitively promising. Recent experiments have provided some relevant results. A basic question asked has been whether people recover the literal meaning of a statement and only subsequently the metaphorical one, or whether the figurative meaning is understood from the beginning.

In a *two-stage model* of metaphor processing, the following steps might be hypothesized. First, a literal meaning is determined. Second, this meaning is checked against context and/or general knowledge; if the results of this checking process make the literal interpretation seem unlikely, the expression is reinterpreted. Verbrugge and McCarrell (1977) investigated this process by studying prompted recall of metaphorical sentences such as *Billboards are warts on the landscape*. Verbugge and McCarrell argue that comprehending such sentences involves determining the shared meaning of the 'topic' (*billboard*) and the metaphorical 'vehicle' (*warts*). They reasoned that if comprehension required determination of this shared meaning, then this should be an effective retrieval cue. This was indeed found to be the case in their experiments. For example, the shared meaning in the example given, *ugly protrusion on a surface*, was a much better retrieval cue than *tell you where to find business in the area*, which was, in turn, more effective for a control metaphor, *Billboards are the yellow pages of a highway*. This suggests that in a reconstructive task, subjects can make good inferences from what the common ground for a metaphor is. Those inferences would not be needed to comprehend more literal statements such as *Billboards are ugly protrusions on the landscape*.

Currently, however, there is little evidence for such a two-stage model. Harris (1976) presented subjects with metaphors and their non-metaphorical equivalents and recorded their latencies to initiate paraphrases. No speech onset difference between the two sentence types was obtained, nor was there any difference found in paraphrase adequacy. Verbrugge and McCarrell (1977) suggest that two-stage models are unparsimonious and propose that metaphorical and literal language are both understood through elaboration processes constrained by context. Ortony, Schallert, Reynolds and Antos (1978) argue along much the same lines that whether or not sentences require a relatively great amount of processing is a function of how easily they can be interpreted in the light of contextually evoked expectations, rather than their degree of literalness. In one of Ortony *et al.*'s (1978) experiments, target sentences were preceded by short or long contexts which induced literal interpretations or metaphorical ones. The results indicated that only in the short context condition did subjects take reliably longer to understand metaphorical than literal targets. In a second experiment, target phrases studied could be given either an idiomatic or a literal interpretation. It was found that idiomatic interpretations took no longer to form than literal interpretations. The Ortony *et al.* results thus provide only limited evidence for a two-stage process. Glucksberg, Gildea, and Bookin (1982) argue that the serial model implies that people can and do ignore the non-literal meanings of sentences whenever the literal meanings are plausible. To test this prediction they asked subjects to take rapid decisions about the *literal* truth of sentences such as *Some jobs are jails*. Subjects correctly judged such sentences as literally false, but the availability of a metaphorical interpretation slowed responses as compared with performances on control sentences like *Some birds are apples*. People do not seem to have an option to ignore non-literal meaning of sentences. Glucksberg *et al.* therefore conclude that people process both the non-literal and literal meanings of sentences in the same way and at the same time. In general, the evidence available from experiments both on indirect requests and metaphorical expressions speaks for a process in which different meanings become available at roughly the same time and context allows selection of one possible reading, or suppression of others.

LEXICAL ACCESS DURING SENTENCE PROCESSING

The isolation and identification of single word units is an essential phase in the process of understanding a sentence. Whatever the psychological status of the word in perception and comprehension may be, at some point we have to isolate and recognize the words in sentences and look up their meanings in our mental lexicon. In this section we will deal with the question of how lexical access occurs during sentence processing.

Models and experimental data on the process of recognizing words in isolation abound in contemporary cognitive psychology. Some of these models can be accommodated in a model of lexical access. However, different requirements and constraints may need to be met. Two important questions are the following: (a) Is word identification facilitated by the prior occurrence of semantically related words and, if so, how? For words presented in isolation there is ample evidence that this is the case, but how do things work for a word in a sentence? (b) Is lexical access affected when words are processed in linguistic structures, such as full sentences or sentence fragments, and does this effect differ from the effect of facilitation of single isolated words? These two questions bear directly on the choice between general classes of lexical access models, and are also relevant to the issue of lexical ambiguity in sentence processing which will be considered later. The two classes of models on lexical access can be tagged *search models* and *activation models* respectively.

The first class of models we would like to consider is exemplified by Forster's (1976) *autonomous search* model. In this model, when a word is perceived, its perceptual attributes are used to select an initial subset of lexical items. The items in this subset are then serially examined to see whether stored properties in each entry can be matched to the input word. The subsets are selected from so-called access files (Forster, 1976, 1979). There are two independent types of access files, permitting access to the lexicon from a visual or from an acoustic stimulus. The word entries in the access files contain no more than pointers to the appropriate entry in the lexicon. When a subset from an access file is selected, the order in which the entries are examined is determined by the basis of their frequency of occurrence.

Because the phonetic and orthographic access files in Forster's model are organized purely according to form and frequency, sentence context can have no effect on lexical access. The model is strictly bottom-up; top-down information is used only at the post-access stage of word recognition. In the model, lexical entries which are semantically related have cross-references. So, for example, it is possible from the lexical entry of *doctor* to access *nurse* directly, by-passing the access files. This possibility does not violate the assumption of autonomous lexical processing because in Forster's view semantic priming is an *intralevel* effect, rather than an interlevel effect. According to this model, priming does not influence levels of processing other than the lexical one.

Our second question raised above concerns the effects of facilitation on word recognition of preceding sentence fragments. Forster's model does not predict facilitation of such fragments on subsequent lexical access, because the way such fragments constrain possible words is not likely to be specified by the set of cross-references between lexical entries. Thus, the autonomous search model predicts facilitatory effects only for prior semantically related *words*, and not for sentence context generally.

The second class of models is best exemplified by Morton's (1969, 1970) *logogen* model and by Marslen-Wilson and Welsh's (1978) *cohort* model. Each lexical entry in Morton's model corresponds to a *logogen*. A logogen is characterized by a threshold value which specifies the amount of information that must be received for the logogen to be activated and automatically make a response available. Logogens can be accessed by both sensory and conceptual information, but cannot send information directly to one another. Only conceptual information is received from the cognitive system. Because the meaning of a sentence fragment affects the cognitive system, this meaning can indirectly influence later lexical access. All logogens which share semantic properties with the sentence fragment will then become partially activated. This has the effect of decreasing the amount of sensory information needed for word recognition, and predicts, in appropriate conditions, facilitatory effects of context.

The *cohort* model (Marslen-Wilson and Welsh, 1978) is also an activation type of model, but, in contrast to Morton's logogen theory, no thresholds are assigned to lexical units. By the time two or three phonemes of a word have been heard, the cohort model holds, there will be parallel activation of an entire class of word-candidates. Each element in this initial cohort will then continue to monitor subsequent input signals. Unlike logogens these recognition elements have the ability to respond actively to mismatches in the input signal. When the input diverges sufficiently from the internal specification for some element, it removes itself from the pool of word-candidates. (It may still remain activated, however.) The size of the original cohort will thus be progressively reduced, until a single candidate remains; at this point the word is recognized. Each memory element has, furthermore, the ability to determine what contextual requirements are meant. Marslen-Wilson and Welsh give no detailed account how this might be accomplished, but mention semantic procedures associated with lexical elements as a way context might be monitored.

Let us briefly consider the three models mentioned in the light of some empirical evidence. Facilitatory effects of sentence context have been found by Morton and Long (1976) in a phoneme monitoring task in which they varied the transitional probability between the first half of a sentence and an unambiguous target word. Monitoring latencies were shorter for high transitional probabilities. Effects of sentence context on lexical retrieval seem to include both facilitation and inhibition (Fischler and Bloom, 1979). Other positive results are reported by Schubert and Eimas (1977), and Underwood (1977). All these results pose serious problems for Forster's autonomous search model, which does not predict facilitation from sentence fragments. Forster (1981) obtained evidence that a purely *lexical* context is capable of facilitating lexical access without inhibitory cost. With sentence contexts, however, the only facilitatory effect he obtained was restricted to highly predictable targets in a lexical decision task. Since this effect did not extend to a *naming* task, Forster concluded that its locus was in making a decision and not in access *per se*. These results are compatible with the notion of autonomous lexical processing. However, exactly the opposite results were obtained by Stanovich and West (1981), who found clear facilitatory effects for naming, both for congruent targets and 'difficult' ones (i.e. unpredictable, low frequency completions of the context). Forster (1981) suggests that this discrepancy arose because the neutral condition in the two experiments was different.

Which empirical evidence favours the logogen and which the cohort model? The logogen model encounters a serious difficulty in explaining performance in tasks in which subjects are asked to detect mispronunciations. Morton (1970) suggests that when the logogen system fails to produce an output, *all* thresholds in the system will be lowered and the original input recirculated, this process is repeated until some logogen responds. This output can then be matched against a copy of the original input. However, Cole (1973) obtained results showing that latency to detect mispronunciations decreased with an increase in the degree of phonetic deviation. Morton's position would predict the opposite because, under the assumption that progressive lowering of the threshold takes more time, with large phonetic deviations, thresholds would have to be lowered more than in the case of small deviations. The logogen model can account for a large part of the findings of Marslen-Wilson, Tyler, and their associates (Marslen-Wilson, 1973; Marslen-Wilson and Welsh, 1978; Marslen-Wilson and Tyler, 1980) on fluent restoration and failure to detect mispronunciations, but the threshold notion central to the logogens does not offer a plausible explanation of the perception of *non*-words. In the cohort model, on the other hand, large deviations could quickly result in very short word-candidate lists, *vis-à-vis* words mispronounced with only small deviations. For a further account of these and related problems, see Marslen-Wilson and Welsh (1978). We end this section with a short remark on semantic relatedness between words and lexical access in sentence perception.

Evidence for effects of semantic priming on retrieval of *unambiguous* words during sentence processing is surprisingly not very abundant. In phoneme monitoring, Blank and Foss (1978) showed that facilitation takes place, and that facilitatory effects are roughly additive. Similar results were obtained by Foss, Cirilo, and Blank (1979). These results are consistent with most context-dependent models of lexical access, and not with theories in which prior semantic context is assumed to affect not the process of access itself but only the selection of one meaning from a series of meaning already retrieved. Such selection models are typically formulated to account for results obtained in experiments on the processing of sentences containing ambiguous words. This issue will now be considered.

ACCESS OF AMBIGUOUS LEXICAL ITEMS

We will consider two questions here: first, whether both (or all) meanings of a lexically ambiguous item are computed in recognition, and second, what effect context has. The two issues are closely related, because context normally is available to a listener.

Experiments on lexical ambiguity often deal with homophones or homographs. However, the same questions about retrieval of different semantic interpretations and context effects hold for words with multiple meanings but the same form. On the other hand, whether models which account for resolution of ambiguity for homophones or homographs can be applied when specific semantic interpretation of a polysemous word needs to be selected has not yet been answered.

We will begin by discussing the 'classical' approach to lexical ambiguity. That lexical ambiguity results in increased perceptual complexity is a well established finding in almost all experiments (see, e.g. Levelt 1978). Why this is so, of course, is another question. Is it because we compute all interpretations of an ambiguous word? The explanations offered have been given a variety of labels. Basically, two classes of models can be distinguished. One model predicts *selective access to meaning*, the other *multiple access to meaning*. In selective access models, context constrains the lexical retrieval process in such a way that usually only a single, contextually appropriate, meaning is found. In multiple access models, on the other hand, all (common) readings of a word are retrieved and an interpretation is selected on the basis of contextual information. Studies on access of ambiguous words presented in isolation show mixed results. For example, Schvaneveldt, Meyer, and Becker (1976) found evidence for selective access, while Warren, Warren, Green, and Bresnick (1978) found clear indications of multiple access.

Results from studies of lexical ambiguity in sentence context also show mixed results. Evidence for a biasing effect of context was obtained by Lackner and Garrett (1972) in a dichotic study. Presentation of a semantically related word to the not attended channel (one ear) led to a disambiguating effect in a sentence presented at the other ear. Several studies by Foss (1970) and his associates (e.g. Foss and Jenkins, 1973) have shown that reaction times to detect a target initial phoneme on a word following an ambiguous word are higher relative to unambiguous control words. Foss and Jenkins did fail to find a decrement in the ambiguity effect when a biasing context was introduced. Such a decrement would be expected if access to meaning was selective. Failure to obtain it might be taken as support for multiple access. As Swinney (1979) notes, however, failure to obtain the effect is not very strong support. A more substantial problem deserves consideration, however. Claims based on phoneme monitoring data about lexical access usually assume that lexical access and not some other process following it is the main determinant of response differences observed. Why should it not be the case, however, that phoneme monitoring reflects some *post*-access decision processes? Other methodological questions about the results of Foss and his associates have been raised by Mehler, Segui, and Carey (1978) and Swinney (1979). Results obtained by Swinney and Hakes (1976) support the second type of theory, that is, they favour selective access to meaning. A way out of these conflicting results has recently appeared, however. Tanenhaus, Leiman, and Seidenberg (1979) using a new method—a variable time delay naming latency paradigm—presented ambiguous words (e.g. *watch* as a noun or verb) in unambiguous contexts. Target words to be named and related to either the noun or to the verb reading were presented at variable delays following these words (which were sentence-final). At zero msec delay, facilitation of naming times took place for *both* readings, regardless of context. At a delay of 200 msec, however, facilitation was obtained only for targets which were related to the meaning of the ambiguous words in the context. Essentially the same results (time-dependent effects of context) were obtained by Swinney (1979) using another experimental paradigm in which subjects performed a lexical decision task for visually presented stimuli strings while hearing a sentence containing lexical ambiguities. Together, such findings suggest a two-stage process in which all reading of ambiguous words are first accessed an inappropriate readings are later suppressed.

Such results pose difficulties for context dependent models of lexical access. Other studies (e.g. Marslen-Wilson, 1976; Marslen-Wilson, Tyler, and Seidenberg, 1978) however, seem to show that the word recognition process is affected by context; subjects seem to identify some words within a few hundred milliseconds from their physical onset, and well before the full word has been heard. Context seems to facilitate this speeded recognition, via semantic expectancies. Why, then, should all meanings of a word still be accessed?

The main facts which we need to reconcile are the following:

(a) There are effects of context in lexical decision tasks.
(b) The presence of a biasing context does not seem to suppress the 'secondary', i.e. non-biased, meaning of a lexically ambiguous word both in cross-model lexical decision (Swinney, 1979) and naming latency tasks (Tanenhaus, Leiman, and Seidenberg, 1979).
(c) Context allows speeded selection of an appropriate lexical entry before it

is complete physically (e.g. in Marslen-Wilson's, 1976, shadowing experiments).

The questions we need to ask are, again (a) What is the locus of the contextual effects? and (b) How does this arise?

Consider a situation in which a person is presented with the following:

(12) John needed to cash a cheque. He went therefore to a bank. . . .

'Now, any dictionary will list several possible meanings from the word *bank*, among them the following:

(a) a place where money is kept and paid out, or can be borrowed;
(b) a long bench on which one can sit;
(c) the land along the side of the river;
(d) a great mass of material, such as of clouds or snow;
(e) sloping ground at the bottom of the sea or of a river.

Will these, or even more, meanings of *bank* be instantly available to the listener, or perhaps only one or two more frequent ones? And how long will they be available? Or will context restrict immediately the alternatives available to one, namely, in our example, to (a)?

On the basis of the evidence reviewed, we would like to propose the following. In doing so we will make a distinction between activation of *lexical* units and activation of *conceptual* units. Context we take to act on the word recognition process by activating a particular conceptual domain. Sentence (12), up to the point where *bank* will be uttered, will already have activated such a domain—that concerned with concepts such as *money*, *saving*, *accountant*, *payment*, etc. One of the results of this arousal is also a pre-activation or activation of all the lexical units associated with this domain, for example temporary activation of all words having to do with *money*, *saving*, etc., with a consequent lowering of their excitation threshold. The threshold for *bank* will also be temporarily lowered. At this moment, a minimum of stimulus information should be sufficient to make the word unit available. Even 'reduced' stimulus information—a degraded stimulus, a tachistoscopic presentation, etc., or, as in Marslen-Wilson's experiments, the first part of a word—will be enough to make the full word *bank* available.

Activation of the lexical unit, however, carries with it *automatic activation* of all its meanings, *including* those not biased by the context. Thus 'secondary' meanings would also be available. Being available, even for a short period of time, the secondary meaning of a word might be retrieved or detected in an appropriate task. For example, at short intervals one could expect a priming effect of *bank* or words of *furniture*, such as *chair*, *couch* or the like, or, for the third reading of the word above mentioned, on words such as *river*, *boat*, etc. This effect, however, would be of short duration and/or rather weak, while the activation effect of the first would be stronger and/or of longer duration.

The first, appropriate meaning of *bank* can be more easily available and will be used by the listener in his interpretation because of one or more of the following reasons: (a) the other meanings are secondary; (b) the other meanings become available later in time or have a faster decay rate; (c) the other meanings are not selected because a single interpretation is made, or because they do not fit in the conceptual structure biased by the context. This is not the place to take a position favouring a single one of these alternatives. For our purposes, it is sufficient to show how the range of known results might be accommodated in one theoretical framework.

In summary, empirical results and theoretical considerations strongly support context-dependent models, in which at an initial stage automatic activation of all meaning is taking place, even of the meaning which is not related to the context. The context does not affect the access of the meaning, but the selection of the appropriate reading, either by putting constraints on the response to be selected; by lowering the criterion for the appropriate response; or simply because as a result of the semantic activation by the context, which biases one reading, the inappropriate reading will not be strong enough to be selected for response, or will decay before it is capable of affecting the selection process.

THE COMPREHENSION OF CONNECTED DISCOURSE

As we pointed out in our introductory comments, recent psycholinguistic work has tended to move away from the study of sentence processing in isolation, and toward consideration of both the effects of larger contexts and those of various pragmatic factors on understanding. For a large part, interest has turned to the study of comprehension of connected discourse. This has become a flourishing and rapidly expanding topic of research especially in the last decade. In the present section, we will try to point out some important features of models of discourse comprehension currently available.

Research on the comprehension of connected discourse has been a point of convergence between several disciplines. Within linguistics, most progress directly related to discourse comprehension has been made in the areas of text linguistics, text analysis, text grammars, and story grammars. Modern text grammars have their roots in structuralism in American linguistics and in the work by Hjelmslev (1943), and owe much to Harris's (1952) studies of text and to his concern with the analysis of connected speech. Text linguistics, on the other hand, has been initially more a European achievement, and this still holds for recent work (e.g. Petöfi 1971; Dressler, 1970, 1973; van Dijk, 1972; etc.). Story grammars have largely been influenced by the analysis of literary texts, such as Propp's (1968) classic study of the Russian folktales.

In psychology, interest in text comprehension and the processing of connected speech has blossomed mainly during the last decade. One of the few notable early predecessors in early experimental psychology is Bartlett (1932). Bartlett's contribution to the study of memory for stories and his notion of *schema* are a standard source of inspiration in contemporary models. Much recent work on discourse comprehension has been facilitated by rapid expansion in the field of semantic memory and, more generally, in theories of representation of knowledge. These, in turn, have been a typical product of artificial intelligence research, which has provided the core for several discourse comprehension algorithms.

As the name implies, text grammars are intended to account for the formal structure of *texts*, as opposed to sentence grammars (cf. van Dijk, 1972). Parallel to recent work by linguists on text grammars, there have been a number of contributions in cognitive psychology to our understanding of discourse processing.

The theories available carry a variety of names: text comprehension models, story grammars, and so forth. It would be simplistic to consider all these models, with the range of connotations their labels carry, as variations on a single type. There are clear differences between them in both organization and scope. On the other hand, they all seem to share some basic assumptions. For example, that the structure of the story or of the discourse is essentially hierarchical, and the story can be represented as an organized set of elements or propositions interrelated within this structure. Most models try to give a formal description of the structure of the narratives and make claims about the psychological reality of these structures. Their empirical aim is to predict how a reader or a listener will use his knowledge about the structure of narratives to comprehend and recall a story. For this reason, most such models make predictions about recall of texts based upon them, for example hierarchical form of the representation and connections between their elements or propositions. For example, a proposition high in the representation hierarchy is more likely to be recalled, as being more central in the story structure. Or, two propositions closely related in a story's structure will more likely be recalled together.

Roughly speaking, the main models available fall into few groups. One of the first explicit models of story comprehension was Rumelhart's (1975) story grammar. Two more recent accounts by Thorndyke (1977) and Mandler and Johnson (1977) are in their basic structure not unlike Rumelhart's proposal and can to some extent be taken as extensions, simplifications, and variations on it. Another type of model is that Kintsch and van Dijk (1975, 1978), and still another type has been proposed by Warren, Nicholas, and Trabasso (1979).

Let us briefly consider some features of Thorndyke's (1977) story grammar, as an example of the first type. In this model, as well as in Mandler and Johnson's (1977), the underlying structure of a story is represented as essentially analogous to that of a sentence in generative grammar, namely as a tree structure in which constituents and the relations between them are made explicit. The corresponding surface structure of the story consists of the sequences of sentences which constitute the narrative. This kind of story grammar uses conventional rewriting rules, with 'units' of a higher and more abstract level then the standard generative rules. For example, Thorndyke's model uses rules such as the following:

STORY → SETTING + THEME + PLOT + RESOLUTION
SETTING → CHARACTERS + LOCATION + TIME

The rules are applied recursively and yield a hierarchical structure similar in form and organization to a phrase marker for a sentence. The terminal nodes are the story's actual *propositions*. In the 'surface structure' of the story, these propositions are mapped into clauses or sentences containing an active or stative verb.

In the model proposed by Kintsch and van Dijk (1978), comprehension of a text is taken to be a process operating on several interconnected levels. Briefly, the process of comprehension is assumed to proceed as follows. The text is analysed by a *parser* which yields semantic structures representing a *propositional* level of organization. The propositions become organized in the *text base*. From this structured data base *macrostructures* are derived, which constitute the *general* meaning of the narrative. All processes interact with knowledge sources, and inferences can be made continuously to obtain a coherent representation of the meaning of the text. The two central processes in the model are the construction of a text base from the propositions, and the derivation of macrostructure from the text base.

In somewhat more detail, the model functions as follows. As parts of a narrative are read, propositions are generated. When enough of these propositions are available, they are organized in a text base. In this process one proposition is taken as being superordinate, and the other as subordinate. The propositions are organized into a hierarchical structure, which is progressively refined by inferences, until a coherent network remains available in working memory. For the next phase of processing, working memory is cleared and the representation is sent to a long-term store, except for a few propositions which are needed to connect the 'old' network with the next one to be built, and allow a coherent representation to be formed. The macrostructure of the text is derived from the text base using macro-rules. The model distinguishes three main types of macro-rules: deletion, generalization, and construction. Operations of these rules transform the propositions in the text base through *inferences* or leave them as they are to form macropropositions, which are themselves then stored in long-term memory.

The model allows for rather specific predictions concerning recall of propositional information, and several experiments by Kintsch and his associates have yielded data which fit reasonably well with these predictions. Seen from these studies, the model appears to have more to say about memory for narratives than about comprehension processes. For psycholinguistic theory at large, the model is particularly limiting in the sense that the level of representations with which it starts is that of the propositions, and all 'lower' processing, such as parsing, is taken for granted.

In Warren, Nicholas, and Trabasso's (1979) theory, a story is reconstructed by representing a causal chain. The reader is seen actively as constructing a coherent representation by filling in gaps in the information given on the basis of his knowledge of the world and what is said or is provided by the text. Again, the reader does this by making *inferences*. The story is represented, as the name of the model implies, as a 'causal chain' of meaningful elements (essentially propositions).

As is implicit in most models like those above, comprehending a story does not consist simply of a process whereby the different elements derived from the text are accumulated in memory. Rather, the reader tries to account for the sequence of actions and events described, to follow the development of a plan, which serves as a framework for interpreting and organizing the events. The beliefs and the attitudes of the reader will influence the representation he constructs and the inferences he makes about the events. Recall of stories, as Bower (1978) has argued, is a complex product of several such factors, of processes of reconstruction, of inference, which continuously interact with the information actually provided in the narrative. In approaches such as Bower's, models of story comprehension and story recall are seen as more directly related to other fields including social psychology.

The approaches we have mentioned are in the first place models about the *structure* of the text. On the other hand, they claim that story structures represent useful schemata for comprehension and recall. Moreover, they try to offer specific predictions about the parts or elements of the story which will be recalled better or worse, and the distortions, additions, or deletions which are likely to take place between presentation and recall. This chapter is not the appropriate place to try to point to the strong or weak features of the particular models mentioned. (For a criticism of contemporary story grammars see, e.g. Black and Wilensky, 1979; and replies by Rumelhart, 1980, and Mandler and Johnson, 1980; see also Frisch and Perlis, 1981.) One important question, with regard to the different models available, concerns their relative merits in making non-trivial, specific predictions about recall. With the exception of a few very specific differences, they seem to make largely equivalent predictions about memory for the different propositions of the narrative. Another problem is that most of them have not been seriously tested in on-line comprehension situations, but rather have been supported using experimental tasks producing gross measures such as rating of comprehensibility.

It is interesting to ask to what extent models of story and text comprehension *can* contribute to, and be integrated with, a psycholinguistic theory of language understanding. Some notions central to text comprehension models seem rather congenial with current ideas in psycholinguistics. A few are the following: comprehending language requires processing structures larger than sentences; comprehending a narrative consists of using knowledge about the world and schemata about what a normal or 'plausible' story should include; understanding involves filling in gaps, introducing consistencies, and eliminating implausible interpretations, with a steady use of inference to assemble the different elements in the story into a congruent structure.

Recent developments have widened the domain of psycholinguistics to include the contribution of broader linguistic and extralinguistic context in the process of language understanding. But psycholinguistic models proper and models of story comprehension are by no means united. While the latter have been constrained and stimulated by progress made in the study of semantic memory and, more generally, by theories of the representation of knowledge in cognitive science, they have neither influenced nor been influenced in large degree by mainstream research on sentence processing. A well integrated theory of language comprehension processes at all levels, from word perception to the understanding of complete discourses, is still distant.

REFERENCES

Abrams, K., and Bever, T. G. Syntactic structure modifies attention during speech perception and recognition. *Quarterly Journal of Experimental Psychology*, 1969, **21**, 280–290.

Bartlett, F. C. *Remembering*. Cambridge: Cambridge University Press, 1932.

Bever, T. G. The cognitive basis for linguistic structures. In J. R. Hayes (Ed.), *Cognition and the Development of Language*. New York: Wiley, 1970.

Bever, T. G., Lackner, J., and Kirk, R. The underlying structures of sentences are the primary units of speech processing. *Perception and Psychophysics*, 1969, **5**, 225–234.

Black, J. B., and Wilensky, R. An evaluation of story grammars. *Cognitive Science*, 1979, **3**, 213–230.

Blank, M. A., and Foss, D. J. Semantic facilitation and lexical access during sentence processing. *Memory and Cognition*, 1978, **6**, 644–652.

Bower, G. H. Experiments on story comprehension and recall. *Discourse Processing*, 1978, **1**, 211–231.

Bransford, J. D., and Franks, J. J. The abstraction of linguistic ideas. *Cognitive Psychology*, 1971, **2**, 331–350.

Bresnan, J. A realistic transformational grammar. In M. Halle, J. Bresnan, and G. A. Miller (Eds), *Linguistic Theory and Psychological Reality*. Cambridge, Mass.: M.I.T. Press, 1978.

Caplan, D. Clause boundaries and recognition latencies for words in sentences. *Perception and Psychophysics*, 1972, **12**, 73–76.

Carroll, J. M., and Bever, T. G. Sentence comprehension: A case study in the relation of knowledge to perception. In E. C. Carterette and M. P. Friedman (Eds), *The Handbook of Perception.* Vol. 7: *Language and Speech.* New York: Academic Press, 1976.

Carroll, J. M., and Tanenhaus, M. K. Functional clauses and sentences segmentation. Unpublished manuscript, 1975.

Carroll, J. M., Tanenhaus, M. K., and Bever, T. G. The perception of relations: The interaction of structural, functional and contextual factors in the segmentation of sentences. In W. J. M. Levelt and G. B. Flores d'Arcais (Eds), *Studies in the Perception of Language.* Chichester: Wiley, 1978.

Chapin, P. G., Smith, T. S., and Abrahamson, A. A. Two factors in perceptual segmentation of speech. *Journal of Verbal Learning and Verbal Behavior,* 1972, **11,** 164–173.

Clark, H. H. Responding to indirect speech acts. *Cognitive Psychology,* 1979, **11,** 430–477.

Clark, H. H., and Clark, E. *Psychology and Language: An Introduction to Psycholinguistics.* New York: Harcourt, Brace, Jovanovich, 1977.

Clark, H. H., and Lucy, P. Understanding what is meant from what is said: A study in conversationally conveyed requests. *Journal of Verbal Leaning and Verbal Behavior,* 1975, **14,** 56–72.

Clark, H. H., and Schunk, D. H. Polite responses to polite requests. *Cognition,* 1980, **8,** 111–143.

Cole, R. A. Listening for mispronunciations: A measure of what we hear during speech. *Perception and Psychophysics,* 1973, **13,** 153–156.

Cole, R. A., and Jakimik, J. Understanding speech: How words are heard. In G. Underwood (Ed.), *Strategies of Information Processing.* New York: Academic Press, 1978.

Danks, J. H., and Glucksberg, S. *Psycholinguistics. Annual Review of Psychology,* 1980, **31,** 391–417.

Dijk, T. A. van. *Some Aspects of Text Grammars.* Den Haag: Mouton, 1972.

Dressler, W. Textsyntax. *Lingua e Stile,* 1970, **2,** 191–214.

Dressler, W. *Einführung in die Textlinguistik.* Tübingen: Niemeyer, 1973.

Engelkamp, J. *Satz und Bedeutung.* Stuttgart: Kohlhammer, 1976.

Fischler, I., and Bloom, P. A. Automatic and attentional processes in the effects of sentence contexts on word recognition. *Journal of Verbal Learing and Verbal Behavior,* 1979, **18,** 1–20.

Flores d'Arcais, G. B. The perception of complex sentences. In W. J. M. Levelt and G. B. Flores d'Arcais (Eds), *Studies in the Perception of Language.* Chichester: Wiley, 1978(a).

Flores d'Arcais, G. B. Syntactic and semantic interaction in processing complex sentences. Research Report. Department of Psychology, University of Leiden, 1978(b).

Flores d'Arcais, G. B. Automatic syntactic computation in sentence comprehension. *Psychological Research,* 1982, **44,** 231–242.

Fodor, J. A., and Bever, T. G. The psychological reality of linguistic segments. *Journal of Verbal Learning and Verbal Behavior,* 1965, **4,** 414–420.

Fodor, J. A., Bever, T. G., and Garrett, M. F. *The Psychology of Language: An Introduction to Psycholinguistics and Generative Grammar.* New York: McGraw-Hill, 1974.

Fodor, J. D. Superstrategy, In W. E. Cooper and E. C. T. Walker (Eds), *Sentence Processing: Psycholinguistic Studies Presented to Merrill Garrett.* Hillsdale, N. J.: Lawrence Erlbaum Associates, 1979.

Forster, K. I. The role of semantic hypotheses in sentence processing. In F. Bresson (Ed.), *Problèmes actuels en psycholinguistique*. Paris: Centre Nationale de la Recherche Scientifique, 1974.

Forster, K. I. Accessing the mental lexicon. In R. J. Wales and E. C. T. Walker (Eds), *New Approaches to Language Mechanisms*. Amsterdam: North-Holland. 1976.

Forster, K. I. Levels of processing and the structure of the language processor. In W. E. Cooper and E. C. T. Walker (Eds), *Sentence Processing: Psycholinguistic Studies Presented to Merrill Garrett*. Hillsdale, N.J.: Lawrence Erlbaum Associates, 1979.

Forster, K. I. Priming and the effects of sentence and lexical contexts on naming time: Evidence for autonomous lexical processing. *Quarterly Journal of Experimental Psychology*, 1981, **33A**, 465–495.

Forster, K. I., and Olbrei, I. Semantic heuristics and syntactic analysis. *Cognition*, 1973, **2**, 319–347.

Forster, K. I., and Ryder, L. A. Perceiving the structure and meaning of sentences. *Journal of Verbal Learning and Verbal Behavior*, 1971, **9**, 699–706.

Foss, D. J. Decision processes during sentence comprehension: Effects of lexical items difficulty and position upon decision times. *Journal of Verbal Learning and Verbal Behaviour*, 1969, **8**, 457–462.

Foss, D. J. Some effects of ambiguity upon sentence comprehension. *Journal of Verbal Learning and Verbal Behavior*, 1970, **9**, 699–706.

Foss, D. J., Cirilo, R. K., and Blank, M. A. Semantic facilitation and lexical access during sentence processing: An investigation of individual differences. *Memory and Cognition*, 1979, **7**, 346–353.

Foss, D. J., and Jenkins, C. M. Some effects of context on the comprehension of ambiguous sentences. *Journal of Verbal Learning and Verbal Behavior*, 1973, **12**, 577–589.

Frazier, L., and Fodor, J. D. The sausage machine: A new two-stage parsing model. *Cognition*, 1978, **6**, 291–325.

Frisch, A. M., and Perlis, D. A re-evaluation of story grammars. *Cognitive Science*, 1981, **5**, 79–86.

Garnes, S., and Bond, Z. W. The relationship between semantic expectation and acoustic information. Paper presented at the Third International Congress of Phonology, Vienna, 1976.

Garrett, M. F. Sentence production. In R. J. Wales and E. C. T. Walker (Eds), *New Approaches to Language Mechanisms*. Amsterdam: North Holland, 1976.

Garrett, M. F., Bever, T. G., and Fodor, J. A. The active use of grammar in speech perception. *Perception and Psychophysics*, 1966, **1**, 30–32.

Glucksberg, S., Gildea, P., and Bookin, H. B. On understanding nonliteral speech: Can people ignor metaphors? *Journal of Verbal Learning and Verbal Behavior*, 1982, **21**, 85–98.

Green, D. W. Psycholinguistics: Cognitive aspects of human communication. In G. Claxton (Ed.), *Cognitive Psychology*. London: Routledge & Kegan Paul, 1980.

Greene, J. M. Syntactic form and semantic function. *Quarterly Journal of Experimental Psychology*, 1970, **22**, 14–27.

Harris, R. J. Comprehension of metaphors: A test of the two-stage processing model. *Bulletin of the Psychonomic Society*, 1976, **8**, 312–314.

Harris, Z. S. Discourse analysis. *Language*, 1952, **28**, 1–30.

Herriot, P. The comprehension of active and passive sentences as a function of pragmatic expectations. *Journal of Verbal Learning and Verbal Behavior*, 1969, **8**, 166–169.

Hjelmslev, L. *Omkring sprogteoriens grundloegselse.* Copenhagen: Munksgaard, 1943.

Holmes, V. M. Some hypotheses about syntactic processing in sentence comprehension. In W. E. Cooper and E. C. T. Walker (Eds), *Sentence Processing: Psycholinguistic Studies Presented to Merrill Garrett.* Hillsdale, N.J.: Lawrence Erlbaum Associates, 1979.

Holmes, V. M., and Forster, K. I. Detection of extraneous signals during sentence processing. *Perception and Psychophysics*, 1970, **7**, 297–301.

Jarvella, R. J. Effects of syntax on running memory span for connected discourse. *Psychonomic Science*, 1970, **19**, 235–236.

Jarvella, R. J. Syntactic processing of connected speech. *Journal of Verbal Learning and Verbal Behavior*, 1971, **10**, 409–416.

Jarvella, R. J., and Herman, S. J. Clause structure of sentences and speech processing. *Perception and Psychophysics*, 1972, **11**, 381–384.

Jarvella, R. J., and Nelson, T. R. Focus of information and general knowledge in language understanding. In J. F. Le Ny and W. Kintsch (Eds) *Language and Comprehension.* Amsterdam: North-Holland, 1982.

Johnson, N. F. Sequential verbal behavior. In T. R. Dixon and D. L. Horton (Eds), *Verbal Behavior and General Behavior Theory.* Englewood Cliffs, N.J.: Prentice-Hall, 1968.

Kaplan, R. Augmented transition networks as psychological models of sentence comprehension. *Artificial Intelligence*, 1972, **3**, 77–100.

Kaplan, R., and Bresnan, J. Lexical-functional grammar: A formal system for grammatical representation. Occasional paper N.13, Center for Cognitive Science, M.I.T., 1980.

Kemper, S. Comprehension and the interpretation of proverbs. *Journal of Psycholinguistic Research*, 1981, **10**, 179–198.

Kimball, J. Seven principles of surface structure parsing in natural language. *Cognition*, 1973, **2**, 15–47.

Kintsch, W., and Dijk, T. A. van. Recalling and summarizing stories. *Language*, 1975, **40**, 98–116.

Kintsch, W., and Dijk, T. A. van. Toward a model of text comprehension and production. *Psychological Review*, 1978, **85**, 363–394.

Kornfeld, J. F. Clause structure and the perceptual analysis of sentences. *Quarterly Progress Report, Research laboratory of Electronics*, M.I.T., 1973, **108**, 277–280.

Lackner, J. R., and Garrett, M. F. Resolving ambiguity: Effects of biasing contexts in the unattended ear. *Cognition*, 1972, **1**, 359–372.

Ladefoged, P. *Three Areas of Experimental Phonetics.* London: Oxford University Press, 1967.

Levelt, W. J. M. A survey of studies in sentence perception: 1970–1976. In W. J. M. Levelt and G. B. Flores d'Arcais (Eds), *Studies in the Perception of Language.* Chichester: Wiley, 1978.

Mandler, J. M., and Johnson, N. S. Rememberances of things parsed: Story structure and recall. *Cognitive Psychology*, 1977, **9**, 111–151.

Mandler, J. M., and Johnson, N. S. On throwing out the baby with the bathwater: A reply to Black and Wilensky's evaluation of story grammars. *Cognitive Science*, 1980, **4**, 305–312.

Marslen-Wilson, W. D. Linguistic structure and speech shadowing at very short latencies. *Nature*, 1973, **244**, 522–523.

Marslen-Wilson, W. D. Sentence perception as an interactive parallel process. *Science*, 1975, **189**, 226–228.

Marslen-Wilson, W. D. Linguistic descriptions and psychological assumptions in the study of sentence processing. In. R. J. Wales and E. C. T. Walker (Eds), *New Approaches to Language Mechanisms*. Amsterdam: North-Holland, 1976.

Marslen-Wilson, W. D., and Tyler, L. K. The temporal structure of spoken language understanding. *Cognition*, 1980, **8**, 1–71.

Marslen-Wilson, W. D., Tyler, L. K., and Seidenberg, M. Sentence processing and the clause boundary. In W. J. M. Levelt and G. B. Flores d'Arcais (Eds), *Studies in the Perception of Language*. Chichester: Wiley, 1978.

Marslen-Wilson, W. D., and Welsh, A. Processing interactions and lexical access during word recognition in continuous speech. *Cognitive Psychology*, 1978, **10**, 29–63.

Mehler, J. Some effects of grammatical transformations on the recall of English sentences. *Journal of Verbal Learning and Verbal Behavior*, 1963, **2**, 250–262.

Mehler, J., Segui, J., and Carey, P. W. Tails of words: Monitoring ambiguity. *Journal of Verbal Learning and Verbal Behavior*, 1978, **17**, 29–35.

Morton, J. The interaction of information in word recognition. *Psychological Review*, 1969, **76**, 165–178.

Morton, J. A functional model of human memory. In D. A. Norman (Ed.), *Models of Human Memory*. New York: Academic Press, 1970.

Morton, J., and Long, J. Effect of word transitional probability on phoneme identification. *Journal of Verbal Learning and Verbal Behavior*, 1976, **15**, 43–51.

Ortony, A., Schallert, D. L., Reynolds, R. E., and Antos, S. J. Interpreting metaphors and idioms: Some effects of context on comprehension. *Journal of Verbal Learning and Verbal Behavior*, 1978, **17**, 465–477.

Petöfi, J. S. *Transformationsgrammatiken und eine kontextuelle Texttheorie*. Frankfurt: Athenäum, 1971.

Propp, V. *Morphology of the Folktale*. Austin, Texas: Texas University Press, 1968.

Reber, A. S. Locating clicks in sentences: Left, center, and right. *Perception and Psychophysics*, 1973, **13**, 133–138.

Riesbeck, C. K., and Schank, R. C. Comprehension by computer: Expectation based analysis of sentences in context. In W. J. M. Levelt and G. B. Flores d'Arcais (Eds), *Studies in the Perception of Language*. Chichester: Wiley, 1978.

Rumelhart, D. E. Notes on a schema for stories. In D. Bobrow and A. Collins (Eds), *Representation and Understanding: Studies in Cognitive Science*. New York: Academic Press, 1975.

Rumelhart, D. E. On evaluating story grammars. *Cognitive Science*, 1980, **4**, 313–316.

Savin, H. B., and Perchonok, E. Grammatical structure and the immediate recall of English sentences. *Journal of Verbal Learning and Verbal Behavior*, 1965, **4**, 348–353.

Schubert, R. D., and Eimas, P. Effects of context on the classification of words and nonwords. *Journal of Experimental Psychology: Human Perception and Performance*, 1977, **33**, 27–36.

Schvaneveldt, R., Meyer, D., and Becker, C. Lexical ambiguity, semantic content, and visual word recognition. *Journal of Experimental Psychology: Human Perception and Performance*, 1976, **2**, 243–256.

Slobin, D. E. Grammatical transformations and sentence comprehension in childhood and adulthood. *Journal of Verbal Learning and Verbal Behavior*, 1966, **5**, 219–227.

Stanovich, K. E., and West, R. F. The effects of sentence processing on ongoing word recognition: Tests of a two-process theory. *Journal of Experimental Psychology: Human Perception and Performance*, 1981, **7**, 658–672.

Steedman, M. J., and Johnson-Laird, P. N. A progammatic theory of linguistic performance. In R. N. Campbell and P. T. Smith (Eds), *Recent Advances in the Psychology of Language*. New York: Plenum Press, 1978.

Steen, P. A. van der. *Syntactic and semantic effects in sentence processing.* Unpublished undergraduate dissertation. Department of Psychology, University of Leiden, 1978.

Suci, G. J., Ammon, P. R., and Gamlin, P. The validity of the probe-latency technique for assessing structure in language. *Language and Speech*, 1967, **10**, 69–80.

Swinney, D. A. Lexical access during sentence comprehension: (Re)consideration of context effects. *Journal of Verbal Learning and Verbal Behavior*, 1979, **18**, 645–659.

Swinney, D. A., and Cutler, A. The access and processing of idiomatic expressions. *Journal of Verbal Learning and Verbal Behavior*, 1979, **18**, 523–534.

Swinney, D. A., and Hakes, D. T. Effects of prior context upon lexical access during sentence comprehension. *Journal of Verbal Learning and Verbal Behavior*, 1976, **15**, 681–689.

Tanenhaus, M. K., and Carroll, J. M. The clausal processing hierarchy and nouniness. In R. Grossman, J. San and T. Vance (Eds), *Papers from the Parasession on Functionalism*. Chicago: Chicago Linguistic Society, 1975.

Tanenhaus, M. K., Leiman, J. M., and Seidenberg, M. S. Evidence for multiple stages in the processing of ambiguous words in syntactic contexts. *Journal of Verbal Learning and Verbal Behavior*, 1979, **18**, 427–440.

Thorndyke, P. W. Cognitive structures in comprehension and memory. *Cognitive Psychology*, 1977, **9**, 77–110.

Tyler, L. K., and Marslen-Wilson, W. D. The on-line effects of semantic context on syntactic processing. *Journal of Verbal Learning and Verbal Behavior*, 1977, **16**, 683–692.

Underwood, G. Contextual facilitation from attended and unattended messages. *Journal of Verbal Learning and Verbal Behavior*, 1977, **16**, 99–106.

Verbrugge, R. R., and McCarrell, N. S. Metaphoric comprehension: Studies in reminding and resembling. *Cognitive Psychology*, 1977, **9**, 494–533.

Wanner, E., and Maratsos, H. An augmented transition network model of relative clause comprehension. Mimeo. Havard University, Cambridge, Mass., 1975.

Warren, R. E., Warren, N. T., Green, J. P., and Bresnick, J. H. Multiple semantic encoding of homophones and homographs in contexts biasing dominant and subordinate readings. *Memory and Cognition*, 1978, **6**, 364–371.

Warren, R. M. Perceptual restoration of missing speech sounds. *Science*, 1970, **167**, 392–393.

Warren, W. H., Nicholas, D. W., and Trabasso, T. Event chains and inferences in understanding narratives. In R. Freedle (Ed.), *New Directions in Discourse Processing*, Vol. 2. Norwood, N. J.: Ablex, 1979.

Wilks, Y. Computational models for language processing. *Cognitive Psychology: Language*. Milton Keynes: Open University Press, 1978.

Wingfield, A., and Klein, J. F. Syntactic structure and acoustic pattern in speech perception. *Perception and Psychophysics*, 1971, **9**, 23–25.

Woods, W. A. Transition network grammars for natural language analysis. *Communications of the ACM*, 1970, **13**, 591–606.

The Process of Language Understanding
Edited by G. B. Flores d'Arcais and R. J. Jarvella
© 1983 John Wiley & Sons Ltd.

2

Lexical Complexity and Sentence Processing

ANNE CUTLER

M.R.C. Applied Psychology Unit, Cambridge CB2 2EF, U.K.

INTRODUCTION

In the mental lexicon of speakers who know it, the word *wombat* should have a relatively simple entry, in which a single sound representation—[wDmbæt] or something more abstract—is linked to a meaning representation along the lines of 'small Australian marsupial mammal'. The lexical representations of many other words, however, are likely to be a great deal more complex. Ambiguous words, such as *bark*, for instance, must have more than one semantic representation associated with a single sound representation. Idiomatic expressions, such as *break the ice*, convey a meaning which is not expressible as a direct function of the words which comprise them, and if they are listed as single units, then their lexical representation incorporates a degree of syntactic complexity. Derived words, consisting of a stem with prefixes and/or suffixes, may represent this morphological structure in their lexical entry: on this dimension the lexical representation of, say, *emit* would be more complex than that of *emir*.

Loosely speaking, then, lexical representations can vary in complexity on at least three dimensions: semantic, syntactic, and morphological. The existence of complex representations of all three types has been specifically claimed: 'Both (all) interpretations of an ambiguous word are always activated' (Foss and Jenkins, 1973); 'Idioms are stored and accessed as lexical items' (Swinney and Cutler, 1979); 'Morphological decomposition is involved in the storage and retrieval of lexical items' (Taft and Forster, 1975).

Clearly, there are fundamental differences between the phenomena which have here been given the summary title 'lexical complexity'. Ambiguous words, and idioms, are complex in the sense that they can call up more than one semantic representation in the lexicon; morphologically complex words, on the other hand, have a unitary semantic representation, but are complex in that different parts of the word may correspond to different parts of the semantic representation. Nevertheless, in this chapter 'lexical complexity' will for the purposes of the argument be treated as a unitary phenomenon. A negative definition is that lexical complexity occurs wherever lexical entries are not simple; lexical simplicity is the case when a phonetic representation of a word evokes a single lexical entry which contains only a single word class representation and a single semantic representation. The existing evidence on this heterogeneous phenomenon (plus some fresh evidence to be presented below) does in fact, it will be argued, produce a coherent picture; these vastly different kinds of complexity indeed have something in common. Two questions will be posed in this investigation: (a) can there be mental representations of words which are complex in the way that has been claimed? and (b) if so, are words with complex lexical entries in any way more difficult to retrieve from the mental lexicon than words with simple entries? It will be argued, to cut the next twenty-odd pages short, that the answer to (a) is 'yes', the answer to (b) 'no'.

The evidence on which these conclusions are based is extensive and varied. Clearly, the two questions raise different methodological issues; whereas an answer to (a) can be sought via a variety of tasks which measure priming and interference, (b) requires the use of specific techniques to assess lexical access difficulty. Since it is to be argued that lexical complexity exerts *no* effect on difficulty of lexical access, it is appropriate to establish at the outset that other variables do have such an effect. The two tasks which have been most frequently used as measures of lexical access time, for example, are lexical decisions (in which subjects make a word–nonword judgement on a string of letters presented in isolation) and phoneme-monitoring (in which subjects listen within sentences for a word beginning with a specified sound). For the former, Whaley (1978) has presented a comprehensive review of the relative effects of a number of variables on lexical decision time; frequency of occurrence, meaningfulness, word length, and several other factors exert strong effects on response time in this task. For the latter, both Cutler and Norris (1979) and Foss and Blank (1980) have argued strongly that phoneme-monitoring response time can provide a measure of the time required to understand the word which precedes the target-bearing word in the sentence[1]; Foss and Blank show, for instance, that phoneme-monitoring responses are sensitive both to frequency of occurrence and word–nonword status of the word preceding the target-bearing item. In the following sections it will be seen that measures of lexical access time consistently fail to show effects of lexical complexity; but the reliable effects of frequency and other factors demonstrate that this failure simply is not due to the lack of a suitable metric by which to assess variations in lexical access time.

SEMANTIC COMPLEXITY

Semantic complexity covers a fairly wide range of variations between words. Firstly, there is lexical ambiguity, cited above as an example of semantic complexity; but ambiguity itself is not a unitary phenomenon. It includes: (a) unsystematic ambiguity, i.e. words with multiple quite unrelated senses (*bear*); (b) systematic ambiguity, i.e. words with related senses in different categories (*glue*); but also (c) words with closely related senses which nevertheless have quite distinct referents (e.g. *run* of people, water, or roads). Secondly, the meanings of words contain information of more central and less central nature; thus the most important part of the definition of the words *beer* and *brandy* is that they each describe a kind of alcoholic drink; but in the sentence 'This container holds the equivalent of a bottle of ——', they call up our knowledge that beer comes (in civilised countries at least) in small bottles and brandy in large ones; while 'He drank brandy in everyone else's round but beer in his own' appeals to our stored knowledge that brandy is a comparatively expensive drink, beer a relatively cheap one.

Certain words carry implications about their surrounding sentence context as part of their intrinsic meaning. Selection restrictions work this way: only horses can be *piebald*, only round things can *roll*. Factive verbs imply, similarly, the truth of their complements: 'I regret that Australian beer bottles hold 26 fluid ounces' is factive; 'I think that Australian beer bottles hold 26 fluid ounces' is not. Finally, the negative element of otherwise unmarked negative words such as *doubt* or *reluctant*, or the causative element in verbs such as *kill* or *dye*, could be held to make the semantic representations of such words more complex than those of words which are neither negative nor causative.

Again it should be made quite clear that disparate phenomena are being treated as if they were alike. Having more than one meaning, as ambiguous words do, is not at all the same thing as having, say, a meaning which can only be conjoined with a very few other concepts, as is the case with the meaning of *piebald*. But selection restrictions, factive presuppositions and negative implications are indisputable components of the meaning of words, with clear distributional and syntactic consequences, just as ambiguity is indisputable. The evidence to be cited in this section will show that the processing of a word necessarily involves access of whatever such indisputable information is associated with it in the lexicon. In this the different varieties of semantic complexity are alike. The case of causativity, however, involves lexical structure which is not indisputable but highly contentious; and, indeed, the review of the evidence on this issue will suggest that there is no validity to the claim that semantic decomposition is a lexical reality analogous to the other types of semantic complexity.

Lexical ambiguity

This is one of the most heavily investigated topics in psycholinguistics. There is good evidence, particularly from quite recent research, that multiple meanings of a lexically ambiguous word are stored together in the lexicon. The evidence is provided by studies which show that occurrence of an ambiguous word makes both its relevant and its irrelevant senses momentarily available, even if sentence context makes it quite clear which sense is appropriate. Swinney (1979) presented listeners with sentences containing an ambiguous word, and required them to make a word–nonword decision about a string of letters presented visually exactly at the point at which the ambiguous word occurred in the auditory channel. The letter strings might be nonwords, words unrelated in meaning to the ambiguous word, or words related to one or the other meaning. For example, a sentence might contain the ambiguous word *bug*, with the visually presented words being *ant*, *spy* or *sew*. Both the related words (*ant* and *spy*) were responded to faster than the unrelated word (*sew*) even when the context resolved the ambiguity; Swinney argued that both meanings of the ambiguous word must have been activated since associates of both meanings have been primed. Similarly, Lackner and Garrett (1972) presented listeners dichotically with two competing messages, one of which was a sentence to which the listeners were required to attend and which they had to paraphrase immediately after hearing it. Some of the sentences contained ambiguous words. In the unattended channel other material was presented (which subjects could not later report), and this material resolved the ambiguity. Lackner and Garrett found that subjects' paraphrases reflected the particular sense expressed by the disambiguating unattended message, and argued that since either meaning could be chosen according to which biasing context was presented, both meanings of the lexically ambiguous word must have been momentarily accessed from the lexicon. Finally, an experiment by Conrad (1974) required subjects to name the colour of the ink of printed words, some of which expressed meaning related to the ambiguous word which had occurred in a previously heard sentence; colour naming time was longer for words related to *either* meaning of the ambiguous word than to unrelated words.

Thus there is a good deal of support for the contention that accessing a lexically ambiguous word involves accessing all its senses. There is no evidence, however, that accessing a word with more than one sense incurs greater processing cost than accessing a word with a single sense. Phoneme-monitoring studies which claimed to demonstrate an increase in processing load associated with the occurrence of a lexical ambiguity (Foss, 1970; Foss and Jenkins, 1973; Cairns and Kamerman, 1975) appear to have confounded the ambiguity variable with physical differences between ambiguous words and their unambiguous controls (Mehler, Segui, and Carey,

1978; Newman and Dell, 1978); when these factors are controlled, sentences containing lexical ambiguities produce phoneme-monitoring reaction times no longer than those for matched unambiguous control sentences (Newman and Dell, 1978; Norris, 1980), and manipulation of the physical factors can make sentences containing an ambiguous word produce *shorter* reaction times than their controls (Mehler, Segui, and Carey, 1978).

The currently available evidence therefore suggests that lexical ambiguity is not associated with an increase in the difficulty of lexical access. It should be noted, however, that judging a string of words to be an acceptable sentence is more difficult if the sentence contains an ambiguous word than if it does not (Mistler-Lachman, 1975; Holmes, Arwas, and Garrett, 1977). Similarly, if a subject is required to comprehend time-compressed sentences presented at a very rapid rate and also to recall a list of words presented after each sentence, then fewer words from the list are recalled correctly when the sentence contains a lexical ambiguity than when it does not (Chodorow, 1979). These results perhaps reflect the development of an interpretation of the sentence as a whole. That is to say, although tasks which specifically measure lexical access difficulty show that ambiguous words are no harder to access than unambiguous words, it may well be the case that it is more difficult to construct a semantic representation of the sentence as a whole when the sentence contains an ambiguous word, and it is thus more difficult to integrate the sentence into actual or potential context. A similar suggestion has recently been put forward by Onifer and Swinney (1981) to account for the effects of frequency of meaning. It has been claimed (Hogaboam and Perfetti, 1975; Holmes, 1979) that the various senses of an ambiguous word are accessed in order of their frequency (i.e. the 'blow' reading of *punch* before the 'drink' reading) and that access of more than one sense only occcurs when a less frequent sense is required. However, Onifer and Swinney showed that priming of words related to both senses of a lexically ambiguous word occurs even when the context demands the most frequent reading; they argued that the apparent effects of frequency of meaning reflected a 'post-access decision process'. If the lengthened acceptability judgement times which Mistler-Lachman and Holmes *et al.* found for sentences containing an ambiguity indeed reflect difficulty of integrating the ambiguous word into sentence context, then it is reasonable to expect that there should be less difficulty in the sentence acceptability judgement tasks when the sentence expresses the more frequently used meaning of the ambiguous word than when it embodies the less frequently used meaning. Exactly this was found to be the case by Holmes (1979). Similarly when a word is used in its most frequent sense, and is therefore easily integrated into its context, it may be difficult to make judgements upon it with relation to other contexts, for example to decide whether or not it is ambiguous. This is what Hogaboam and Perfetti (1975) found.

The processing of semantically complex words in sentence context will be discussed again below. With regard to lexical access alone, the ambiguity studies strongly indicate that all senses of an ambiguous word are accessed but that lexical access itself is no more difficult for ambiguous than for unambiguous words. Lexical ambiguity thus offers a standard against which other types of semantic complexity, on which there is much less evidence available, can be compared.

Factivity

A predicate is said to be factive when it implies that its sentence complement expresses a true proposition. Factivity is thus an instance of lexical presupposition (see Morgan, 1969, on the distinction between lexical and sentential presupposition). There exists a whole class of factive words (Kiparsky and Kiparsky, 1971) comprising verbs such as *regret* and *know*, and adjectives such as *important* and *crazy* (cf. 'Bruce thought the decision crazy' versus 'Bruce thought the decision likely'). It is reasonable to assume that lexical presupposition in general, and factivity in particular, is an inseparable part of the definition of such words (the *Concise Oxford Dictionary*, for example, defines *regret* as 'be distressed about or sorry for (event, fact)'). Hence it should be incorporated in the mental representation of a factive verb or adjective, and when such a word occurs in a sentence, retrieval of its meaning from the internal lexicon should include retrieval of its presuppositional implications with respect to its complement. It thus becomes legitimate to query whether the occurrence of a factive is associated with greater processing difficulty as a result of the implications it involves, in comparison with otherwise similar but non-factive words. No existing evidence on this question is available in the literature; the data below come from studies of my own.

Again, it appears that lexical complexity does not imply difficulty. In a phoneme-monitoring experiment run by David Swinney and myself in Swinney's laboratory at Tufts University, response time was compared to target sounds preceded (a) by factive verbs or adjectives, or (b) by non-factive control words matched with the factives on frequency and length in syllables. An example sentence is:

(1) The retired general deplored/declared a continued readiness for war on the part of the NATO partners.

In this example the target sound is /k/ and the target-bearing word therefore 'continued'. The factive words produced reaction times not significantly different from those produced by the non-factives (see Table 2.1), $(F_1(1;30) = 1.25, p > .25)$.

Thus lexical access of a factive word seems to involve no greater processing difficulty than access of a non-factive. In contrast to the ambiguity case,

Table 2.1   Phoneme   monitoring   latencies
(msec) to target words preceded by a factive
or a non-factive verb or adjective

Average latencies	
Factive	Non-factive
515	506

however, factivity also exhibits no effect on the time required to judge whether or not a sentence is acceptable. In a follow-up to the previous experiment, conducted at Sussex University, I used the same set of factive words in a sentence classification experiment; again each sentence occurred in two versions, one containing the factive and another a non-factive verb or adjective matched on frequency and length in letters, for example:

(2) The retired general deplored/declared the army's readiness for war.

The response time to classify the sentences as acceptable or not did not differ significantly across the two conditions (Table 2.2) ($F_1 < 1$).

Thus factivity, unlike ambiguity, does not appear to be associated with any difficulty of integration into an overall representation of the sentence. Factive verbs and adjectives are as easy to process at all levels as non-factive verbs and adjectives.

Table 2.2   Time (msec) required to classify
sentences containing factive versus non-factive
verbs or adjectives

Average classification time	
Factive	Non-factive
2068	2064

Selection restrictions

Many verbs and adjectives are severely constrained with respect to the nouns of which they are predicated. Only liquids can *spray*, for example, or be *lukewarm*, whereas only adult females can be *pregnant*. When such words are applied to nouns not meeting the relevant restrictions ('pregnant silence', 'a lukewarm reception') they are understood to be used metaphorically, i.e. the restrictions are observed in the breach.

Selection restrictions of this kind must form part of the restricted word's lexical entry. (Again we can call on the testimony of printed dictionaries, which commonly state the selection restrictions at the outset of a definition: 'of liquids'; 'of a woman or a female aninal'; etc.) Thus the lexical entry for a word which involves selection restrictions is more complex than for one which does not, in that accessing the word will automatically produce the information that the set of nouns of which it can be predicated is severely limited. Is a restrictive lexical representation more difficult to process at any level than a non-restrictive one?

Once more, the answer is no. In fact, the reverse is true: words embodying selection restrictions can be very efficient at selecting a set of appropriate associates, and the consequent priming between words can result in sentences containing restrictive verbs or adjectives being easier to process than sentences with similar but non-restrictive words. Again the evidence is provided by unpublished work from the University of Sussex laboratory. Norris (1980) compared sentences like (3a), in which the verb embodies selection restrictions, with sentences like (3b), containing a non-restrictive verb, in a sentence classification task.

(3) a. The ink sprayed the customer. b. The ink annoyed the customer.

Norris found that the acceptability judgement times were shorter for the restrictive-verb versions. That is, construction of an overall sentence representation appears to be easier when the sentence contains a restrictive rather than a non-restrictive verb. This implies that retrieval of words from the mental lexicon does include retrieval of any selection restrictions associated with them; but the extra complexity of the information retrieved does not mean that linguistic processing becomes harder as a result.

Lexical negatives

Negation increases response time in a large number of psycholinguistic tasks (Wason, 1959, 1961; Just and Carpenter, 1971; Chase and Clark, 1972). Single lexical items can be in themselves negative—for instance, when they have a negating prefix (*unhappy*, *dislike*), or when they imply a negative (*doubt* = not believe; *vacant* = not occupied). The syntactic behaviour of affixed and implicit negatives is in many cases exactly like that of explicit negative elements (Klima, 1964). One must ask therefore whether negative lexical items are by themselves associated with an increase in processing difficulty, since they would seem to constitute an outstanding instance of lexical complexity which is likely to imply processing complexity.

Indeed, Clark and Clark (1977) have reported that the familiar response time deficit assocated with negation also appears when implicit negatives are used in a verification task (in which subjects judge whether or not a sentence accurately describes the content of a visual display, whether a sentence is true or false, or whether or not two sentences have the same meaning). A series of experiments by Sherman (1973, 1976) has investigated the contribution of explicit, implicit, and affixal negatives to reaction time to judge the 'reasonableness' of a proposition. He found that all types of negative elements, including lexical negatives, led to an increase in time to make the decision, in comparison with latency to judge the reasonableness of a sentence which contained no negative elements.

None of these tasks, however, measured direct lexical access or even sentence comprehension time. All of them required the subject to make a judgement about the content of the sentences presented—truth, reasonableness, accuracy in describing a picture, or identity with another sentence's content. Thus the effect of negation on response time might apply to any of several components of the subject's task: comparison or verification time as well as comprehension time. It does not necessarily follow from these results that affixed or implicit negatives are more difficult to access from the mental lexicon than non-negative words, or that sentences containing affixed or implicit negatives are more difficult to comprehend than sentences without any such words.

Again the only specific investigations of lexical access and sentence processing time with this variable are unpublished studies from the University of Sussex laboratory. The evidence indicates that negative lexical items, like other semantically complex words, are no more difficult to process than comparable simple words. In a phoneme-monitoring study, I measured reaction time to targets preceded by afffixed or implicitly negative verbs or adjectives in comparison with non-negatives matched on frequency and length in syllables, as in (4) and (5), in both of which the target sound is /b/:

(4) The recommendations of the environmental impact study were sure to disappoint/gratify backers of the new development.

(5) The dog sniffing round the yard stuck its nose into the empty/yellow bucket under the hedge.

As can be seen from Table 2.3, the effect of negation was not significant

Table 2.3   Phoneme monitoring latencies (msec) to target words preceded by implicit and affixed negative and non-negative verbs and adjectives

	Average latencies		
	Negative	Control	Average
Implicit	434	417	423
Affixed	436	447	441
Average	435	432	

Table 2.4   Lexical decision latencies (msec) to implicit and affixed negative and non-negative verbs and adjectives

	Average latencies		
	Negative	Control	Average
Implicit	635	659	647
Affixed	708	710	709
Average	672	684	

$(F_1 < 1)$. Since no attempt was made to match across the two sets of negative words, no estimate of the comparative difficulty of affixed and implicit negatives can be made on the basis of these data.

The same negative words were also included in a simple visual lexical decision (word-nonword) experiment, along with three sets of control words: one set matched with the negatives on length in letters and frequency; another set matched on length but not on frequency; and a third set matched on frequency but not on length. Although both the length $(F_1(3,57) = 4.23, p < 0.01)$ and frequency $(F_1(3,57) = 15.95, p < 0.001)$ manipulations produced the predicted significant effects, there was no significant effect of negation $(F_1(1,19) = 1.71, p > 0.2)$ as Table 2.4 shows.

Thus it is clear that lexical access *per se* takes no more time for a negative than for a non-negative word. Nor, it appears, is the process of simply understanding a sentence containing a lexical negative difficult in itself. The same 24 negative words used in the preceding two experiments were also incorporated in a sentence classification experiment in which subjects were asked to judge the acceptability of sentences containing either one of the negative words or a non-negative word matched on frequency and length in letters, for example:

(6) The headmaster will forbid/compel the boys to stay at school.

(7) The conservative vicar disliked/approved the choice of hymns.

Response time did not vary significantly as a function of the presence or

Table 2.5   Classification times (msec) for sentences containing implicit and affixed negative and non-negative verbs and adjectives

	Average classification times		
	Negative	Control	Average
Implicit	1912	1983	1947
Affixed	2114	2088	2102
Average	2013	2035	

absence of a lexical negative, as is clear from Table 2.5, ($F_1(1,26)$ = 2.05, $p > 0.15$).

We can summarize the evidence on lexical negation as follows: the fact that implicit and affixed negatives behave like explicit negative elements in verification tasks argues strongly that the processing of such lexical negatives involves processing of the negative element. That is, it is apparent that part of the lexical representation of an affixed or implicit negative is a representation of negation. Nonetheless, no reflection of additional processing complexity as a result of the presence of a single negative element shows up in tasks which measure lexical access or sentence comprehension time. From this we are forced to conclude that the response time decrement associated with single negative lexical items in verification tasks must result from other requirements of the task than sentence comprehension *per se*. Lexical negatives, like other semantically complex words, contain additional information (a negative element) in their lexical entry, but are not by virtue of this more difficult to understand.

However, although a sentence containing a single negative item is no more difficult to understand than an all-affirmative sentence, it is well known that as the number of negatives in a sentence increases, the sentence rapidly becomes extremely hard to interpret:

(8) Few Australians would fail to deny their reluctance not to doubt that the Tasmanian devil no longer exists.

But again, this effect appears to operate on the construction of a semantic representation of the sentence as a whole. Conceivably, construction of an overall sentence representation involves setting a truth index (one model incorporating such an index is given by Clark and Clark, 1977), and each additional occurrence of a negative item would require that the truth index be reset. If it were the case that this setting and resetting process is hard to keep track of, then competing representations of the sentence might become simultaneously available, leading to difficulty in deciding upon a final interpretation. In any case, it is clear that the difficulty associated with the occurrence of negation in sentences like (8) inheres in the construction of an integrated sentence representation; the experiments on single lexical negatives demonstrate convincingly that it is not a lexical access effect.

Semantic decomposition

Some linguists, Lakoff (1965), for example, or Postal (1970), have argued that the lexical representations of several classes of single words are expressed in terms of the meaning of other words or phrases, specifically, concepts corresponding to components of their semantic representation. Thus causative verbs such as *kill* or *dye* might be expressed as CAUSE (die) or

CAUSE (acquire colour). More generally, word meanings might be defined in terms of superordinate concepts, e.g. *man* as (adult) (male) (human) (animate), etc.

A good deal of controversy has surrounded this claim, both in linguistics and in psycholinguistics. It is discussed here because it makes clear predictions about added complexity resulting from the lexical access of, for instance, causative verbs. That is, if the correct semantic analysis of a sentence such as 'the dingo killed the wombat' is a structure containing two propositions, one with an explicit verb of causation and the other with an inchoative (unanalysed) verb, i.e. 'The dingo caused (the wombat die)', then a listener's comprehension of this superficially single-proposition sentence must involve reconstruction of the two-proposition underlying representation and must therefore involve greater perceptual complexity than comprehension of a sentence not containing a causative. But a number of experiments, mainly by Kintsch (1974), have failed to show any effect on processing difficulty of semantic complexity of this kind. For instance, Kintsch found that causative verbs were not associated with any increase in difficulty in comparison with inchoative verbs when processing difficulty was measured by sentence initiation time, sentence completion time, or phoneme-monitoring response latency. Similarly, unpublished experiments in our laboratory at Sussex have failed to find an effect of semantic complexity of verbs on (a) time to read a sentence, (b) latency to answer a question, and (c) lexical decision response time, i.e. lexical access time.

This is not more than the previous catalogue of findings on multiple meanings, presuppositions, selection restrictions, and negative marking would have led us to expect; all of these types of information are incorporated in lexical representations, are activated in the course of lexical access, but do not lead to an increase in processing difficulty. Yet there are strong reasons for believing that semantic decomposition is a very different case from the other four kinds of semantic complexity discussed above: to wit, there is no evidence that the lexical representations of, say, causative verbs are in fact decomposed, and there is even a certain amount of evidence that they are not decomposed. Fodor, Garrett, Walker, and Parkes (1980), for instance, conducted a series of experiments in which they elicited subjects' judgements of how closely related were two words within a sentence. This test proved sensitive to differences in underlying structure, for instance between sentences with *expect*-type verbs and *persuade*-type verbs. Thus, in (9) the underlying structure of the *expect* version has the two words, 'captain' and 'passengers', in different clauses (9'), whereas in the *persuade* version both words occur in the main clause (9").

(9)   The captain expected/persuaded the passengers to stay calm.
(9')   The captain expected (the passengers stay calm).
(9")   The captain persuaded the passengers (the passengers stay calm).

As predicted, the words 'captain' and 'passengers' were judged significantly more related in the *persuade* version than in the *expect* version of (9). However, no corresponding differences were found between the relatedness judgements for 'workers' and 'paint' in a comparison of causative verbs with matched non-causatives, as in (10):

(10) The workers spilled/found some paint.

although if the causative verb had been decomposed in comprehension, the underlying structure of the causative sentence would presumably have contained the two tested words in different underlying clauses:

(10') The workers caused (paint spill).

Similarly, Fodor, Fodor, and Garrett (1975) found standard performance decrement effects of negative marking in affixed and implicit negatives in a verification task similar to that used by Sherman (1973), but found no such effects for words whose decomposed definitions should contain a negative element, e.g. *bachelor*. Fodor *et al.* concluded that since these words do not act as though they contain a negative element in their semantic representation, they are presumably not decomposed into simpler elements in the process of being understood.

Kintsch (1974) found that words with decomposable definitions did not produce more errors than matched inchoative words on a simple memory task, although in prior research (Kintsch, 1972) he had found evidence that other kinds of lexical complexity (see the discussion of morphological complexity in the following section) were associated with poorer memory task performance. In another experiment, Kintsch used sentences containing decomposable words (e.g. *convince*) in a recall task and found that words representing a base component of the meaning of the experimental words (in this instance *believe*) were effective recall cues—as effective as high associates (e.g. *persuade*) though not as effective as the complex word itself. (None of the components were themselves high associates of the experimental words; but note that Fischler, 1977, has shown that any semantically related word will prime as efficiently as a high associate). Thus definitional elements of the decomposable word's meaning are effective primes for that word, but the processing (understanding and memory storage) of a decomposable word does not necessarily involve decomposition into its components; if it did, one might have expected Kintsch's component words to have provided as effective a recall cue as the complex words themselves.

The evidence seems clear: semantic decomposition, like other forms of semantic complexity, is not associated with added processing difficulty. In fact, it appears that it may not even be analogous to other kinds of semantic complexity discussed above, since not even an indirect reflection of decomposition in sentence comprehension has been found. Decomposable words such as *kill*, *bachelor*, or *convince* may have lexical representations which overlap enough with those of other words to evoke these other words as associates; but there is no evidence that the component concepts are actually contained in the definition of complex words. Certainly the strongest possible version of the decomposition hypothesis is not valid—decomposable words are not accessed via the lexical representation of other words corresponding to components of their semantic representation. And like other semantically complex words, words with decomposable definitions are not more difficult to access from the lexicon than words with simpler definitions.

MORPHOLOGICAL COMPLEXITY

Morphological complexity has not always been considered as an issue separate from semantic complexity. In the same way that the lexical representation of *kill* was hypothesized to be constructed from the lexical representation of *cause* and *die*, so for instance the lexical form of a derived word such as *wisdom* was hypothesized to be constructed from that of its base word, in this case *wise*. It should be noted that all of Kintsch's experiments described in the previous section examined morphologically complex words (abstract and agent nouns such as *ability* and *speaker*) as well as causatives and other decomposable words; the results reported did not differ significantly across type of word. But the two cases have been separated in this discussion for a good reason, namely that whereas there is no evidence that decomposable words contain within their lexical entry a representation of the base words which supposedly comprise their meaning, there is abundant evidence that morphologically complex words do contain within their lexical representation the details of their morphological structure.

Prefixed words

This topic has attracted a number of recent studies: Taft and Forster (1975); Taft (1979); Stanners, Neiser, and Painton (1979); Fay (in press); Rubin, Becker, and Freeman (1979). Taft and Forster's study investigated the time to reject nonwords in a lexical decision tasks as a function of whether or not the nonwords were stems of existent prefixed words: e.g. *juvenate* from *rejuvenate* was compared with *pertoire* from *repertoire*, which is not prefixed. The *juvenate* type of nonwords took significantly longer to reject than the *pertoire* type. This response time difference also held when the items were presented bearing pseudoprefixes (*dejuvenate* versus *depertoire*). Taft and Forster argued that prefixed words are stored in the lexicon under a heading which corresponds to their stem, that is, *rejuvenate* is actually stored as *juvenate*. In direct support of this conclusion they reported another experiment in which they examined real words which occurred also as stems. In some cases the prefixed form was much more common than the stand-alone form (as is the case with *prevent* versus *vent*), in others the prefixed form was less common than the stand-alone form (e.g. *card* versus *discard*). Lexical decision reaction time to words like *vent* was slower than reaction time to words which only occurred alone; but this was not the case for words like *card*. Taft and Forster's explanation of this finding involved interference from the higher-frequency forms which could not stand alone and on which a 'yes' response could therefore not be based. This particular result, however, is highly likely to be artefactual. The stand-alone roots were matched with their controls on frequency of the surface form alone, not including the frequencies of other regular inflected forms. In this experiment 16 of the 20 *vent*-type words were matched with controls which had a much higher frequency when other inflections are taken into account. *Pending* and *picking*, for instance, have a surface frequency of 14 each, but the combined frequency of *pick* plus *picked* plus *picking* plus *picks* is 151, whereas the combined frequency of all forms of *pend* is still 14 (Kučera and Francis, 1967). This fact alone could have accounted for the reaction time difference found in this condition; in the *card* condition, where no reaction time difference was found, there was also no imbalance between roots and controls on the combined frequency measure. (As will be seen in the following section, the evidence is very clear that regular inflections for tense and number do not produce separate lexical representations for each form. It is therefore very important to take this fact into account when constructing frequency-matched materials).

Taft (1979) reported a further experiment in which pairs of words were compared which themselves had the same frequency of occurrence (e.g. *reproach* and *dissuade*) but differed in the frequency of occurrence of their same-stem relatives (*approach* is more frequent than *persuade*). In each case the relatives were higher in frequency than the stimulus words (though higher by different amounts) so that the interference effects as claimed in the Taft and Forster experiment should have been equivalent in this case. The words with comparatively high-frequency same-stem relatives were responded to significantly faster than their frequency-matched controls with comparatively low-frequency relatives. Thus the reaction time advantage of a high-frequency word can carry over to its morphological relatives, indicating that, according to Taft, the lexical representations of morphologically related words are closely connected with the frequency rating for the entire group determined most probably by the aggregate of all the related forms.

Stem defined lexical representation is also postulated by Fay (in press) on the basis of a study of prefix errors in spontaneous speech. Substitution errors often occur in which a prefixed word is replaced by another word with the same stem but different prefix (11), or by a non-occurring combination of prefix with the target stem (12):

(11) . . . the sewing *constructions* (Intended: *instructions*)
(12) . . . to which I would like to become *concustomed* (Intended: *accustomed*).

Fay argued that these errors are best explained in terms of a model of the mental lexicon in which prefixed words are accessed via their stems; in the production case, the correct stem is accessed but the wrong prefix attached to it, resulting in a typical prefix error.

However, there are two recent pieces of evidence which indicate that it may not be the case that the lexical representation of a prefixed word is simply and only in terms of its stem. Stanners, Neiser, and Painton (1979) used the repetition priming effect (the reaction time to the second presentation of a particular word in a list of lexical decision items is speeded; Forbach, Stanners, and Hochhaus, 1974) to investigate the effectiveness of morphological components as primes for a morphologically complex word. They found that stem and prefix presented separately (either alone, or as part of other words) earlier in the list significantly facilitated lexical decision response time to a later representation of a prefixed word in comparison with the same word presented without preceding primes. However, they also found that priming with the word itself was significantly more effective than priming with its morphological components presented separately. They argued that the model of the lexicon best supported by their results was one in which each prefixed word had a unitary undecomposed representation—so that the word itself was its own best prime—but the representations of all words with the same stem were connected, perhaps via a representation of the stem, so that accessing any one activated, to some extent, the others; thus the morphological components were also effective primes. In another experiment Stanners *et al.* found that words with independently meaningful prefixes (e.g. *un-*, *de-*) were as effective at priming their stem words as the stem words themselves; that is, *unaware* was as good a prime for *aware* as *aware* itself.

A similar conclusion to that drawn by Stanners *et al.* was suggested by Rubin, Becker, and Freeman (1979). Lexical decision reaction times were found by Rubin *et al.* to be faster for prefixed words (*remark*) than for pseudo-prefixed words (*reckon*) when the rest of the list consisted of prefixed words and 'prefixed' nonwords (*retext*), but not when the rest of the list consisted of non-prefixed words and nonwords. More recently, Taft (1981) found a *naming* reaction time deficit for pseudoprefixed words, even when subjects saw no really prefixed words at all; but Henderson, Wallis and Knight (1983) failed to find any *lexical decision* reaction time deficit for pseudoprefixed words in a mixed list. Rubin *et al.* proposed morphological decomposition of a prefixed word in lexical access as an optional strategy—not necessary, since prefixed words have a unitary representation, but possible, since they *can* be accessed via their stem. For this mode of access to be at all possible the morphological structure information must be incorporated in the lexical representation; either all words with one stem are listed conjointly, with access to the stem activating them all, or prefixed words have two unconnected representations, one unitary and one headed by the stem. The former alternative is the one most compatible with the Stanners *et al.* results as well as with those of Taft, of Fay, and of Rubin *et al.*

Finally, another experiment by Fay (1980) supports this kind of mixed model. In a lexical decision experiment, prefixed words (*institute*) did not differ in response time from non-prefixed words (*assassin*), but prefixed nonwords composed of nonexistent combinations of real stems and prefixes (*abvention*) were significantly more difficult to reject than non-prefixed nonwords. Fay interpreted this finding as indicating that prefixed words could be accessed holistically, but that access via the stem was also possible; this latter option was responsible for the interference effect with nonwords, as the entry for *vention* would have to be checked out to ensure that it could not occur with *ab-*. Taft, Forster, and Garrett (1974, cited by Taft and Forster, 1975) also found that, other things being equal, prefixed words are no more difficult to access from the lexicon than non-prefixed words. The results reported in the section on *Lexical negatives* above also include a parallel finding: in our studies of negation, words with negative prefix were no more difficult to process than non-prefixed controls. That is to say, whatever activation of morphological structure goes on in the recognition of a prefixed word, it does not make the process of recognition more difficult.

Suffixed words

Inflections

There is abundant evidence that words inflected for tense or number do not have lexical representation independent of their base form, and that base word and inflection are separated in language processing. In tachistoscopic presentation inflected words seem to be perceived as two units (Gibson and Guinet, 1971). Recall of adverbs ending in -*ly* is affected by the frequency of the base adjective rather than the frequency of the inflected adverb form (Rosenberg, Coyle, and Porter, 1966). Regular inflected forms (*pours*) show a repetition priming effect on their base words (*pour*) as strong as that of the base word itself (Stanners, Neiser, Hernon & Hall 1979; Fowler & Napps 1982), while priming with irregular inflected forms (*hung*) is less effective than priming with the base word itself (*hang*) though still significantly better than no prime at all (Stanners, Neiser, Hernon, and Hall, 1979). This kind of morphological priming is, also, somewhat more robust over time than semantic priming (Henderson, Wallis & Knight, 1983). Pretraining with an inflectional variant (e.g. *sees*) significantly facilitates later learning of a word (e.g. *seen*) in comparison with no pretraining, or pretraining with a word with as much visual similarity to the target word as the morphological relative (e.g. *seed*; Murrell and Morton, 1974). Only *regular* inflections provide effective priming, however, when the dependent variable is accuracy of report of a degraded auditory signal (Kempley and Morton, 1982). Plural morphemes tend to get detached in memory representations (van der Molen and Morton, 1979). Lexical decision reaction times are sensitive both to the frequency of occurrence of the surface form and to the combined frequency of base plus inflectional variants (Taft, 1979). Neither lexical decision reaction times nor word naming times, however, are affected simply by whether or not a word embodies an inflection (Fowler and Napps, 1982).

An argument in favour of a stemorganized lexicon has been advanced by Jarvella and Meijers (Chapter 3 of this volume). Jarvella and Meijers primed target verbs either with differently inflected forms of the same stem, or with similarly inflected forms of different stems; subjects in their experiments performed same and different stem judgements significantly faster than inflection judgements, a result which they interpreted as evidence against the independent lexical representation of inflected forms.

Similarly, it has been claimed that inflected forms are actually generated by rule during speech production. This argument has chiefly been made on speech error evidence (Fromkin, 1973; Garrett, 1976; MacKay, 1979); errors in which inflections are misplaced in an utterance are common, and the inflectional form applied in the error is usually that appropriate to the word to which it has actually been attached rather than to the word to which it was intended to be attached:

(13) I'd hear one if I knew it. (Intended: I'd know one if I heard it.)
(14) . . . in little yellow bag from the banks(s). (Intended: bags(z) from the bank.)

MacKay (1976) has made the same claim on the basis of his experimental finding that translating a present into a past tense form takes longer and is more subject to error the more complex the relation between base and inflected form. The evidence is, however, also quite compatible with representation of the appropriate inflected forms in the lexicon: not as independent, unitary entries, but as a sub-part of the lexical entry for the base word. Such a representation would have to allow for differential degrees of closeness between base and inflection, to account for the lesser effectiveness of irregular forms as primes in comparison with regular forms (Stanners, Neiser, Hernon, and Hall, 1979) and greater difficulty of translation from one to the other (MacKay, 1976); it would also account for the finding of Jarvella and Snodgrass (1974) that reaction time to judge that the same base word was involved in a pair of words (base + inflected form) was longer when the inflection was irregular (*sing-sang*) than when it was regular (*sail-sailed*). Finally, a recent experiment by Lukatela, Gligorijević, Kostić, and Turvey (1980) investigated noun inflections in Serbo-Croatian; from the fact that lexical decision responses to nominative forms were consistently faster than responses to genitive or instrumental forms, the authors argued for a model of lexical representation of inflected forms in which the nominative comprises the nucleus of a cluster of separate entries, one for each form.

Derivational suffixes

As was mentioned above, Kintsch (1974) failed to find on-line processing effects of the derivational complexity of agent and abstract nouns. Two studies, it is true, do report a reaction time deficit associated with morphological complexity, but in each case there is reason to believe that the result may have been due to other factors. Snodgrass and Jarvella (1972) found lexical decision reaction time to be longer to prefixed and suffixed forms in comparison with their base forms; but the comparison strings were matched neither on frequency nor on length. Holyoak, Glass, and Mah (1976) found that reaction time to judge whether or not a string of words expressed a true proposition (a task which, it will be recalled, was found by Sherman, 1973, to be sensitive to lexical negation) was longer when a morphologically complex word was involved, e.g. 'knights have strength' versus 'knights are strong'. However, since the effect persisted (for some items) even when the predicate was presented (and processed) before the sentence subject, Holyoak *et al.* claimed that it constituted evidence *against* morphological decomposition; and indeed, since the authors had failed to control for length, frequency or syntactic structure, there is no lack of alternative explanations for their results. Similarly open to criticism is the finding of Kintsch (1972) that derived nouns produce poorer performance in a paired-associate learning task; when the additional variable of concreteness was controlled, the effect disappeared (Richardson, 1975). In fact, such factors as concreteness and imageability seem to have been confounded with morphological complexity in a number of other early studies of this topic; see Richardson (1977) for a review.

Thus, not suprisingly in view of all the evidence summarized hereto, there is no indication that suffixed words are more difficult to process than matched simple words. But there is evidence that morphological structure of this kind is represented in the lexicon. Kintsch (1974) found that base components of abstract and agent nouns such as *ability* and *attendant* (*able*, *attend*) were as effective recall cues as high associates of the same words (*skill*, *gas station*). Stanners, Neiser, Hernon, and Hall (1979; replicated by Fowler & Napps 1982) found that derived words (*selective*, *destruction*) produced a significant repetition priming effect for their base words (*select*, *destroy*), though not as large an effect as that produced by the base word itself. Bradley (1979) found that a combined frequency measure obtained by adding the frequency of the baseword to that of its derivatives was a better predictor of lexical decision response time for derived words ending with -*ness*, -*er* or -*ment* than was the frequency of occurrence of the stimulus word alone. Thus there is evidence that suffixed words, like prefixed words, have lexical entries closely connected with, but not simply subordinate to, the entries of their base words. The entries can be accessed via the base word or independently. In support of this suggestion one can cite the finding of Manelis and Tharp (1977) that reaction time to decide whether or not a pair of letter strings are both words is slower if one is suffixed and the other not (*printer slander*) than if both are suffixed (*printer drifter*) or both simple (*slander blister*); although pseudo-suffixes (*vegetable*, *rubbish*) do not increase response time (Henderson, Wallis & Knight, 1983). Morphological decomposition is an optional strategy; if applied inappropriately (e.g. when the processor is misled by *print* + *er* to think that *slander* can be similarly analysed), it can result in increased processing difficulty.

Independent evidence in favour of conjoint storage of suffixed words derived from the same base comes from studies of errors in spontaneous speech. Firstly, errors of lexical stress show a curious pattern, as seen in (15)–(17):

(15) . . . so we don't have any conflícts.
(16) . . . and all the syntáx texts be lost.
(17) . . . from my prósodic colleagues.

The stress is always erroneously applied to a syllable which bears stress in a morphological relative of the target word (*conflict* (verb), *syntactic*, and *prosody* respectively). Cutler (1981a) proposed that this pattern is a result of the way such errors arise: namely from confusion within the lexicon between the stress-marked syllables of conjointly stored morphological derivatives from the same stem. Interestingly, the direction of interference in these errors does not appear to be random. A subset of the lexical stress errors involves confusion between the syllable stress marking of a base word and a morphologically more complex word, and within this subset more than two-thirds involve a derived word produced with stress on the syllable which bears it in the base word (as in (17) above); fewer than one-third involve a base word stressed on a syllable which bears stress in a derivative (as in (16)), a statistically significant difference (Cutler, 1980).

Word formation errors also occur (Fromkin, 1977; McKay, 1979; Cutler, 1980), in which the wrong suffix can be applied (e.g. *self-indulgement* for *self-indulgence*) or the correct suffix can be wrongly applied (e.g. *expection* for *expectation*). Again, these errors argue that base and suffix are separable in speech production. In word formation errors, there is a significant tendency for the erroneous derived form to be more transparent with respect to its base form than the target form would have been (Cutler, 1980); thus the base word *expect* is better preserved in *expection* than in *expectation*. Similarly, the fact noted above that stress errors tend to be derived words erroneously pronounced with the stress of their base rather than vice versa also suggests that derived forms may be preferred which are closer to their base. Some experimental evidence also indicates a possible difference between transparent and opaque derived forms. For instance, the effect that Bradley (1979) found for derivations ending with *-ness*, *-er*, or *-ment* (all of them transparent), namely that the combined frequency of all derivatives better predicted lexical decision reaction time than the individual item frequency, did not hold for derivatives with *-ion*, which are opaque. Similarly Jarvella and Snodgrass (1974) found that pairs of words in which the derivation and the base had different spelling (*defend–defensive*) took longer to classify as being derived from the same stem than pairs in which the base-to-derivation relation was transparent (*attain–attainable*). Bradley argued that a possible explanation of her result was that transparent forms were subordinate to the lexical representation of their base forms whereas opaque forms had independent representations. However, a more conservative explanation is simply that the lexically specified relation between transparent derivatives and base is closer than that between opaque derivatives and base; this explanation is analogous to the account of lexical representation of regular and irregular inflections suggested above.

Productive morphology

Not only do speakers make errors of word formation, they also regularly create their own neologisms, that is, use their internalized knowledge of morphological structure. Examples of spontaneous neologisms from my own collection include:

(18) What I need is a de-mad-ifier.
(19) He just context-free-ized it.
(20) . . . retreat even further from empiricity.

In all such cases, the produced form is transparent with respect to its base (with certain apparent exceptions, such as (20), which will be discussed below). That this pattern reflects a real preference for transparent derivations can be shown in experiments in which subjects are asked to choose between alternative derived forms of the same base. Speakers prefer, for instance, *-ness* derivations to *-ity* derivations when the latter are opaque, i.e. result in a change in vowel quality, shift of primary stress, etc. (*sinisterness, sinisterity*), but show no preference between the two suffixes when both derivations are transparent (*jejuneness, jejunity*; Cutler, 1980). Similarly, when subjects are asked to judge whether or not possible words formed from base plus suffix are in fact English words, they accept more words formed with *-ness* than with *-ity* if the *-ity* derivatives are opaque (Aronoff and Schvaneveldt, 1978), but show no preference either way if both *-ness* and *-ity* derivatives are transparent (Cutler, 1980). However, there are exceptions to this generalization; in some cases derived words which do not preserve all of the base word, or which bear primary stress on a syllable different from the stressed syllable of the base word, prove to be quite acceptable. For instance, in an experiment reported by Cutler (1980), subjects did not show a significant preference between *excusement* and *excusion*, although the latter fails to preserve the final phoneme of the base word. Also, Aronoff and Anshen (1981) showed that possible nouns formed from adjectives ending with *-ible* are accepted more often when they are derived with *-ity* (*suppressibility*) than when they are formed with *-ness* (*suppressibleness*).

Nevertheless, it can be shown that such words are also *functionally* transparent. Thus although *suppressibility* bears primary stress on the fourth syllable, the second syllable (which bears primary stress in the base) still carries a secondary stress. And it is important to note that listeners can distinguish stressed from unstressed syllables, but not, in the absence of full information about the word, multiple levels of stress (Lieberman, 1965). Thus a listener hearing *suppressibility* registers the second syllalbe as stressed without any way of knowing that a yet more highly stressed syllable is about to come. Consonants have not been lost and vowel quality has not changed; thus the first two syllables of *suppressibility* presumably suffice to enable the listener to access the lexical entry (group of lexical entries) for *suppress*. Analogously, *empiricicity* in (20) above preserves the first syllables of *empirical*, with the second more highly stressed than the first or third.

The case is different, of course, for *suppressivity*. Adding *-ity* to *suppressive* shifts the primary stress back onto the first syllable, resulting in a change in vowel quality. Instead of beginning with [səp] like the rest of the morphological relatives of *suppress, suppressivity* begins with [sʌp] like *supper, supplement* and *suppurate*, and could initially mislead the language processor towards the lexical entries for these words. The criteria for functional transparency appear to be crucially concerned with the initial portions of the word. It has been suggested (Cutler, 1981b) that it might be possible to specify exactly how much of the base word has to be preserved for a derived word to be functionally transparent. For each word there is a theoretically earliest point at which it can be identified, namely that point at which it becomes distinguishable from other words in the language beginning with the same sequence of sounds; Marslen-Wilson (1980) calls this the *recognition point*. In all of the *-ibility* derivatives which Aronoff and Anshen (1981) found to be acceptable, the segmental values and relative syllable stress of the base word were preserved up to the base word's recognition point (for *suppress*, for instance, this is the final sound, at which it diverges from *supremacy*). In Cutler's (1980) experiments, too, all of the non-transparent but acceptable neologisms preserved relative stress and segmental value up to the recognition point of the base (for *excuse* the recognition point is [j]).

Preserving the base word up to the recognition point allows the hearer enough information to be sure of accessing the base word's lexical entry. Thus when speakers have to choose neologisms, they prefer those which contain transparently within them their base word or, at least, those segments which are crucial for auditory recognition of the base word. The implication of this preference is that speakers possess general criteria for the acceptability of neologisms which are based on what will be most convenient for the hearer. As long as the hearer can access the base word's lexical entry, the neologisms can be understood by the application of morphological principles to the base word's meaning, despite the fact that no specific lexical representation for the particular nonce-form exists. Not only does the production of neologisms draw on a speaker's internalized knowledge of morphological structure, but it expresses the speaker's knowledge of how words are represented in the lexicon and how a morphologically complex word may be accessed via its base.

SYNTACTIC COMPLEXITY

This final section considers three ways in which lexical representations may incorporate syntactic complexity. Firstly, there is systematic ambiguity—one word with more than one form class. Secondly, there is the holistic representation of multi-word units. And thirdly, there is the case of subcategorization restrictions on verbs, a lexically specified syntactic constraint.

Systematic ambiguity

A special case of lexical ambiguity arises when one considers ambiguity across form class. Words with multiple unrelated meanings do not necessarily maintain form class across meanings (e.g. *bear*); moreover, huge numbers of words can be used—with closely related meanings—in more than one form class, particularly as nouns and verbs (*doubt*, *crown*, *fuse*, etc.). Syntactic structure usually constrains interpretation completely with respect to form class; one might think that syntactic structure would provide sufficient cues on the basis of which to select the correct, and only the correct, reading of a word ambiguous across form class where the only alternative interpretation was of a form class different from that demanded by the context. Therefore, it might be expected that no evidence of lexical activation of the alternative interpretations should be found. However, Prather and Swinney (1977), using Swinney's cross-modal priming task described earlier, found that when ambiguous words of this type were incorporated in sentences in which the syntactic context completely constrained which reading was appropriate—the noun readings were preceded by *the*, the verb readings by *to*—words related to both the appropriate and the inappropriate (different form class) meaning were primed. Moreover, this was true both of unsystematic (non-meaning-related) and systematic (meaning-related) ambiguities. This finding suggests that multiple meanings of words may be stored together irrespective of form class, i.e. the lexicon can contain syntactically heterogeneous word conglomerates.

A similar finding to Prather and Swinney's is that of Tanenhaus, Leiman, and Seidenberg (1979), who found that presentation of a syntactically ambiguous word in an unambiguous syntactic context (e.g. 'they all rose') significantly facilitated naming latency to an associate of the contextually inappropriate meaning of the ambiguous word (e.g. flower). Again, this suggests that despite constraining syntactic context both noun and verb readings of the ambiguous word were momentarily activated.

A somewhat different picture is offered by an experiment conducted by Ryder and Walker (1982). Subjects were asked to judge whether or not two words were semantically related. When one of the words was semantically ambiguous (*duty–tax*) reaction times were longer than when both words were unambiguous (*city–town*). Moreover, this was true irrespective of whether the dominant or infrequent meaning was required for the relatedness judgement (*duty–responsibility*; *duty–tax*). Systematic (cross-category) ambiguities, on the other hand, only produced an interference effect when the judgement involved the infrequent reading (*cart–carry*), not when it involved the dominant reading (*cart–wagon*); the latter type of pair was responded to as quickly as unambiguous pairs. Ryder and Walker argued that in the access of cross-category ambiguities only the primary meaning (that is, the primary form class) is activated at first, in contrast to the case of semantic ambiguity, where all meanings are automatically activated at once.

An analogous conclusion can be drawn from an experiment by Forster and Bednall (1976), who measured subjects' reaction time to judge the acceptability of two-word strings, in each case a noun or verb preceded by *to* or *the*. When systematically ambiguous words were presented in their dominant sense (*the cage*, *to blame*), reaction time was as fast as to unambiguous words (*the wife*, *to greet*); but reaction times to the infrequent senses of systematically ambiguous words (*to cage*, *the blame*) were significantly slower.

How are these results to be reconciled with the findings that appear to show that all meanings of a systematic ambiguity are activated? It should be noted that both the Prather and Swinney and the Tanenhaus *et al.* studies demonstrated an effect of semantic priming due to the contextually inappropriate meaning, the dependent variable in each case being time to respond to a word which was not itself the systematically ambiguous word. As such they constitute robust evidence that priming did occur. The Ryder and Walker and the Forster and Bednall studies, on the other hand, measured reaction time to some judgement made about the systematically ambiguous word itself—its relatedness to another word, or its acceptability in combination with a preceding function word. Their findings are quite compatible with the suggestion that although both meanings are accessed, the dominant form class interpretation is retrieved first and is therefore able to be judged more rapidly than the later-activated infrequent interpretation. In this there seems to be a real difference between non-systematic and systematic ambiguity: although in both cases all meanings of a word constitute part of the same lexical grouping, in the case of systematic ambiguity the less frequent interpretation may only be accessed via the dominant interpretation.

Multi-word units

A second way in which a lexical entry may be syntactically complex is that a single meaning may be associated with a string of words. An obvious instance of a multi-word unit expressing a single meaning is that of idioms; the meaning of an idiom cannot by definition be expressed as a concatenation of the meanings of its component parts. The idiomatic meaning of 'let the cat out of the bag', for instance, has nothing to do with cats or bags. Linguists (e.g. Fraser, 1970) have claimed that idioms function in the language not as phrases but as single lexical items, and that they are listed in the lexicon just as any other word is listed. Indeed, evidence that idioms are represented as holistic units in the mental lexicon was presented by Swinney and Cutler (1979) using a task which was analogous to lexical decision and sentence classification, namely phrase classification, in which subjects were presented with strings of words and asked to determine whether or not they were acceptable English phrases. Idiomatic phrases were matched with control phrases which were constructed by substituting for one word in the idiom another word of equal length and equal or higher frequency (e.g. for 'break the ice' the control was 'break the cup'). Reaction time to classify idioms was significantly faster than classification time for the control phrases, a result which was interpreted as evidence that the idioms had been accessed, in their idiomatic sense, as units; no extra time was required to integrate the separate word meanings and arrive at an acceptable interpretation of the phrase, as would have to have been done for the control phrases.

Note that an alternative view of the lexical representation of idioms has been proposed by Bobrow and Bell (1973), namely that idioms are indeed represented as units, but in a separate idiom list; when an idiom is comprehended, a literal reading is first computed and only when that fails is the phrasal meaning accessed from the idiom list. The Swinney and Cutler results provide definite evidence against this claim. Bobrow and Bell based their suggestion not on results of an on-line processing task, but on which interpretation subjects reported for a string like 'kick the bucket' (which can be meant either literally or idiomatically). The strings were presented under biasing conditions which consisted of prior presentation of (a) a number of idioms, or (b) a number of literal phrases; idiomatic readings tended to be reported when idioms had been presented, literal readings when literal phrases had been presented. Bobrow and Bell claimed that their subjects could adopt or abandon a special idiom mode of processing; but Swinney and Cutler pointed out that Bobrow and Bell's results could equally well be explained as reflecting a mental decision about the most appropriate meaning on which to base a response.

In a second experiment, Swinney and Cutler compared idioms with different levels of syntactic frozenness. Frozen idiomatic phrases convey their idiomatic meaning in only one syntactic form (e.g. 'jump in the lake' cannot undergo the simplest syntactic operations: 'Joylene's jumping in the lake was desired' does not convey the idiomatic reading), whereas others are less frozen or virtually unfrozen ('bury the hatchet', for instance, retains its idiomatic interpretation through most syntactic permutations). No difference was found between more frozen and less frozen idioms; all showed an equivalent advantage over literal control strings.

In a further unpublished experiment carried out at the University of Sussex, idioms with literal interpretations (such as 'break the ice' and 'kick the bucket') were compared with idioms which have no literal interpretation (e.g. 'by and large', 'in the know'); again both types of idiom showed an equivalent reaction time advantage in comparison with literal strings.

Thus it appears to be the case that multi-word idioms have unitary lexical representation. Supporting evidence for this model comes from an experiment by Ortony, Schallert, Reynolds, and Antos (1978) who found that comprehension of idiomatic phrases in contexts which demanded their idiomatic reading took no longer (in fact was often faster) than comprehension of the same phrases in contexts requiring a literal interpretation. Moreover, Gibbs (1980) found that paraphrase judgements were faster for the idiomatic than for the literal reading of an idiom irrespective of whether the idiomatic string had been preceded by appropriate preceding context, or no context. These results indicate that accessing the idiomatic lexical entry may be easier than accessing the multiple entries for the separate items in the string; which in turn suggest that there should in general be a bias to perceive idiomatic readings. This is indeed the case. Van Lancker and Canter (1981) had subjects record idioms in contexts which forced either literal interpretation or the idiomatic reading, then excised the relevant strings from context and played them to listeners in an attempt to determine whether the productions had included disambiguating acoustic information. They found that listeners could readily distinguish the idiomatic and literal interpretations one from the other when they were presented together; but when the productions were presented in isolation, listeners showed a strong preference for the idiomatic interpretation irrespective of the context from which the utterance had been taken. And in another unpublished study by Swinney and Cutler, carried out at Tufts University, phoneme-monitoring reaction time was measured to targets immediately following idiomatic phrases: in contexts which were biased towards the idiomatic interpretation of the phrase, no difference was found between the idiomatic and matched control phrases, but when the context was biased towards the literal interpretation, reaction time to targets following the potential idioms was somewhat longer than to targets following the unambiguous controls—indicating interference from competing access of the idiomatic reading.

This is not to say that when an idiomatic entry is available, no activation of the component words' literal meaning takes place; it does, as has been shown by another cross-modal priming study by Swinney (1981), in which words in an idiomatic string (e.g. 'kick the bucket') primed related words as they occurred ('hit' was primed as subjects heard 'kick', 'pail' was primed as they heard 'bucket'), as well as words related to the idiomatic meaning of the whole phrase ('die'). But as we would expect from all the evidence cited in this chapter, it is not the lexical access process itself which becomes more difficult—resulting in a reaction time decrement—but post-access decisions of one kind or another.

A further reflection of the unitary lexical status of idiomatic strings appears in the results of another unpublished study by Swinney and myself. We reasoned that if idioms are unitarily represented, then their syntactic structure (particularly for the more frozen idioms) is predictable. This fact might be then expected to be reflected in speech production processes. It is established, for example, that the relative strength of syntactic boundaries influences the amount of phrase-final lengthening which occurs immediately before a boundary, so that speakers produce a greater amount of lengthening before boundaries dominated by high nodes in the syntactic structure tree of an utterance than before boundaries dominated by lower nodes (Cooper, Paccia, and Lapointe, 1978). Thus we predicted that speakers would treat syntactic boundaries occurring within an idiom as less strong than the same boundaries occurring within the same phrase used in a non-idiomatic sense, and that this difference would result in less phrase-final lengthening before the boundary in the idiom than in the literal version. We chose seven idioms which could also be interpreted literally, and embedded each in two disambiguating paragraph contexts, one appropriate for the literal and the other for the idiomatic reading. An example is given in (21); the idiom 'let the cat out of the bag' contains an internal boundary before the prepositional phrase 'out of the bag'.

> (21) a. We have to keep the animals apart while we're in the car or they might start fighting and distract the driver. So please be careful not to let the cat out of the bag. I'll keep the dog in this basket.
> b. We want the party to be a complete surprise to her, and we'd be really upset if she found out. So please be careful not to let the cat out of the bag. I'll be responsible for getting her there on time.

Six speakers who were unaware of the purpose of the experiment recorded all fourteen paragraphs. The durations of the syllables preceding the syntactic boundary (in (21), the duration of 'cat' which preceded the prepositional phrase 'out of the bag') were measured with the aid of a waveform editing program. Table 2.6 presents the results. This difference was statistically significant ($F_1(1, 5) = 9.68$, $p < 0.03$) and thus provided support for the prediction that syntactic boundaries within idioms have less strength in speech production than boundaries within comparable non-idiomatic phrases.

Similar results were reported by van Lancker, Canter and Terbeek (1981), who also found that other phonological processes sensitive to syntactic boundary strength produced evidence that the same boundaries were weaker in an idiomatic than in a literal version of a given phrase.

Finally, there is an interesting parallel between idioms and ambiguous words to be noted. Recall (from the section on *lexical ambiguity* above) that sentence classification time for sentences containing an ambiguous word is longer than for unambiguous sentences. This is also the case with sentences containing an idiom which could also have a literal interpretation; and idioms are also associated with longer reaction time for same–different meaning judgements on pairs of sentences (both results from Brannon, 1975). As we would expect on the basis of the earlier explanations, this was true only of idioms which could also be literal phrases. Idioms which had no literal sense ('in the know'), produced significantly *faster* reaction times in the sentence classification task than strings which could be either literal or idiomatic. Like ambiguous words, therefore, idioms can take longer to integrate into the

Table 2.6 Mean duration (msec) of syllable produced before a syntactic boundary in idiomatic and literal use of the same phrases

Average duration	
Idiom	Control
228	240

context of a whole sentence—as long as they allow more than one interpretation.

The idiom studies show that multi-word units can have holistic lexical representation. We should suspect that idioms are not the only such syntactically complex unit; for instance, compound nouns (*hotrod, garbage truck*) are similarly very likely to have unitary entries. The same goes for many familiar phrases ('How do you do?'). No relevant experimental evidence has as yet been collected on these types of phrase.

Verb subcategorization

Another possible case of syntactic complexity in the lexicon arises in the form of restrictions on syntactic contexts in which a word can occur, of which verbs provide the classic case: transitive versus intransitive, complementizing versus non-complementizing. Some verbs can take no object or complement: 'Bazza exists', but not 'Bazza exists a peanut', or 'Bazza exists that the peanut was rotten'. Others can take an object or not: 'Bazza eats'; 'Bazza eats a peanut'. Still others can take a complement or not: Bazza stated his name'; Bazza stated that the peanut was rotten'. Others must have a complement: 'Bazza seems to be a peanut'. Others can have all three modes: 'Bazza believes'; 'Bazza believes me'; 'Bazza believes that the peanut is edible'. Is this kind of constraint incorporated in the lexical entries of verbs, and if so, does it affect the ease with which different kind of verbs are processed?

Fodor, Garrett, and Bever (1968) compared complementizing with non-complementizing verbs and found that sentences containing complementizing verbs were more difficult to paraphrase. Subjects also made more errors with sentences containing complementizing verbs on a task in which they had to rearrange shuffled sentences—although there was no difference between the two types of sentence with respect to time taken to complete rearrangement. Fodor *et al.* argued that lexical access reveals whether or not the verb can take a complement and proposed an on-line effect of this type of complexity of the following kind: if a verb allows more than one possible syntactic continuation (e.g. *believe*), then more hypotheses will be computed about the syntactic structure of the sentence than in the case of a syntactically simpler verb (e.g. *eat*). This was also argued by Bever (1970).

However, on the balance of the evidence it appears most likely that verb complexity does not exercise its effects on lexical access time. Hakes (1971) replicated Fodor *et al.*'s paraphrase results, but failed to find any effect at all of verb complexity on phoneme-monitoring reaction time. Hakes (1972a) again failed to find a phoneme-monitoring effect of verb structure, and also reported an unpublished result of Garrett and Chodorow, in which verb complexity had no effect on time to decide whether or not a given word had appeared in a sentence.

In line with our earlier arguments, we would therefore suspect that if no effect of verb complexity on lexical access time can be detected, then the added difficulty associated with complementizing verbs in the paraphrase and sentence rearrangement tasks must be due to post-access processes—integration of a complete sentence representation. Indeed, Chodorow (1979) reported that lists of words were recalled worse when recall was also required of sentences with indeterminate structure, in comparison with sentences with simple transitive verbs, or with complementizing verbs followed by the complementizer *that* (which resolves the ambiguity). Recall that lexical ambiguity was also associated with a performance decrement in this task. Thus the existence of more than one possible sentence interpretation seems to be a factor which causes processing difficulty; the locus of the difficulty is however not at the lexical access level, either—as argued earlier—in the case of lexical ambiguity or in the case of verb structure ambiguity. (Note that complementizing verbs did not produce a performance decrement when they were followed by *that*, only if the structure of the sentence was temporarily indeterminate. Not surprisingly, the performance deficit for complementizing verbs in the paraphrase task also disappeared when the explicit complementizer was included (Hakes, 1972b).)

Verb subcategorization thus appears to be yet another case in which variable amounts of lexically represented information do not have an effect on difficulty of lexical access *per se*; yet the same information can lead to multiple possible interpretations of a sentence becoming available, which in turn can result in added processing difficulty in a task requiring computation of and/or decision about the meaning of a sentence as a whole.

CONCLUSION

The purpose of this chapter was to consider all the various ways in which lexical representation of words could deviate from simplicity, and to determine whether it would be possible, despite the heterogeneity of the phenomena involved, to draw some generalization from the available evidence. This indeed proved possible, and two clear conclusions have emerged, namely that lexical representations are very rarely simple, but that the process of lexical access is not made easier or more difficult by the complexity of the contents of the lexical entry. In the first section it was shown, for instance, that processing an ambiguous word involves access to all its semantic representations. Similarly, access of the entry for a lexical negative provides the information that its meaning includes negation, and access of the lexical entry for a restrictive verb selects the set of concepts of which it can be predicated. An exception to the representation of semantic complexity in the lexicon, however, is the disputed case of semantic decomposition, which, it was argued, is not lexically represented at all; not only are decomposable words no harder to process in any way, they simply do not seem to be decomposed at any level of processing. In no case was any type of semantic complexity found to be associated with greater difficulty of lexical access, when all confounding factors were controlled.

In the second section it was seen that morphologically complex words are also no more difficult to access from the lexicon than morphologically simple words; but there was abundant evidence that the mental representations of words contain information about morphological structure, and that speakers draw on this information in creating new words. The third section showed that a single lexical entry can embrace more than one form class and even a phrasal unit, and that information about the complement structure of verbs is also lexically represented; again, none of these factors was found to cause lexical access to become more difficult.

On the other hand, it was shown that many types of lexical complexity can lead to greater processing difficulty just in the case that (a) the task taps the time to construct a representation of an entire sentence and/or to make a judgement about it, *and* (b) the effect of the lexically complex word is to enable more than one representation of the sentence to be acceptable. The locus of the processing difficulty is not, however, at the level at which the information is retrieved from the lexicon; it is at the level at which it is integrated into a representation of the sentence as a whole.

The chapter began with a reference to a lexically simple word, *wombat*. Let us now consider what the lexical representation of a complex word might be like. *Discount* is a word which is semantically ambiguous: it can mean 'deduction from price' or 'not take seriously, not consider'. It has more than one form class, with all meanings originally systematically related; but the verb-meaning 'deduct from price' is closer to the noun-meaning than is the verb-meaning 'not take seriously'. It is morphologically complex, consisting of a prefix plus stem. The prefix incorporates a representation of negation (see Figure 2.1).

Although *discount* can be stressed on either the first or second syllable, segmental quality remains the same (there is no vowel reduction), so that we can consider the string [dískaʊnt] as a fair representation of all interpretations of the word. Stress varies with the speaker: some give the word initial stress in all readings; others give the noun initial stress and the verb final stress irrespective of meaning; still others give initial stress to the verb, as to the noun, in the 'deduct from price' reading ('they gave me a discount'; 'they discounted it for me'), but use final stress in the other verb reading ('We discounted the tobacco firm's lung cancer statistics'). I am one of the latter group; in my lexicon the price-deduction verb and noun are closely connected, with the 'not consider' verb separate.

Let us consider, then, that *discount* has three basic nodes (lexical entries), two of which are systematically related. Any of these nodes can be separately

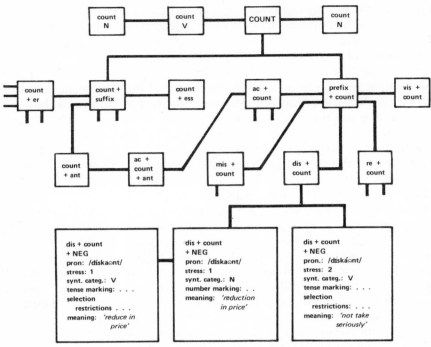

Figure 2.1   The lexical representation of *discount*

accessed; but if *discount* is heard with initial stress, of the two possible meanings to be activated the noun one will be first, the verb second (see '*Systematic ambiguity*'). On the other hand, access of any node activates the others (see '*Lexical ambiguity*'). *Discount* can also be accessed via its stem, *count* (see '*Prefixed words*'); this itself is a node of the conglomerate lexical entry for *count*, which is semantically and systematically ambiguous, having one noun reading ('nobleman') unrelated to the main verb meaning ('enumerate'), which itself has a closely associated noun ('enumeration'). Thus *count* has three major lexical nodes associated with it, plus a node for *count + prefix* and another for *count + suffix*; the former has a major branch for *dis-*, another for *ac-*, another for *mis-*, and a fourth which leads to *viscount*; the suffix node is connected to entries for *counter* (itself with half a dozen different readings), *countable, countess* etc.; the prefix and suffix nodes together dominate nodes for *accountant, uncountable,* etc. Entries for any kind of multi-word unit which includes *count* (*lose count; no-account; don't count your chickens*) will also be associated with the conglomerate. Semantic groupings include a separate cluster of *count* (nobleman), *countess,* and *viscount*; a major grouping of every word that has anything at all to do with the numeration meaning of *count* (including all the readings of *discount*); a 'negative' grouping comprising only the various readings of *discount* and *miscount*, etc. Within each node for *discount* there will be, at least, its sound representation and its meaning, a representation of its syntactic category, and any further refinements of this (*discount* the verb can only be transitive, for instance), how it should be inflected, its stress pattern, a negative marker. Besides all the structural connections within the lexical conglomerate, each word and semantic grouping will have associative connections with semantically related words, *rebate*, *disregard*, *number*, *baron*, *token*, or whatever.

In contrast, a word like *wombat* may have a number of associative connections (*emu*, *muddle-headed*, etc.), but no structural connections at all. It is clear, however, that the *wombats* are in the minority—there are many more words like *discount*. Lexical complexity is the norm. Under these circumstances, it is fortunate that lexical complexity does not in itself cause language processing difficulty.

NOTE

1. Under appropriate conditions phoneme-monitoring response time also provides a measure of the time required to understand the target-bearing word itself; see Cutler and Norris (1979) and Foss and Blank (1980) for further discussion of these issues. In all the phoneme-monitoring studies reported below, the target-bearing item followed the word on which the independent variable was manipulated.

ACKNOWLEDGMENTS

This research was supported by the Science Research Council. For discussions over many years of the issues raised in this paper I am very greatful to Phil Johnson-Laird, Dennis Norris, Dave Swinney and Ed Walker; to Ino Flores d'Arcais, David Fay, Phil Johnson-Laird and Dennis Norris thanks for useful comments on an earlier version of the manuscript. None of the above should be held responsible for the imperfections of the resulting product.

REFERENCES

Aronoff, M., and Anshen, F. Morphological productivity and phonological transparency. *Canadian Journal of Linguistics*, 1981, **26**, 63–72.

Aronoff, M., and Schvaneveldt, R. Testing morphological productivity. *Annals of the New York Academy of Science*, 1978, **318**, 106–114.

Bever, T. G. The cognitive basis for linguistic structures. In J. R. Hayes (Ed.), *Cognition and the Development of Language*. New York: Wiley, 1970.

Bobrow, S., and Bell, S. On catching on to idiomatic expressions. *Memory and Cognition*, 1973, **1**, 343–346.

Bradley, D. C. Lexical representation of derivational relation. In M. Aronoff and M. L. Kean (Eds), *Juncture*. Cambridge, Mass.: M.I.T. Press, 1979.

Brannon, L. *On the understanding of idiomatic expressions*. Unpublished doctoral dissertation, University of Texas, 1975.

Cairns, H. S., and Kamerman, J. Lexical information processing during sentence comprehension. *Journal of Verbal Learning and Verbal Behavior*, 1975, **14**, 170–179.

Chase, W. G., and Clark, H. H. Mental operations in the comparison of sentences and pictures. In L. W. Gregg (Ed.), *Cognition in Learning and Memory*. New York: Wiley, 1972.

Chodorow, M. S. Time-compressed speech and the study of lexical and syntactic processing. In W. E. Cooper and E. C. T. Walker (Eds), *Sentence Processing: Psycholinguistic Studies Presented to Merrill Garrett*. Hillsdale, N.J.: Lawrence Erlbaum Associates, 1979.

Clark, H. H., and Clark, E. V. *Psychology and Language: An Introduction to Psycholinguistics*. New York: Harcourt, Brace, Jovanovich, 1977.

Conrad, C. Context effects in sentence comprehension: A study of the subjective lexicon. *Memory and Cognition*, 1974, **2**, 130–138.

Cooper, W. E., Paccia, J. M., and Lapointe, S. G. Hierarchical coding in speech timing. *Cognitive Psychology*, 1978, **10**, 154–177.

Cutler, A. Productivity in word formation. *Papers from the Sixteenth Regional Meeting, Chicago Linguistic Society*, 1980, 45–51.

Cutler, A. Errors of stress and intonation. In V. A. Fromkin (Ed.), *Errors in Linguistic Performance: Slips of the Tongue, Ear, Pen and Hand*. New York: Academic Press, 1981(a).

Cutler, A. Degrees of transparency in word formation. *Canadian Journal of Linguistics*, 1981(b), **26**, 73–77.

Cutler, A., and Norris, D. Monitoring sentence comprehension. In W. E. Cooper and E. C. T. Walker (Eds), *Sentence Processing: Psycholinguistic Studies Presented to Merrill Garrett*. Hillsdale, N.J.: Lawrence Erlbaum Associates, 1979.

Fay, D. A. *Morphology and stress in the mental lexicon*. Final Report to National Institute of Mental Health, NIMH Grant No. R03MH32912, 1980.

Fay, D. A. The mental representation of prefixed words: Evidence from prefix errors in spontaneous speech. *Journal of Verbal Learning and Verbal Behavior*, in press.

Fischler, I. Semantic facilitation without association in a lexical decision task. *Memory and Cognition*, 1977, **5**, 335–339.

Fodor, J. A., Garrett, M. F., and Bever, T. G. Some syntactic determinants of sentential complexity, II: Verb structure. *Perception and Psychophysics*, 1968, **3**, 453–461.

Fodor, J. A., Garrett, M. F., Walker, E. C. T., and Parkes, C. H. Against definitions. *Cognition*, 1980, **8**, 263–367.

Fodor, J. D., Fodor, J. A., and Garrett, M. F. The psychological unreality of semantic representations. *Linguistic Inquiry*, 1975, **6**, 515–531.

Forbach, G. B., Stanners, R. F., and Hochhaus, L. Repetition and practice effects in a lexical decision task. *Memory and Cognition*, 1974, **2**, 337–339.

Forster, K. I., and Bednall, E. S. Terminating and exhaustive search in lexical access. *Memory and Cognition*, 1976, **4**, 53–61.

Foss, D. J. Some effects of ambiguity upon sentence comprehension. *Journal of Verbal Learning and Verbal Behavior*, 1970, **9**, 699–706.

Foss, D. J., and Blank, M. A. Identifying the speech codes. *Cognitive Psychology*, 1980, **12**, 1–31.

Foss, D. J., and Jenkins, C. M. Some effects of context on the comprehension of ambiguous sentences. *Journal of Verbal Learning and Verbal Behavior*, 1973, **12**, 577–589.

Fowler, C. A., and Napps, S. E. *Lexical forms*. Unpublished manuscript, Dartmouth College, 1982.

Fraser, B. Idioms within a transformational grammar. *Foundations of Language*, 1970, **6**, 22–42.

Fromkin, V. A. (Ed.), *Speech Errors as Linguistic Evidence*. The Hague: Mouton, 1973.

Fromkin, V. A. Putting the emPHAsis on the wrong sylLABle. In L. M. Hyman (Ed.), *Studies in Stress and Accent*. Los Angeles: University of Southern California, 1977.

Garrett, M. F. Syntactic processes in sentence production. In. R. J. Wales and E. C. T. Walker (Eds), *New Approaches to Language Mechanisms*. Amsterdam: North-Holland, 1976.

Gibbs, R. W. Spilling the beans on understanding and memory for idioms in conversation. *Memory and Cognition*, 1980, **8**, 149–156.

Gibson, E. J., and Guinet, L. Perception of inflections in brief visual presentations of words. *Journal of Verbal Learning and Verbal Behavior*, 1971, **10**, 182–189.

Hakes, D. T. Does verb structure affect sentence comprehension? *Perception and Psychophysics*, 1971, **10**, 229–232.

Hakes, D. T. Verb complexity and sentence comprehension: Further data and reflections. Unpublished manuscript, University of Texas, 1972(a).

Hakes, D. T. Effects of reducing complement constructions on sentence comprehension. *Journal of Verbal Learning and Verbal Behavior*, 1972(b), **11**, 278–286.

Henderson, L., Wallis, J., and Knight, D. Morphemic structure and lexical access. In H. Bouma and D. G. Bouwhuis (Eds) *Attention and Performance X*. Hillsdale, N.J.: Lawrence Erlbaum Associates, 1983.

Hogaboam, T. W., and Perfetti, C. A. Lexical ambiguity and sentence comprehension. *Journal of Verbal Learning and Verbal Behaviour*, 1975, **14**, 265–274.

Holmes, V. M. Accessing ambiguous words during sentence comprehension. *Quarterly Journal of Experimental Psychology*, 1979, **31**, 569–589.

Holmes, V. M., Arwas, R., and Garrett, M. F. Prior context and the perception of lexically ambiguous sentences. *Memory and Cognition*, 1977, **5**, 103–110.

Holyoak, K. J., Glass, A. L., and Mah, W. A. Morphological structure and semantic retrieval. *Journal of Verbal Learning and Verbal Behavior*, 1976, **15**, 235–247.

Jarvella, R. J. and Meijers, G. Recognizing morphemes in spoken words: Some evidence for a stem-organized mental lexicon. Chapter 3, this volume.

Jarvella, R. J., and Snodgrass, J. G. Seeing ring in rang and retain in retention: On recognizing stem morphemes in printed words. *Journal of Verbal Learning and Verbal Behavior*, 1974, **13**, 590–598.

Just, M. A., and Carpenter, P. A. Comprehension of negation with quantification. *Journal of Verbal Learning and Verbal Behavior*, 1971, **10**, 244–253.

Kempley, S. T., and Morton, J. The effects of priming with regularly and irregularly related words in auditory word recognition. *British Journal of Psychology*, 1982, **73**, 441–454.

Kintsch, W. Abstract nouns: Imagery versus lexical complexity. *Journal of Verbal Learning and Verbal Behavior*, 1972, **11**, 59–65.

Kintsch, W. *The Representation of Meaning in Memory*. Hillsdale, N.J.: Lawrence Erlbaum Associates, 1974.

Kiparsky, P., and Kiparsky, C. Fact. In D. D. Steinberg and L. A. Jakobovits (Eds), *Semantics: An Interdisciplinary Reader in Philosophy, Linguistics and Psychology*. Cambridge: Cambridge University Press, 1971.

Klima, E. S. Negation in English. In J. A. Fodor and J. J. Katz (Eds), *The Structure of Language.* Englewood Cliffs, N.J.: Prentice-Hall, 1964.

Kučera, H., and Francis, W. N. *Computational Analysis of Present-day American English.* Providence, R.I.: Brown University Press, 1967.

Lackner, J. R., and Garrett, M. F. Resolving ambiguity: effects of biasing context in the unattended ear. *Cognition*, 1972, **1**, 359–372.

Lakoff, G. On the nature of syntactic irregularity. *Mathematical Linguistics and Automatic Translation. Report No. NSF-16.* Cambridge, Mass.: Harvard University Computation Laboratory, 1965.

Lieberman, P. On the acoustic basis of the perception of intonation by linguists. *Word*, 1965, **21**, 40–54.

Lukatela, G., Gligorijevic, B., Kostic, A., and Turvey, M. T. Representation of inflected nouns in the internal lexicon. *Memory and Cognition*, 1980, **8**, 415–423.

MacKay, D. G. On the retrieval and lexical structure of verbs. *Journal of Verbal Learning and Verbal Behavior*, 1976, **15**, 169–182.

MacKay, D. G. Lexical insertion, inflection and derivation: Creative processes in word production. *Journal of Psycholinguistic Research*, 1979, **8**, 477–498.

Manelis, L., and Tharp, D. A. The processing of affixed words. *Memory and Cognition*, 1977, **5**, 690–695.

Marslen-Wilson, W. Speech understanding as a psychological process. In. J. C. Simon (Ed.), *Spoken Language Generation and Understanding*. Dordrecht: Reidel, 1980.

Mehler, J., Segui, J., and Carey, P. Tails of words: Monitoring ambiguity. *Journal of Verbal Learning and Verbal Behavior*, 1978, **17**, 29–35.

Mistler-Lachman, J. L. Queer sentences, ambiguity and levels of processing. *Memory and Cognition*, 1975, **3**, 395–400.

van der Molen, H., and Morton, J. Remembering plurals: unit of coding and form of coding during serial recall. *Cognition*, 1979, **7**, 35–47.

Morgan, J. L. On the treatment of presupposition in transformational grammar. *Papers from the Fifth Regional Meeting, Chicago Linguistic Society.* 1969.

Murrell, G. A., and Morton, J. Word recognition and morphemic structure. *Journal of Experimental Psychology,* 1974, **102**, 963–968.

Newman, J. E., and Dell, G. S. The phonological nature of phoneme-monitoring: A critique of some ambiguity studies. *Journal of Verbal Learning and Verbal Behavior*, 1978, **17**, 359–374.

Norris, D. G. *Serial and interactive models of comprehension.* Unpublished doctoral dissertation, University of Sussex, 1980.

Onifer, W., and Swinney, D. A. Accessing lexical ambiguities during sentence comprehension: Effects of frequency-of-meaning and contextual bias. *Memory and Cognition*, 1981, **9**, 225–236.

Ortony, A., Schallert, D. L., Reynolds, R. E., and Antos, S. J. Interpreting metaphors and idioms: Some effects of context on comprehension. *Journal of Verbal Learning and Verbal Behavior*, 1978, **17**, 465–477.

Postal, P. M. On the surface verb 'remind'. *Linguistic Inquiry*, 1970, **1**, 37–120.

Prather, P., and Swinney, D. A. *Some effects of syntactic context upon lexical access.* Paper presented at the American Psychological Association Convention, San Francisco, 1977.

Richardson, J. T. E. Imagery, concreteness and lexical complexity. *Quarterly Journal of Experimental Psychology*, 1975, **27**, 211–223.

Richardson, J. T. E. Lexical derivation. *Journal of Psycholinguistic Research*, 1977, **6**, 319–336.

Rosenberg, S., Coyle, P. J., and Porter, W. L. Recall of adverbs as a function of the frequency of their adjective roots. *Journal of Verbal Learning and Verbal Behavior*, 1966, **5**, 75–76.

Rubin, G. S., Becker, C. A., and Freeman, R. H. Morphological structure and its effect on visual word recognition. *Journal of Verbal Learning and Verbal Behavior*, 1979, **18**, 757–767.

Ryder, J., and Walker, E. C. T. Two mechanisms of lexical ambiguity. In J. Mehler, E. C. T. Walker, and M. F. Garrett (Eds), *Perspectives on Mental Representation. Experimental and Theoretical Studies of Cognitive Processes and Capacities*. Hillsdale, N.J.: Lawrence Erlbaum Associates, 1982.

Sherman, M. A. Bound to be easier? The negative prefix and sentence comprehension. *Journal of Verbal Learning and Verbal Behavior*, 1973, **12**, 76–84.

Sherman, M. A. Adjectival negation and the comprehension of multiply negated sentences. *Journal of Verbal Learning and Verbal Behavior*, 1976, **15**, 143–157.

Snodgrass, J. G., and Jarvella, R. J. Some linguistic determinants of word classification times. *Psychonomic Science*, 1972, **27**, 220–222.

Stanners, R. F., Neiser, J. J., Hernon, W. P., and Hall, R. Memory representation for morphologically related words. *Journal of Verbal Learning and Verbal Behavior*, 1979, **18**, 399–412.

Stanners, R. F., Neiser, J. J., and Painton, S. Memory representation for prefixed words. *Journal of Verbal Learning and Verbal Behavior*, 1979, **18**, 733–743.

Swinney, D. A. Lexical access during sentence comprehension: (Re)considerations of context effects. *Journal of Verbal Learning and Verbal Behavior*, 1979, **18**, 645–659.

Swinney, D. A. Lexical processing during sentence comprehension: Effects of higher order constraints and implications for representation. In T.F. Myers, J. Laver, and J. Anderson (Eds), *The Cognitive Representation of Speech*. Amsterdam: North-Holland, 1981.

Swinney, D. A., and Cutler, A. The access and processing of idiomatic expressions. *Journal of Verbal learning and Verbal Behavior*, 1979, **18**, 523–534.

Taft, M. Recognition of affixed words and the word frequency effect. *Memory and Cognition*, 1979, **7**, 263–272.

Taft, M. Prefix stripping revisited. *Journal of Verbal Learning and Verbal Behavior*, 1981, **20**, 289–297.

Taft, M., and Forster, K. I. Lexical storage and retrieval of prefixed words. *Journal of Verbal Learning and Verbal Behavior*, 1975, **14**, 638–647.

Taft, M., Forster, K. I., and Garrett, M. F. Lexical storage of derived words. Paper presented at the Experimental Psychology Conference, Melbourne, 1974.

Tanenhaus, M. K., Leiman, J. M., and Seidenberg, M. S. Evidence for multiple stages in the processing of ambiguous words in syntactic contexts. *Journal of Verbal Learning and Verbal Behavior*, 1979, **18**, 427–440.

Van Lancker, D., and Canter, G. J. Idiomatic versus literal interpretations of ditropically ambiguous sentences. *Journal of Speech and Hearing Research*, 1981, **24**, 64–69.

Van Lancker, D., Canter, G. J., and Terbeek, D. Acoustic and phonetic correlates of idiomatic and literal utterance contrasts. *Journal of Speech and Hearing Research*, 1981, **24**, 330–335.

Wason, P. C. The processing of positive and negative information. *Quarterly Journal of Experimental Psychology*, 1959, **11**, 92–107.

Wason, P. C. Response to affirmative and negative binary statements. *British Journal of Psychology*, 1961, **52**, 133–142.

Whaley, C. P. Word-nonword classification time. *Journal of Verbal Learning and Verbal Behavior*, 1978, **17**, 143–154.

The Process of Language Understanding
Edited by G. B. Flores d'Arcais and R. J. Jarvella
© 1983 John Wiley & Sons Ltd.

3

Recognizing Morphemes in Spoken Words: Some Evidence for a Stem-organized Mental Lexicon

ROBERT J. JARVELLA

*Max Planck Institut für Psycholinguistics, Nijmegen,
and N.I.A.S., Wassenaar, Netherlands*

and

GUUST MEIJERS

University of Tilburg, Netherlands

A central question in the psychology of language is whether the mental lexicon —the dictionary in our heads—is a lexicon of words. By 'words', we simply mean those entities which we conventionally talk about as if they were lexical items, can stand alone in speech or writing, have some identifiable meaning, and belong to a form class such as nouns or verbs. The answer to this question is not obviously 'yes'. For although practically any lexical theory will be preoccupied with these items on some level, there is no compelling reason why they should be considered the most basic or elementary structures in this respect in our minds. For word *meanings*, this kind of issue has perhaps been most systematically explored by Miller and Johnson-Laird (1976). Though assuming words are the meaning conveying elements of discourse, Miller and Johnson-Laird arrive at a theory of procedural semantics in which lexical representations are defined and tests conducted partly in terms of semantic and conceptual primitives, and in which word meanings are composed of, or linked to, several kinds of information.

In the present chapter, we are interested in a largely similar issue, but more on the level of lexical *form*, namely, what should be considered the phonological and orthographic primes in the internal lexicon, and how may words be constructed from these? Our main concern is to ask which words have their own lexical entries. The answer to this question is neither obvious nor uncontroversial. In general, those words which are also free or unbound morphemes would be the first and principal contenders for this status. Then perhaps 'derived' forms would be counted; and, after that, possibly inflected words. The most dubious candidates perhaps would be the forms of grammatical morphemes. But beyond those morphemes whose forms can stand alone, and perhaps some bound roots, which lexical items have independent lexical entries is largely open. To answer this question, it may be necessary to ask others, such as 'How *might* morphologically complex words be represented and organized?' and 'How would such representations be *reached* in perceiving and producing speech and writing?'

Linguistic considerations largely by themselves (see, e.g., Vennemann, 1974; Linell, 1979) suggest some restrictions on how words might be listed or formed in the lexicon, based on considerations such as what linguistic generalizations might be captured, and naturalness, but only incidentally the problem of access. Thus, one possibility is that the mental lexicon contains purely morphological form representations, and not words as most people learn to think of them at all, since words always appear as superficial variants of morphemes, as a phonetic (or orthographic) realization. This is the kind of view to which one supposes generative phonology à la Chomsky and Halle (1968) would be most sympathetic. In a sufficiently abstract morphemic theory, lexical access might be thought of as occurring by a perceiver first detecting potential morphs present in a word, and then looking up the root hypothesized and perhaps other morphemes in some way which allows checking for its internal well-formedness. Within psycholinguistics, one theory compatible with this hypothesis is that of Taft (Taft and Forster, 1975; Taft, 1979, 1981), from which it might be extrapolated that root morphemes are main lexical entries and affixed forms either subentries or constructed. In speech production, morphemic forms might be thought to be accessed by grammatical and semantic information (cf. Forster, 1976), constructed, and articulated using some kind of phonetic realization rules.

A second possibility for lexical representation is one which is maximally redundant: where all words have separate entries and their lexical forms are highly superficial. According to Vennemann (1974), this kind of representation would best satisfy what he calls the 'strong naturalness condition': that the only lexical forms be (made up of) allomorphs, that for non-alternating parts of morphemes these be identical to their *phonetic* representation, and that lexical representations of roots be identical to particular allomorphs, with rules for suppletion only when absolutely necessary (e.g. *go* vs. *went*). Within such a framework, in speech production there would be no need to generate words by rule, although this still might be used to explain word innovations and some slips of the tongue. Instead, phonetic representations would serve word production directly. Such superficial representation of words seems consistent with a perceptual theory of lexical access such as proposed by Marslen-Wilson (Marslen-Wilson and Welsh, 1978; Marslen-Wilson and Tyler, 1980), in which the acoustic signal is compared from left to right against a set of internal, phonetically coded recognition elements, and these elements can receive further inputs at *non*-speech defined levels of processing.

A third possibility is that the lexicon contains just a *subset* of surface phonetic or shallow phonemic forms, for example, free-standing allomorphs and word stems, plus for each, some listing or procedure for generating its inflections. This view, which takes for granted fairly concrete forms but also the likelihood of word (re-)construction by rule, has been argued by Linell (1979) to have the greatest face validity, as well as to represent the most favoured treatment in traditional accounts of the lexicon. Perceptually, once a main lexical entry is reached, one might argue that its list of inflections is consulted (or generated) to further reference the perceived form's grammatical properties. Words could be produced on the basis of such features either by generating affixes needed by rule, or by looking them up, and then amalgamating them with their roots. In contrast to the position endorsed by Vennemann, morphological processes in Linell's conception thus can be thought of as being creative. In contrast to Chomsky and Halle, the representations they are taken to work on (or at least the phonological ones) are closer to the level of speech.

The above considerations, of course, are not *just* linguistic. The three viewpoints mentioned above are in fact variants of a psychological theory of lexical access and representation. But to the extent that they were not originally intended by their advocates to be this, they are process or performance *metaphors*, and can serve best as a kind of linguistic backdrop for discussing experimental investigations of word and morpheme perception. A reading of the literature in the latter area suggests that we are still not very far beyond such a rough level of theorizing, however. For spoken words, there is little that can be said about how stems and affixes in inflected forms are recognized in any language. The experimental part of this paper tries to ask some such questions about the perception of verbs in modern Dutch: how such words may be represented in the internal lexicon, how their representations are reached, and how they might be checked against a developing percept. The most relevant prior research on inflected word forms comes from studies of recognition of printed language. We will not attempt to review this material very exhaustively (see also Cutler, Chapter 2 of this volume), but rather present and discuss some major findings and ideas which arise from it.

Inflected word forms contain by definition both stem and non-stem information. The latter usually is conveyed by affixation, root alternations, and the like. One major question of interest in a morphological theory of the lexicon is whether information of these two kinds is processed independently and in parallel. This kind of issue was investigated over several age levels by Gibson and Guinet (1971) for printed English verbs and pseudo-verbs having the inflections, -s, -ed, and -ing, and Ø (their stem forms alone). The words presented were exposed only briefly, and subjects were simply asked to write down what they saw. (They were told that some of the forms were not real words, but to try to read these anyhow.) Recognition accuracy increased as the stimuli became more wordlike (e.g. going from *nrai*, which is unpronounceable, to *nair*, which is a possible word, to *rain*), and with age of the subject. When stems and inflected forms of the same length were compared (e.g., *start* vs. *rains* or *listen* vs. *rained*), it was found that recognition was poorer at the ends of the verb *stems*; this tendency increased in strength as the stems shown became less acceptable English. Some verb stems standing alone were also perceived as being inflected. From their data, Gibson and Guinet conclude that the stem (base form) and inflections of a printed word are perceptually separable features: 'that they are picked up independently; that each is a unit, but that the base, if it is meaningful, i.e., a word itself, has some priority for the actively engaged reader' (1971, p. 187). Murrell and Morton (1974) obtained some additional results consistent with this hypothesis, although recognition of the root forms of the words they studied was intentionally biased. We mention their experiment again below, in a slightly different context.

Inflected words need be recognized in some way which allows determination that they are inflected. A second main question of interest thus concerns how such word forms might be analysed or decomposed in perception, and these relationships actually ascertained. From a series of lexical decision experiments using printed English words and nonwords, Taft and Forster (1975) put forward an hypothesis that readers will attempt to decompose a word morphologically to gain access to lexical memory *via* its stem. Taft and Forster performed three studies relevant to this question. In one study, it was found that nonword judgements were slower, and more errors occurred, on items whose stems in English do not occur as free forms (e.g., *juvenate* from *rejuvenate*), than on items stripped of similar non-prefixes (e.g., *pertoire* from *repertoire*). In a second study, it was found that free forms more frequent than prefixed words having the 'same' root (e.g., *card* vs. *discard*) are recognized faster than control items of equal length and frequency, while free forms less frequent than similar prefixed forms (e.g., *vent* and *prevent*) are recognized more slowly than control items. And in a third study, prefixed nonwords with arguably real stems (e.g., *dejuvenate*) were found to be recognized as nonwords more slowly and less accurately than prefixed nonwords with pseudo-stems (e.g., *depertoire*).

Taft and Forster took these data to suggest that prefixed words are accessed through their stems rather than directly, and themselves do not have independent lexical representations; secondly, when more than one lexical entry exists for different stems of the same form, these entries are examined from most to least frequent. Thus, they argue that in making lexical decisions, subjects initially make an attempt to divide an incoming letter string into prefix and stem. The candidate stem is then searched for in the central lexicon. If decomposition was successful and the stem is found, the combination of prefix and stem is checked, and if determined to be a word, the subject responds that it is a word. If the stem hypothesized after decomposition is not found, if the combination is not found to occur, or if no hypothesis for decomposition could initially be supported, the whole word is searched for in the lexicon. If if is located and found to be a free lexical form, the subject also responds 'yes, this is a word'. And if it is not found, or determined not to be a free form, the subject responds 'no, it is not a word'.

This model of lexical access, and Taft and Forster's interpretation of their final experiment (the only one *using* prefixed forms), have been disputed by Rubin, Becker, and Freeman (1979) on the grounds that subjects may have been *artificially* led to decompose the words seen because they were presented *only* prefixed and pseudo-prefixed forms. Rubin *et al.* showed their own subjects 20 prefixed English words (e.g., *recover, unknown*) and 20 matched 'pseudo-prefixed' words (e.g., *reckon, uncle*) in the context of 140 other words and nonwords which were *entirely* prefixed or non-prefixed. In each of two experiments reported, the critical prefixed words were judged to be words more rapidly than the matched pseudo-prefixed words, but in each case the advantage found on real prefixed items was greater, and reliable only in the 'all prefixes' context.

Taft (1981) has recently answered these objections by arguing that, if two routes of lexical access are possible, for prefixed words, it would have been counterproductive for subjects in Rubin *et al.*'s 'all prefixes' context to do decomposition, and pointed out that in the non-prefix context, positive responses on the critical items might themselves have been made even *before access*, by checking whether a potential prefix was present. Taft also provided evidence that adjusted naming latencies for real prefixed words (e.g., *replica*) were faster than for pseudo-prefixed words (e.g., *precipice*), as the decomposition theory would predict. A further problem with the Rubin *et al.* studies is that, while these authors balanced their prefixed and pseudo-prefixed stimuli for length and initial syllable, the matching done on frequency did not take into account how frequent the 'real' prefixed forms without *stems* occur in English. In most cases, the free form apparently was more frequent than the prefixed one, and in Taft's theory, the two would not plausibly occur as subentries of the same lexical item (e.g., *absent* vs. *sent, define* vs. *fine*, etc.). By the logic of Taft and Forster's general model, and as shown by Taft (1979) to be empirically supported, the first stem entry to be examined in these cases would not be the prefix-related one, but the *non*-prefix-related one (e.g., *sent* and *fine*). This means that, assuming the forms studied were decomposed, their speed advantage vs. non-decomposable forms should have been be partly offset by multiple attempts to locate the proper lexical entry.

Another set of lexical decision experiments aimed at inferring the nature of memory representations for prefixed English words has been conducted by Stanners, Neiser, and Painton (1979). Using a measure of priming as an index of lexical activation, these authors tried to ask whether prefixes and stems have separate representations in the mental lexicon (i.e., where *revive* is internally 'present' as two forms, *re* and *vive*), or whether they occur together as a single, morphologically marked form (e.g., *re + vive*). In the studies conducted, the critical comparisons made were between lexical decision times for prefixed words such as *revive* when (a) no prior occurrence had occurred, (b) the words had been primed by a prior occurrence, and (c) the prefixed words had been primed only by their stem, or by their prefix and stem on different trials. In general, Stanners, Neiser, and Painton did find some facilitation of lexical decision times in the (c) case, when a prefixed word's stem alone had served as a prime, or when the stem and prefix had been presented separately. However, only about half as such time gain with respect to the control condition was obtained there as in the case where the prefixed word itself had previously been presented. The conclusion Stanners, Neiser, and Painton draw is that prefixed words have joint 'prefix plus stem' representations in memory rather than independent ones.

As Taft (1981) has pointed out, however, the Taft and Forster model includes *three* stages: the stripping-off of prefixes, the location of stems, and the determination that combined prefix plus stem items hypothesized actually occur as word forms. Since the Stanners, Neiser, and Painton stem priming technique did not call for anything resembling this last stage before the critical test words were shown, one should perhaps not *expect* the same amount of facilitation as for 'repetition' priming. Presenting a prefixed word first, and the stem second, which Stanners, Neiser, and Painton (1979) also tried, but with inconclusive results,[1] seems to be a less objectionable basis for comparison, though in both cases, there is still a further complication. Namely, it may make a difference whether the lexical decision reached on a priming or test item is positive (e.g., for *revive*) or negative (for *vive*).

Other results by Stanners and his colleagues suggest that the printed forms of some *suffixed* English words may be partitioned into morphemes when read. Using the same priming–lexical decision technique, Stanners, Neiser, Hernon, and Hall (1979) found that regular third person singular present and past tense forms of verbs and their present participles (e.g., *calls*, *called*, *calling*) were as effective in priming the verbs' unmarked ('infinitive') forms as the verb stems themselves (e.g., *call*). However, only about half of the corresponding 'repetition' priming effect (seeing the same verb earlier in a stimulus list) was obtained for past-tense forms of strong verbs (e.g. *shook*), adjectives derived from verbs (e.g., *predictable*), and nouns derived from verbs (e.g., *disturbance*). From this work, Stanners, Neiser, Hernon, and Hall suggest two access mechanisms to verbs in memory: direct access to base forms for regularly inflected verbs, and indirect access for other forms, including the 'irregular' (ablaut) forms of strong verbs.

As an explanation for the fact that priming with morphologically related forms seems to have an *absolutely* greater effect than priming with words which are only semantically related to probes, Stanners, Neiser, Hernon, and Hall suggest that 'activation of the base verb (may be) a necessary operation in processing the variation (the morphologically related word) rather than an automatic by-product' (1979, p. 411). If this conclusion is correct, the representation allowing lexical access to a word like *shook* would contain a reversible ablaut rule or information such as 'see *shake*' or '*shake* plus past', without specifying the meaning (or perhaps the form) of *shake* itself. But for a word like *called*, this would be unnecessary; its lexical representation would include (or be found with) the stem itself. It should be noticed that in both the 'regular' and ablaut cases, the same result might be accomplished by indirect access via a morphological pre-analysis which serves to locate a verb's stem in memory, if its different forms are listed and explained there, or capable of being generated by rule. Only a single mechanism would then be needed; the lack of any difference in priming found for English weak verbs by Stanners *et al.* might be regarded as accidental, or taken to reflect degrees of linguistic recoding needed at the initial or final, pre-comparison stage of processing.

Another closely related study in the literature is that of recognition for briefly presented printed words by Murrell and Morton (1974). The English words studied by Murrell and Morton were morphologically related pairs including *reader–reading*, *see–seen*, and *pains—pained*. About half of the sixteen pairs used were made up of one uninflected word and one inflected one. Murrell and Morton found than when subjects were given one word from each pair to study in advance, they were nearly as good at recognizing the words' stems in the other version as they were in recognizing them in the words they had learned. A changed inflection, on the other hand, was not well recognized. To demonstrate that the effect found was not simply one of spelling similarity, Murrell and Morton employed a control condition in which words were pre-learned which began with the same letter sequence but were morphologically unrelated to the words of interest (e.g., *ready*, *seed*, and *paint*). There was no effect of training observed for these words. The results of this study are thus consistent with Stanners, Neiser, Hernon, and Hall's (1979) findings for weak verbs in English.

The experimental data reviewed above concern the reader rather than the listener. In fact, there appear to be few or no published experiments in which the recognition of inflected verb forms in spoken language has been tested. Written language is, of course, very different from spoken language. In the one case, a number of characters or larger units may be perceived together, while in the other acoustic information is received inevitably from left to right. Marslen-Wilson and Welsh (1978) and Marslen-Wilson and Tyler (1980) have developed a model for the recognition of spoken words which tries to account for the fact that this process rapidly takes place and permits a listener to keep pace with a fluent speaker. Underlying their own model of word cohorts is the principle that a listener will identify and distinguish a word from other words he knows as early as is theoretically possible in the speech signal, choosing an initial set of word candidates after hearing as little as two or three phonemes. In this model, in normal utterances structural and inter-pretative knowledge sources are taken to interact with this set of word candi-dates and further phonetic information perceived to allow selection of the appropriate word. For words heard in isolation, choice of the correct alterna-tive should depend on phonetic input alone. Each phoneme heard should eliminate some candidates from the initial set (the whole lexicon) at the word's beginning, and the word is recognized when only one candidate remains. An exact point of recognition can thus be predicted, and the proce-dure in general explains how it is possible to identify a word before it has been completely heard. Since Marslen-Wilson seems to have considered only free morphemes in his word perception research, one may wonder in what way the mechanism proposed might apply to inflected words or ones subject to inter-nal morphophonemic changes (e.g., the past tense of strong verbs). It would also be interesting to know whether morphemes in general are recognized at the earliest moment they can theoretically 'be found in' the speech signal.

A COMPOSITE MODEL OF SPOKEN WORD RECOGNITION

In light of the above discussion, and anticipating the force of our own results, a model like the following might be suggested as a first approximation to the process of auditory word recognition, i.e., of how spoken words are rep-resented and reached in the mental lexicon (for related proposals for the perception of printed and spoken words, see Hudson, 1981; Meijers and Jarvella, 1982). In the perception of spoken word forms, a left-to-right analysis is performed, perhaps along the general lines suggested by Marslen-Wilson (1980). Secondly, however, the *central* files of the mental lexicon themselves are organized in terms of words' roots. Thus (at least many) morphologically complex words will not be present there as separate entries, but rather as subentries (or subprocedures). We take the principal or main lexical entries to be the words' roots, and also to function as the primary nodes or pathways connecting lexical meaning with lexical form. This means that the 'lexical' part of speech perception will be concerned above all with the identification of morphological elements which may be accessible princi-pally via other kinds of representations (cf. Forster's (1976) peripheral files). To locate stem entries, peripheral processes are needed.

We suggest that spoken words are first pre-analysed in a way that a hypothesis can be made about what their morphs are, and it is via morphs recognized as possible roots that access to main lexical entries usually occurs. The amount of abstraction in this process leading (a) from spoken word forms to such hypotheses and (b) from these to lexical access *per se*, may however be considerable. What seems potentially most critical is that a perceiver should know quickly and accurately when, for example, enough of a word is heard to determine its principal morph, and look up this or its corresponding root morpheme in memory. Prefix-stripping such as proposed by Taft and Forster (1975) may have its analogue in this auditory process, as a way of locating the beginning of the morph most relevant for lexical access, and for grammatical prefixes, and affixes generally, might also serve some non-lexical parsing function. Thus, following Gibson and Guinet (1971), it could be interesting to ask whether the processing of, for example, the Germanic verbal prefix *ge-* (e.g., in German *geschlossen* or Dutch *gesloten*) operates alongside stem processing, with usable results at high speed. The question is not so much whether one can identify such a form as a past participle independently of its stem (as we might say that *schlumped* is a possible past tense form in English, though *schlump* (or *schlimp*) is not found in the English lexicon—the capacity to recognize and generate such forms clearly is there). Rather, the issue is whether we recognize such words functionally as a form of some lexical item (or non-item). If stem and affix morph(eme)s are not differentially processed in this sense, one could expect that decisions about the two in real words would unfold about equally fast, measured from some relevant point in time such as their speech offset, but that there might be context effects (e.g., priming of root meaning or past-tenseness). A stem-organized mental lexicon would appear to make different predictions, because the stem's role would be central both in form recognition, and in determining words' meanings. A further critical question is, of course, how words changed by ablaut (as in the root vowel of *spoken* or *geschlossen*) are recognized. In such cases, affix-stripping alone leaves a different stem allomorph; some further pattern-recognizing algorithm may be required.[2]

SOME ASPECTS OF VERB MORPHOLOGY IN GERMANIC LANGUAGES

Before presenting and discussing our own experiments, it may be useful to briefly sketch the morphology of verbs in Dutch, the language that was used in them.

Verb morphology in Germanic languages as a whole provides a useful testing ground for hypotheses on lexical access and representation in the internal lexicon. These languages have different classes of verbs, the different classes are inflected in partly different ways, and one might expect them to be, at least in part, processed in different ways. Earlier forms of Germanic languages would probably provide better insights into word recognition processes than their modern ones, if they could be studied. At one time, use of verbal prefixes and suffixes was far more productive and elaborate than it is today. Language psychologists, however, usually cannot test their theories on written records or reconstructions. Secondly, for the question of interest, English presents still further limitations. In its modern form, its verb morphology may be the least rewarding among the Germanic languages to study. This is partly due to history and partly to linguistic change accompanying it.

Consider past participles. In Old English (like modern Dutch and German), past participles were generally formed with a prefix ge-[3] and a suffix containing a dental consonant. Before the eleventh century, our Anglo-Saxon forbears usually said *gerunnen* for (have) 'run', *geholpen* for 'helped', *gelufod* for 'loved', and *geboren* for 'born'. This prefix, whose meaning in proto-Germanic was probably something like 'with' or 'together', developed in time into a notion of event completeness or perfectivity. Originally (cf. Wright, 1925), it was not applied to the past participles of verbs already having such meaning, such as *cuman* ('come') or *findan* ('find'). But in Old English it had become usual to use *ge-* irrespective of this distinction, perhaps partly in contrast to a durative interpretation of other forms for expressing pastness (Strang, 1970). Later the system of verbal prefixes in English entered a period of decline and these were partly supplanted by new forms (cf. Marchand, 1969; Baugh and Cable, 1978). In the case of *ge-*, the prefix was reduced and transcribed in Middle English dialects as *i-* or *y-* (Clark, 1957). It appears as such in the literature of that period (the opening sentence of *The Canterbury Tales* contains *yronne* ('run')), but was also used later by Spencer and other poets of the sixteenth century, often in 'archaic' forms of their own creation. Traces of the *ge-* prefix have nearly vanished from modern English. It is currently used primarily dialectally (as *a-*) and in a few obsolete forms like *yclept* and *yclad* known principally to lexicographers. It may be only in Nordic languages that the prefix reconstructed by philologists as *ga-* in proto-Germanic found a more rapid demise. There, it has already disappeared as a productive morpheme prehistorically, and in records of Old Norse appears only in a few fossilized forms such as *glíkr* ('like').

Why should the *ge-* past participles in modern Germanic be of interest to modern psychologists? Simply put, it is the fact that these verb forms *have* a grammatical prefix and thus *do not* begin with their stem or root morphemes. This may have certain perceptual consequences when one hears such a word. It is worth asking how a German understands an utterance of *gemacht*, or a Dutchman of *gemaakt*. Do speakers of these languages first determine what verb the word comes from and only then what form it is of this verb? Or do they, for example, analyse morphological information from left to right, in a way that enables them to determine that a verb is a past participle no later than to decide *what* verb it is a past participle of? In these languages, it is often the case, namely, that the prefix plus part of the stem is sufficient in principle to uniquely identify either stem or form. This is one of the issues we attempt to resolve in the present chapter.

The gradual erosion of *ge-/y-* past participles is not the only feature of modern English verbs which distinguishes them from their West Germanic neighbours. In some respects, this development was just a special (but grammatically interesting) instance of a more general phenomenon. The *ge-* prefix on Old English past participles was just one of a set of verbal prefixes which were productive in word formation. This set included, among others, *a-*, *be-*, *for-*, *fore-*, *on-*, *under-* and *wip-*. As Baugh and Cable (1978, p. 66) point out, with the aid of these prefixes, many verbs could be formed with the same root, e.g., from *settan* ('set'), *besettan* ('appoint'), *forsettan* ('obstruct'), *onsettan* ('oppress'), *wipsettan* ('resist'), and so on. Verbs constructed with these prefixes, like those formed with *ge-* (which was also still used lexically, e.g., in *gesettan*, 'people' or 'garrison'), also declined gradually in use. In the fourteenth to sixteenth centuries, a second set of verbal prefixes largely of Latin and Old French origin entered the language and probably competed with the Germanic ones, further undermining the old system (see, e.g., Strang, 1970, p. 191). These 'newer' prefixes are dominant in English today, and what remains of the pre-Germanic system is largely remnants (e.g., *withstand, beget, forgive*), where the prefixes' meanings have been lost.

Again, Dutch and German provide a contrast, and a pattern of verb formation more consistent with the older Germanic forms. Both have preserved a set of fairly productive verbal prefixes, and neither was 'colonized' to quite the same extent by Latinate prefixes such as *circum-*, *dis-*, *inter-*, *pre-*, and *re-*. German and Dutch each possess a set of unstressed verb prefixes including *ver-*, *be-*, and *ge-* which still combine with verb roots rather productively, and have some fairly consistent meaning (or meanings).[4] From a psychological point of view, these verbs are interesting for two reasons. First of all, their prefixes do not detach (vs. for example most *stressed* prefixes). It is an interesting question whether they are also 'inseparable' in the internal lexicon. For example, could some kind of 'prefix stripping' plausibly take place in word recognition for these items? Secondly, these verbs, unlike practically all others, do not take the *ge-* prefix as part of their past participle. They thus do not begin with a morpheme in this form which provides information as to what kind of verb form it is. In fact, this form of these verbs is ambiguous and can stand for (non-first person) singular present as well. The nature of the hearer's perception of these '*ge-* minus' verbs was another general question entertained in the research we report.

English is more like Dutch and German (and Nordic languages, for that matter) in a third respect: it still contains a reasonable number of strong as well as weak verbs. The root-vowel alternation and *-en* suffix of strong verbs might be considered among the more durable morphological traits in modern Germanic.[5] In Old English, the past tense of strong verbs was marked by a root vowel change (and in the plural by a suffix and sometimes a still different vowel change), and their past participle formed (usually) by a vowel change, the prefix *ge-*, and the suffix *-en*. Thus, for, e.g., the verb *sprecan* ('speak') one said *spræc* for (he) 'spoke' and *gesprecen* for 'spoken', and for *helpan* ('help'), *healp* for (he) 'helped' and *geholpen* for (have) 'helped'. Dutch and German continue until today to exhibit highly regular processes of ablaut. In English, on the other hand, there has been a tendency for the past participles to lose their inflections (compare Old English *gerunnen* with modern *run*) and also for strong verbs to become weak (witness the case of *help* above).

In the course of history, English weak verbs have also been subject to change. In the cases corresponding to those above, the past tense of, e.g., *lufian* ('love') was *lufode* and the past participle *gelufod*; the past of *libban* ('live') was *lifde* and the past participle *gelifd* (Baugh and Cable, 1978). In general, the past tense was formed by the verb stem plus a suffix containing an open syllable beginning with a dental consonant (cf. modern German *liebte, lebte*), while the past participle was formed by the *ge-* prefix, the verb stem, and a suffix ending in a dental consonant (cf. German *geliebt, gelebt*). What remains of this system is the stem plus English suffix spelled *-ed*, used for both functions.

This concludes our remarks on verb morphology in Germanic languages. We have presented a brief historical–modern comparison for two reasons. One is to help give the modern reader unspecialized in diachronic linguistics an idea of some of the verb forms he would have used in English up to about the time of Chaucer. The other is to help him understand what it still is like to form simple verb constructions in German or Dutch, and provide a kind of mnemonic aid for understanding the research reported in the final sections of the chapter.

TWO EXPERIMENTS

Selection of materials

The words studied here were spoken past tense forms and past participles in Dutch. Dutch verbs have both a singular and a plural past tense form, the latter being marked by a word-final suffix *-(e)n*.[6] Here, all past tense forms used were in the singular. The verbs chosen as cueing words and as targets came from three classes:

(a) *Regular strong verbs.* The strong verbs studied were of the ABB-type (Extra, 1978), meaning that there was the same change in the stem vowel of the infinitive form in the past and past participle (e.g., *vechten–*

vocht–gevochten = *fight–fought–fought*). This is the largest class of strong verbs and the easiest to use for controlling factors like word frequency. The singular past tense includes only the verb stem with the change in stem vowel, and no suffix. In the past participle form, the prefix *ge-* and the suffix *-en* are also present. The *ge-* prefix is also characteristic of past participles in one of the two classes of weak verbs studied.

(b) *+ge weak verbs.* Weak verbs in this class have past participles which begin with the *ge-* prefix and end with a suffix *-t* or *-d* (e.g., *spelen–speelde–gespeeld* = *play–played–played*). (Word-final /d/ in Dutch is devoiced.) The singular simple past is formed with the verb stem plus the suffix *-te* or *-de*, depending on whether the stem ends in a voiced or unvoiced consonant. Formation of the past tense in this way is also characteristic of the second class of weak verbs studied.

(c) *-ge weak verbs.* The singular past tense of these verbs is also formed by addition of the suffix *-te* or *-de* to the verb stem (e.g., *bereikten–bereikte–bereikt* = *reach–reached–reached*). On the other hand, the past participles do not take the *ge-* prefix, but only the *-d* or *-t* suffix. The past participle forms of weak verbs in this class are homophonous with their third person present forms, e.g., *bereikt* also means 'reaches'.

Overall frequency of use of the singular past tense and of past participles in Dutch does not greatly differ. In a recent spoken word count (de Jong, 1979), there were about 22 per cent more singular past tense forms than past participles (2,244 vs. 1,841). From a corpus of 600,000 printed words (Uit den Boogaart, 1975), van Heuven (1978) determined that singular past forms were 26 per cent more frequent than past participles used as verbs (17,156 vs. 13,625 occurrences respectively). On the basis of the latter sample, about 2.9 per cent of all word tokens in Dutch are past singular forms, and 2.3 per cent are past participles. For the present studies, 40 different verbs from each of the three classes described above were selected. In each case, 20 were presented as a target verb in the singular past, and 20 in the past participle. The target verbs used had between 10 and 200 occurrences in the Uit den Boogaart corpus. (This was the frequency of all their forms *together.*) Examples are shown in Table 3.1, together with the mean frequency and range per experimental condition.

Test items

The basic test items in both experiments conducted were the same: the 120 verb targets placed at the end of word strings of variable length. Two word sequences ending in each target word were constructed. These sequences contained the same words, and were preceded by the same cue word, but varied in grammaticality. One sequence had grammatical word order, and the other random word order. In Experiment 1, each subject tested heard each sequence once, or a total of 240 in all. In Experiment 2, each subject was tested on each sequence twice.

Of the 120 basic items, 48 contained different forms of the same verb as cue and target (e.g., *gekookt–kookte*, *stapte–gestapt*), 48 contained the same form of different verbs (e.g., *prees–bereikte*, *gestudeerd–gefloten*), 12 contained the same form of the same verb (e.g., *steeg–steeg*, *bewerkt–bewerkt*), and 12 contained different forms of different verbs (e.g., *geschoten–studeerde*, *vocht–gedankt*). To the extent permitted under the experimental design (including balancing for word frequency), pairing of verbs, and which verb in a pair was chosen as cue and which as target, were decided randomly.

The spoken verbs and filler words used in the experiments were pre-

Table 3.1   Examples of stimuli (cueing and target verbs) used in the experiments

Form of target		Example	N	Verb frequency	
				Mean	Range
STEM SAME, FORM DIFFERENT					
Past	Strong	*gestonken–stonk*	8	52	12–124
singular	Weak+ge	*gekookt–kookte*	8	48	12–144
	Weak–ge	*begeerd–begeerde*	8	48	10–108
Past	Strong	*gleed–gegleden*	8	50	14–156
participle	Weak+ge	*stapte–gestapt*	8	64	15–112
	Weak–ge	*ontdekte–ontdekt*	8	55	16–143
STEM DIFFERENT, FORM SAME					
Past	Strong	*verraste–prees*	8	45	13–132
singular	Weak+ge	*klom–bouwde*	8	61	18–114
	Weak–ge	*prees–bereikte*	8	70	18–181
Past	Strong	*gestudeerd–gefloten*	8	42	12–114
participle	Weak+ge	*erkend–gegooid*	8	49	18–98
	Weak–ge	*gestopt–verrast*	8	41	17–109
STEM SAME, FORM SAME					
Past	Strong	*steeg–steeg*	2	57	57–58
singular	Weak+ge	*wisselde–wisselde*	2	33	27–39
	Weak+ge	*beperkte–beperkte*	2	69	46–93
Past	Strong	*gegrepen–gegrepen*	2	64	62–67
participle	Weak+ge	*gepakt–gepakt*	2	52	37–67
	Weak–ge	*bewerkt–bewerkt*	2	26	21–32
STEM DIFFERENT, FORM DIFFERENT					
Past	Strong	*gezakt–vocht*	2	52	49–55
singular	Weak+ge	*gedanst–telde*	2	46	38–55
	Weak–ge	*gebogen–besefte*	2	33	26–41
Past	Strong	*vierde–gesprongen*	2	54	53–56
participle	Weak+ge	*plaatste–gerookt*	2	43	38–48
	Weak–ge	*leed–behaald*	2	41	26–57

recorded on master tapes, and mounted by re-recording onto stimulus tapes. On each test trial, a cueing verb was presented first, followed by a pause of 2.5 sec. The word string ending in the second verb (the target form) then began, with each word in this sequence beginning 1 sec following the beginning of the previous word. The word strings used were 3, 4, 5, and 6 words in length. The target verb, as mentioned, always occurred last.

To permit detecting possible effects of grammatical context, two kinds of word sequences were developed as mentioned, using the identical lexical material. On the one hand, Dutch subordinate clauses were used, of which versions were constructed of length two to five words excluding the target verb. In such clauses, the verb group is final, and either past participles or past tense forms made appropriate continuations. Random word strings were then formed by permuting the words in the corresponding grammatical strings. Examples of the three kinds of subordinate clause constructions used (using the subordinating conjunctions *omdat*, 'because'; *dat*, 'that'; and *waarom*, 'why') are shown below, together with randomizations used. Corresponding to our decision not to use plural past tense forms here, the subjects of these 'clauses' were always singular. The first Dutch sequence shown in each case

Type I $\overset{0}{-}$ omdat hij $\overset{3}{-}$ ze $\overset{4}{-}$ vroeger $\overset{5}{-}$ helemaal $\overset{6}{-}$
          – because he – them – earlier – completely –
          – hij helemaal – ze – vroeger – omdat –

Type II $\overset{0}{-}$ dat hij $\overset{3}{-}$ ze $\overset{4}{-}$ gisteren $\overset{5}{-}$ al $\overset{6}{-}$
          – that he – them – yesterday – already –
          – gisteren hij – ze – al – dat –

Type III $\overset{0}{-}$ waarom hij $\overset{3}{-}$ toen $\overset{4}{-}$ zo $\overset{5}{-}$ snel $\overset{6}{-}$
          – why he – then – so – quickly –
          – hij waarom – snel – zo – toen –

is the grammatical sequence, and the one shown below the translation is the random one. The place marked 0 corresponds to the location of the cueing verb before the word list *per se*. The places marked 3, 4, 5, and 6 are the serial positions within the word list at which, on a given test trial, the target verb might have occurred.

In preparing the stimulus tapes, a pulse concomitant with the onset of each target verb was placed using a voice key onto the non-speech channel. During the experiment, these pulses were used to start a timer used to measure subjects' reaction times. The length of target verbs and certain temporal locations within them were determined from oscillograms made of the speech wave. Using the word form list found in Uit den Boogaart (1975), we determined the earliest phoneme within each target at which only one verb remained as a possible continuation, and similarly, the earliest point in the

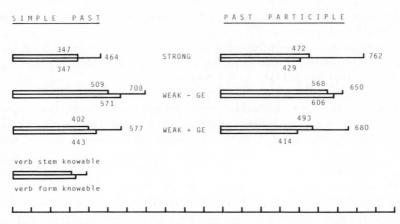

Figure 3.1   Lengths of verb targets differing in stem or form from cueing words, for simple past and past participle, and for the three verb forms

form at which it would be possible to know positively that it was a past tense form or a past participle. The centre of the decisive phonetic segment was then determined from the oscillogram for each target verb. The results obtained are illustrated in Figure 3.1 for verb targets differing in stem or form their cueing verbs, and also reported with verb length in Tables 3.2 and 3.3, where the reaction times obtained in the two studies are summarized. The measurements based on length of the spoken verb targets were used to calculate RT from the within-word points and from word offset.

Testing procedure

In Experiment 1, subjects were asked to register decisions if the verb targets shown were *alike* in stem or in form with the cueing verbs. Stem decisions were registered with one hand, and form decisions with the other hand. (One push button was labelled 'stem', the other 'tense'.) Thus, on most trials only one response was appropriate, but there were also trials where no response was called for, or both responses. A random order of the stimulus items was recorded for playback on two tapes. Half of the sixteen subjects tested (students at the University of Tilburg) heard one tape first, and the other half the other tape first. Similarly, half of the subjects pressed 'stem' with their right hand, and half pressed 'tense'. All subjects were right-handed.

In Experiment 2, subjects were asked to judge the stimulus materials presented twice, in two different tasks. The tasks were to make 'same' and 'different' judgements based on the verb target's stem, and to make them based on its form type *vis-à-vis* the cueing verb. Judgements were registered by pushing a button marked 'yes, same' with one hand, or a button marked 'no, different' with the other hand. The subjects were eight right-handed students from the University of Tilburg who had not taken part in the first experiment. Half judged stem identity in the first of two test sessions, and half judged form identity, and vice versa in the second half of the experiment. Independently, half of the subjects made 'same' judgements with their right hand in the first test sessions and with their left in the second, and the other half the other way around.

All subjects were given written instructions before starting the experiment. They were told that the study was meant to investigate perception of verb forms, and that two kinds of forms—third person past tense and past participles—had been selected with that aim in mind. To familiarize subjects with the experimental task, they were first shown some examples, and then practised on eight items orally with the experimenter. They were told that their decisions should be made and registered as quickly as possible. The subjects then put on headphones and the experiment started. The first 24 items presented on the tape were additional training items. Subjects were told on these items if they had made errors. During the remainder of the experiment, no feedback on accuracy was given.

FINDINGS

The experiments performed here included test items of two general kinds, one in which the cueing and target verbs were alike in stem or form (e.g., *bel+de−ge+bel+d*, *verdien+de−bel+de*) and the other in which both features were shared (the target and cue were identical) or neither feature was (e.g., *bel+de−ge+reken+d*). The former types of item outnumbered the latter by a ratio of 4 to 1; the analyses preformed of the data in the two cases were independent. The data themselves are in each case a distribution of errors made and a set of latency measures to correct response. (Reaction times greater than 3 sec measured from word onset were removed and estimated.) It will be seen that the errors are predicted by the latencies and vice versa. Three points during the presentation of a target word were used to define the beginning of the response interval: the word's physical onset, its offset, and the earliest point within the word when the stem or form type could be theoretically known. In practice, this was the midpoint of a phonetic segment.

Experiment 1

We will briefly consider first the errors recorded, then the latency of response on non-identical cue-target word items, and finally RT on trials where the two verb forms were the same.

An error could be made in this experiment by pressing either response button or by not pressing it. Together, this happened on only about 5 per cent of test trials. Subjects made the highest percentage of errors on form decisions: about 8 per cent both on pressing falsely and not pressing falsely, compared with less than 2 per cent for stems in each case. Secondly, there were proportionally the most errors made on weak, inseparable prefix verbs, then on strong verbs, and finally on other weak verbs. Thirdly, there were somewhat more errors made on targets which were past participles than which were past tenses. And fourthly, errors were most prevalent of all in judging -ge weak verbs for form equivalence. On these items (e.g., *verplaatst*, *verplaatste* = 'moved'), the false alarm rate was more than 11 per cent.

When a target verb had the same stem (e.g., *zwom–gezwommen* = English *swam–swum*), or was a form of the same type as the cue used (e.g., *verklaarde—drukte,* the past tenses of *explain* and *press*), RT in this first experiment averaged about 1.3 sec measured from word onset. The major results obtained for response latencies on these items were: (a) same stem judgements were made faster than same form judgements, (b) judgements on -ge

Table 3.2   Mean word length and reaction time (sec) in Experiment 1 for targets sharing verb stem or verb form with cueing word

Form of target	Length	Point for determining reaction time		
		Word onset	Word-internal	Word offset
STEM SAME, FORM DIFFERENT				
Past tense singular				
Strong (e.g., *stonk*)	.46 (.35)	1.04	.69	.58
Weak+ge (*kookte*)	.59 (.40)	1.08	.68	.48
Weak−ge (*begeerde*)	.71 (.48)	1.31	.83	.60
Past participle				
Strong (*gegleden*)	.78 (.50)	1.13	.63	.35
Weak+ge (*gestapt*)	.66 (.49)	1.12	.63	.46
Weak−ge (*ontdekt*)	.65 (.61)	1.42	.81	.77
FORM SAME, STEM DIFFERENT				
Past tense singular				
Strong (*prees*)	.47 (.35)	1.35	1.00	.88
Weak+ge (*bouwde*)	.57 (.44)	1.29	.85	.72
Weak−ge (*bereikte*)	.71 (.57)	1.53	.96	.83
Past participle				
Strong (*gefloten*)	.74 (.41)	1.43	1.02	.69
Weak+ge (*gegooid*)	.70 (.39)	1.37	.98	.67
Weak−ge (*verrast*)	.65 (.59)	1.67	1.08	1.02

Note: The length shown in parentheses corresponds to the part of the stimulus word prior to the within-word measuring point for 'same' judgements.

weak verbs were made relatively slowly with respect to strong and other weak verbs, and (c) RT was positively correlated with word length measured from word onset but negatively correlated from word offset. Word lengths and reaction times for these same stem, different form, and same form, different stem items are given for all relevant subconditions in Table 3.2. We summarize the main effects and interactions found by analysis of variance, and the correlations obtained, in the text below.

Same-stem judgements were made about 250 msec faster than same-form judgements for the items represented in Table 3.2 measured from any of the three points shown (p(Min F'_{obs}) < .002 in each case). The differences were 1183 vs. 1441 msec from word onset, 712 vs. 984 msec word internally, and 540 vs. 802 msec from word offset. The effect of verb class, secondly, was also statistically reliable each way the response latency was estimated (p(Min F'_{obs}) < .01 in all cases). Measured from word onset, RT on -ge weak verbs averaged 1483 msec, vs. 1214 msec for other weak verbs and 1238 msec for strong verbs. Using the word-internal measuring points, the corresponding means were 921, 785, and 836 msec. And from word offset, they were 805, 585, and 625 msec respectively.

The only remaining significant findings from this analysis were a main effect of type of verb form for RT calculated from word *onset* (1267 msec on past tense vs. 1357 on past participles, Min $F'(1,52) = 7.99, p < .01$) and an interaction for RT measured from word *offset* between type of verb form and verb class (Min $F'(2,103) = 13.90, p < .001$). Faster decisions from words' ends were taken on participial forms (e.g, *gezongen* = *sung*) than past tense ones (e.g., *zong* = *sang*) for strong verbs (520 vs. 730 msec), while decisions were faster on past tense forms (*bereikte* = *reached*) than past participles (*bereikt* = *reached*) for -ge weak verbs (716 vs. 895 msec)[7]. For other weak verbs, RT for past and past participle forms (*rekende* vs. *gerekend* = *figured*) was closer to being equal (602 vs. 565 msec respectively).

Further, as mentioned, RT and word length were rather weakly correlated for these partly same–partly different target verbs. From word onset, the correlation observed was positive, both for same-stem items (.28) and same form-type items (.34) ($p < .025$ and .01 respectively). From word offset, the correlation in each case was negative: −.40 and −.29 respectively ($p < .01$ and .025).

Finally, the results for items where both stem and form type matched are more difficult to evaluate. There were only two items used per subgroup, and a correct reaction called for pushing both response buttons. Only an analysis of variance by subjects was performed. The difference in speed of stem vs. form-type judgements (1190 vs. 1254 msec respectively measured from word onset) was nôt statistically reliable. Second, there was a verb class effect found using all three measures of time to response ($p < .001$ for each). In each instance, -ge weak verbs elicited, as before, the slowest responses.

Measured from word onset, these took 1457 msec on average, vs. 1089 msec for strong verbs and 1177 msec for other weak verbs. Third, from word onset, there was again a main effect of verb form: past tense items were responded to faster than (prefixed) past participles (1193 vs. 1266 msec respectively, $p = .01$). And fourth and last, again measured from word onset, verb form and verb class interacted ($p < .001$). In this case, strong past tense forms (which were one syllable in length) were reacted to about 300 msec faster than the corresponding (three-syllable) past participles, whereas responses on the past participles of weak verbs were slightly faster (by 75 msec for both classes) that those on the past tense forms.

Experiment 2

We follow the same pattern in reporting results here as used above. First, errors are considered, then responses where the target word differed in one respect from the cue, and finally the RT data where the target repeated the cueing verb or differed from it in both relevant respects.

Table 3.3   Mean word length and reaction time (sec) in Experiment 2 for targets sharing verb stem or verb form with cueing word

Target form	Length	Stem judgement from			Form judgement from		
		Onset	Within	Offset	Onset	Within	Offset
STEM SAME, FORM DIFFERENT							
Past singular							
Strong	.46 (.35)	.57	.22	.11	.89	.54	.43
Weak+ge	.59 (.45)	.59	.20	−.00	.93	.48	.33
Weak−ge	.71 (.57)	.72	.24	.01	1.13	.56	.43
Past participle							
Strong	.78 (.45)	.75	.25	−.03	.89	.44	.11
Weak+ge	.66 (.44)	.70	.21	.04	.91	.47	.25
Weak−ge	.65 (.62)	.76	.15	.11	1.29	.67	.64
STEM DIFFERENT, FORM SAME							
Past singular							
Strong	.46 (.35)	.71	.36	.24	1.14	.79	.67
Weak+ge	.57 (.41)	.77	.36	.21	1.00	.56	.43
Weak−ge	.71 (.54)	.82	.28	.11	1.22	.65	.51
Past participle							
Strong	.74 (.44)	.85	.41	.11	1.20	.79	.46
Weak+ge	.70 (.50)	.84	.34	.14	1.10	.71	.41
Weak−ge	.65 (.52)	.85	.33	.20	1.42	.83	.77

Note: The length shown in parentheses corresponds to the part of the stimulus word prior to the within-word measuring point for 'different' judgements.

Subjects in this study judged whether a target verb stem was the same or different as in the cueing verb, and whether the form type was the same or different, in separate tasks. This led to a somewhat lower error rate, especially on form judgements. Errors on stems occurred on 2.7 per cent of relevant test trials, vs. 3.4 per cent of those for form. Form decisions on fully different target verbs (8 per cent) and in making same form judgements on -ge weak verb past participles (14 per cent) and on strong verbs (about 7 per cent for both form types) were the only categories of responses where more than a nominal number of errors were made.

The main findings for RT on same stem, different form and same form, different stem items were: (a) both same and different judgements were made faster in judging stems; (b) judgements on -ge weak verbs were made relatively slowly, except as measured within the target verbs; and (c) RT was positively correlated with word length when measured from word onset but negatively correlated with it from word offset. These findings are similar to those reported above for the first experiment. As before, the effect of verb form type changed with the measurement point used. Vis-à-vis Experiment 1, responses were considerably speeded, averaging about .9 sec measured from word onset, and for 'different' as well as 'same' judgements. The mean reaction times in the various subconditions are shown for both in Table 3.3.

First, same-stem judgements were made about 500 msec faster than same-form judgements for the items in Table 3.3 using any of the three bases of measurement. The respective differences were 681 vs. 1180 msec measured from word onset, 210 vs. 722 msec word internally, and 37 vs. 546 msec from word offset ($p(F'_{obs}) < .001$ for each). Different-stem judgements were made about 200 msec faster than different-form judgements for these items ($p(F'_{obs}) < .02$ for all three measures). Given the distribution of items to conditions, this means further that stem judgements were made on the same words about 300 msec faster than form judgements, and that the difference between 'same' and 'different' judgements was positive for stem decisions but negative for form decisions.

Second, turning to verb class as a factor, of the six comparisons defined by point of measurement and response executed ('same' vs. 'different') on these items, four—those from word onset and from word offset—yielded significant results beyond the .005 level. For 'different' judgements, response on -ge weak verbs were simply slower than those on strong and other weak verbs. For 'same' judgements measured from these two points, -ge verbs were again the slowest to respond to, but strong verbs also elicited slower responses than +ge weak verbs. Word-internally, on the other hand, for 'different' judgements, there was little difference between classes. From here, mean RT was 441 msec for strong verbs, 458 msec for -ge weak verbs, and 413 msec for +ge weak verbs. These differences do not approach significance. For 'same' judgements, a weak effect was obtained ($F'(2,40) = 3.23, p < .05$), but it did not involve -*ge* weak verbs. The corresponding means measured from within words were 512 msec for strong verbs, 465 msec for -*ge* weak verbs, and 421 msec for other weak verbs. Only the largest difference among these means was reliable when tested *post hoc*.

Third, in five of the six analyses carried out, verb class interacted with stem vs. form judgements. For 'different' judgements, these interactions appear to have a simple basis: form judgements were slower to make on -*ge* weak verbs than the others, but stem judgements were not. Measured from within words, on -*ge* verbs these were actually made fastest. For 'same' judgements, the situation is less clear. The interaction between stem/form and verb class from word onset was just significant ($F'(2,25) = 3.34, p = .05$); word-internally, it was not significant; from word offset, it was again reliable ($F'(2,71) = 5.14$, $p < .01$). The most obvious generalization which can be given for these results is that stem judgements for strong and +*ge* weak verbs took about the same amount of time, but form judgements took considerably longer (120–150 msec) for strong verbs.

Fourth, speed of response also varied as a function of the past–past participle distinction, but the relative advantage found changed as the measurement point was moved from word onset to word offset. From word onset, past participles were slower to respond to than past tense forms: by 989 vs. 872 msec for 'same' judgements, and 939 vs. 875 msec for 'different' judgements ($p(\text{Min } F'_{obs}) < .02$ for both cases). Word-internally, the corresponding difference for same judgements (490 vs. 442 msec) just missed significance at the .05 level, and that for 'different' judgements (444 vs. 431 msec) became significant. From words' ends, 'same' judgements were about equally fast in the two cases (288 vs. 295 msec), and 'different' judgements were actually faster (240 vs. 294 msec) for past participles ($F'(1,28) = 4.33, p < .05$).

Fifth, the only remaining statistical interactions found in these analyses were from word offset between verb class and verb form. This interaction was significant ($p(F'_{obs}) < .001$) for both same and different judgements. In each case, past tense forms were slower to respond to than past participles for strong verbs, but past participles were slower to respond to than past tense forms for -*ge* weak verbs. The magnitude of the differences can be best seen from Table 3.3.

Sixth and finally, word length and RT were found as in Experiment 1 to be correlated positively on same form or stem items measured from word onset, and negatively correlated from word offset. Of the eight correlations reported in Table 3.4, all are significant beyond the .01 level except those measured from word onset for 'same' and 'different' judgements on form.

The remaining data from Experiment 2 are the response times obtained on target verbs which were identical to cues, and on targets which differed from the cueing word in both stem and verb form. Because of the small number of items involved, only a by-subject analysis of variance was again performed.

Table 3.4   Correlation coefficients (Pearson r) between word length and RT on targets sharing stem or form with cueing verbs in Experiment 2

Stimulus judgement	Point for determining reaction time	
	Word onset	Word offset
Stem same	.36	−.47
Stem different	.44	−.49
Form same	.22	−.36
Form different	.16	−.47

This time, however, 'same' vs. 'different' judgements were included as a factor. The results of this analysis were quite straightforward: there were two large main effects and besides these only some suggestive trends. First, stem decisions were made much faster than decisions on verb form: 759 vs. 1168 msec on average from word onset, and by 399 msec word-internally and from word offset ($p < .001$ in each case). Second, same judgements were made faster than different judgements, on average by nearly 200 msec from each measuring point ($p < .001$ in each case). And third, a pair of trends were observed mirroring the previous results reported. RT on -*ge* weak verbs was slower than on other verbs from word onset ($p < .05$), but word-internally the three verb classes had almost identical average latencies (about 525 msec). And judgements on past participles were made slower by about 80 msec from word onset and within words ($.05 < p < .1$ in each case), but from word offset, were made slightly faster than those on past tense forms.

Syntax

We have not mentioned any findings above for grammatical vs. ungrammatical word order in test items. This is because in neither Experiment 1 nor 2 were there any very striking differences found for this factor. In both studies, moreover, what small difference was observed tended to favour faster, more accurate performance when verb targets were heard in ungrammatical sequences. measured from word onset, the grand means in Experiment 1 for targets sharing stem or form with their cueing verbs were 1327 msec when heard in grammatical sequences and 1305 msec when heard in ungrammatical ones. The corresponding means in Experiment 2 were 948 vs. 913 msec for 'same' judgements, and 909 vs. 905 msec for 'different' judgements. In each case, there were also more errors made when test sequences were grammatical: 89 vs. 61 in Experiment 1, and, across 'same' and 'different' judgments, 67 vs. 28, in Experiment 2. The RT differences found were not reliable tested from any point; the only one even approaching significance was as measured from word offset in Experiment 2 for 'same' judgements, where the difference observed was 43 msec ($F'(1,72) = 3.62, p = .06$). Although the error rate was very marginal, subjects consistently made more errors on verb targets in grammatical sequences ($t(15) = 1.97, p < .05$ in Experiment 1; $t(7) = 8.41, p < .001$ in Experiment 2).

INTERPRETATION

We will try to describe the present results in terms of existing theories, but also imply that a composite model involving features of several of these may be more satisfactory than any of them alone. The ideas we rely on from the literature come primarily from Taft and Forster (1975), Forster (1976), Marslen-Wilson (1980; Marslen-Wilson and Welsh, 1978; Marslen-Wilson and Tyler, 1980), Stanners (Stanners, Neiser, Hernon, and Hall, 1979; Stanners, Neiser, and Painton, 1979), Hudson (1981), and Meijers and Jarvella (1982). Subjects were asked here to perform what might be labelled, following Forster (1979), a speeded same–different classification task. They first heard one spoken verb form and then, in the course of a short list of words, a second verb form. When the second verb form was presented, it was their task to determine as quickly as possible whether the verb was the same or different in some sense as the first verb. In Experiment 1, subjects registered a decision only if the second verb was the same as the first in one (or both) of two respects. In Experiment 2, they registered both 'same' and 'different' decisions, in different test sessions, for the verbs' stems and their forms. The forms studied were Dutch past participles and third person singular past tense forms. A range of these forms were studied from three verb classes. The word sequences they were placed in constituted well-formed clauses or were grossly ungrammatical.

Only a stem-organized mental lexicon would appear to be able to explain the most striking and consistent result found here: that subjects' decisions were almost invariably taken faster in judging identity or non-identity of verbs' stems than in judging properties of the verbs' forms reflected by prefixes and suffixes and stem-internal vowel changes. Marslen-Wilson's 'cohort' model does not take into account words' morphology, and thus may make no prediction whatsoever here. Taft and Forster's model (1975) does presuppose a stem-organized central lexical file, and would predict the present result insofar as recognizing what a word is entails prior access to its stem, and that determination of its form requires search through (or generation of) the subentries of the stem and some kind of post-lexical comparison with the stimulus. In a model in which a word's form and its stem are recognized independently, conversely, the first process would need to run much slower than the second to account for the present findings. There are reasons to believe that a word search based on grammatical form would not be very efficient (see, e.g., Forster, 1976; Knuth, 1973).

It is, of course, possible that something else about the task or the words used in it makes this first result unrepresentative, or even trivial. To us, this seems unlikely. The words that were studied were made up of both verb roots and other grammatical morphemes, and either (or neither) by themselves may in principle have been sufficient for the decisions obtained in the respective conditions to be made. Secondly, serial order of the stem and grammatical morphemes in the words studied varied. On a purely left-to-right basis, there were cases present for which it could theoretically be said that what form a verb had could be known before it could be known what its stem was. Subjects did not appear to be able to take advantage of this fact, even when they were asked to make stem and form decisions in completely separate tasks (Experiment 2). Relatively speaking, their performance actually deteriorated, *vis-à-vis* a situation (Experiment 1) where identity judgements on each criterion were made at the same time. Thirdly, this result did not depend on a comparison using items where the two verbs presented had the same stem, and one might argue that lexical access for a stem decision but not a form decision was possible before the target verb was heard. Subjects were also faster in Experiment 2 in deciding that a stem was different than they were in deciding that a form was different where, in the latter case, the form was a different form of the same verb. The faster 'no, different' decisions than 'yes, same' ones on form in that experiment, however, may reflect such prior access, though still some 300 msec slower than 'same' stem judgements on the identical items. A genuine increase in the speed of form decisions did appear to occur when a positive decision on the stem was made at the same time (Experiment 1, identical items). Fourthly, the stem and form judgement tasks do not seem to differ in such a way that one should be *intrinsically* easier than the other. In our view, stem judgements in the main part of our experiments may have been faster partly because roots are a main point of contact between linguistic form and lexical meaning. However, it begs the question to say that it is the stems' meaning, independent of lexical access, which explains the result. To argue this, one would need further to show that, for example, the perception of meaning similarity or difference was more salient for stems, that semantic priming would produce similar effects, and so on. In general, this first and major result thus suggests that the most efficient way to access information in the central lexicon is to first reference the main lexical entry for *lemmas*, or the main lexical entries for morphologically related words; that this happens via a process whereby the stem is first identified.

It can be shown that the kind of theory proposed by Stanners makes essentially wrong predictions with respect to lexical access here. Stanners would hypothesize that different forms of the same lemma have different basic lexical entries rather than being different subentries or reconstructed. For this reason, it should be faster to access (and compare, etc.) two words which have the same stem and the same form than two words which have the same stem but different forms. This was the case in neither study that was performed. Measured from target onset, 'same'-stem judgements in Experiment 1 were made on average in 1190 msec when the target verb and cue were identical, vs. 1183 msec when one was a past participle and the other a third person past tense form. Again, Stanners would predict that, even if same-stem judgements were not always faster for identical cue and target verbs, they would certainly be faster where the principal form of the verb (assumed to be the infinitive or its stem) differed from the forms of the verbs being tested. That is, *sang* and *sung* in English according to Stanners have different base lexical entries than *sing*, and there is not reason to expect anything different in the mental representation of strong verbs in Dutch or any other Germanic language. This prediction is again wrong. In Experiment 1, decisions on strong verb targets identical to cues averaged 1053 msec from word onset, vs. 1084 on non-identical cue-target pairs. In Experiment 2, the corresponding means were 687 and 660 msec. In neither case did the difference approach being significant.

To be fair, one might argue, of course, that this is not exactly what Stanner's position would be. On the last point made, for example, while not having the same phonetic or orthographic form of the stem in the infinitive (e.g., *zingen*), the past tense and past participle forms of strong verbs studied shared the same 'change' from the infinitive (e.g., *zong* vs. *gezongen*). Now, if *zong* and *gezongen* do not fall in the lexical entry for *zing(en)*, but the past and past participle forms of weak verbs do fall together with their infinitives in one lexical entry (e.g., *koken–kookte–gekookt = cook–cooked–cooked*), then the comparisons made on strong verbs should be made, for example, less directly, access to the same lemma might not re-arise, etc. One would probably predict that, *vis-à-vis* performance on 'comparable' weak verbs, judgements on strong verbs where the stem is 'repeated' in the target form should be made more slowly. There is some evidence from Experiment 2 that this is so, but it is not the strongest kind of evidence. Latencies on strong verbs in general in Experiment 2 were longer than those for +*ge* weak verbs, i.e., measured from all three points used to define the start of the response interval when the judgement called for was 'same'. Inspection of Table 3.3, however, plus the significant interaction obtained between verb class and verb form from word's end for 'same' judgements, shows that this effect was limited by and large to judgements on form and not on stem identity. This does not rule out the possibility that lexical entries for different forms of strong verbs include cross-listings which identify the stem in their lemma (e.g., *zong*: form of *zingen*; look there for further information). But it does make it seem unlikely that their grammatical form would be cross-listed as well (e.g., *gezongen*: past participle of *zingen*).

Let us turn to the more general issue of how access to a (largely) stem-organized central lexicon might occur. A second major finding here, smaller in magnitude but almost as uniform as that of relative speed of stem over form decisions, was relative slowness of response on *-ge* weak verbs, that is verbs which begin in Dutch with the bound 'prefixes' *be-*, *her-*, *er-*, *ont-*, and *ver-* (and *ge-*, which we did not use). In Experiment 1, responses on *-ge* weak verbs were slower than those on both *+ge* weak verbs and strong verbs, measured from all starting points used for calculating RT. In Experiment 2, responses on *-ge* weak verbs were slower measured from target on- and offset than those on *+ge* weak verbs for both 'same' and 'different' judgements, and, for 'different' judgements, were also slower from these two points than responses on strong verbs. The model proposed by Taft and Forster (1975) appears to be able to account for this result in two different ways, depending on whether one regards this set of verb 'prefixes' as real or only apparent. As mentioned earlier, they propose that words are morphologically decomposed to locate their stem, which then permits the words to be accessed in the central lexicon. Suppose that this process of morphological decomposition has the effect of stripping the 'prefixes' off *-ge* weak verbs. Now, if they are regarded as real prefixes, there will be a multiplicity of lexical entries 'addressed' by their stems, e.g., for *verwerken* ('process') reduced to the stem '*werk*', a set of forms for *werken* ('work'), *verwerken*, *bewerken* ('work over'), *werkelijk* ('really'), *werkloos* ('unemployed') and many others. If one searches this list of entries to confirm that the target belongs to the same entry as the cue, more time can be expected to be consumed the longer the list is. Suppose, on the other hand, that *verwerken* is not included in this list, and, for simplicity's sake, that only the verb *werken* is accessed when *ver-* is stripped from *verwerken*. In this case, *verwerken* will not be addressable at all under this stem, and a new attempt may be launched to access the correct verb without removal of the 'prefix'. Again, more work will be called for than where success is immediate; this can be presumed to be reflected in RT. On either account, then, one may need to access more than one lexical entry to locate a *-ge* weak verb. And only when the stem does not permit looking only under the simple verb entry will this be so, for example, for *+ge* weak verbs. In that case, to explain the relative speed of judgements on these verbs here, one would need to hypothesize, following Forster (1976) or Taft and Forster (1975), that other factors, such as word frequency, determine the order in which different entries with the same 'peripheral' code are looked up, and show that *-ge* verbs do not receive high priority in this process.

An alternative hypothesis for access to a stem-organized central lexicon is that words heard are initially matched from left to right against a kind of peripheral word list. Forster (1976), Marslen-Wilson and Tyler (1980), and Hudson (1981) all propose some kind of comparable matching procedure based on the temporal structure of information in word tokens. The general assumption made is also that lexical access will be attempted (or occur) before all of the information in a stimulus word has been placed in a usable format and matched against the internal set of codes. Especially in spoken words, this gives early information heard more emphasis, but perhaps most of all (or only) when that phonetic information serves sufficiently to reduce uncertainty over alternatives. There is reason to believe that prefixes would word against early decisions being made in this way, since the information needed to distinguish one prefixed word from others would follow the prefix.[8]

In the present context, one would predict on this basis that, for example, past participles will be slower to respond to than simple past tense forms in Dutch if they take the prefix *ge-* before their stem. This prediction is generally supported in our data: measured from word onset, RT on past participles was in most analyses about 80 msec slower than on past tense forms. This effect included performance on *-ge* weak verbs, which do not take this prefix. However, the 'inseparable prefixes' which these verbs do take in all their forms would have the same function of delaying the point in a word when sufficient information has been heard for lexical access to occur. In Experiment 1, there is still an overall effect of slowness on *-ge* weak verbs *vis-à-vis* the other classes studied of about 110 msec if the initial part of the word hypothetically necessary to making an unambiguous decision is subtracted from RT. However, in Experiment 2, this difference shrinks to about 20 msec overall, and stem decisions are actually made about 40 msec earlier, relatively speaking, than on the other two classes. The fact that longer reaction times from word beginning also tended to occur generally for longer forms here similarly reflects indirectly the fact that the shorter words studied were not prefixed forms but the longer ones were. Finally, this theory could be supported by the fact that the non-suffixed forms studied tended to have the longest RTs measured from word offset. In these cases (the strong past tense forms such as *zong*, 'sang'), proportionally speaking, the largest part of the word needs to be heard before it becomes clear what verb is involved. If checking of a verb's morphological form proceeds via access to its stem, one would expect the same negative correlations for form judgements here, and these were, of course, obtained (even, again, where verb form was theoretically knowable earlier in a target word). Although there is greater risk in interpreting negative findings, the fact that, measured from the word-internal point, 'same stem' judgments in Experiment 2 had about equal latencies (roughly 200 msec.) over verb types and forms studied might also be argued to favor the same general hypothesis.

It should be clear that morphological decomposition and left-to-right comparison of a word against a list of word forms are not incompatible hypotheses. A pre-morphological analysis (where the subject is not aware that affixes are being stripped off, and cannot use the information to decide immediately what morphological form is involved) might be conducted on-line in the word recognition process. Since it is the information in word stems which allows access to the lexicon, and such a process would help mark the boundaries of stems, prefix-stripping might help both initially in lexical access, and in checking whether an inflected form found in the mental lexicon in fact corresponds to the word presented post-lexically.

The negative findings obtained here for the syntactic factor we included are difficult to interpret. On the one hand, they might be taken to support a theory of lexical access free of syntactic influences (i.e., Forster over Marslen-Wilson and Tyler)[9]. Both the correlations of word length with RT here, and the slopes for these correlations obtained, happened to go in the opposite direction of those found by the latter authors in a study of English monosyllabic nouns (1980). The stimuli here were not recorded in the context of connected speech, however. At least Marslen-Wilson and Tyler used a lead-in sentence; their stimulus materials were spoken as single utterances. It might also be argued on other grounds that the present studies do not lend themselves ideally to uncovering effects on word processing of a listener's decisions made at other linguistic and non-linguistic levels.

There may be, for example, a situation in which some of the main trends found in the present data might be largely offset, and perhaps even reversed. In the studies we have reported, either a past tense or a past participle of a verb could occur at any of the test points used in grammatical sequences. If a past participle occurred, however, the following word would have had to be an auxiliary. In Dutch, however, the auxiliary in subordinate clauses with a non-finite main verb may either immediately follow or precede this verb. Thus, *dat hij het had gedaan* and *dat hij het gedaan had* are two equivalent ways of saying the same thing ('that he had done it'). And, in a broader context, in both cases it may often largely be a foregone conclusion that a perfect construction is being used after only the first verb form is heard. To that extent, for the aux-first case, results considerably different from those found here with respect to stem and verb form judgements might be obtainable. Stem judgements, in particular, might be no longer so fast compared to form judgements, and decisions on past participles might, even measured from word onset, be no slower (or even faster) than those made on past tense forms. We note in this regard that in an unpublished study, L. M. Goldstein found that phoneme-monitoring latencies for word initial /g/ in Dutch (which is phonetically a velar affricate) were shorter for the relatively small class of Dutch -ge weak verbs having the (permanent) ge- prefix when these were presented in a context demanding their infinitive than when presented in a context calling for a past participle, *vis-à-vis* other verbs (Lew Goldstein and Sieb Nooteboom, personal communications). While Goldstein's result is quite consistent with the present findings—the ge- prefix being more lexically, and less grammatically informative when part of an infinitive than a past participle—it does suggest that recognition of non-finite verb forms in spoken Dutch will be sensitive to preceding finite verb forms heard. The question is then whether, under appropriately biasing conditions, this kind of effect might be sufficiently powerful to suggest word processing which does not depend fully on stem-based lexical access.

NOTES

1. We refer to their Experiment 4. There is a printing error or some other discrepancy in the results reported for this study. (Compare Table 1, p. 737 with the description of *post hoc* significant results on p. 741.) In this study, the same tendency as found in the others Stanners *et al.* report (which the table but not the text suggests) might simply mean that the priming words, apparently most of which began with *dis-* or *un-* (e.g., *disinfect–infect*, *unsafe–safe*), had some inhibitory effect on recognizing the target words.
2. Bybee and Slobin (1982) approach this problem for English past tense forms like *struck* and *snuck* and the *speaking* process by making the following suggestion. In coming upon a verb being sought, the speaker will produce a regular past tense if it is not marked as being irregular. If it is marked as irregular, the meaning/syntax based search will continue until the right form of the verb is found. Bybee and Slobin suppose that the search process cannot bypass the base form, but that once this is found, other information needed will be immediately available. They consider strong verbs having past forms in one vowel but derived from verbs having different root vowels to be psychologically rote forms rather than constructed by rule.
3. The phonetic realization of the consonant in the *ge*-prefix in Old English was probably the palatal [j]. The vowel is given by Clark (1957) as [ɛ] and not schwa.
4. Thus, there are really two morphemes in Dutch and German with the spelling (and corresponding phonology) *ge*-, one a lexical prefix and the other a grammatical prefix. In some contexts, it would be important to study both together (see the reference to Goldstein at the end of the chapter). In the present study, where our interest was focused on the difference between the two kinds of prefixes, we did not wish to further complicate the task by doing this. It is obvious that our failure to use foils such as *gebruikte* ('used') may have had some slight effect on the results.
5. In Scandinavian, many verbs with inseparable prefixes were re-introduced under German commercial influence during the Hanseatic period. Unlike West Germanic, strong verbs in, e.g., Swedish have a root vowel change in the past and supine (e.g., *springa–sprang–sprungit = spring–sprang–sprung*), but, in the latter case, a different suffix (*-it* vs. *-(a)t* for weak verbs.)
6. The dental nasal in most Dutch plurals is not normally pronounced.
7. The long average decision latencies for form judgments on items such as *verstrekte–verstrekt* possibly reflects the latter (past participial) forms falling within those for past tense. Similar results have apparently been found in work on same–different judgments for Morse code (Marcel Just, personal communication).
8. Marslen-Wilson (1983) reports some data which seem to support this notion for the English prefix *in-*. Nonword judgments for items beginning with *in-* were found to be unusually slow, and most predictable when their stem portion alone was used to estimate a theoretical point of earliest recognition.

ACKNOWLEDGMENT

We wish especially to thank Gerard Kempen for his long-term interest and moral and intellectual support in the research reported here, and for making available technical facilities when they were needed. The simplification of the decision task in Experiment 2 was first suggested by William Marslen-Wilson. Significant technical assistance was received from Pieter Huybers in the data analyses reported, and from Paul Hendrikx in the instrumentation developed for the testing. Construction of the experimental tapes was fostered by help from the audio-visual center of Tilburg University. Finally, Charles Fillmore and Carolyn White graciously made available their libraries, allowing significant improvements in the text at a critical time; Claus Heeschen also provided useful historical information. Order of authorship here is based on relative contribution to the paper's final form only.

REFERENCES

Baugh, A. C., and Cable, T. *A History of the English Language*, Englewood Cliffs, N.J.: Prentice-Hall, 3rd edition, 1978.

Bybee, J. L., and Slobin, D. I. Rules and schemas in the development and use of the English past. *Language*, 1982, **58**, 265–289.

Clark, J. W. *Early English*. New York: Norton, 1957.

Chomsky, N., and Halle, M. *The Sound Pattern of English*. New York: Harper and Row, 1968.

Extra, G. *Nederlands voor buitenlanders: psycholinguistische aspecten van vreemdetaalverwerving*. Unpublished doctoral dissertation, University of Nijmegen, 1978.

Forster, K. I. Accessing the mental lexicon. In R. J. Wales and E. Walker (Eds), *New Approaches to Language Mechanisms*. Amsterdam: North-Holland, 1976.

Forster, K. I. Levels of processing and the structure of the language processor. In W. E. Cooper and E. C. T. Walker (Eds), *Sentence Processing: Psycholinguistic Studies Presented to Merrill Garrett*, Hillsdale, N.J.: Lawrence Erlbaum Associates, 1979.

Gibson, E. J., and Guinet, L. Perception of inflections in brief visual presentation of words. *Journal of Verbal Learning and Verbal Behavior*, 1971, **10**, 182–189.

Heuven, V. van *Spelling en lezen: Hoe tragisch zijn de werkwoordsvormen?* Assen: van Gorcum, 1978.

Hudson, P. T. W. *Repetition, semantic priming and the mental lexicon*. Unpublished manuscript, University of Nijmegen, 1981.

Jong, D. de *Spreektaal: woordfrequenties in gesproken Nederlands*. Utrecht: Oosthock Scheltema en Holkema, 1979.

Knuth, D. E. *Art of Computer Programming*, Vol. 3: *Sorting and Searching*. Reading, Mass.: Addison-Wesley. 1973.

Linell, P. *Psychological Reality in Phonology*. Cambridge: Cambridge University Press, 1979.

Marchand, H. *Categories and Types of Present-day English Word Formation: A Synchronic-diachronic Approach*, 2nd edition. New York: Adler, 1969.

Marslen-Wilson, W. D. Speech understanding as a psychological process. In J. C. Simon (Ed.), *Spoken Language Generation and Understanding*. Dordrecht: Reidel, 1980.

Marslen-Wilson, W. D. Function and process in spoken word recognition. In H. Bouma and D. Bouwhuis (Eds), *Attention and Performance X*. Hillsdale, N. J.: Lawrence Erlbaum Associates, 1983.

Marslen-Wilson, W. D., and Tyler, L. K. The temporal structure of spoken language understanding. *Cognition*, 1980, **8**, 1–71.

Marslen-Wilson, W. D., and Welsh, A. Processing interactions and lexical access during word recognition in continuous speech. *Cognitive Psychology*, 1978, **10**, 29–63.

Meijers, G., and Jarvella, R. J. La perception des racines et des flexions verbales en langue parlée. In J. F. Le Ny and W. Kintsch (Eds), Langage et compréhension.: *Bulletin de Psychologie*, 1982.

Miller, G. A., and Johnson-Laird, P. N. *Language and Perception*. Cambridge, Mass.: Harvard University Press, 1976.

Murrell, G. A., and Morton, J. Word recognition and morphemic structure. *Journal of Experimental Psychology*, 1974, **102**, 963–968.

Rubin, G. S., Becker, C. A., and Freeman, R. H. Morphological structure and its effect on visual word recognition. *Journal of Verbal Learning and Verbal Behavior*, 1979, **18**, 757–767.

Stanners, R. F., Neiser, J. J., Hernon, W. P., and Hall, R. Memory representation for morphologically related words. *Journal of Verbal Learning and Verbal Behavior*, 1979, **18**, 399–412.

Stanners, R. F., Neiser, J. J., and Painton, S. Memory representation for prefixed words. *Journal of Verbal Learning and Verbal Behavior*, 1979, **18**, 733–743.

Strang, B. M. H. *A History of English*. London: Methuen, 1970.

Taft, M. Recognition of affixed words and the word frequency effect. *Memory and Cognition*, 1979, **7**, 263–272.

Taft, M. Prefix stripping revisited. *Journal of Verbal Learning and Verbal Behavior*, 1981, **20**, 289–297.

Taft, M., and Forster, K. I. Lexical storage and retrieval of prefixed words. *Journal of Verbal Learning and Verbal Behavior*, 1975, **14**, 638–647.

Uit den Boogaart, P. C. *Woordfrequenties in geschreven en gesproken Nederlands*. Utrecht: Oosthoek, Scheltema en Holkema, 1975.

Vennemann, T. Words and syllables in natural generative grammar. In A. Bruck, A. Fox and M. W. Lagaly (Eds), *Papers from the Parasession on Natural Phonology*, Chicago: Chicago Linguistic Society, 1974.

Wright, J. *Old English Grammar*. London: Oxford University Press, 1925.

The Process of Language Understanding
Edited by G. B. Flores d'Arcais and R. J. Jarvella
© 1983 John Wiley & Sons Ltd.

4

How On-line is Language Processing?

MANFRED BIERWISCH

Akademie der Wissenschaften der D.D.R. Berlin

THE PROBLEM

A fair amount of research on the nature of language understanding has been devoted to the role of grammatically defined, especially syntactic, structures in the processing of linguistic utterances. Recently, some of the assumptions which seem to be inherent in this 'structural approach' have been brought into question, in connection with a shift in research interests towards the actual processes involved in language comprehension. A fairly radical version of this 'process approach' has been developed by Marslen-Wilson, Tyler and others in a series of interesting papers, (e.g. Marslen-Wilson, 1975, Marslen-Wilson and Tyler, 1980; Marslen-Wilson, Tyler and Seidenberg, 1978, etc.). The strictly on-line, left-to-right character of language understanding is summarized by Marslen-Wilson *et al.* (1978, pp. 242–243) as follows:

> The listener is seen as attempting a direct word-by-word mapping of the input onto a single internal representation. In its most developed form, this representation could correspond to what we call comprehending a sentence, and would not be describable in strictly linguistic terms, since it would have to contain the products of inferences drawn from the listener's non-linguistic knowledge. So it would not, in itself, be either a syntactic or a semantic representation, although for its construction it would draw upon both syntactic and semantic aspects of the input.

In order to shape the following discussion, I will formulate three claims that seem to me to be distinctive for this conception with respect to alternative views it is meant to replace:

(A) The interpretation of the speech signal is a strictly on-line, left-to-right, word-by-word process, using all types of information available at any given point.
(B) The interpretation of the speech signal does not result in internal representations of separable syntactic and semantic structures, but rather in one uniform representation of a partially non-linguistic character.

(C) This interpretation results from the application of both linguistic and non-linguistic knowledge so that normally no purely linguistic parts of the process can be singled out.

Claim (A) is directly opposed to all conceptions which assume that certain syntactically determined constituents—usually clauses of some type—must be assembled before semantic and pragmatic interpretation can proceed. More generally, (A) denies that sentence perception proceeds through a series of levels, in which for reasonably sized chunks of an utterance, first a syntactic, then a semantic, and finally a contextual representation is constructed.[1] Claim (B) is directed against the assumption that the various levels of structure specified by a linguistically adequate grammar are directly realized during the process of sentence comprehension. In other words, (B) denies that any structure other than the 'final' one, representing the comprehension of an utterance, is built up. Finally, (C) is directed against the assumption that the actual processes of language understanding divide in a natural way into purely linguistic and extralinguistic parts.

Although Marslen-Wilson, Tyler, and their co-workers argue in a fairly general and definite sense for a coherent conception of language understanding along the lines indicated by (A) to (C), their proposal is crucially flawed; clarification of the shortenings present is an indispensable prerequisite for any assessment of the conception being offered. The main weakness of the proposal is the lack of any specification of the internal representation onto which the input is mapped. Without such a specification, claims (A) to (C) remain vague and are in danger of equivocation or triviality. Thus, the aim of this paper is to consider claims (A) to (C) on the basis of certain minimal and hopefully non-debatable assumptions about conditions which internal representations must meet. I will argue in particular that (C) is basically correct, that (B) is essentially wrong, and that (A) is in need of clarification and modification. As to the more specific part of my arguments I will consider as a crucial component of language understanding the requirements involved in scope determination. Certain conclusions for process oriented conceptions of language understanding will be formulated as a result.

Three other points should be made in advance. Firstly, claims (A), (B), and (C) are only loosely connected.[2] There is no logical necessity to accept or reject all three of them together. Some weaker connections among the three claims will be discussed in due course.

Secondly, the highly interesting experimental evidence Marslen-Wilson, Tyler, and their collaborators have produced is relevant only with respect to claim (A), indicating that semantic and contextual interpretation need not await completion of particular syntactic processing. It has, strictly speaking, no bearing whatsoever on claims (B) and (C). It is, in fact, hard to see what kind of evidence could be produced in their favour, since the non-existence of structures which are not directly accessible can never be proved, and there is, on the other hand, ample evidence indicating that the structures in question do play some role in processing. As to (C), which is not the main concern of the present paper, things are somewhat more complicated, and will be briefly discussed below.

Finally, the proposals made by Marslen-Wilson and others do not represent the only contemporary approach conforming to claims (A) to (C). The artificial intelligence approach to language comprehension developed, e.g., in Riesbeck and Schank (1978), although based on fairly different general considerations, has similar aims with respect to (A) to (C).[3] Here, I will not discuss the differences among various possible conceptions meeting conditions (A) to (C), but rather concentrate on the claims themselves.

LEVELS OF UNDERSTANDING

In order to clarify the discussion, I will introduce a number of preliminary notions. To begin with, a listener obviously can achieve various levels of understanding. For present purposes, the following possibilities might be distinguished: for a given hearer H and and utterance u it may be the case that:

(1) H understands u phonetically,
(2) H understands u syntactically,
(3) H understands u semantically,
(4) H understands u contextually.

Each of these types of understanding can be construed as the hearer receiving a sensory signal s and interpreting it as a linguistic utterance u by assigning to it an internally represented structure of some kind. More specifically, the resulting structure will be called the phonetic structure P of u in case (1), the syntactic structure S of u in case (2), the logical form LF of u in case (3), and the contexual meaning C of u in case (4). Thus, clarifying levels of understanding (1) to (4) obviously will depend on a more precise characterization of the relevant types of structure. For the moment, I will take P to be some version of phonetic feature representation. (I will not bother with the question of whether (1) could or should be split up into phonetic and phonemic understanding.) I will have to say more about S and LF in Section 4. As to (4), it might eventually be necessary to distinguish two possibilities: in addition to, or often instead of, a literal interpretation, u might be assigned a non-literal (indirect, figurative, metaphorical, etc.) interpretation. Hence (4) might be further split up as follows:

(5) (a) H understands u literally.
    (b) H understands u non-literally.

Accordingly, we have to distinguish between a literal and a non-literal contextual meaning C_l and C_n for (5a) and (5b), respectively.[4] Notice that both C_l and C_n are versions of contextual meaning, being alternatively instances of what Clark (1978) calls 'intended interpretation'. Although they are arrived at by sometimes rather different processes and determined by different types of rules, they are structures of the same general type, and they are alike in that both are dependent on information about the context and background in terms of which u is interpreted. In what follows I will talk simply about contextual meaning C whenever the distinction between literal and non-literal meaning is not at issue.[5] I will briefly return to the character of contextual meaning below.

The different levels of understanding distinguished in (1) to (4) are to be conceived of as purely intuitive notions whose purport can best be indicated by considering the various ways in which a hearer H might fail to understand u. Thus, one might fail to understand u phonetically just because there is too much noise or the speech producing signal s is too inarticulate. Similarly, one might fail to understand u syntactically because of its syntactic complexity. The well-known cases of higher-order self-embedding as in (6) are but one example.

(6) The girl the man the cats and one of the dogs belong to adopted recovered.

Neither phonetic nor semantic nor contextual factors are relevant in cases of this type. Third, one might fail to understand u semantically, for instance, in logically unperspicuous cases like (7), which incidentally pose no problem syntactically:

(7) (a) No disease is small enough not to be ignored.
    (b) The cathedral is much too wide in order to be higher than it is long.

Finally, one might fail to understand an utterance contextually in a large number of ways. Failure to find appropriate referents for pronouns or definite descriptions constitutes just one class of cases. Another type is illustrated by instances like (8), where in spite of its obvious syntactic and semantic structure, the hearer might fail to find an appropriate literal or non-literal contextual interpretation for the phrase *language of the sculpture*.

(8) He tried to eliminate the language of the sculpture.

Statements (1) to (5) do not exhaust the different levels and ways an utterance may or may not be understood. One might, for instance, understand all the sentences of a poem, a philosophical essay, or a mathematical argument on virtually all of the levels discussed here, and still fail to understand it in crucial respects. For obvious reasons, these 'higher' levels of understanding fall outside the scope of this paper.

Different types of misunderstanding provide additional illustration of the levels of understanding that were distinguished above. Misunderstanding, in fact, is only a particular type of understanding, where H assigns an internal representation to u that differs, on one or more levels, from the representation which the speaker intended to be assigned to it. It is easy to see that each type of misunderstanding can be traced to the level of structure from which it originates. For discussion of some more specific problems involved in certain types of misunderstanding, see Section 7 below.

In the sense discussed so far, understanding (including misunderstanding) can be construed as a process that realizes a particular function which specifies the mapping of the input information onto the pertinent internal representation. Thus, in line with statements (1) to (4), we have the following functions:

$$(1') \; F_1(s) = P \qquad (2') \; F_2(s) = S$$
$$(3') \; F_3(s) = LF \qquad (4') \; F_4(s, c) = C$$

Just as before, P, S, LF, and C represent phonetic structure, syntactic structure, logical form, and contextual meaning, respectively, and s represents the acoustic signal on which the utterance is based. A crucial point is that F_4 depends on two inputs, i.e. it maps s together with the contextual information c on the contextual meaning C.

There seems to be a clear intuitive sense in which F_1 to F_4 form an order ascending from phonetic to contextual understanding. I will argue below that this order is best construed as an implication to the effect that computing the value of F_i normally implies the computation of F_{i-1} for $i > 1$, but not necessarily the other way around. (This does not mean, however, that the construction of P, S, LF, and C proceeds in this order.) Anticipating this assumption, we can define syntactic, semantic, and contextual understanding in a somewhat different way:

$$(2'') \; F_2'(s) = \langle P, S \rangle \qquad (3'') \; F_3'(s) = \langle P, S, LF \rangle$$
$$(4'') \; F_4'(s, c) = \langle P, S, LF, C \rangle$$

It seems to me that the distinction between F_3' and F_4' corresponds by and large to the distinction that is often made—for the most part implicitly—between language perception and language comprehension: the study of the former is mainly concerned with the processes realizing the various aspects of F_3', the study of the latter is concerned with the realization of F_4'. Notice, however, that a distinction between perception and comprehension corresponding to F_3' and F_4' specifies research attitudes and not necessarily separable parts of the processes normally involved in language understanding: even though it is possible to investigate the assignment of P, S, or LF to a given signal s by controlling only stimulus s, there is no reason to exclude the possibility that at least certain components of general background knowledge, and hence certain pieces of contextual information, are involved automatically in the process.

In order to account for the distinction between literal and non-literal understanding, a corresponding differentiation with respect to F_4' would be necessary. As I am only marginally concerned with the problem of non-literal interpretation in this paper, I will not go into details.

On the basis of the discussion so far, it would be simple to define the concept of partial understanding, again with respect to different levels of understanding, and the corresponding notions of partial misunderstanding and partial lack of understanding. The basic idea would be that H understands u partially with respect to one of the levels in question, if H assigns an incomplete representation to u on that level. Although a more realistic account of normal situations in language understanding would certainly require the availability of such concepts, I will refrain from giving a more detailed specification in the present paper.

BASIC ASSUMPTIONS

In this section I will formulate a number of basic assumptions concerning the processes involved in language understanding, and certain consequences which follow from these assumptions.

The first assumption is a fairly uncontroversial one: the process of language understanding necessarily involves the assignment of a phonetic structure P to the input signal s.[6] Less obvious is the precise nature of P and the processes by which it is arrived at. Two points seem to be sufficiently clear, however. Firstly, phonetic representations, though based on features and segments, are organized in higher-order units, with words (or rather word forms) being the perceptually prevalent units. To the extent to which these units are built up from the sequences of more elementary events, even at the lowest level of processing, speech perception is not strictly on-line but rather organized in terms of memory-based, integrated patterns. Secondly, phonetic representation contains important cues or indicators as to the eventual syntactic organization of an utterance being perceived. Suprasegmental features, mainly accent and intonation, are the more obvious indicators in this respect, but segmental properties such as the duration of vowels also contribute to this aspect, as Nooteboom, Brokx and de Rooij (1978), among others, have shown. To sum up, we obtain the following first assumption:

(A1)   Normal language understanding involves the mapping of a speech signal s onto a phonetic representation P that is organized as a sequence of phonetically specified word forms plus relevant suprasegmental specifications.

Notice that (A1) does not imply that a given utterance must be phonetically understood in the sense discussed above before higher-level processes can start. In fact, the construction of P often will depend on higher-level structures, as is borne out by the fact that we often understand things we do not hear and even things not present in the speech signal. The identification of word forms is also generally accompanied by activation of their lexical meaning. This is actually the core of the experimental results obtained by Marslen-Wilson and his associates. I will argue below that this is a necessary, but not a sufficient, condition for achieving normal semantic and contextual understanding of an utterance.

The second assumption is simply that language understanding normally requires a contextual interpretation C. Without going into the enormously complex and controversial details of the precise character of C, I will take it for granted that the contextual meaning of a sentential utterance has to specify at least the internal representation of a more or less complex state of affairs plus a certain attitude towards this state of affairs expressed by the utterance. As a first approximation, one might take the representation of the state of affairs in question—the 'propositional content' of a sentential utterance—as characterizable in terms of a set theoretical structure based on a system of individuals and various types of attributes and operations.[7] Of the alleged attitudes, no satisfactory account is yet available.[8] With these provisional remarks in mind, the second assumption might be formulated as follows:

(A2) Normal language understanding involves the internal represen- tation of a contextual meaning C depending on the structure assigned to the speech signal s and the contextual information c.

The structure assigned to s includes, besides the phonetic representation P, the syntactic structure S and the logical form LF. Before turning to these structures and the way they mediate the connection between s, c, and C, I would like to clarify the following point: although (A2) does not imply that a full phonetic, syntactic, and semantic representation must be constructed before a contextual meaning can be built up, the construction of C cannot in general proceed in a strictly on-line manner in any reasonable sense of this term. This can be shown, for example, by means of the referential inter- pretation of pronouns, which is clearly a part of the specification of C. Consider sentences (9) and (10):

(9) Mary asked Sally where to go, but, you know, she isn't the right person to give a clear answer.

(10) Mary asked Sally where to go, but, you know, she isn't the right person to wait for an answer.

Given normal background knowledge, the only way to understand (9) is to make *she* coreferential with *Sally*, while the only way to understand (10) is to make *she* coreferential with *Mary*. Clearly, this decision cannot be made until the predicate *give a clear answer* or *wait for the answer* is interpreted. Hence, in cases like (9) and (10), crucial parts of the contextual meaning are not available in the manner of an immediate on-line interpretation. This phenomenon is of course not restricted to the referential interpretation of pronoun. In a similar way, the interpretation of *book* as specifying a 'type' or a 'token' in (11) is possible only after the last word of the sentence:[9]

(11) In preparing the lecture, he badly missed the book, as it was full of important $\left\{\begin{matrix} \text{notes} \\ \text{insights} \end{matrix}\right\}$

Although the formulation of (A2) is neutral with respect to literal or non-literal interpretation, my remarks on (9) to (11) concern only literal interpretations. It is easy to see, however, that in a wide variety of cases a non-literal interpretation is even more outside the range of strict on-line, real-time processing. I will not go into these problems here, but rather turn to the assumptions concerning the mediating syntactic and semantic structure.

As already suggested, I take it that the syntactic structure and the logical form of a sentence mediate between its phonetic and contextual interpretation. As to syntactic structure, this yields the following assumption:

(A3) Natural language understanding involves the assignment of a syntactic structure S to the speech signal s so that S determines the way P is related to the logical form LF.

I am inclined to consider (A3) as obvious or even trivial. As it is explicitly challenged by claim (B) in Section 1 above, let me emphasize that there is a large variety of cases where the assignment of S as an independent level of structure directly can be seen as an indispensable condition for understanding an utterance u. To give just one type of example, compare (12) and (13):

(12) The girl you mentioned recently came to the office.
(13) The girl you mentioned recently has visited the office.

With appropriate intonation, (12) is ambiguous, with *recently* modifying either the relative clause or the main clause. (Notice that these two readings can, but need not, be distinguished by different suprasegmental indicators.) (13), however, is not open to the second interpretation, which would have to be expressed, for example by (14):

(14) The girl you mentioned has recently visited the office.

The crucial point is that the assignment of *recently* in (13) is a purely syntactic phenomenon, as shown by the semantic well-formedness of (14), and is, of course, an indispensable condition for the correct understanding of (13).

The assignment of S, and hence the more detailed specification of (A3), has been the main concern of a large number of studies in language under-standing, as indicated above. It is worth pointing out, however, that by no means all the conceptions developed in this connection imply the assumption that a complete syntactic structure must be developed before semantic interpretation begins. To take just one recent example, the two-stage parsing system proposed by Frazier and Fodor (1978), although coping only with the syntactic aspects of language understanding, leaves open various ways in which subsequent, parallel, or even anticipating semantic processing might proceed. Hence (A3) contradicts claim (B), but not claim (A). It is a separate issue to what extent claim (A), i.e. strict on-line processing, can be main-tained with respect to S. Fodor (1978) discusses a systematic class of cases—the assignment of preposed Wh-phrases to their 'original' syntactic positions—that can hardly be managed in a strictly on-line fashion, but rather needs some kind of intermediate storage.[10] Sentences like (15) provide another example of a similar phenomenon:

(15) *Darüber* wünscht *sich* der Direktor *genauer zu informieren*.
('About that the director wants to make more detailed enquiries'.)

The italicized words of this sentence must be identified as constituents of the subordinate infinitival clause as indicated in (16) in order to assign a logical form to it.

(16) Der Direktor wünscht (darüber genauer sich zu informieren).

Notice that (16), which is related to (15) by topicalization and clitic-placement, does not itself represent the logical form of (15), but merely the clausal structure in terms of which the constituent connections within (15) are organized.[11] It is clear that the assignment of S in cases like this cannot be an on-line process without intermediate storage of some kind.

Although the delimitation between syntactic and semantic structures is in general far from being clear, I will take for granted a principled distinction between these levels of structure, and formulate the following assumption:

(A4) Natural language understanding involves the assignment of a logical form LF to the speech signal s in accordance with P and S such that LF determines the contextual meaning C with respect to the context c.

That LF cannot be identified either with syntactic structure or contextual meaning can be seen from simple cases like (17):

(17) John has only seen him.

Here S specifies, among other, the domain or focus of *only*, viz. the verb *see*; LF specifies the semantic effects of this focus assignment, viz. the denial that someone called John did something more than (or besides) seeing the person referred to by *him*; and *C* contains the context dependent information of what this something turns out to be. It should be obvious that to the extent to which the identification of *LF* depends on the specification of *S*, the assignment of *LF* cannot in general proceed in a strictly on-line fashion. Sentences like (15) provide simple illustrations. I will argue below that the assignment of *LF* often involves additional deviations from strict on-line processing. This claim depends on the fact that *LF* by no means consists of a sequence of word meanings (or rather meanings of lexical expressions), but sometimes requires fairly complicated interrelations which do not correspond to the linear ordering of lexical elements in a sentence.

Before turning to these problems, I will formulate two assumptions that provide a certain perspective for interpreting and justifying (A1) to (A4).

(A5) Natural language understanding is a highly automatized and largely spontaneous process.

The impact of this general, though obvious assumption is this: if it is true that in certain cases the identification of the syntactic structure of a sentence is an indispensable condition for its semantic and contextual interpretation— and it is easy to multiply pertinent examples like (13), (15), and (17)—then a natural consequence of (A5) would be that the syntactic structure of a sentence is automatically computed even if its full specification might not be required to identify its contextual interpretation. Similar considerations apply, of course, to phonetic structure and logical form. This type of reasoning is by no means strange and artificial. It is rather a natural extension of what we know from other types of highly structured behaviour. It is in fact the automatic character of structure assignment that renders speech production and perception possible, and it is only on this basis that all kinds of de-automatized processes are to be analysed. These considerations are, moreover, very much in line with the well-known fact that under normal conditions the structures in question are not (or not fully) accessible to conscious reflection, just as the components in terms of which the visual field is organized are not generally amenable to such reflection.

I have argued, and will argue in still more detail, that the assignment of *S*, *LF*, and *C* (and possibly even *P*) does not generally proceed in a strictly on-line manner, but requires various degrees of intermediate storage providing delays and anticipations. I do not mean this as a retreat to the position, rejected by claim (A) above, that language understanding proceeds from *P* through *S* and *LF* to *C*, even in cases where decisions on 'higher' levels depend on previous information from 'lower' levels. I will rather make the following assumption:

(A6) Normal language understanding is a multi-level parallel process developing structures on all pertinent levels, such that the eventual result is the specification of the structural interpretation P, S, LF, C of s with respect to c.

The remainder of this paper is an attempt to give somewhat more substance to (A6), thereby implicitly clarifying claim (C), rejecting claim (B), and modifying claim (A) presented in Section 1. Two questions have to be raised in this attempt: First, how is the parallel processing interrelated in order to yield the appropriate structural interpretation of the signal with respect to its context? Second, how can gaps in on-line processing be reconciled with the basically left-to-right nature of the input, especially in cases where the different levels are not 'synchronized'?

The answer to both questions depends on both structural and process aspects, which will be discussed in Sections 4 and 5, respectively. It will then be illustrated in somewhat more detail with respect to the problem of scope determination.

THE CHARACTER OF STRUCTURAL REPRESENTATIONS

As any reasonable discussion of the problems clustering around (A6) depends, among others, on the characterization of the structures involved, some remarks on the formal nature of P, S, LF, and C are appropriate here.

To begin with, I will assume that P, S, and LF are structured and inter-related according to a system G of grammatical rules and conditions. That means that G determines the result of $F'_3(s)$, insofar as a level of semantic understanding can be singled out, but it by no means implies that G determines the actual steps through which this result is eventually achieved. (I will return to this problem in Section 5.) Without any principled discussion of the form of G, I simply assume that it consists of the phonological, morphological, syntactic, semantic, and lexical rules of the language. The tacit knowledge represented by these rules is fixed during the process of language acquisition. I will furthermore assume that C, as well as the contextual setting c, belong to the realm of conceptual structure and that the determination of C by LF on the basis of c is governed by general principles of contextual interpretation.

Turning then to the character of structural representations determined by G, let me repeat that P is to be construed as an essentially linear representation of phonetic attributes specifying the segmental, suprasegmental, and boundary information assigned to s in accordance with the rules and conditions of G. Although P includes a grouping of the basic attributes in terms of segments, syllables, phonological words and phrases, and intonational clauses,[12] its character is inherently sequential, according to the temporal dimension of the signal s. In spite of this fairly close correspondence between the external stimulus s and its internal interpretation in terms of P, this does not mean that $F_1(s)$ could assign P in a strictly on-line fashion as was already pointed out in connection with (A1) above. To give just two examples: Whether the initial stretch of a particular signal s is to be represented as [hiz] as in (18a) or as [hi:+z] (where '+' indicates a morpheme boundary) as in (18b) might be dependent on information available only several words later.

(18)(a) His coming to the unexpected, highly informative . . .
    (b) He's coming to the unexpected . . .

In a similar way, but for different reasons, assignment of the appropriate degrees of stress on the first two nouns in (19a) and (19b) might be possible only after the coordinate structure and the relative clause construction, respectively, have been identified:

(19)(a) The girl, the boy, and a little dog were still waiting.
    (b) The girl the boy was looking for was still waiting.

Retrograde identification of properties of P is certainly a widespread phenomenon, due to the fact that, on the one hand, P is frequently underdetermined by the actual signal s, and on the other hand, is determined not only by the phonological rules of G, but may also depend in part on morphological, syntactic, and even semantic rules and conditions. Examples like (18) and (19) thus indicate that even a phonetic interpretation of s often goes beyond the identification of a sequence of word forms. As I am not concerned in the following discussion with special problems of phonetic understanding, usual orthographic notation will be sufficient as a substitute for P, and its linear ordering might be taken as corresponding approximately to the time parameter of s.

Turning next to the syntactic representation S, I will assume that it provides basically two types of information: firstly, a constituent hierarchy imposed on the string of lexical items whose phonological specification underlies P, and secondly, certain binding relations holding among particular constituents. S might contain empty places which play a role in the constituency and binding relations, although they are not filled with lexical items phonetically realized in P. In order to be more concrete, I will assume that S can be represented essentially in the form of surface structures as discussed in Chomsky (1977) and related work. Thus something like (21) would be a description of the syntactic structure S of (20), with identical indices indicating the above mentioned binding relations and the unity element e specifying empty places:

(20) Who promised you to stay?

(21)

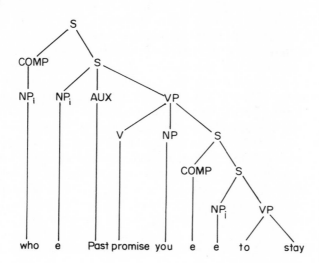

Representations such as (21) embody quite a number of assumptions with respect to principle and detail which have to be clarified and motivated within the theory of syntactic structure. For the present purpose, particular claims can be restricted to fairly uncontroversial facts that will be discussed in due course. The general assumption that something like (21) is both necessary and sufficient to account for the properties of S leaves open various options as to the type of rules that generate S and relate it to the other grammatically determined representations.[13] It also leaves open the question of how syntactic categories are defined, although I will suppose for the sake of concreteness that some version of $\bar{X}$-theory as developed in Jackendoff (1977) accounts for the general nature of syntactic categories. It must be assumed, however, that G does not only generate a class of syntactic representations S, but that its rules and conditions also determine two mappings: a mapping A of S into P and a mapping I of S into LF.

The mapping A relates S to (one of) its phonetic realization(s) and consists basically of the morphological spelling rules (as studied e.g. in Bierwisch, 1967), and the phonological rules, alongside certain deletion rules and filters in the sense of Chomsky and Lasnik (1977).[14] On the basis of A we can define an inverse mapping A' such that $A'(P)$ is a syntactic analysis S assigned to P on the basis of G. Obviously, neither A nor its inverse A' are unique mappings, their non-uniqueness corresponding to free variation in the case of A and syntactic ambiguity in the case of A'. Before turning to LF and the way it is related to S by the interpretive function I, let me add two general remarks about the nature of S and its relation to P.

The first remark concerns the linear and non-linear aspects of S. On the one hand, S has an inherent linear order, insofar as its terminal elements—modulo certain morphological and phonological adjustments—correspond to sequentially ordered parts of P. This aspect is formally captured by the fact that S is represented by an ordered tree. By virtue of this ordering, S is correlated to the temporal dimension of the speech signal s to the extent to which P is related to it. On the other hand, S goes inherently beyond linearity as it consists of a constituent hierarchy determining dominance and command relations and has certain binding relations assigned to its constituents. Hence A maps a linearly ordered hierarchy on a linear structure, while A' assigns non-linear relations to a linear structure. From the point of view of language understanding, the linear aspect of S can be more or less directly inferred from s, whereas the non-linear properties have to be supplied on the basis of grammatical knowledge. All of this is trivial, but has still to be kept in mind in view of claim (A) above concerning the on-line character of language understanding.

A less trivial side remark concerns the relations between syntactic and prosodic hierarchies. As mentioned above, prosodic organization provides a certain built-in hierarchy even to P, which may but need not pave the way to the syntactic constituency. Besides the fact that prosodic and syntactic hierarchies do not coincide structurally, there seems to be a crucial difference as to their perceptual status: prosodic units are by and large manifested in perceptually amenable properties of the speech signal—fundamental frequency, energy distribution, pauses—whereas syntactic constituents and relations are basically abstract in the sense that they are not directly related to sensory information. The ambiguity of sentences like (22) or minimal pairs like (23) are simple examples in this respect:[15]

(22) (a) [$_S$ John will [$_{VP}$ buy [$_{NP}$ the book] [$_{PP}$ for Susan]]]
      (b) [$_S$ John will [$_{VP}$ buy [$_{NP}$ the [$_{\bar{N}}$ book [$_{PP}$ for Susan]]]]]
(23) (a) Who$_i$ did you expect [$_S$ e$_i$ to stay at the meeting]
      (b) Who$_i$ did you$_j$ expect [$_S$ e$_j$ to see e$_i$ at the meeting]

The situation is fairly obvious in cases like (23): besides the distinction of [stey] and [si:] there is no contrast in the phonetic representation corresponding to the syntactic difference between the two sentences. Things are slightly more complicated with (22), as one might try to discern an optional phonetic distinction corresponding to the difference in constituency for the two readings. But even if there is such a possibility, the putative distinction is not obligatory. In other words, there is at least one systematic realization on which the difference in constituency in (22) is not paralleled by any systematic property of s.[16]

The second remark concerning S and its relation to P is prompted by the fact that grammatical descriptions usually posit various intermediate levels of structural representation. Thus the phonological theory of Chomsky and

Halle (1968), which I have presupposed as a framework for specifying P, assumes an underlying phonemic level of representation mediating between syntactic and phonetic representations. Additional steps might be taken into consideration. Hence the question arises: Why postulate just P and S as relevant for language understanding? I would like to make three points in this respect.

(i) P and S (as well as LF and C) are taken to be necessary levels of representations characterizing structural aspects of normal, automatic language understanding. This does not exclude, however, the possibility that additional aspects of structural organization might turn out to be relevant.

(ii) Although the format of representation developed within the framework of generative linguistics provides the most reasonable starting point for characterizing aspects of language understanding, there is no *a priori* necessity to identify P or S with exactly one level of representation in a derivation determining the structure of the utterance u in accordance with G. Thus P might correspond essentially to the systematic phonetic representation in the sense of Chomsky and Halle (1968), containing however additional information about those characteristics that are reflexes of phonemic invariants as opposed to free or conditioned variants. Similar considerations apply to S and its relation to grammatical surface structure.[17] In short, then, internal representations relevant to the processes of language understanding need not correspond in a simple one-to-one manner to levels of representation posited for the most explicit specification of structural properties and interrelations of the expressions of a given language. (See Section 5 for further comments.)

(iii) Whatever amendments in the sense of (i) might turn out to be necessary, I take P and S as levels of organization that are necessary and presumably sufficient to account for the structural properties of normal syntactic understanding. The particular status of these two levels is motivated by fairly general organizational properties, notably the inherent linearity of P corresponding to its sensory (and motoric) correlates, and the abstract hierarchical character of S imposed on its terminal string.

It should be obvious that considerations like those in (i) to (iii) apply in a similar vein to LF and C and their relation to corresponding levels of grammatical derivations.

Turning then to LF, I will assume as a starting point that its formal characterization should depart as little as possible from standard predicate logic. This is, of course, more a heuristic orientation than a substantive claim, which has, however, a number of advantages. First, it provides a fairly well understood frame of reference with respect to formal properties as well as referential (or rather contextual) interpretation. Second, it allows one, for the time being, to avoid a large number of still unsettled problems concerning the details of logical form and semantic structure of natural languages by leaving open just to what extent and in which way familiar versions of predicate logic need to be extended. Third, as a tentative orientation it keeps the theoretical apparatus as restricted as possible, denying it arbitrary expressive power.

Taking this orientation as a heuristic background, the following more specific assumption will be made. According to the basic character of predicate logic, LF is built on functional structure, i.e. functor-argument relations integrating primitive elements into higher-order units. This presupposes a categorization of primitive and complex units by means of appropriate functor and argument categories which is most naturally expressed in terms of some version of categorial grammar deriving from Ajdukiewicz (1935).

For the sake of illustration, consider the following system of categories:

(24) (a) n and p are basic categories (for names and propositions, respectively);

(b) if $c_0, c_1, \ldots, c_k$ are categories, then $\langle c_0/c_1 \ldots c_k \rangle$ is the category of a k-placed functor that takes arguments of category $c_1, \ldots, c_k$ respectively forming a complex entity of category c_0.

The primes of LF are either constants or variables in the usual sense, represented in the following by capital and lower case letters respectively. As an example, one might consider (27) as a first approximation to LF of (25), for which (26) indicates the syntactic structure;

(25) Who promised you to melt the gold?

(26) $[_S \text{who}_i [_S e_i \text{ Past } [_{VP} \text{ promise you } [_S e_i \text{ to melt the gold}]]]]$

(27)

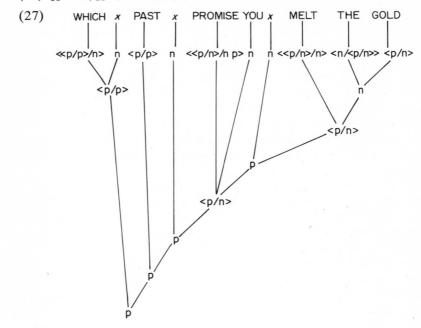

It should be obvious from this rough outline that (24) specifies what might be called the syntax of *LF*. It imposes what is essentially a categorized hierarchy on the primitive elements of *LF*. Furthermore, it requires binding of variables according to usual principles of quantificational theory. A case in point in (27) is WHICH x, a kind of quantifier, which binds the first argument of both PROMISE and MELT. As can be seen from comparing (26) and (27), there is a fairly close correspondence between S and LF with respect to hierarchy and binding relations.[18] There are, however, a number of basic differences.

First of all, constituents in S do not in general coincide with the compositional structure of *LF*, as we will see below in a number of relevant cases.[19] Secondly, S and LF seem to differ with respect to the nature of categories, even if there are levels of corresponding constituents. Thus while *who* is an NP on a par with *you* or *the gold* in S, its interpretation WHICH x in LF is a propositional operator, which has a rather different categorial status. Other differences could easily be listed and have to be accounted for by the different principles underlying the constituency of S on the one hand and the functional character of LF on the other hand.

A third difference is probably the most important in the present context. As already pointed out, S has an inherent linear order, i.e. it is formally based on a concatenation system. In contrast, LF constitutes a hierarchy without linear order and is thus formally based on a set system. Thus, while the sequential ordering in syntactic trees reflects an inherent property of the represented structures, ordering in semantic trees is a purely notational choice. (28a) to (28c) therefore represent the same *LF*:

(28) (a) $[_p [_n \text{JOHN}] [_{\langle p/n \rangle} [_n \text{MARY}] [_{\langle \langle p/n \rangle /n \rangle} \text{LOVE}]]]$
      (b) $[_p [_n \text{JOHN}] [_{\langle p/n \rangle} [_{\langle \langle p/n \rangle n \rangle} \text{LOVE}] [_n \text{MARY}]]]$
      (c) $[_p [_{\langle p/n \rangle} [_{\langle \langle p/n \rangle /n \rangle} \text{LOVE}] [_n \text{MARY}]] [_n \text{JOHN}]]$

The assumption that *LF* has no left-to-right order is motivated by a number of facts. To mention just one of them, sentences like (29) and (30) should have essentially the same logical form in spite of their different syntactic structure, a condition that is most naturally met by a purely hierarchical structure for *LF*:

(29) Who$_i$ will you$_j$ try $[_s$ e$_j$ to sell e$_i$ the book$]$
(30) Wem$_i$ willst du$_j$ $[_s$ e$_j$ e$_i$ das Buch zu verkaufen$]$ versuchen.

For a discussion of further aspects of the non-linear nature of *LF* see Wexler and Culicover (1980).[20] Consequences with respect to the left-to-right character of language understanding will be considered below.

Three further points concerning the nature of *LF* should be mentioned. The first point relates to the primes of *LF* and the degree of dissolution of lexical items to be postulated. So far, I have by and large identified primes with lexical items. Now, lexical items are characterized by semantic relations, which, among others, play a crucial role in word identification, as one of the major findings in work on lexical access clearly shows. Two ways of capturing these relations are currently under debate: (a) meaning postulates, and (b) componential analysis. According to (a), the primes of LF are meanings of lexical items, interrelated by a complex system of axioms or rules determining the logical inferences that can be drawn from sentences in which the lexical items occur. According to (b), lexical items are decomposed on LF into more elementary primes, and it is this compositional structure which determines the semantic relations in question, and by the same token the potential logical inferences. Approach (a) is strongly advocated by Fodor (1975) and subsequent work,[21] while (b) is inherent in most linguistic work in semantic analysis. For a recent, fairly elaborate version, see e.g. Miller and Johnson-Laird (1976). It should be noted, furthermore, that the two approaches are not mutually exclusive, i.e. meaning postulates might be assumed to interrelate semantic primes, even if these are not in general identical to meanings of lexical items, but turn out to be components of their meanings.

As a certain amount of lexical decomposition must be assumed for reasons to be discussed below in more detail, I will briefly illustrate its consequences for LF. Suppose that the semantic structure of (transitive) *melt* is composed in the following way:

(31) $\hat{y}[\hat{x}[\exists z[[DO \; x \; z] \wedge [CAUSE \; z \; [CHANGE[SOLID \; y]$
$[LIQUID \; y]]]]]]$

In order to simplify the notation of LF, here and in the following I omit the indication of categories. According to what has already been said, ordering within brackets, i.e. within complex components of LF, is arbitrary. For expository reasons, I follow usual conventions, placing functors before their arguments. Although DO, CAUSE, CHANGE, SOLID, and LIQUID are not to be identified with the meaning of the corresponding English lexical items, I take the labels to be sufficiently self-explanatory and will not add any further remarks. $\exists$ and $\wedge$ indicate existential quantification and logical conjunction in the usual sense. In order to change the complex preposition composed of these constants and the variables x, y, and z into an operator of the same category as MELT in (27), lambda abstraction over the variables x and y is used, where $\hat{x}$ is of category $\langle\langle c_1/c_2\rangle/c_1\rangle$ if x is of category c_2. In other words, $\hat{x}$ takes an argument of category c_1 and makes it into a functor of category $\langle c_1/c_2\rangle$. Given the usual rule for lambda conversion, viz. (32), it follows that (33a) is equivalent to (33b), if MELT is replaced by (31):

(32) $[\hat{x}[\ldots x \ldots]]a = [\ldots a \ldots]$ if x and a are of the same category.

(33) (a) $\exists z[[DO \; x \; z] \wedge [CAUSE \; z[CHANGE \; [SOLID \; G]$
$[LIQUID \; G]]]]$
(b) $[MELT \; G] \; x$

If we assume that G abbreviates the representation of *the gold* on *LF*, then (33b)—and hence (33a)—is the representation of [e *to melt the gold*] thus giving a reasonably more fine-grained *LF* of the example (25) above.

For the time being, these suggestions might be sufficient. It will be left open to what extent they are to be followed in order to come as close as possible to the representation of *LF* actually involved in spontaneous language understanding. Notice that it might very well be the case that there is a variety of options from which a choice is to be made according to intervening conditions, i.e. *melt* may sometimes translate into a defined constant MELT, sometimes into a complex structure like (31), and sometimes into an even more detailed representation, analysing, for example, CHANGE into a complex functor relating states and time intervals. See Miller (1978, p. 92 ff.) for some considerations to this effect.

The second point to be made with respect to *LF* concerns the distinction between those parts which are usually called assertion and presupposition. Without going through the lengthy and complicated discussion dealing with this problem,[22] I will simply make the following two assumptions: First, the logical form *LF* of an utterance u consists of a pair [*PR*; *AS*] where *PR* is the presupposition and *AS* is the assertive part of u. Both *PR* and *AS* are categorized hierarchies over primitive elements of *LF* in the sense described so far. Secondly, *PR* might be taken as a complex condition specifying the class of contexts c allowing a contextual interpretation C of u. Intuitively speaking, *PR* connects u to certain properties of the context that are relevant for the interpretation of u. To illustrate the point, we might paraphrase (34) roughly by (35), where (a) and (b) express approximately the presupposition and the assertive part of (34):

(34) Mike also has problems with him.
(35) (a) Someone other than Mike has problems with him.
     (b) Mike has problems with him.

These hints are not meant as an even remotely adequate account of the problems of presupposition, but they will serve the purpose of spelling out certain aspects of scope determination to be taken up below.[23]

The third and final point with respect to *LF* shall only be mentioned for the sake of completeness. All comments made so far on the structure of *LF*—including the distinction of presupposition and assertive part—relate to propositional content, which must be distinguished from the various attitudes or intentions directed towards that content which might also be expressed in an utterance. For some discussion of the problems involved see Bierwisch (1980b). As I am not going to consider the specific role this distinction might play with respect to language understanding, I will simply ignore it.

To conclude my remarks concerning *LF*, I will add two comments on the mapping I relating S to *LF*. Firstly, as already mentioned, I take this mapping to be determined by the rules of the grammar G. More specifically, two sets of rules are responsible for I. The first set is just the system of lexical rules associating a phonological matrix with its syntactic characteristics and semantic interpretation. Within the componential analysis approach, a rule that relates *melt* to (31) would be a case in point. The corresponding rule in the meaning postulates approach would simply map *melt* into a prime of LF, viz. MELT. The second set comprises various types of rules operating on syntactically organized structures. This set includes rules of construal in the sense of Chomsky (1977 and elsewhere), conditions on binding, and rules of lambda conversion, deriving jointly the compositional hierarchy of LF from the syntactic representation S. The details depend on specific properties of the organization of G which need not be discussed here.

Secondly, it is clear from the foregoing discussion that I maps an ordered, categorized hierarchy over syntactic primes onto an unordered one over semantic primes. In other words, while A—the mapping from S to P—relates a string to a hierarchy, I relates an ordered to an unordered hierarchy.

I finally turn to some remarks on the contextual interpretation C. These will be rather sketchy, firstly because in this respect very little beyond mere generalities is sufficiently clear to reach general agreement, and secondly because I am not going to discuss specific problems related to contextual understanding. I am concerned with C mainly insofar as it is helpful or even necessary in clarifying the perspective for 'lower' levels of understanding.[24] As mentioned above, C is not within the range of G, i.e. it does not belong to the levels of linguistic structure. This means that C might contain elements and relations that are not determined by grammatical rules and knowledge of language. However, as C is obviously involved in the spontaneous process of contextual understanding, there must be a systematic interaction between grammar and those rules and conditions that inherently determine the structure of C. For some preliminary considerations with respect to the status and character of C, see my remarks on 'situational structure' in Bierwisch (1980c); a more specific account is to be found in Johnson-Laird (1980) in terms of what he calls 'mental models'.

A rather general characterization of C might ascribe to it a set theoretical structure of some sort that does not in general exhibit a hierarchical or tree structure. I take this to be one of the major differences between C and LF. To illustrate the point, suppose that on the level of mental models, objects or individuals are represented by (possibly complex) entities to which properties, relations, etc., can be ascribed. Suppose furthermore, as seems to be reasonable, that on this level any particular individual is represented just once, no matter how often reference is made to it, in how many states of affairs it is involved, etc. This assumption also is inherent, by the way, in the conception of model theoretic semantics, the formal apparatus of which might be taken as a first approximation to a formal account of the notion of mental world and mental model. Given these assumptions, it is obvious that for a sentence like (36), *C* contains only one occurrence of the individual to which *John* and *himself* refer. In *LF*, there are at least four occurrences referring to that individual, as (37) indicates:

(36) John expected to be able to nominate himself.

(37) [For *x* = JOHN] [*x* EXPECT [*x* BE ABLE [*x*[NOMINATE *x*]]]]

Clearly, whatever format of representation is chosen for *C*, it cannot be a hierarchical structure if it is to correspond on the one hand to the multiplicity of conditions contained in (37), while reducing on the other hand the various instances of the individual involved in these conditions to one entity. Hence *C* must be organized in terms of a generalized type of set theoretical structure. For independent arguments to the same effect based on the interpretation of quantifiers and definite descriptions, see e.g. Johnson-Laird and Garnham (1980).

To say that mental models are not trees—and, of course, not linearly ordered—does not help very much in saying what they are. To answer that question would require, among others, an account of the way in which such models are related to visual and other modes of perception, a specification of the mental operations they are subject to,[25] and a clarification of the ontology inherent in this level of representation. All this goes far beyond the present paper and will not be pursued any further.

There is one point to be added, however. The level of representation we are talking about is relevant not only for *C*, but also for the specification of its context *c*. This means that the context *c* with respect to which an utterance is to be interpreted is a mental representation, even if an actual, 'external' situation is responsible for the contextual interpretation. (In such cases it is the mental reflection of the external situation that functions as the relevant context *c*.) A moment's thought shows that this is not merely a methodological unification bringing together real, fictional, past, future and all other types of conceivable contexts, but corresponds to the fact that we can refer even to an actual situation only insofar as we have created a mental structure interpreting it.

We must finally postulate a mapping *V* that relates the logical form *LF* of an utterance *u* to its contextual interpretation *C* with respect to *c*. Basically, *V* is determined by principles of reference and denotation that specify the interpretation of constants and variables in *LF*, taking into account the compositional structure of *LF*. We might assume that *V* is to be developed at least in part along the lines pursued in model theoretic semantics specifying conditions of truth and satisfaction for *LF* with respect to a model, the relevant model being provided by *c*. From this point of view, *V* is a function mapping *LF* and *c* into *C*, that is $V(LF, c) = C$, where *C* is a configuration either within or to be added to *c*.[26] Considering the composition of *LF* in terms of the pair $[PR; AS]$, we might assume more specifically that $V(PR, c)$ identifies a configuration within c, usually called the pragmatic presuppositions, whereas $V(AS, c)$ specifies what is to be added to or changed within c. In a sense, therefore, $V(AS, c)$ determines the new information of an utterance with respect to the context c. In other words, $V(PR, c)$ is a structure that satisfies PR in c, while $V(AS, c)$ is a structure, determined relative to c, that potentially enriches or modifies c.

Notice, incidentally, that $V(LF)$, and especially $V(PR)$ might be much more specific in an intuitive sense than LF or PR. Instantiation of a quantified variable is a case in point. Consider for example the sentence (34) again, whose PR was paraphrased by (35a). Most contexts will yield a pragmatic presupposition that provides a particular instance for *someone other than Mike*. Sentence (35c) could be a paraphrase of one such possibility:

(34) Mike has also problems with him.
(35) (a) Someone other than Mike has problems with him.
     (c) The speaker and the addressee have problems with him.

Although these are fairly vague hints as to the nature of V, they can presumably be made precise in terms of usual principles of variable assignment, denotation, and satisfaction. It should be noted, however, that V must rely also on less well established principles. To illustrate the problem, we might consider sentences like (38) or (39):

(38) (a) I left the university about ten in the morning.
     (b) I left the university in the early sixties.
(39) (a) He badly missed the book, as it was full of notes.
     (b) He badly missed the book, as it was full of insights.

In (38a) *university* must be interpreted as a physical object, in (38b) as an institution. A parallel distinction applies to *leave*, which refers to a physical act in (38a) and to a change in social milieu in (38b). Although these are conceptually clearly distinct entities, *university* and *leave* are certainly not lexically ambiguous in the sense of, e.g. *bank* or *post*. Hence the whole sentence *I left the university* is not ambiguous between two different LF's, but its interpretation C differs according to the context that makes sense of the specification either of the hour or of the year. Analogous considerations apply to the interpretation of *book* in (39). The problem illustrated by these examples has many ramifications, the proper treatment of which is anything but clear. For some discussion see Nunberg (1979). It should be obvious, however, that, if the building and the institution are conceptually distinct (and hence different in C) while *university* is not lexically ambiguous and hence not different on LF, then V must account for the difference in interpretation. Therefore, V must be based not only on principles of reference and denotation, but also on principles of what might be called conceptual specification. Notice, incidentally, that these principles again do not allow for a strictly on-line interpretation: which specification is to apply to *leave* and *university* in (38) or to *book* in (39) might be undecidable until the end of the sentence.[27]

Let me finally point out that according to the general characteristics of *LF* and *C*, *V* must be a mapping from unordered hierarchies into set theoretical structures that are neither ordered nor hierarchical. In other words, while under *I* linearity is dropped, under *V* tree structure is dissolved.

To summarize these lengthy—though still rather incomplete—remarks, we have the following general characteristics of the structural representations corresponding to the levels of understanding introduced in (1) to (4) in section 2 above:

(40) *P*: sequence of (bundles of) phonetic attributes, grouped in terms of perceptually accessible larger units (such as syllable, phonological word, intonation group).

(41) *S*: categorized, ordered tree imposed on syntactic formatives, which correspond to subsequences of *P* (including the empty string *e*), subject to binding relations.

(42) *LF*: categorized, unordered tree imposed on semantic primes, which are either constants or variables, organized according to functor–argument relations with variable binding.

(43) *C*: set theoretical structure not subject to ordering and tree conditions, determined by the inherent ontology of the mental world (whatever that turns out to be).

Ignoring otherwise interesting details, the general characteristics that are of primary relevance with regard to on-line processing can be schematized as follows:

(44)

	P	*S*	*LF*	*C*
linear ordering	yes	yes	no	no
tree structure	no	yes	yes	no

Bearing in mind the gross oversimplification of this schema, we might say that language understanding maps a strictly linear, time-dependent structure via hierarchization—first ordered, then unordered—into a timeless representation of free dimensionality. Although this is commonplace, it has important consequences for any account of language understanding. (Trivially, the inverse mapping characteristics hold for speech production.) The mapping between these structures are determined by *A*, *I*, and *V*, as discussed above. We can reconstruct the functions F_2 to F_4 of Section 2 in terms of these mappings as follows:

(45) (a) $A'(P) = S$
    (b) $I(S) = LF$
    (c) $V(LF, c) = C$

Inserting these mappings into F_2 to F_4 we get:

(46) $F_1(s) = P$ (see $(1')$ above)
(47) $F_2(s) = A'(F_1(s)) = S$
(48) $F_3(s) = I(A'(F_1(s))) = LF$
(49) $F_4(s,c) = V(I(A'(F_1(s))), c) = C$

Analysed in this way, F_2 to F_4 automatically turn into F_2' to F_4' as all preceding (or 'lower') levels of representation must be identified, in order to apply the rules constituting the next mappings. (Remember that a full computational account of these mappings might derive intermediate steps between P, S, LF, and C, which however do not appear to be relevant as separate representations in language understanding.)

GRAMMAR AND PROCESSING

Although many problems remain and others need further clarification, suppose that something like the representations and mappings discussed in the previous section is required as a framework for understanding language comprehension. Even if all the missing details and eventual corrections were added, the framework would not, of course, in itself provide an account of the processes of language understanding, since the representations P, S, LF, and C as well as the mappings A (or A', for that matter), I, and V are purely structural entities and relations which are clearly to be distinguished from the actual processes by which they are produced or identified. This distinction brings us back to the venerable and persistent issue concerning the relation between competence and performance or grammar and processing.[28]

It is clear at least since the paper of Fodor and Garrett (1966) that any attempt to identify grammatical rules with steps of processing is doomed to failure. The fate of the so-called derivational theory of complexity (DTC) which tried to explain complexity of comprehension in terms of number of transformations, is only the most explicit example for this kind of failure.[29] The conclusion that Fodor and Garrett drew from this observation was that the relation between grammar and processing is abstract.

Without adding much to the substance of this claim, I will replace it by the following slightly more specific assumption:

(A7) The grammar G specifies potential targets for the levels of language understanding and the structural mappings between them.

In other words, assuming that phonetic, syntactic, semantic, and contextual understanding are involved in spontaneous processing—a claim that has to be justified on independent empirical and theoretical grounds—G defines the structure and mappings eventually realized in the pertinent processes. (This assumption will be specified more precisely below.) Seen in this perspective, clarifying how grammars and processes are related amounts to the task of specifying mechanisms whose operations are to be controlled by grammatically defined structures and mappings. It seems to me that much of the work following the breakdown of DTC and similar conceptions is best to be understood in this vein.

A fairly rigid program to this effect could be formulated as follows:

(D) There are mechanisms M_1 to M_4 such that M_1 realizes F_1, M_2 realizes A', M_3 realizes I, and M_4 realizes V.

The task, according to (D), would be to specify the different characteristics of M_1 to M_4 as well as the manner of their interaction. Notice, first of all, that (D) does not require that syntactic processing has to be completed before semantic interpretation can start, etc., as the different mechanisms can be assumed to work in a parallel manner. Hence (D) would not be in conflict with claim (A) above (although it clearly contradicts (B) as well as (C)).

Let me briefly explain why I take (D) to be wrong. Consider the putative mechanism M_1 accounting for the interpretation of s in terms of P. Under normal conditions, the identification of P involves, of course, lexical access, organizing P in terms of a sequence of word forms. Now lexical rules, however they might be organized in detail, clearly provide not only phonetic but also syntactic and semantic information. As syntactic categorization is relevant for S, and semantic properties of lexical items constitute part of the mapping I, it would thus be absurd to postulate mechanisms M_2 and M_3 realizing A and I independently from M_1. I therefore assume that A, I, and V, in spite of their essential differences discussed above, cannot be realized by strictly independent processing mechanisms. Notice, incidentally, that (D) is not a strawman position altogether. In fact, most of the work on models for parsing mechanisms must be conceived as attempting a characterization of M_2, which maps P (or rather a sequence of word forms) into S. The various versions of augmented transition network (ATN) grammars in particular have developed fairly detailed mechanisms clarifying the way in which phrase structure rules (and even certain transformations) might control an actual mapping process from strings to categorized trees. To the extent to which ATN grammars are construed as partial models of real processes of language understanding, they are bound to a program like (D) at least with respect to M_2.[30] Without arguing about the more technical aspects of ATN grammars such as the debatable adequacy of push-down storage as part of a processing model, I would simply say that there is little reason to assume that language understanding is mediated by separate mechanisms along the lines indicated by (D). To mention just one well known type of problem, the difference in acceptability between sentences like (50) and (51) cannot be explained in terms of ATN grammars:

(50) The teacher who the boy you visited mentioned left.

(51) The ice cream that the boy you mentioned bought melted.

Although both are difficult to comprehend for purely syntactic reasons, (51) is somewhat easier to parse, as the nested clauses are more readily separated on semantic grounds.[31] In order to account for these and similar, less artificial phenomena, the notion of autonomous mechanisms responsible for phonetic, syntactic, semantic, and contextual interpretation must be abandoned.

It must be emphasized, by the way, that the issue of separate processing mechanisms in the sense of (D) is not to be confused with the autonomy of the grammar G and its various components. It might very well be the case that the rules of G constitute modular, autonomous systems in the sense discussed, for example, in Chomsky (1980a), determining the targets for various types of processing, while the processing operations carried out interact in various ways across levels of structural organization. This possibility is in fact crucially inherent in the very distinction between competence and performance.

Before turning to the problem of how to replace (D) by alternative notions, I will insert some consideration of the way in which temporal characteristics of processing relate to the dimensionality of the different types of representations summarized in (44). Let us start with the general, fairly vague and almost trivial assumption (A8):

(A8) Any processing operation O is characterized by a real time interval t. Two operations O_1 and O_2 are temporally connected iff there is a time interval t such that $t = t_1 t_2$.

This assumption can be made precise in a number of ways. It does not make any claim as to the character and complexity of O_i, the order of magnitude of t_i, the degree of variability of operation time, or a number of other parameters. It also leaves open the question whether temporally connected operations merely follow one another, or whether they are operationally connected in some sense to which we will turn below. It simply relates operations to the time axis and defines the notion of temporal sequence of operations. All this is trivial. (Notice, however, that something like (A8) is presupposed by all kinds of chronometric analysis.) Less trivial is the problem of specifying the range of possibilities for parallel processing: sequences of operations might overlap or merge, a sequence might split into two or more parallel sequences, parallel sequences might be independent or dependent on each other, to mention the more obvious examples. Even a superficial systematization would require additional concepts besides temporal connectedness. I will not go into these problems here and simply assume that temporal ordering plays a crucial role in all these cases.

It is now straightforward to relate the temporal ordering of processing operations in the sense of (A8) to the linear character of P and S. This at least seems to me the most reasonable, if not the only way to construe the notion of left-to-right processing accepted in claim (A) in Section 1. This does not mean, though, that the relation in question is simple and obvious.[32] Putting aside intricate details, we are still left with a number of principled problems, of which two are of primary importance: firstly the relation of non-linear—including hierarchical—aspects of structure to the temporal ordering of processing, and secondly the relation of storage or retention to the temporal character of processing. I will discuss these in turn.

Logically, there are two ways in which linear processing can cope with non-linear structures:

(52) Sequential processing. Operations scan (or construct) a non-linear structure in sequential order according to certain conditions of linearization.

(53) Parallel processing. Operations scan (or construct) a non-linear structure in parallel according to certain conditions of interaction.

For the sake of illustration, consider a structure like (54), which could be processed according to (52), e.g. as indicated in (55a), or according to (53) as indicated in (55b):

(54)

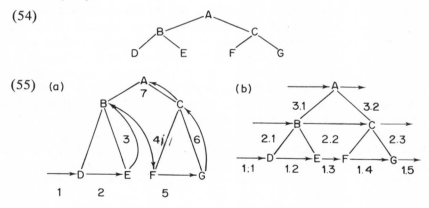

(55) (a)   (b)

In (55), an arrow with index i represents an operation O_i with time interval t_i. Any arrow points to the result of O_i. Thus O_1 in (55a), as well as $O_{1.j}$ in (55b), result in identifying (or constructing) D, whereas O_3 as well as $O_{2.1}$ result in identifying B and its connections to D and E. It follows from the latter condition that $O_{2.1}$ can operate only after $O_{1.2}$. (Hence a certain temporal relation is defined even for the parallel sequence $O_{1.i}$, $O_{2.j}$, and $O_{3.k}$ in (55b), a problem to which we will return.) Depending on the 'content' of the different operations to be defined below, other ways of processing (54) according to either (52) or (53) can be imagined. Even combinations of parallel and sequential processing are possible, for example by processing DEFG sequentially, and in parallel sequence the nodes BCA (in that order).[33] Notice that neither (55a) nor (55b) suggests an actual procedure for processing a syntactic or semantic tree. They are merely meant as illustration of the principles (52) and (53). It should be pointed out, however, that ATN grammars are essentially an implementation of (52), with operations defined in such a way that the resulting sequence would be that of (55c) in footnote 33 rather than (55a).[34]

Four further remarks are to be made. Firstly, if applied to an ordered tree (or any other linearly ordered hierarchy), the sequence(s) of operation times for both (52) and (53) can still be related to the linear order of terminal elements, and hence to the time coordinate of s. The relation is by far less direct than for purely linear structures, but the principles are fairly obvious.[35] Secondly, both (52) and (53) can be extended to unordered trees, the crucial difference being the fact that the sequence of operations is then not determined by linear properties of the structure to be processed. As, however, the very notion of processing is intrinsically bound to the time dimension, a certain ordering will be imposed on the structure by the way it is processed. This holds, of course, for both sequential and parallel processing. We need to expand on this point below. For the time being, I will merely point out that the sequence of operations may be determined in part by linear properties of other structures whose processing interacts with that of unordered structures. Linear aspects of S in particular may induce a kind of secondary linearity into LF according to the interaction of processing on the two levels. It is in this sense that intuitively the meaning of initial words of an utterance comes earlier than that of later ones although LF in itself does not make sense of ordering among its components. (Actually, things are less simple than the intuitive notion suggests, as will be seen below.) Thirdly, neither (52) nor (53) is restricted to trees. In fact, both can be generalized in the same vein to arbitrary structures according to the content of available operations. This then includes in particular structures of the type hypothesized for C (and mental models in general). Obviously, the remarks made above with respect to linearization carry over under this generalization. Fourthly, the generalization of (52) and (53) to arbitrary structures includes as well the case of two or more structures that are related by structurally defined mappings. Hence, it encompasses not only LF and C, but even complete structural representations $\langle P, S, LF, C \rangle$ whose levels are interrelated by A, I, and V, as described in Section 4.[36] Below we will rely crucially on this notion which, of course, requires giving an appropriate characterization to the operations involved.

I have referred various times to the 'content of operation O', a notion that now requires some clarification. Without aiming at a serious, complete theory of processing operations, one must take it as a necessary—though by no means sufficient—specification that O reaults in some change in the internal state of the processing system. More specifically, O might result in adding or deleting a certain unit A and/or relating A to other units. This, of course, presupposes that internal states are to be characterized in terms of units and relations. I take this to be a claim so vague and general that it can hardly be rejected by any attempt to make sense of the notion of processing. I will call the change brought about by an operation O the target of O. On this basis, assumption (A7) specifying the relation between grammar and processing can be made more precise in the following way:

(A7') The target of an operation O involved in language processing is defined by a unit or configuration within a structure determined by G.

Thus the target of O_1 in (55a) would be defined by D, the target of O_3 would be defined by $[_B DE]$, provided that G determines (54) as a possible representation.

Assumption (A7') achieves two things. First, it provides a somewhat more precise notion as to how grammar and process are to be related. Second, it restricts operations in language processing to those changes that can be defined in terms of grammatical primes (or rather grammatical and conceptual primes, in order to include C). In other words, although there might be operations involved in language processing whose targets cannot be defined grammatically, they are not operations of language processing. Rather, they are either parts of the operations in question (which are then complex operations in a different respect), or they are operations of accompanying processes (such as, say, identifying the speaker's emotional state according to certain parameters of s).

To elaborate the topic one step further, we need to recognize that O may be dependent on certain conditions in order to achieve its target. Thus O_3 in (55a) as well as $O_{2.1}$ in (55b) both operate on the condition that D and E are already given in order to arrive at the target $[_B DE]$. Hence O is characterized obligatorily by its target, and optionally by its condition. This, then, leads to the following more complete specification:

(56) An operation O is characterized by the pair $\langle OC, OT \rangle$ where OC is the condition, OT the target of O.

We will call $\langle OC, OT \rangle$, where OC can be empty, the structural content of O. On the basis of (56) we can modify (A7) as follows:

(A7'') The content of an operation O involved in language processing is defined by structural configurations determined by G.

The characterization arrived at in (56) is formally close to the notion of productions that has proliferated following the influential work of Newell and Simon (1972), especially to artificial intelligence (AI) approaches to cognitive processes. In fact, as we have made no particular claims with respect to OC and OT (except that they can be defined in structural terms), even grammatical rules formally fall under (56). It is therefore important to emphasize the difference between processing operations and grammatical rules underlying (A7″). Rules determine structural properties and relations, and have no temperal characteristics whatsoever, while operations are subject to real time flow.[37] It seems to me to be one of the deep conceptual difficulties with artificial intelligence that it persistently tends to ignore the difference in question.

Notice furthermore that the structural content as defined in (56) does not fully characterize an operation in all cases. In general, O will achieve its target OT on the basis of a certain input or cause, which is not automatically to be identified with its condition OC. A clear case in point is the mapping of s into P. Whatever the elementary operations might be, they must be released by the sensory input s which, by definition, cannot be defined in grammatical terms. As I am not attempting a full characterization of operations, I will not state this point more formally and merely point out the incompleteness of (56).

What is of more concern in the present context is the connection between operations in terms of condition and target, which can be defined as follows:

(57) O_j is operationally connected to O_i if the target of O_i is contained in the condition of O_j.

Notice that operational connection is independent of temporal connection as introduced in (A8) above, although there is a relation between the time intervals of operationally connected operations. This relation can be stated as follows:

(58) If O_j is operationally connected to O_i, then t_i precedes t_j.

The reason for (58) is obvious and has already been illustrated. Notice that we must not require operationally connected operations to be also temporally connected, as can already be seen from our simple example (55a): O_3 is operationally connected to O_1 (it presupposes the target of O_1), although O_2 intervenes and thus prevents temporal connection. Things are a bit more complicated with respect to operationally connected operations in parallel processing. For the sake of illustration, consider once more (55b), the relevant part being produced here as (59):

(59)

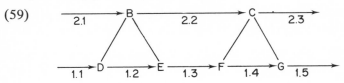

$O_{2.1}$ is operationally connected to $O_{1.1}$ and $O_{1.2}$, and it is temporally connected to $O_{1.2}$. Besides $O_{2.1}$, $O_{1.3}$ is temporally (though of course not operationally) also connected to $O_{1.2}$, this being a crucial point of parallel processing. What about $O_{2.2}$? It is, of course, operationally connected to both $O_{1.3}$ and $O_{1.4}$, and furthermore temporally to $O_{1.4}$. What we cannot account for so far is the intuitive notion that $O_{2.2}$ should be connected to its 'predecessor' $O_{2.1}$, in order to achieve parallel processing in the intended sense.[38] What seems to be necessary is a characterization of O not only by its content OC and OT, but also by the state from which it starts. This is a fairly natural assumption, that can be added in a straightforward way:

(60) On operation O is characterized by a triple $\langle OS, OC, OT \rangle$ with OC and OT as in (56), and OS is a (partial) characterization of the initial state of O.

If we redefine 'structural content of O' by $\langle OS, OC, OT \rangle$, (60) immediately carries over to (A7″). Again, I assume that OS is defined in structural terms by G. With this amendment, $O_{2.2}$ would be characterized by $\langle B, FG, [_C FG] \rangle$, giving the intended connections. To summarize, in order to relate grammatical structures of various types of formal dimensionality to temporal characteristics of processing, we have introduced a system Q of operations O defined by (60) and related to time and structure by (A7″) and (A8).

Before leaving this topic, I will add three general remarks. Firstly, Q is, of course, of almost amorphous complexity, allowing for all kinds of absurd operations. What is interesting, however, is that one way to restrict it in a reasonable way is indicated by (A7″): the structural content of admissible operations is defined by G. Restrictions on G thus automatically imply restrictions on Q. Although this is still a rather vague condition, it might suggest at least a certain perspective for construing Chomsky's fundamental claim that a theory of performance should have a theory of competence as a proper part. Secondly, a further way to restrict Q would be in terms of general conditions on possible operations, independently of the pertinent types of structures. Time, complexity, and space of processing indicate tentative parameters of such general conditions.[39] These would have to be justified on empirical grounds, which cannot be afforded independently of G, however, as Q, though characterized by independent properties, is always bound to structural conditions defined by G (or other systems of cognitive structures). Thirdly, Q can be differentiated (and thus enriched rather than restricted) by properties like relative strength or probability of operations, accounting for preferred or even stereotyped sequences of operations. This yields a fairly plausible possibility to account for a number of different, though probably related phenomena, which are dependent on linguistic structures but cannot reasonably be attributed to linguistic (or other) competence. For one thing, perceptual strategies in the sense discussed by Bever (1970) might be construed as more or less integrated sequences of operations. Another point is that a fairly wide range of aphasic phenomena fall naturally into different types of disintegration or interference within parts of the processing system Q without implying the loss or disturbance of G. I cannot expand on these issues, which deserve careful consideration in their own right and are mentioned only to indicate further perspectives that might be pursued in this connection.

Returning to the main theme of relating temporal characteristics to different types of structural representations, let me repeat that we have recognized two cases:

(a) Structural linearity: temporal order of processing is by and large related to concatenation properties of structural representations.
(b) Processing order: temporal order of processing induces linear ordering into representations that are structurally unordered.

With crucial exceptions to be discussed immediately, (a) holds for P and S. Case (b), on the other hand, holds for LF and C. It entails, of course, the question of which order is induced, and how it is induced. Two factors are to be distinguished. First, there are ordering effects of structure in non-linear representations. They are determined by operational connections and their relation to time intervals, as stated in (58) above. Thus, for example, $O_{2.1}$ would have to follow $O_{1.1}$ and $O_{1.2}$ in our example (59), even if (59) is construed as an unordered hierarchy, just because OC of $O_{2.1}$ requires the previous identification of D and E in one order or the other. Let us call this factor the 'internal condition'. The second factor would correspondingly be an 'external condition'. It intervenes, if there is no internal condition, just because operations have to have some time relation to each other. Thus if we construe (59) as an unordered structure, $O_{1.1}$ and $O_{1.2}$—which are not operationally connected—might be applied in any order.[40] Whatever ordering eventually shows up, does not depend on any internal, structural condition of (59). Putting aside for the moment problems of storage and display, it seems to me in fact that the notion of an unordered representation is tantamount to the possibility that it be processed in alternative orders that are equivalent as to internal conditions. Thus if we consider a functional expression $f(a)$ where f is the functor and a the argument, it amounts to the same thing whether first f is identified and then applied to a, or first a is identified and then f applied to it. It is precisely in this sense that LF as well as C, but not S, is unordered.

The crucial point now is that LF is subject to external conditions on processing order if we consider LF separately from other structural representations; these conditions are turned, however, into internal ones, as soon as we consider LF as the value of the structurally defined mapping I from S into LF. To see the point, it is sufficient to consider I insofar as it is determined by lexical rules. If we continue to assume that identification of a word W is a (complex) operation that has as its target the phonetic as well as the syntactic and semantic properties of W, then clearly the structural linearity of P and S becomes an internal condition on processing order with respect to $\langle P, S, LF, C \rangle$, and hence also for LF and C. We thus get at least some left-to-right processing order even for LF and C as a consequence of structural linearity. The basic idea of this consideration is almost trivial, but its details are anything but simple, as will be seen in the next section.

To conclude the discussion of structural and processing order, I will consider the notion of on-line processing. We are dealing here, of course, with a metaphor imported from computer jargon. It means roughly that input and processing are running simultaneously. Its demarcation in the present context is not very precise, however. For the sake of argument, I will therefore adopt a more specific notion to the effect that processing ceases to be on-line if there are intervening operations that require previous results to be retained for later processing. More specifically, I am interested in what might be called 'strict on-line processing' in roughly the following sense:

(61) O_i is a strict successor of the sequence $O_1, \ldots, O_{i-1}$ iff
    (a) O_i is temporally connected to O_{i-1}, and
    (b) if O_i is operationally connected to some O_j for $1 \leqslant j < i$ then there is no O_k with $k > j$ to which O_i is not operationally connected.

(62) A sequence of operations $O_1 \ldots O_n$ is a strict on-line process iff O_i is a strict successor of O_{i-1} for $1 < i \leqslant n$.

Condition (61a) is straightforward; condition (61b) excludes all intervening operations from strict on-line processing. To put it the other way around, a strict successor may collect any number of targets achieved by previous operations, as long as there are no operations whose target is irrelevant for the strict successor. The point is that strict on-line processing would not admit the processing of any material that interrupts operational connections. Although (62) applies only to sequential processing, it can easily be extended to parallel processing, for example by saying that Q is strictly on-line, iff all parallel sequences of operations constituting Q are strictly on-line.

We have introduced a rather special concept, which can be modified in a number of ways. While it does not make, of course, any empirical claim, it can be used in clarifying certain empirical issues. One point of interest is this. On the one hand, a given structure (such as our simple example (54)) can be processed in a number of different ways, some of which are strictly on-line, others of which are not.[41] It *is* now an empirical question whether and to what extent (up to which price in terms of complexity of operations for example) language tends to be strictly on-line in case of alternative possibilities. On the other hand, there are structures that do not allow for any strictly on-line mode of processing. This again is an empirical point, concerning the relation of structures of natural language to conditions of processing. Cases of binding like (63) are obvious examples:

(63) Who$_i$ did you$_j$ expect [e$_j$ to see e$_i$ at the meeting]?

The operation identifying and binding e_i has *who$_i$* as part of its condition and is thus operationally connected to an operation that is separated by a large amount of intervening processing. The case is similar for e_j. That is obvious enough, and we could have arrived at this conclusion without the expense of definitions like (61). There are, however, more intriguing cases exhibiting similar properties, as we will see below.

Turning next ot the thorny problem of memory in processing, I will restrict myself to three general remarks, as there is practically nothing I have to add to the vast literature on aspects of memory, which is, moreover, to a large extent based on either technological or intuitive metaphors in interpreting the very notion of memory.

First remark: It is a logical necessity that the result of understanding an utterance must be kept in one way or the other in memory. That is simply the moral of the fact that at least for a certain time there is something in the mind which was not there before the utterance was processed. There are, however, important differences as to what is retained and for how long. Thus, as Jarvella and Herman (1972) have shown, verbatim recall—based on retention of P (or P and S?)—is in general possible for the last clause heard only. Different conditions hold for other levels of representation. Thus it might be that, for example, LF is not retained at all except for the time of processing itself. It seems to me that considerations like this are the rationale behind claim (B) above, that no separate syntactic and semantic representations are developed in language understanding: They play no independent role in storage and retrieval. I need not go into further details here, as I am not specifically concerned with problems of recall.[42]

Second remark: Besides retention for eventual recall, intermediate storage during the process of understanding is necessary, a function of what is usually called working memory. Evidently, all processes that are not strictly on-line in the sense defined above crucially rely on intermediate storage. If working memory in this sense is to be distinguished from short-term memory as mentioned before, that cannot be done in terms of memory span or temporal characteristics, as can be seen from cases like this:

(64) Hört$_i$ der Pianist . . . noch vor der Probe $\left\{ \begin{array}{l} \text{zu üben auf e}_i \\ \text{die Bänder an e}_i \end{array} \right\}$?

'Does the pianist . . . $\left\{ \begin{array}{l} \text{stop practising} \\ \text{listen to the tapes} \end{array} \right\}$ before the rehearsal?

Here the dots can be filled by arbitrarily complex relative clauses expanding the interval between the separated parts *hört* and *auf/an* of the German lexical entries *aufhören* and *anhören*, respectively. Hence the time span required for working memory can easily exceed the time normally admitted for verbatim recall, for example. In other words, the distinction in question can only be made in terms of structural and/or processing characteristics.[43] One favoured idea in this respect is the characterization of working memory in terms of push down stacks or other rather limited forms of storage. Other proposals, such as that of Arbib and Caplan (1979), rely instead on a kind of overall display that is not restricted in any particular way.[44] Although I am sceptical with respect to the metaphor of push-down storage, I have no special claims to make, except that intermediate storage needs somehow to be guaranteed for handling the widespread deviations from strict on-line processing.

Third remark: Something like an overall or simultaneous display seems to be a necessary assumption, at least with respect to mental models (i.e. the level of c and C) allowing for a variety of accesses in processing subsequent (parts of) utterances. Although it is fairly unclear what this kind of 'internal display' (a metaphor again!) should be, it seems to play a guiding role in language understanding. (See Section 7 below for some illustration.) In fact, the internal representation envisaged in claim (B) above as *the* result of language understanding can best be made sense of in terms of this kind of freely accessible display.

Notice that the three aspects of storage I have commented on—short-term memory for recall and recognition, working memory, and simultaneous display—are all distinct from what is usually called long-term memory. They are interrelated in crucial ways in terms of processing operations, but I have nothing to add with respect to this problem beyond the assumptions already inherent in (A7) and its refinements.

We are now ready to formulate an alternative to the notion of separate processing mechanisms assumed in (D) above. The basic idea is simply this: the function F'_4 defines the levels of structure and their interrelations developed in understanding an utterance u based on the signal s with respect to the context c. These levels of structural representation are developed by parallel processing that is as strictly on-line as possible with respect to s, c and the content of available operations. To formulate this idea more precisely, let me introduce the following auxiliary notions.

> (65) $F'_4(s, c)$ is maximal relative to G and V iff it contains all the specifications that are compatible with s, c, and G, and the principles of reference and denotation constituting the mapping V.

Thus if $F_1(s)$ is the phonetic representation of a word W then $F'_4(s, c)$ is maximal, if it consist of W's phonetic characteristics, its syntactic categorization, its lexical and contextual meaning with respect to c. Similarly, if

$F_1(s)$ is for example the phonetic form of a noun phrase like *some of the boys*, then the maximal F_4' provides also its full syntactic, semantic, and contextual representation, as far as these can be determined on the basis of s, c, G, and V. Two points need be taken note of. The first is that $F_4'(s, c)$ might be incomplete in certain respects. This problem will be considered below. The second point is that F_4' need not be uniquely determined even with respect to a particular context, although many ambiguities will be removed by reference to c. In order not to obscure the discussion, let us ignore for the time being problems of ambiguity. As we will see, these can ultimately be reduced to a particular case of the former point.

Suppose next that s is a proper initial part of s', that is, there is some s'' such that $s' = ss''$. We will then define completeness as follows:

(66) $F_4'(s, c)$ is complete relative to G, V, and s' iff the maximal $F_4{}'(s', c)$ neither modifies nor further specifies any specifications in $F_4'(s, c)$.

Some refinements are still required to spell out the notion of modifying and specifying a representation, but the main point of (66) should be clear enough: F_4' is complete if and only if it is not affected by processing of further parts of the utterance. The relation between completeness and maximality is obvious:

(67) For any initial part s of s': if $F_4'(s, c)$ is complete relative to G, V, s', then it is maximal relative to G, V, but not necessarily vice versa.

All cases that cannot be processed in a strictly on-line fashion for structural reasons contain instances of initial parts that might be maximal, but cannot be complete. We have discussed a large number of them. To take just the last example (64): F_4' cannot be complete for all initial parts until the separated prefix *auf* or *an* (and hence the lexical unit *aufhören* or *anhören*) is identified.[45] The definition of completeness does not make any claims as to where during the processing operations completeness is achieved. Thus the missing prefix might be anticipated rather early because of the role of c, and it will at least be predicted if the infinitive *zu üben* is processed.

This, then, leads to a more explicit formulation of the idea that language understanding is as on-line as possible:

(A9) $F_4'(s, c)$ is normally maximal, but not necessarily complete for any initial stretch s of the incoming signal s' of an utterance u.

This formulation is an empirical assumption which, if correct, sets a number of conditions for any theory that purports to be an explanation of language understanding. It does not outline such a theory, however. Rather, it can be met by various theoretical models making specific claims with respect to properties of the operation system Q, of storage and display, and, of course, of G and V. Assumption (A9) does not strictly exclude claim (D), but it is not subject to the objections which can be raised against (D), and can in fact be pursued in a number of ways that are incompatible with the claim of separate processing mechanisms.

Two final remarks. Firstly, the definitions in (65) and (66) can easily be extended to 'lower' levels of understanding defined by F_1, F_2', and F_3'. (A9) will accordingly hold also for deprived cases of extra-contextual, purely syntactic or semantic understanding. Secondly we can capture disambiguation by the notion of completeness in the following sense: any ambiguity in the interpretation of an initial part of u that is ruled out by processing further parts of u amounts to a particular type of specification, which thus completes F_4' of the part in question. Generalized in this way, (A9) implies that language understanding is as unambiguous as possible.

SCOPE DETERMINATION

In this section I will briefly illustrate the previous considerations by discussing somewhat more intricate cases of structural limits for strict on-line processing. More specifically, I will be concerned with two types of cases that fall under the notion of scope. For practical reasons, I will restrict the analysis to F_3', i.e. I will largely ignore the role of contextual interpretation. The notion of scope is imported from logical terminology, where it characterizes the domain of operators like negation, quantifiers, and modal operators. In terms of the functional structure that we have assumed for LF in Section 4, the following definition can be given:

(68) A is the scope B in LF iff A is of category a, B is of category $\langle b/a \rangle$ and $[BA]$ is of category b.

This yields a generalization of the notion of scope, as it includes, for example, the argument(s) of a predicate; this generalization is natural in all relevant respects, however.

The roots of the notion of scope are thus traced to LF, but scope must also be defined for S, in order to be applicable in the usual way. This can be done as follows:

(69) x is the scope of y in S iff $I(S) = LF$ and A and B are the respective images of x and y in LF under I, and A is the scope of B in LF.

The intriguing point now comes from the fact that in natural language the tree structures of LF do not in general coincide with those of S, thus turning phenomena of scope into a fairly intricate, two-level matter. Consider for instance the sentences (70a) and (b), which have the same syntactic structure, except for the modals *can* and *must*. They differ, however, in LF in a way that brings them close to synonymity, as indicated by the paraphrases in (71a) and (b), respectively:

(70) (a) John cannot distribute the monograph.
     (b) John must not distribute the monograph.
(71) (a) It is not possible for John to distribute the monograph.
     (b) It is necessary for John not to distribute the monograph.

Intuitively speaking, the modal is within the scope of *not* in (70a) while the relation is inverse in (70b). That is an idiosyncratic fact about English modal verbs, which is relevant in the present context for two reasons.

Firstly, although the different scope behaviour of *can* and *must* depends on the lexical items in question, it cannot be represented on the level of word forms, nor on the full syntactic representation S alone. It rather involves S and its mapping into LF. (Notice incidentally that it would not help either to claim that what is at issue is just the construction of C on the basis of the sequence of words, since the problem is precisely how C depends on P.) Hence, contrary to claim (B), S and LF are crucially involved in the process of language understanding.

Secondly, while syntactic and semantic scope roughly coincide in the case of *must*, they differ with respect to order and hierarchy in the case of *can*. The relevant parts of S and LF are these:

(72) (a) S: [. . . can not [. . .]. . .]
         LF: [. . . NEG [CAN[. . .]]. . .]
     (b) S: [. . . must not [. . .]. . .]
         LF: [. . . MUST [NEG[. . .]]. . .]

The crucial point is that (72a) cannot be constructed in a strictly on-line fashion, since *not* follows an element that is part of its scope. Notice that the problem arises not because of different ordering in S and LF—there is no order in LF as such—but rather because of the hierarchy of scopes. In other words, F_3' for *John cannot* . . . cannot be complete, even if it is maximal.

One might object that these are minor problems, since *can* and *not* are direct neighbours, which might even be turned into a single item *can't* under contraction. The same phenomena show up, however, with any number of intervening constituents. Consider the following examples:

(73) (a) John can distribute only the monograph.
     (b) John must distribute only the monograph.

The crucial interaction is between the modals and *only*, which contains a negative element, as exhibited by its close paraphrase *nothing but*. Now, that negative element has the same scope properties in LF as ordinary *not*. Thus using approximate paraphrases as in (71), we get (74):

(74) (a) It is not possible for John to distribute anything but the monograph.

(b) It is necessary for John to distribute nothing but the monograph.

As (74a) shows, *can* is in the scope of (part of) *only* in (73a). In fact, it is essential for understanding (73a) to recognize that negation applies to the modality. But here the elements in question are no longer adjacent. And they can be separated even further:

(75) John can distribute the monograph you are so urgently looking for only once.

As we will see below, things are further complicated by the fact that *only* requires not only scope determination for its negative component, but induces at the same time a presupposition for the entire clause.

In general, then, scope recognition is an intrinsic requirement for language understanding. The pertinent phenomena crucially depend on the interaction of S and LF, more precisely on the mapping of S on LF. Hence contrary to claim (B), both S and LF are necessarily involved in language understanding. Furthermore, syntactic and semantic scope (as defined in (68) and (69)) do not necessarily coincide in natural language. Divergencies in this respect are usually barriers against strict on-line processing, the minimal case being illustrated by (72a). This then yields in part the initially mentioned modification of claim (A).

Taking these conclusions for granted, I will discuss other cases of scope determination, showing that we are not dealing with marginal curiosities, but rather with a central phenomenon of language understanding. The most frequently discussed problem in this connection is the scope interaction of quantifiers. I will not enter this field, though, and rather deal with one problem that is much simpler, and another that is still more complicated than the scope of quantifiers.

I have defined scope in a rather general way so that it includes all types of functor–argument structures in LF. A particularly simple case of this type are attributive adjectives as in *green chair* or *rapid move*. Putting aside intricacies irrelevant in the present context, S and LF of *the green house* are as follows:[46]

(76) S: $[_{NP}[_{Det}$ the] $[_{\bar{N}}[_A$ green] $[_N$ house]]]
(77) LF: $[_n[_{\langle n/cn \rangle}$ THE] $[_{cn}[_{\langle cn/cn \rangle}$ GREEN] $[_{cn}$ HOUSE]]]

Thus *chair* is the scope of *green*, and *green house* is the scope of *the*. So far, scope in S and LF are exactly parallel. Consider next adjectives like *big*, *tall*, *narrow* (and in general so called 'relative adjectives'), which imply comparison with a certain average or standard. Thus *large house* means something like *house larger than the average*, the average or standard being provided by the modified noun. A first, simplified approximation to the LF of *the large house*—whose S is exactly as in (76) with *large* substituted for *green*—would be (77):

(77) [$_n$ THE$_{cn}$[$_{(cn/cn)}$ LARGER THAN AVERAGE HOUSE]
[$_{cn}$ HOUSE]]]

This structure is based among other things on a lexical rule for *large* whose semantic part is roughly (78):

(78)

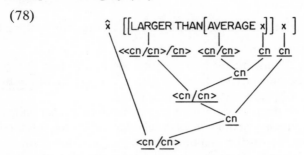

If (78) is applied to the meaning of *house*, lambda conversion yields the *cn*-part of (77).[47] Two interesting observations can now be made. First, F_3' of the initial part *the large . . .* must be incomplete, since the variable providing the standard cannot be instantiated until *house* is identified. Second, this does not prevent, in the present case, the possibility of strict on-line processing, since the internal structure of *large* as given in (78) is not related sequentially to parts of *s*. Thus although syntactic and semantic scope are related in a non-trivial way, they are not divergent.

The situation becomes different if we consider cases like *the large green house*. Actually, there are two variants to be distinguished here that differ with respect to *S* and *LF* and optionally also with respect to *P*. They are also distinguished orthographically:

(79) (a) the large, green house
      (b) the large green house

Simplifying a bit, (79a) refers to a house that is large and green, while (79b) refers to a house that is larger than other green houses. Ignoring irrelevant details, *S* and *LF* of (79a) and (79b) are given in (80) and (81), respectively:

(80) *S*:   [$_{NP}$ the [$_{\bar{N}}$[$_A$ large] [$_A$ green] [$_N$ house]]]
      LF: [$_n$ THE [[LARGER THAN [AVERAGE HOUSE]]
             [GREEN HOUSE]]]
(81) *S*:   [$_{NP}$ the [$_{\bar{N}}$[$_A$ large] [$_{\bar{N}}$[$_A$ green] [$_N$ house]]]]
      LF: [$_n$ THE [[LARGER THAN [AVERAGE[GREEN
             HOUSE]]] [GREEN HOUSE]]]

As with *the large house*, F_3' of the initial *the large . . .* is incomplete. But, now, the further processing cannot be strictly on-line, for reasons that differ with respect to (80) and (81). Consider first the 'coordinative' case (80). Although the second modifier *green* does not affect the specification of the variable *x* in the semantics of *large*, its presence requires an intermediate item to be processed which does not contribute to the target of the operation that identifies the missing specification for *x*. In other words, the identification of the standard for comparison is delayed by the intervening, coordinate modifier.

Consider next the 'subordinate' case (81). Here *green* is involved in specifying the variable in question, but only as a modifier of *house*. It is within the scope of *large*, but is itself a functor, whose scope is *house*. This nesting of scope leaves us with two logically possible modes of processing. One option is first to combine *large* with *green* into a complex functor which is then applied to *house*. The other option is first to apply *green* to *house* and insert the result for the variable in *large*. The intermediate result for *the large green* . . . in the two cases is indicated in (82) and (83), respectively:

(82) $[_n$ THE $\hat{x}$ [[LARGER THAN [AVERAGE[GREEN x]]] [GREEN x]] . . .]

(83) $[_n$ THE $\hat{x}$ [[LARGER THAN [AVERAGE x]] x] GREEN . . .]

Which way is followed under which conditions is an empirical question to be decided by suitable testing. I suspect that in general (82)—integration from the centre outwards—is followed. However that may turn out to be, notice that the second, though not the first, option is incompatible with strict on-line processing, as the operation which integrates *green* with *house* intervenes before the interpretation of *large* is completed.

The problems discussed with respect to (79) also show up in cases with intervening material of various degrees of complexity:

(84) (a) The large, frequently visited house of Lord Nobody.
     (b) The large, gorgeous, but ridiculous house of Lord Nobody.

Turning next to the fairly complex problems of scope determination for *even*, *only*, *also*, and a number of related particles, I will restrict the discussion to the core problems relevant in the present context.[48] The pertinent facts can be illustrated by the following examples:

(85) (a) John even visited Mary.
     (b) John didn't even visit Mary.

Stress placement is a crucial condition for the interpretation of these sentences. Their meaning would be different, if *Mary* instead of *visit* were stressed. With stress as indicated, the interpretation can be paraphrased as follows:

(86) (a) John visited Mary, although it was less likely for him to visit her than to *x* her.

(b) John didn't visit Mary, although it was less likely for him not to visit her than not to x her.

What *even* adds to the meaning of a sentence in which it occurs is a presupposition whose content is indicated in (86) by the *although* clauses. In order to represent the *LF* of these sentences more formally, we need a probability function p applicable to propositions, and an ordering of probabilities $>$. On that basis, we get the following representation of *LF* for (85a) and (85b):

(87) $[\forall x : x \in X [p[\text{PAST}[\text{JOHN}[x \text{ MARY}]]] > p[\text{PAST}[\text{JOHN}$ $[\text{VISIT MARY}]]]]]; [\text{PAST}[\text{JOHN}[\text{VISIT MARY}]]]$

(88) $[\forall x : x \in X [p[\text{NEG}[\text{PAST}[\text{JOHN}[x\text{MARY}]]]] > p[\text{NEG}$ $[\text{PAST}[\text{JOHN}[\text{VISIT MARY}]]]]]]; [\text{NEG}[\text{PAST}[\text{JOHN}$ $[\text{VISIT MARY}]]]]$

Here X is a set over which the alternatives to visiting range. It is to be specified by the context c, with respect to which the sentence is interpreted. The part before the semicolon represents the presupposition, as defined in Section 4.

In order to show how *LF* in cases like these relates to S, we need the notion of focus in addition to that of scope. With much simplification, it can be characterized as follows:

(89) The focus x of y in S is a constituent x within the scope of y that is bound by y.

There is still much to be clarified in order to arrive at a uniform and satisfactory concept of focus. For the time being, (89) will suffice. The scope of *even* and particles of the same type is the clause they appear in; their focus is the constituent marked by the main stress of the clause.[49] With this characterization in mind, the following provisional lexical representation for *even* can be given:

(90) S: PARTICLE, $[_S \alpha - \beta [_{+MS} \gamma] \delta]$
LF: $\hat{f}_{\text{scope}}[\hat{v}_{\text{foc}}[[\forall x : x \in X[p[f'(x)] > p[f'(v)]]]]; [f'(v)]]]$

As to S, PARTICLE indicates the syntactic categorization for *even* and it is followed by a subcategorization frame, which tentatively indicates that *even* precedes its focus γ, marked by $+\text{MS}$ (main stress). In order to represent *LF*, I have assumed that f is a variable for the scope of *even* (i.e. the *LF* of the entire clause besides *even*), v is a variable for the *LF* of γ, and $f = f'(v)$.

Consider now, how the processing of (85b) works. For the sake of illustration, let me indicate F_3' for the initial part. Suppose that F_3' of *John didn't . . .* is roughly this:

(91) S: $[_S[_{NP} \text{ John}] [_{Aux} \text{ did not}] . . .]$
LF: $\text{NEG} [\text{PAST}[\text{JOHN} . . .]]$

Now, identification and integration of the subsequent item *even* according to (90) yields something like (92):

(92) *S*: $_\text{s}[_\text{NP}$ John] $[_\text{Aux}$ did not] $[_\text{VP}[_\text{PRT}$ even] . . .]]

   LF: $\hat{v}_\text{foc}[[\forall\, x : x \in X[p[\text{NEG}[\text{PAST}[\text{JOHN}\, x \ldots]]] > p[\text{NEG}$
      $[\text{PAST}[\text{JOHN}\, v \ldots]]]]]; [\text{NEG}[\text{PAST}[\text{JOHN}\, v \ldots .]]]]$

The dots in *LF* indicate the remaining part of the scope variable *f* to be filled in by further processing. As *LF* has no intrinsic linear order, this might be thought of as the result of parallel processing.

The representation (92) looks rather complicated. In fact it might be readily reduced if it becomes related to the context of interpretation, since all it amounts to is the assignment of a contextually determined probability to the focus of *even* relative to other eventualities. Nevertheless, that simple result cannot be achieved without the intermediate steps discussed. I need not spell out the limitations for strict on-line processing in detail. Suffice it to say that, besides the intricate 'projection' leading from (91) and (90) to (92), any intermediate material between *even* and its focus would constitute a case in point. This would already be the case, if *Mary* instead of *visit* were stressed in (85).

It was the aim of this section to exemplify in a somewhat schematic way the crucial and ubiquitous role of scope, its consequences for the interaction of genuine syntactic and semantic structures, and for the limitations of strict on-line processing. I will finally turn to some fairly vague remarks on the crucial role of interactive processing on all levels.

SLIPS OF THE EAR

Slips of the tongue have become a useful source for insights into the mechanisms of speech production. There are at least two main obstacles that will prevent slips of the ear from playing an equally helpful role in understanding language comprehension. One problem is pure observational: to identify a slip of the ear, both what the speaker actually said and what the listener perceived must be controlled, whereas slips of the tongue can usually be identified by merely controlling the speech signal. To put it bluntly, speech errors can in principle be tape-recorded, listeners' errors must always be 'mind-recorded'. Hence data will remain rare. The second problem concerns the analytic consequences to be drawn. Whereas production errors usually allow for a fairly clear identification of the point of error, leading to fairly clearcut inferences with respect to the structures and mechanisms involved, perception errors do not seem to allow local identification of the error. Consider the following example:

(93) uttered: Da müssen Hunderttausende drinstecken.
     perceived: Da *muß*'n Hunderttausend*er* drinstecken.

Phonetically, there are two misinterpretations at the places marked in (93): [u] is perceived instead of [y] and [ər] instead of [ə]. Grammatically, however, these two errors result in a single number-confusion (singular substituted for plural) that is in turn manifested in three coordinated local errors: *müssen* goes to *muß*, leaving the infinitive ending -*en* for interpretation as the indefinite article (*ei*)*n*, which is to be substituted for the zero article of the plural NP, and finally the singular ending -*er* serves to replace the plural -*e*. One could only speculate which of these errors is cause and which is effect: where, in other words, the decision is located which leads to the (mis)interpretation chosen. Taking the first handicap as a matter of fact, which dooms the analysis of slips of the ear to never being more than an occasional heuristic device,[50] I will turn the second handicap into an argument concerning the nature of language understanding.

Consider the following rather instructive case. At the end of a party, agreements are made between A and B as to who gives whom a ride:

(94) A utters: Wieviel hast'n du getrunken?
                      (How much did you drink?)
      B perceives: Wie fährst'n du betrunken?
                      (How do you drive drunk?)

It would be somewhat artificial to give a phonetic transcription that renders the error acoustically plausible. The initial part should probably be something like [vi:flastn du:]. I don't take the acoustic aspect to be too important, however. What is more revealing, is B's reaction, protesting against the presumed presupposition of A:

(95) B utters: Ich bin gar nicht betruken!
                  (I'm not drunk at all!)

Let us look at the facts more closely. Phonetically, there are two places of mismatch: [fi:lhast] is perceived as [fɛ:rst] (more narrowly [i:lha] is perceived as [ɛ:r]), and [g] is perceived as [b]. (It is not difficult, by the way, to identify the relevant phonetic features that remain unchanged in both interpretations.) The two errors are, of course, correlated, though in a rather intricate way. In terms of word identification, there are two or three errors, depending on the point of view. *Viel* and *hast* is substituted by *fährst* and the past participle of *trinken* is turned into the past principle of *betrinken*. These words are integrated into rather different syntactic structures. On the level of *LF*, there is no point in further sorting out the differences. One should rather say that two shared elements remain. What is at issue is a Wh-question, as indicated by *wie*, and it contains somewhere the element DRINK. The crucial point seems to be that the uttered and the perceived sentence have completely different presuppositions. Sentence A presupposes that the listener has drunk something and asks how much, sentence B presupposes that the listener is going to drive drunk and asks how. It is obvious, that these different presuppositions select (or at least prefer) fairly different contextual features in terms of which the situation is interpreted. It is mere guesswork that this predilection initially determines the interpretation on all other levels, including phonetics, although it seems to be a rather plausible guess, corroborated by the reply (95).

Irrespective of this guess, three conclusions can be drawn. Firstly, even if there are local points to which the error can be traced—in (94) there are two of them—they cannot be identified as the point of error. In some sense, there is in fact no error at all. The listener is just interpreting the signal with respect to his or her context. And the loci of apparent errors are correlated by the general structure the listener proceeds to develop.

Secondly, to the extent to which the original signal is misinterpreted, the conclusion is warranted that language understanding is based in crucial respects on top-down rather than purely bottom-up processing. This conclusion becomes particularly forceful, if two or more phonetic errors are interrelated by common features of resulting higher-level representations. This does not lead one back to a pure analysis-by-synthesis model of language perception. A more plausible interpretation is provided by a model based on parallel processing relying on acoustic input in order to determine the structural decisions to be made.

Thirdly, the character and the interrelation of errors indicated by (93) and (94) clearly demonstrates that language understanding is organized in grammatically determined structures. Their details may differ from those assumed in the previous sections, but their existence cannot be doubted.[51] Otherwise the misidentification of the absent verb *fährst* would be a complete mystery. And the plural concord in (93) is even more cogent in this respect as it is a purely morpho-syntactic phenomenon.

If one accepts the guess as to the 'leading' role of contextual interpretations entertained with respect to (94), a fourth point is to be made. Language understanding is based on two types of input, whose dominance might change according to various external conditions. Sometimes s might be leading and sometimes c might prevail. Language understanding must therefore proceed from both ends according to the potential intermediate structures and mappings provided by G.

CONCLUDING REMARKS

To summarize, I have tried on the basis of a number of assumptions to clarify and substantiate the claims (A) and (C) respectively, and to reject claim (B). I have been concerned in particular with the way in which rules of grammar and grammatically determined structures might be related to processes of language understanding. The assumptions (A1) to (A9) are based on empirical observations and theoretical presumptions that I take to be fairly uncontroversial. Therefore (A1) to (A9) are mainly meant to spell out the consequences of these presuppositions. The concept arrived at in this way centres around (A6), which says that language understanding is normally a multi-level parallel process involving P, S, LF, and C; this might be called the 'luxury position of language understanding', in contrast to what might be called the 'emergency position' advocated for example by Riesbeck and Schank (1978). According to this conception, which does not distinguish between LF and C, syntax is involved only if there is no other way out. It cannot be doubted that there are many ways to get around without syntax and logical form or semantics, for example in a language one does not have full command of. But it seems to be equally obvious that this is the exceptional case (presumably supported by strategies worked out in normal use of fluent language understanding). To sharpen the point, the emergency case is lacking syntax, rather than using it.

It should be obvious that (A1) to (A9) by no means outline a theory of language understanding. They rather aim at a conceptual clarification of conditions to be met in one way or other by theoretical models which attempt to account for processes of language understanding. Besides further clarification of linguistic and conceptual rules and structures, substantial assumptions as to processing operations and characteristics of storage seem to be primary candidates in this respect.

With respect to the latter, progress can be made mainly (or perhaps only) by constructing and testing models for particular aspects of processing. There are two difficulties to be overcome in such attempts, as I have tried to emphasize: first, explicit models of processing are readily tempted to identify grammatical rules with processing, thereby either discrediting linguistic competence or turning performance into the operation of a pseudo-grammar. Second, explicit modelling of particular aspects—though indispensable in principle—nevertheless tends to obscure the essential point that language understanding, though determined by well defined separate levels of structure, is a rather flexible, interactive process. This should be borne in mind.

NOTES

1. An even more extreme position ruled out by (A) would be the claim that utterances (or rather sentences) as a whole must be analysed syntactically before a semantic and pragmatic interpretation can be assigned to them. I will omit any further consideration of this possibility, as nobody could seriously maintain that the semantic interpretation of a sentence would begin only after the completion of its last constituent.
2. Of course, the assumption that, contrary to (A), speech perception must go through a stage of syntactic analysis before proceeding to semantic and pragmatic interpretation implies at least a partial refusal of (B). But the reverse does not

hold: one might assume, contrary to (B), that, normally, a full syntactic and semantic representation is developed for each perceived utterance, without rejecting the one-line nature of that process as claimed by (A).

3. One important difference is that Schank advocates fairly detailed assumptions as to the conceptual representation resulting from the process simulating language comprehension.

4. For some discussion of the distinction between C_l and C_n see Bierwisch (1979) from a linguistic point of view, and Clark (1978) from a psychological point of view.

5. I use 'contextual meaning' rather than, say, 'pragmatic structure', in order to include all kinds of dependencies on the context of use, which might include background knowledge of a general kind besides pragmatic conditions in the narrower sense.

6. I here ignore the particular problems involved in understanding written language, although the relation between phonetic and graphemic structures is anything but trivial.

7. This approach makes available the apparatus of model theoretic semantics, provided that it is construed as an account of cognitive structures and operations in the sense proposed in Bierwisch (1979). It is, however, in need of further elaboration and adaptation, if crucial problems of conceptual and perceptual representations are to be captured.

8. For some discussion, see Bierwisch (1979) and Lang (1979).

9. I do not consider the distinction in question as a true ambiguity in the lexical meaning of *book*, comparable to the ambiguity of, say, *letter* or *trial*, etc., as such ambiguities would also imply different representations on the level of logical form. It is easy to see, however, that the well-known phenomenon of backward disambiguation in cases like 'Finally, I found the paper I was supposed to write on/about' follows the same pattern of processing as the contextual interpretation in cases like sentences (9) to (11).

10. It is of no importance in the present context which of the different types of storage considered by Fodor—first in last out, first in first out, or equal access storage—is accepted.

11. Sentences like (15) also present difficulties for the clausal-processing hypothesis, incidentally. According to this hypothesis, the identification of deep structure clauses is a crucial initial step in sentence understanding. For obvious reasons, the identification of the two clauses in sentences like (15) cannot organize syntactic processing: it rather can only result from it. Marslen-Wilson *et al.* (1978) have critically analysed the clausal hypothesis from a different point of view, whose consequences need not be accepted in other respects, though.

12. For a systematic account of these groupings see Libermann and Prince (1977), Selkirk (1980), and the references cited there. It should be noted that the hierarchical structure imposed by these groupings on the phonetic feature representation developed in Chomsky and Halle (1968) does not coincide with the hierarchy of syntactic constituents to which we next turn. I cannot pursue here the intricate and highly interesting question of how prosodic and syntactic hierarchies interact in the process of sentence perception—a question that has scarcely been raised in any principled way.

13. Thus S might be derived by transformational mapping from an underlying base structure or it might be generated directly by phrase structure rules plus certain conditions on coindexing and binding (see Chomsky, 1977, p. 106, for some remarks on this alternative). S might also be taken as the last line of a Montague-type of syntactic construction tree – provided that constituency is somehow

indicated, perhaps along the lines proposed by Partee (1976, p. 64). Or it might be thought of as the output of an augmented transition network (ATN) grammar of the appropriate type. This is to mention just some of the currently discussed versions of syntactic theory. Although choosing among alternatives like these is by no means an arbitrary matter, but rather a highly significant issue of theory construction, it is of no relevance in the present context, as long as different systems provide descriptively equivalent representations for the pertinent syntactic properties.

14. Notice incidentally that it is essentially this mapping A that accounts formally for the assignment of P to s 'in accordance with the rules and conditions of G', as stipulated above. In other words, the phonetic attributes in terms of which s is interpreted are in accordance with the rules and conditions of G just because P is a value for $A(S)$ for some syntactic representation S.

15. For the sake of simplicity, I will represent S in the sequel in terms of labelled bracketings instead of tree diagrams, omitting specifications that are not directly relevant to the pertinent context.

16. The fact that (22a) is by far the preferred interpretation, overriding probably even the alleged acoustic indicators, is due to totally non-phonetic aspects of (22). See Frazier and Fodor (1978) and Wanner (1980) for alternative attempts to explain this preference in terms of general properties of syntactic processing mechanisms.

17. Actually, the trace theory of movement rules adopted in Chomsky (1977) and related work introduces information about 'earlier' syntactic representations as part of the surface structure representation itself, somewhat in the sense just contemplated with respect to P. S might depart, however, even from an enriched notion of surface structure of this type in certain respects. A case in point might be the status of so called stylistic rules, the effect of which is excluded from surface structure, but should probably be incorporated in S. Since I have no particular arguments in this respect, I leave the question open. As to the status of S, see also note 13.

18. It is not clear how close this correspondence should be, to what extent in particular the binding relations in LF are paralleled by those in S. In view of the rules that provide the mapping from S to LF, Chomsky (1980a, p. 17) makes the conjecture that LF should have the form of a syntactic phrase marker. With regard to the following considerations it seems plausible to adopt a slightly relaxed version of this conjecture to the effect that S and LF show crucial properties of syntactic phrase markers, but differ in certain other respects.

19. One version of strict correspondence in compositionality of S and LF can be taken to be the core principle of Montague grammar. Chomsky (1977, p. 197 ff. and passim) shows this claim to be unwarranted on empirical grounds.

20. Actually, Wexler and Culicover (1980) consider the problem within the context of the so-called standard theory, where LF is supposed to be related to deep structure rather than to surface structure. In principle, however, their considerations carry over to the framework adopted here presupposing enriched surface structures, that can directly be interpreted semantically.

21. One of Fodor's main arguments against componential analysis (or 'definition', as he calls it) relates to the speed of comprehension which does not plausibly allow for representations with complex internal structure of lexical units, all the more so, as differences in compositional complexity are apparently not paralleled by differences in comprehension time. (*He sought it* does not seem to be more difficult to comprehend than *He found it*, although *seek* would be componentially more complex than *find*, in fact, *seek* would have the lexical

representation of *find* as a proper part of its meaning.) Fodor (1975, p. 150 ff.) proposes to account for these observations by stipulating two systems: a sentence understanding system, which assigns representations in *LF* to speech signals, and a logical system which derives potential inferences from these representations by means of meaning postulates. The understanding system is quick and basically on-line, the inferential system operates off-line and without temporal limitations. There are various problems with these proposals, though. Notice first of all that by the same type of argument, not only semantic decomposition, but also analysis in terms of phonetic features would have to be refuted, i.e. phonetic feature matrices would have to be replaced by certain global representations related to each other by something like rules of phonetic similarity. Secondly, the assumption of two different systems for comprehension and inferencing respectively is certainly a fairly plausible one (corresponding in some sense to the distinction between spontaneous and 'higher order' understanding envisioned above). It seems to be rather dubious, however, that inferences are defined only—or even primarily— over *LF*, rather than over the contextual interpretation *C*. I have mentioned these issues, as they relate directly to aspects of language understanding, indicating that the controversy concerning the two approaches in question is anything but settled. I will argue in Section 6 however, that at least some lexical decomposition must be assumed for *LF*.

22. The pertinent literature is too ramified to even be listed. For a recent overview of some of the core problems from the point of view of a unified formal treatment, see Karttunen and Peters (1978). I will not adopt here the formal details of their proposal, but I follow essentially the spirit underlying it. Karttunen and Peters, among others, argue that instead of the notion of presupposition the notion of conventional implicature is more appropriate to capture the relevant phenomena. Although this shift will probably allow for relevant generalizations, I will stick to the traditional terminology.

23. Notice incidentally that the structure [*PR*; *AS*] of *LF* in a sense relativizes the claim that *LF* is a strictly hierarchical structure. Strictly speaking, *LF* must be considered as a set of hierarchies. As nothing of any relevance in the present context follows from this modification, I will continue to consider *LF* as a categorized, unordered hierarchy.

24. Even terminology is extremely varied and sometimes confusing with respect to this level of representation. Thus, whereas Chomsky (1977) distinguishes logical form and 'fuller representations of meaning', which he calls semantic representations, determined by logical form plus other cognitive systems, Jackendoff (1977) does not seems to envisage such a distinction, in spite of otherwise similar conceptions, since what he calls conceptual structure encompasses both logical form and additional cognitive aspects. Difficulties in telling apart similarities and differences in underlying assumptions arise with respect to Fodor's (1975) 'Language of thought', the conceptual representations of Miller and Johnson-Laird (1976), and most of the pertinent work in artificial intelligence. A fairly clear distinction parallel to the one assumed here is expressed in Wexler and Culicover (1980, p. 459 ff.) in terms of semantic representation and mental world, where the former corresponds to our level of *LF*, and the latter ot our level of *C*. Similarly, the more recent work of Johnson-Laird (1980) on 'mental models' or 'discourse models' in Johnson-Laird and Garnham (1980) is fairly close to the notion of contextual meaning *C*, based on general and situational knowledge adduced in interpreting an utterance.

25. These operations would probably include rules of inference and deduction, as most logical operations (in the sense mentioned in footnote 21) are probably

based on representations of this level. See Johnson-Laird (1980) for illustrative examples pointing to this conclusion.

26. The latter alternative has been discussed within a somewhat different framework in an interesting paper by Dahl (1977). According to Dahl's proposal, LF can be interpreted either as a kind of checklist, identifying models that fit the checking conditions, or as an instruction to build up a model according to the conditions in question. Although the two perspectives are equivalent in many respects, as Dahl points out, they allow for a useful distinction, as we will see immediately.

27. In fact, they seem to violate even the much more abstract principle of compositionality in the sense of Frege, as can be seen from (38): $V(LEAVE, c)$ depends on $V(UNIVERSITY, c)$ and vice versa, which is at variance with demands on compositionality of interpretation on any reasonable assumptions about the details of LF.

28. Although the various components of grammar cover only the representations P, S, and LF as well as the mappings A and I, the problem carries over directly to C and the mapping V -just as to any other cognitive system, such as visual perception, music, arithmetic computation, etc. The following discussion of grammar and process therefore applies equally to mental models and the mapping V into these models.

29. It should be noted that although the dispute around the DTC is centered syntactic transformations, an even stronger case can be made for phonological rules. Compare for example German *Bottich* and *zottig*, whose phonetic representations are [botiç] and [cotiç] respectively. As the latter is derived from underlying [cotig] by final devoicing and spirantization. which do not apply to the former, *zottig* would have to be perceptually more complex than *Bottich*, while the plural forms *zottige* and *Bottiche* would not be different in this respect, which is clearly an absurd prediction. More generally, even a superficial glance at phonological derivations clearly shows that there is no correlation whatsoever between derivational and perceptual complexity. It seems to be obvious that similar considerations apply to other levels of representation and mappings between them. (Notice that this casts additional doubts on Fodor's objections against componential analysis mentioned in footnote 21). Notice furthermore that the generality of these considerations renders it irrelevant that modifications with respect to the place of transformations in syntactic theory have drastically reduced the impact of the original version of DTC for independent reasons.

30. This does not hold in the same sense, say, for the parsing system proposed by Frazier and Fodor (1978). This system accounts for the construction of only one aspects of S, viz. its tree structure, in terms of two general assumptions: first the construction of S proceeds in two stages, and second the primary stage is limited to the capacity of up to six words, which are 'packaged' for further integration on the second stage. The system does not account for binding relations of wh-phrases, etc., and does not form, therefore, an autonomous mechanism of syntactic processing. In other words, it attempts to explain certain preferences in assigning categorized tree structures to strings of words by two conditions on processing, which, however, do not constitute a self-contained mechanism. (For further comments see note 34.) This attempt might not be fully successful, as Wanner (1980) points out, but it does not automatically fall under objections that are to be raised against (D).

31. It should be noted that this observation is by no means at variance with the comments made earlier in connection with cases of self-embedding like (6). The difficulties with (50) and (51) are clearly syntactic in origin, as can be seen from the intelligibility of (50') and (51'), which are semantically identical to (50) and (51), respectively, differing only in that they are free of syntactic self-embedding.

(50′) The teacher left who the boy mentioned who you visited.
(51′) The ice cream melted that the boy brought who you mentioned.

The point is that semantic connections might help to some extent to overcome syntactic processing difficulties.

32. Suppose for example that phonetic processing of s is organized as a word-by-word process in some sense, involving word identification as a somehow autonomous operation unit. It is immediately obvious that this would have to be construed as a fairly complex aggregate of operations (even if we ignore for the moment that word identification accomplishes at the same time phonetic and partial syntactic and semantic interpretation). According to the 'cohort' theory of Marslen-Wilson and Tyler (1980), identification of the initial part of a word activates a 'cohort' of related words, which is then stepwise reduced until the target is eventually met. Hence not only a sequence of more elementary operations is involved, but probably a fairly complex array of partially parallel operations. Other models propose different aggregates of elementary operations for word recognition. Let us assume for the sake of argument, however, that phonetic word identification is achieved by operations O_i in the sense of (A8), such that $t = t_1 t_2 \ldots t_k$ is the processing time for mapping s into P where $P = W_1 W_2 \ldots W_k$ is a sequence of word forms and W_i is identified by O_i. We need not assume that the t_i are of identical length, but the O_i should be considered as self-contained operation units, whatever their internal complexity might turn out to be. We might assume that t is related to the time coordinate t' of s in the following way:

(i) For all time points t_j' of t' there is a corresponding time point t_j of t such that $t_j = t_j' - r_j$ where the retardation r varies within very narrow limits.

In other words, we assume that identification of P proceeds roughly synchronously with s subject to some retardation parameter r. These assumptions are contrary to fact in many respects and hold at best if P is to be construed as a list of isolated word forms. In all cases of natural understanding of utterances the O_i are not self-contained, and there are clear effects of anticipation and delay (besides the parameter r) influencing the processing time t as opposed to t' of s. Nevertheless, (i) can serve as a first approximation to the way along which linearity of representations, temporal ordering of processing operations, and time characteristics of s are related to each other. From this point of view, it might be taken to be a crucial task for any theory of actual processes of language understanding to account for systematic deviations form (i) in terms of intervening relations among the O_i as well as between the O_i and higher-order operations.

33. An extensive study of principles underlying sequential processing of hierarchically organized structures (called 'plans') is provided by the seminal book of Miller, Galanter, and Pribram (1960). According to the principles developed there, (54) would be processed in the following way:

(55) (c)

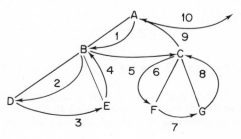

34. This, by the way, constitutes another crucial difference between ATN grammars and the parsing system of Frazier and Fodor (1978) mentioned in note 30: while ATN grammars crucially depend on sequential operation according to (52), no particular claim is inherent in Frazier and Fodor's two-stage system. It does not specify any sequential or parallel processing, but rather defines certain boundary conditions limiting the array of one type of operations.

35. We need not spell out the details. The basic idea is simply this: for (52), the principle (i) of note 32 is to be construed in such a way that t includes the time intervals of all the operations in the sequence, not just those identifying terminal elements. As a consequence, the correspondence between time points of t and t' will be more 'condensed' for some intervals than for others. For instance, if DEFG of (54) were word forms corresponding to stretches of s with time intervals t'_1 to t'_4, then t'_1 would correspond to t_1 of O_1, while $t'_2t'_3$ would correspond to $t_2t_3t_4$, and t_4' would correspond to $t_5t_6t_7$. For (53), the correspondence defined in (i) is to be extended to n overlapping sequences of operation times, which in turn are subject to the inherent time relations hinted at with respect to O_{1i}, O_{2j}, and O_{3k} above.

36. In fact, the idea, rejected by claim (A), that understanding proceeds by first identifying S, then constructing its semantic representation, and finally a contextual interpretation must be construed as a particular version of (52), while the parallel processing implicit in (A) is a version of (53), applied to $\langle P, S, LF, C \rangle$.

37. To clarify the point further, I should add that under particular demands rules may be turned under particular demands into (complex) operations. Thus if in a grammatical task a sentence like *John is here* is turned into *Is John here?*, the question transformation is turned into a part of a complex real-time operation. Notice, however, that this 'application' of a grammatical rule must be clearly kept apart from its original status as part of the grammar defining possible targets for language processing. In fact, it is not only based on a derived interpretation of a grammatical rule, it constitutes a type of mental processing that must be sharply distinguished from relying on the rules of grammar in spontaneous processes of language understanding. Although this is all too obvious, the neglect of the distinction has caused a lot of confusion. This is even more consequential, as there are less clear cases of a merging between rules and operations. To take an interesting point, logical inferences (defined over C and/or LF) in the sense proposed by Fodor (1975) (cf. note 21) might be operations that turn into real-time operations. More generally, we might envisage a distinction between operations that produce structural characteristics of mental states and operations that operate over such structural representations. It is only the latter into which rules of grammar (or other cognitive systems) can be turned. They clearly presuppose the former type of operations.

38. Notice that if we were to represent temporal and operational connections more strictly, (59) would have to be turned into (59'):

(59')

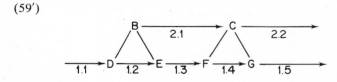

Although there is still some kind of parallel processing, as e.g. both $O_{1.3}$ and $O_{2.1}$ are temporally connected to $O_{1.2}$, the flow of operations resemble more that of (55a) than (55b), thus obscuring the very idea of parallel processing.

39. If I am not mistaken, the proposal of Arbib and Caplan (1979) to develop a computational notion of neurolinguistics is best to be understood as giving a bit more precise content to the general properties of Q in the sense developed here. Seen in this perspective, the basic idea of Arbib and Caplan can even be reconciled with the objections that Kean and Smith (1979) have raised—correctly, as it seems to me—against the undifferentiated, global character of the model, claiming that a modular conception of mental processes is to be preferred on both methodological and empirical grounds. The point is that there might be global characteristics of Q on the one hand, while G, which is strictly modular, imposes modularity on Q in an indirect way because of the connection stipulated by (A7″).

40. This is not quite correct, if we take the initial state of an operation into account. Thus $O_{1.2}$ might be subsequent to $O_{1.1}$ just because D defines its initial state OS. Suppose therefore, that the initial state of all operations $O_{1.1}$ applying in (59) is some structural feature F which is part of all the terminal elements D, E, F, G.

41. Thus both (55a) and (55b) are strictly on-line, while (55c), and therefore processing in ATN grammars in general, is not.

42. For a provisional survey of short-term memory for different levels of structure see Bierwisch (1975).

43. Languages seem to differ with respect to the amount of structurally conditioned intermediate storage they tend to tolerate. Thus the 'splitting' of lexical items in German by finite verb movement in main clauses as exemplified in (64) often produces rather extreme cases where even word identification ceases to be strictly on-line. A comparable phenomenon is produced in English by particle movement in cases like *put NP about*, which is, however, of a much more restricted range, allowing only for simple, non-complex NP's to intervene.

44. A kind of general display is also inherent in the two stage system of Frazier and Fodor (1978) with the additional assumption, however, that the first 'packaging' stage is restricted to about six syntactic primes. This, then, is a third difference of this system as compared to ATN grammars which crucially rely on push-down storage. (For other differences see notes 30 and 34.)

45. There might be intermediate parts that are complete, though. The subject NP *der Pianist* . . . , for example, is not affected by the incompleteness of the verb *hört* (*auf*).

46. The problems I am ignoring here are the proper semantic categorization of noun phrases, the analysis of determiners, and the status of plural noun phrases. I simply continue to categorize noun phrases semantically as *n*. For the sake of perspicuity, $\langle p/n \rangle$ is abbreviated by *cn* (for 'common noun').

47. Actually, (78) is a somewhat misleading simplification in certain respects. A more careful analysis would have to specify the different dimensions on which comparison is based in *large* as opposed to *high, long*, etc. Thus a closer approximation would be:

   (i) $\hat{x}[\hat{y}[[[\text{GREATER}[\text{SIZE-OF}[\text{AVERAGE } x]]][\text{SIZE-OF } y]] \text{ AND } [x \, y]]]$

Here x is a variable of category *cn*, as in (78), and y is of category *n*. We can ignore, however, these refinements, as they do not affect the point at issue.

48. For a more careful, though still incomplete analysis of the syntactic and semantic aspects involved see Karttunen and Peters (1978), whose ideas I follow with slight simplifications.

49. There is a crucial connection between main stress and focus, although the relation is much more complicated in general. Full discussion of the issues involved would go far beyond the present paper.

50. One could, of course, easily produce similar effects by, say, presenting subjects with locally masked speech signals. Systematic variation of structural properties of masked loci could furthermore be used to identify particular conditions on processing. The remaining difference is that between natural and experimental setting.
51. It should be pointed out that this conclusion is not weakened by the accidental character of the data. Methodologically, the existential claim can be substantiated even by one single convincing example. This would not mean to deny the want for more data, though.

ACKNOWLEDGEMENTS

This paper has greatly benefited from discussion with William Marslen-Wilson, whose ideas and exciting experimental findings provided the main challenge to think the issue of on-line processing over. Needless to say that he can't be responsible for faults in my divergent views. I am also grateful to Marie-Louise Kean, Herb Clark, Ino Flores d'Arcais, Hans Geissler, Phil Johnson-Laird, and Walter Kintsch for discussions and comments.

REFERENCES

Ajdukiewicz, K. Die syntaktische Konnexität, *Studia Philosophica*, 1935, **1**, 1–27.
Arbib, M. A., and Caplan, D. Neurolinguistics must be computational. *The Behavioral and Brain Sciences*, 1979, **2**, 449–460.
Bever, T. G. The cognitive basis for linguistic structures. In J. R. Hayes (Ed.), *Cognition and the Development of Language*. New York: Wiley, 1970.
Bierwisch, M. Syntactic features in morphology. In *To Honor Roman Jakobson*. The Hague: Mouton, 1967.
Bierwisch, M. Psycholinguistik. Interdependenz kognitiver Prozesse und linguistischer Strukturen. *Zeitschrift für Psychologie*, 1975, **183**, 1–52.
Bierwisch, M. Wörtliche Bedeutung—eine pragmatische Gretchenfrage. In G. Grewendort (Ed.), *Sprechakttheorie und Semantik*. Frankfurt/Main: Suhrkamp, 1979.
Bierwisch, M. Utterance meaning and mental states. In F. Klix and J. Hoffman (Eds), *Memory and Cognition*. Berlin: Deutscher Verlag der Wissenschaften, 1980(a).
Bierwisch, M. Semantic structures and illocutionary force. In J. R. Searle, F. Kiefer, and M. Bierwisch (Eds), *Speech Act Theory and Pragmatics*. Dordrecht: Reidel, 1980(b).
Bierwisch, M. Sprache und Gedächtnis: Ergebnisse und Probleme. In M. Bierwisch (Ed.), *Psychologische Effekte sprachlicher Strukturkomponenten*. München: Fink; and Berlin: Akademie-Verlag, 1980(c).
Chomsky, N. *Essays on Form and Interpretation*. Amsterdam: North-Holland, 1977.
Chomsky, N. On binding. *Linguistic Inquiry*. 1980(a), **11**, 1–46.
Chomsky, N. *Rules and Representations*. New York: Columbia University Press, 1980(b).
Chomsky, N., and Halle, M. *The Sound Pattern of English*. New York: Harper & Row, 1968.
Chomsky, N., and Lasnik, H. Filters and control. *Linguistic Inquiry*, 1977, **8**, 425–504.
Clark, H. H. Inferring what is meant. In W. J. M. Levelt and G. B. Flores d'Arcais (Eds), *Studies in the Perception of Language*. Chichester: Wiley, 1978.

Dahl, Ö. Games and models. In Ö. Dahl (Ed.), *Logic, Pragmatics and Grammar*. Göteborg: Department of Linguistics, University of Göteborg, 1977.

Fodor, J. A. *The Language of Thought*. New York: Crowell, 1975.

Fodor, J. A., and Garrett, M. Some reflections on competence and performance. In J. Lyons and R. J. Wales (Eds), *Psycholinguistic Papers*. Edinburgh: Edinburgh University Press, 1966.

Fodor, J. D. Parsing strategies and constraints on transformations. *Linguistic Inquiry*, 1978, **9**, 427–473.

Frazier, L., and Fodor, J. D. The sausage machine: A new two-stage parsing model. *Cognition*, 1978, **6**, 291–325.

Jackendoff, R. X̄ syntax: A study of phrase structure. *Linguistic Inquiry Monograph*, 2. Cambridge, Mass.: M.I.T. Press, 1977.

Jarvella, R. J., and Herman, S. J. Clause structure of sentences and speech processing. *Perception and Psychophysics*, 1972, **11**, 381–384.

Johnson-Laird, P. Mental models in cognitive science. *Cognitive Science*, 1980, **4**, 71–115.

Johnson-Laird, P., and Garnham, A. Descriptions and discourse models. *Linguistics and Philosophy*, 1980, **3**, 371–393.

Karttunen, L., and Peters, S. Conventional implicature. In D. A. Dinneen and Choon-Kyu Oh (Eds), *Syntax and Semantics*, Vol. 11. *Presupposition*. New York: Academic Press, 1978.

Kean, M. L., and Smith, G. E. Commentary on 'Neurolinguistics must be computational' by M. A. Arbib and D. Caplan. *The Brain and Behavioral Sciences*, 1979, **2**, 469–470.

Lang, E. Zum Status der Satzadverbiale. *Slovo a Slovesnost*, 1979, **40**, 200–213.

Levelt, W. J. M., and G. B. Flores d'Arcais (Eds), *Studies in the Perception of Language*. Chichester: Wiley, 1978.

Libermann, M., and Prince, A. On stress and linguistic rhythm. *Linguistic Inquiry*, 1977, **8**, 249–336.

Marslen-Wilson, W. D. Sentence perception as an interactive parallel process. *Science*, 1975, **189**, 226–228.

Marslen-Wilson, W. D., Tyler, L. K., and Seidenberg, M. Sentence processing and the clause boundary. In W. J. M. Levelt and G. B. Flores d'Arcais (Eds), *Studies in the Perception of Language*. Chichester: Wiley, 1978.

Marslen-Wilson, W. D., and Tyler, L. K. The temporal structure of spoken language understanding. *Cognition*, 1980, **8**, 1–71.

Miller, G. A. Semantic relations among words. In M. Halle, J. Bresnan, and G. A. Miller (Eds), *Linguistic Theory and Psychological Reality*. Cambridge, Mass.: M.I.T. Press, 1978.

Miller, G. A., Galanter, E., and Pribram, K. H. *Plans and the Structure of Behavior*. New York: Holt, Rinehart and Winston, 1960.

Miller, G. A., and Johnson-Laird, P. *Language and Perception*. Cambridge, Mass.: Harvard University Press, 1976.

Newell, A., and Simon, H. A. *Human Problem Solving*. Englewood Cliffs, N.J.: Prentice-Hall, 1972.

Nooteboom, S. G., Brokx, J. P. L., and de Rooij, J. J. Contributions of prosody to speech perception. In W. J. M. Levelt and G. B. Flores d'Arcais (Eds), *Studies in the Perception of Language*. Chichester: Wiley, 1978.

Nunberg, G. The non-uniqueness of semantic solutions: Polysemy. *Linguistics and Philosophy*, 1979, **3**, 143–184.

Partee, B. H. Some transformational extension of Montague grammar. In B. H. Partee (Ed.), *Montague Grammar*. New York: Academic Press, 1976.

Riesbeck, C. K., and Schank, R. C. Comprehension by computer: Expectation-based analysis of sentences in context. In W. J. M. Levelt and G. B. Flores d'Arcais (Eds), *Studies in the Perception of Language*. Chichester: Wiley, 1978.

Selkirk, E. O. The role of prosodic categories in English word stress. *Linguistic Inquiry*, 1980, **11**, 563–605.

Wanner, E. The ATN and the sausage machine: Which one is baloney? *Cognition*, 1980, **8**, 209–225.

Weigl, E., and Bierwisch, M. Neuropsychology and linguistics: Topics of common research. *Foundations of Language*, 1970, **6**, 1–18.

Wexler, K., and Culicover, P. W. *Formal Principles of Language Acquistion*. Cambridge, Mass.: M.I.T. Press, 1980.

The Process of Language Understanding
Edited by G. B. Flores d'Arcais and R. J. Jarvella
© 1983 John Wiley & Sons Ltd.

5

Great Expectations: Context Effects During Sentence Processing

DONALD J. FOSS and JAMES R. ROSS

University of Texas at Austin, U.S.A.

It is a truism that context affects the processing of sentences and that it does so at many points. For example, determining the reference of a pronoun or of a definite description is often dependent upon the surrounding linguistic context; so too is determining the illocutionary force of an utterance. In this paper we will concentrate upon a commonly studied problem: the role of prior linguistic context on the processing of subsequent lexical items.

It is generally conceded that (within limits) processing a word within a sentence is easier if that word has been preceded by a semantically related one. The limits of the phenomenon are important, as is the theoretical framework within which such facilitation effects are explained. Our aims here are: (1) to evaluate critically the existing models concerned with the facilitation effect; (2) to propose a new theoretical framework within which to examine semantic facilitation effects; and (3) to present data difficult or impossible to reconcile with existing models but consistent with the one suggested here. Along the way we will have something to say about the locus of the facilitation effect, an issue of some current interest.

THE PHENOMENON

For over a decade it has been known that the processing of a word occurring in a word list , e.g., *nurse*, is speeded if that word is preceded by a semantically related one, e.g., *doctor* (Meyer and Schvaneveldt, 1971). Subsequent research has investigated some of the properties of this phenomenon, in particular its time course. It has been shown, for example, that related words can be presented with a very short interstimulus interval while still obtaining a facilitation effect (e.g. Neely, 1977). It has also been suggested that the processing of a word is slowed (inhibited) when immediately preceded by a semantically unrelated one.

More important to our present concern, there is evidence that the processing of a word in a sentence is easier if that word is preceded by a semantically related one. For example, in one such study Blank and Foss (1978) presented sentences like (1) and (2) below to listeners and asked them to comprehend the sentences and to respond by pushing a button to a specified word-initial target phoneme that occurred immediately after the word of interest (phoneme monitoring task). It is assumed that the reaction time (RT) to make the response is directly related to the momentary processing difficulty experienced by the comprehender at the point where the target phoneme occurs. In these examples the critical word is *eye* and the target phoneme is /p/.

(1) The drunk winked his bloodshot eye probably without even knowing it.
(2) The drunk scratched his aching eye probably without even knowing it.

Blank and Foss found that the RT to the target phoneme was significantly shorter in (1), which has the related semantic context, than in (2).

The facilitation of lexical processing has been observed in sentences using a variety of techniques including naming latency for a word in a sentence (e.g. Stanovich and West, 1979), mis-pronunciation detection (e.g. Cole and Jakimik, 1979), shadowing (e.g. Marslen-Wilson and Welsh, 1978), cross-modal lexical decision (e.g. Swinney, Onifer, Prather, and Hirshkowitz, 1979), and a new technique called phoneme-triggered lexical decision (Blank, 1980). These results are not surprising given both the earlier cited data from experiments using lists and our common sense beliefs about language processing. Although the semantic facilitation effect is a robust one in the sense that it has been observed in a number of studies using a variety of techniques, the mechanism(s) underlying the effect are not yet clear.

THE MODELS

Numerous models attempting to account for the facts of semantic facilitation of lexical processing have been proposed. For the present we will merely sketch the outlines of the dominant approaches; the reason for such cursory treatment will become clear presently. The most influential class of models concerned with semantic facilitation (models of spreading activation) puts the burden of the effect on the organization of the mental lexicon. Additionally, assumptions are made about how information is shared among the items stored there. One such model was proposed by Collins and Loftus (1975). They argued that concepts sharing semantic properties are more highly interconnected with one another in the mental lexicon than are concepts sharing few properties. When a concept is activated by outside stimuli, the related concepts, that is, those sharing many properties with it, are also activated to some extent. When a later stimulus is consistent with one of the activated concepts, it becomes available more rapidly than if the prior semantically related word had not occurred. Collins and Loftus provided a set of conditions limiting this generalization; in particular, they proposed that the activation spreading throughout the mental lexicon is reduced as it passes through each item in the semantic network. These important subsidiary assumptions need not concern us for now, however. A model based on spreading activation was also proposed by Meyer and Schvaneveldt (1971), among others.

Meyer and Schvaneveldt proposed and rejected another model to account for their findings in list studies. According to this view, which they dubbed a 'location shift' model, semantically related words are stored 'nearby' one another, more or less analogous to related words being on the same page in the mental dictionary. When a word on a page is retrieved, the dictionary stays open to that page. If the next word to be looked up is on that page, retrieval is rapid; if it is on a different page, retrieval is slower since the page must be turned to a new location. If a third word occurs that is related to the first (i.e. the first and third are on the same page), with an unrelated word in between, the third one will not be found any more rapidly than another, unrelated word since the relevant page is no longer immediately available to the search mechanism. The location shift model was rejected by Meyer and Schvaneveldt because they found that the time to respond to the third word of a trio was somewhat faster when it was related to the first word than when it was unrelated, even when an unrelated word intervened. We will have occasion to consider this model again later.

Another model that speaks to the facilitation effect was proposed by Forster (1979). He argues that the language processor is composed of a set of autonomous components—among them lexical, syntactic, and message processors—organized such that 'lexical processing is unaffected by either syntactic or semantic context' (p. 42). Thus, according to Forster, calculations carried out by higher-level processors cannot affect those carried out by those at lower levels. He proposed that lexical access occurs via one of two independent access files (one phonetic, the other orthographic), and that the searching and matching processes take place within these files. Access speed is affected by the frequency of the word and by its (phonetic or orthographic) form. Thus, his search model of lexical access would seem to preclude a spreading activation account of context effects (see also Rubenstein, Lewis, and Rubenstein, 1971). However, even Forster tentatively adopts such an explanation, suggesting 'that the associative [facilitation] effect occurs at the lexical (central) level, and is produced by the network of cross-references defined over lexical entries' (1979, p 73). Forster concludes that such interconnections are required in order to account for some sentence production effects, but that the interconnections are available for use as a back-up system for word recognition. We will discuss again later the claim about the autonomy of the components in Forster's system. For our present purposes, though, Forster's views fit tidily within the class of spreading activation models.

Perhaps the most influential model in the area of context effects is due to Posner and Snyder (1975). Their model is not concerned directly with the principles of semantic organization nor with the mechanisms of search and retrieval (though it has indirect implications for them), but rather with the attention processes involved in contextual facilitation and inhibition. Posner and Snyder proposed that the effects of context are due to two distinct mechanisms. First, there is a very fast acting 'spreading activation' component. This mechanism does not require attentional resources and it leads only to facilitation of related items, not to inhibition of unrelated ones. Naturally, it requires a lexicon organized in a fashion such that spreading activation can operate. Second, there is a slower acting attentional component: it requires the subject's resources, does interfere with ongoing activities that require attention, and leads to inhibition of words unrelated to the word receiving such attention. Considerable work has been influenced by, and is generally supportive of, this two-factor theory of the context effect (e.g. Neely, 1977; Fischler and Bloom, 1979; Stanovich and West, 1979). We will include the two-factor theory among the general class of spreading activation models since that is how the first factor, at least, is said to operate.

With the exception of the location shift model, then, all of the above described systems operate on the principle of spreading activation. In fact, each of them is really the schema for a model, since there are many particular versions that could be built consistent with the views proposed by the various theorists. Indeed, this flexibility is part of the difficulty involved in painting a single picture of the mechanisms underlying the context effect. Consequently, it is difficult to find data that will wash out one of the models; they are generally easy to retouch.

The approach that we will take to the problem here is not to try pitting one of the spreading activation models against the others, but instead to describe a property common to a sub-class of all such models and to investigate that property. We believe that each of the spreading activation models cited above has an instantiation (often the commonly accepted one) that is consistent with the following description.

MODELS OF LEXICAL–LEXICAL ACTIVATION AND AN ALTERNATIVE

When a stimulus occurs, certain subsets of words in the mental lexicon that are compatible with the stimulus become directly available. According to the spreading activation models we have just reviewed, an additional set of items—those semantically related to the stimulus word(s)—become active.

Let us say that these latter are 'indirectly accessible' from the stimulus. If the next word in a sentence is among those that have become indirectly accessible, its processing is speeded. Further, according to some models, if the next word is not among those that are indirectly accessible, its processing may be inhibited.

As noted, numerous mechanisms and processes may actualize the above description. For the present we are not concerned with these variants but with the fact that versions of each model propose that certain words are indirectly accessible given a single input stimulus word. Each theorist could modify his or her model such that this characterization might be strained. What we are describing is a subset of models within each of the theoretical frameworks. This set can be specified more precisely (see Foss, in preparation), but the present description should suffice for the present. Let us call all models that fit the above characterization lexical–lexical activation (LLA) models. The question that we want to raise is this: is the appropriate model of lexical facilitation a member of the class of LLA models? Our thesis is that the correct answer is no.

Let us consider briefly an alternative sentence processing schema. According to this alternative, listeners rapidly calculate the semantic interpretation (or semantic value; Lewis, 1972) of the phrases or syntactically coherent sub-phrases that they hear. Once the semantic interpretation of a phrase has been computed, the comprehender examines memory to see whether a representation of that interpretation exists there and, if so, the set of concepts and words semantically or pragmatically related to it are then indirectly accessible. Thus, the items that are accessible are those related to the high-level interpretation of the phrase (or higher constituent). Importantly, we suppose that this set need not overlap at all with the set of items that are indirectly accessible from the individual words composing the phrase. Thus, the set of words that are indirectly accessible from a phrase may be different from the set that is indirectly accessible from its constituent words (see Foss and Harwood, 1975, for some evidence supporting this view).

At times a late occurring word in a sentence will be related both to the semantic interpretation of the prior word and to the semantic interpretation that has been computed for the preceding phrase or higher-level unit. In this case we expect facilitation of that next word. When such an event occurs, it will appear as though the processing of the next word has been facilitated by the just prior one. But according to the present view, this appearance is deceiving; the operative relation is that between the semantically interpreted phrase and the next word.

Let us suppose, then, that the next word in a sentence is related to the last word of the preceding phrase, but not to the interpretation of the complete phrase. In this case our schema predicts that the processing of that next word will not be facilitated, a prediction counter to that derived from all LLA models. According to such models the processing of the next word should be speeded because that word is indirectly accessible from the one just preceding it. It is possible to devise a test to examine whether LLA models or the alternative schema presented here is the appropriate one. Experiment 1 was designed to be such a test.

Experiment 1

All LLA models predict that the processing of a word like *camera* will be facilitated if a listener has just processed a closely related word such as *photographer*, since the former is indirectly accessible from the latter. There is no reason to expect that facilitation will occur if *camera* is immediately preceded by a more neutral word such as *man*. In Experiment 1, subjects were presented with a number of trials, each consisting of three sentences composing a very short story or vignette. The materials were presented auditorily and the listeners were asked to comprehend them and to carry out the phoneme monitoring task, pushing a button when one of the words on the trial began with a phoneme that was specified in advance of the trial. We were interested in the relative amount of time needed to process a critical word (e.g. *camera*) in the story. The word carrying the target phoneme occurred immediately after the critical word.

Two independent variables were manipulated. One involved the word just prior to the critical word: it was either semantically related to the critical word (e.g. *photographer's*) or relatively neutral with respect to it (e.g. *man's*). Actually, the words *photographer* and *man* occurred twice in the respective sentences, as can be seen by inspecting examples (3)–(6). The second variable involved what we will call a context or setting word. On half the trials the first sentence contained a neutral context word (e.g. *workroom*). On the other half of the trials the first sentence contained a context word that was biased (e.g. *bakery*). Neutral context words were chosen such that the comprehender could reasonably still attend to or focus upon a typical characteristic of the actor (e.g. a photographer in a workroom encourages the interpretation that photographic equipment is involved). Biased words were chosen so that the comprehender would compute an interpretation of the sentence that was not closely related to the typical characteristics of the actor. For example, in (6) the listener is told essentially that the photographer is in the bakery. The rest of the vignette, up to the word *camera*, permits the listener to continue interpreting the input as having to do primarily with aspects of the setting (e.g. it is bakery related) and not with the canonical aspects of a photographer. When *photographer's* occurs in (6) we believe that words semantically related to it will not be readily accessible and therefore will not be more rapidly processed than in the control sentence (5). The listener will be prepared to process rapidly terms related to bakeries, not photographers, since bakery terms will be indirectly accessible from the interpretation of the high-level semantic analysis of the material up to that point. In contrast, when *photographer's* occurs in (4), words related to it will nearly all be rapidly accessible since they also will be in the set of items indirectly accessible from the high-level semantic representation. In the case of example (4) it is likely that *camera* is in both sets; hence, its processing will be facilitated relative to the neutral sentence (3). We anticipate, then, that the time to process *camera* (and hence to respond to the target phoneme, which is /g/ in these examples) will be faster in (4) than in (3); and, importantly, that processing time will *not* be faster in (6) than in (5).

(3) Time spent looking over things in the workroom was always pleasurable to the man. The sights were very enticing. It was clear that the man's camera gave him an ideal means of capturing pleasant memories.

(4) Time spent looking over things in the workroom was always pleasurable to the photographer. The sights were very enticing. It was clear that the photographer's camera gave him an ideal means of capturing pleasant memories.

(5) Time spent looking over things in the bakery was always pleasurable to the man. The sights were very enticing. It was clear that the man's camera gave him an ideal means of capturing pleasant memories.

(6) Time spent looking over things in the bakery was always pleasurable to the photographer. The sights were very enticing. It was clear that the photographer's camera gave him an ideal means of capturing pleasant memories.

It is important to underscore the critical prediction here. All LLA models predict that subjects will process *camera* more rapidly in (6) than in (5) since it will have been preceded by a semantically related word from which it is indirectly accessible. We hypothesize that there will be no facilitation in this case.

Method

Twenty-four experimental items were constructed, each consisting of three sentences. Each item had four versions: the word just prior to the critical word was either semantically related or neutral with respect to it; and crossed with this variable, the context (setting) word was either neutral or biased *away* from the sense of the critical word. Four material sets were constructed. Each material set contained 24 experimental items, six in each condition. Across the four material sets, each experimental item occurred in all four conditions. Twenty-six filler items were also included in each material set: 15

did not contain the target specified for that trial, while 11 varied the target position, sometimes putting it in the first or second sentence of the trial. Each filler item was similar in style to the experimental items.

The experiment was, then, a 2 × 2 × 4 factorial with the first two variables within subjects and the third (materials) variable between subjects. Sixty undergraduates from the University of Texas at Austin participated in the study, fifteen in each material set.

The subjects were given instructions and a short set of practice trials before the experiment proper. The materials were presented binaurally over the headphones. Immediately after the experiment subjects were given a twenty-item written recognition test; half of the items had been heard earlier and half had not. The subjects were tested in groups of varying size from one to six; each subject was seated in a booth out of sight of the others.

Results

The mean RTs for the subjects in each of the four conditions are shown in Table 5.1. Overall, there was no main effect due to the type of word (related or neutral) that immediately preceded the critical word. The effect of context (biased vs neutral) was significant by subject ($F(1,56) = 5.37, p < 0.03$), but only marginally significant by item ($F(1,23) = 3.05, p < 0.10$). The more important comparison for our purposes concerns the interaction of these two variables. This interaction was significant both by subjects ($F(1,56) = 7.10, p < 0.001$) and by items ($F(1,23) = 4.78, p < 0.05$).

Inspection of Table 5.1 will show that when the sentence context was neutral (e.g., the *workroom* sentences), the presence of the semantically related word just prior to the critical word led to faster RTs than did the neutral word (534 msec vs 561 msec). This difference was significant by subjects ($p < 0.02$) though not by items. Such a difference has been observed in other experiments using considerably different materials (e.g. Blank and Foss, 1978), so we are still prepared to say that the effect is robust. However, when the context was biased away from the agent of the sentence (e.g. the *bakery* cases), the presence of a related word (e.g. *photographer*) just prior to

Table 5.1 Mean phoneme monitoring reaction times (msec), Experiment 1

Context	Just prior word	
	Neutral (e.g. man's)	Related (e.g. photographer's)
Neutral (e.g. workroom)	561	534
Biased (e.g. bakery)	558	572

the critical word (e.g. *camera*) did not facilitate the processing of the critical word in the slightest. Indeed, the longest RTs were observed in such cases.

We had earlier conducted a study using similar materials, techniques, and subjects ($N = 69$). In that study, however, only three of the four conditions present in Experiment 1 were tested; the biased setting and neutral word case (the lower left cell of Table 5.1 involving *man* and *bakery*) was omitted. The pattern of results for the three conditions of that study was identical to the results observed here. In the neutral context (e.g. *workroom*) cases, RTs were significantly faster (by subjects) when the critical word was preceded by a semantically related word (e.g. *photographer's*) than when it was preceded by a semantically neutral word (e.g. *man's*). These RTs were 579 msec and 599 msec, respectively. As predicted, however, when the semantically related word occurred in the biased context (e.g. photographer in the bakery), the average RT was not reduced at all: 604 msec.

Discussion: access vs integration

The results of Experiment 1 seem clear: the processing of a word is apparently not always facilitated when that word is preceded by a semantically related one; the effect of semantic relatedness among lexical items depends upon the linguistic context within which the words occur. This finding is at odds with the class of explanations we described as LLA models. We should note again that many models concerned with semantic facilitation effects can be modified so that they will be able to account for our present results. But to the extent that models have been based on LLA assumptions, they may be inadequate.

The data are consistent with our earlier hypothesis: the degree of facilitation accruing to a lexical item is determined by the semantic value for the input that has been computed up to the point where the item in question occurs. This is not to say, however, that a complete interpretation of the available input is immediately computed, only that the effective context is the highest-level interpretation that has been computed. Since our approach has received some support, it merits further theoretical work.

Up to this point we have been careful not to commit ourselves to assumptions about mechanisms underlying the facilitation effect. Although most theorists assume that the locus of the facilitation effect is at the stage of lexical access (differing on the mechanisms by which access is speeded), it is worth entertaining an alternative hypothesis. The alternative is that the facilitation is due to the speed with which words can be integrated into the ongoing semantic representation. It is intuitive that some words are more readily integrated into the ongoing interpretation of a sentence than are others. Furthermore, it is likely that most of the experiments involving sentence processing and semantic facilitation could be interpreted as being consistent with an integration interpretation as well as with an access interpretation. In particular, the results of Experiment 1 could be interpreted within either an access or an integration framework.

Foss, Cirilo, and Blank (1979) pointed out the existence of these two possibilities. They opted for an access interpretation of their data largely on grounds of parsimony, noting that it would be implausible to interpret the list data in terms of an integration hypothesis. Of course, that is very far from a knock-down argument. Since we consider this to be an important theoretical matter, we will briefly describe two experiments whose results fit rather more neatly into an integration interpretation.

Experiments 2 and 3[1]

One rationale for Experiments 2 and 3 was to examine the effects of semantically related adjectives on the processing of the head noun of a phrase. Earlier research (Cutler and Foss, 1974) had shown facilitation effects, not surprisingly, but some of their data were complex, (e.g. there were interactions with the functional role of the NP). Also, the present studies were conducted in part to examine the mechanisms involved in the phoneme monitoring task itself. This latter issue will not be further explored here (see Foss and Blank, 1980; Foss, Harwood, and Blank, 1980, for fuller discussions of the relevant issues).

Subjects in these experiments were presented sentences like (7)–(9) and were asked both to comprehend them and to respond to a target phoneme. We were interested in the relative amounts of time required to process the subject nouns in the sentences as the preceding adjective was varied. These nouns were immediately preceded by either a relatively neutral adjective, i.e. one that does not elicit the subject noun when presented alone, as in (8); by an adjective that is semantically related to the noun and which elicits it in isolation, as in (9); or by no adjective, as in (7).

(7) In a moment of hopelessness the delinquent contemplated suicide.
(8) In a moment of hopelessness the hostile delinquent contemplated suicide.
(9) In a moment of hopelessness the juvenile delinquent contemplated suicide.

The target phoneme for which the subjects listened occurred on the noun of interest (e.g. the /d/ in *delinquent*) on half the trials and immediately after the noun (e.g. the /k/ in *contemplated*) on the other half. Thus, there were six basic conditions in the experiment defined by crossing the target position and sentence type variables. One sixth of the sentences in each material set came from each of the six conditions. Six material sets were constructed such that across them each basic sentence occurred in all six versions. The experiment was, therefore, a 3 (adjective type: none/unrelated/related) × 2 (target position: on vs after the noun) × 6 (material sets), with the first two variables being within subjects and the last being between subjects.

The frequencies of the related and unrelated adjectives were matched according to the Kucera and Francis (1967) estimates. Also, twenty-four filler sentences were constructed, eight of which did not contain the target phoneme and the remainder of which varied the target position throughout the sentences. The resulting seventy-two sentences were randomized and presented to subjects over headphones under conditions similar to those used in Experiment 1.

The primary difference between Experiments 2 and 3 was in the materials used. The design and procedures were identical for the two studies. In Experiment 2 many of the sentences began with the NP that carried the noun of interest. In Experiment 3 that NP was nearly always preceded by a prepositional phrase, an adverbial phrase or some other modifying phrase. Some of the basic sentences were also different across the two studies.

After the subjects had listened to the sentences a brief recognition comprehension test was administered. Subjects who did no better than chance on this test were excluded from the experiment. In each experiment the data from sixty remaining subjects were analysed, ten from each material set.

Results

The mean reaction times to respond to target phonemes in the two studies are shown in Figures 5.1 and 5.2. Overall there were significant effects due to target position and to adjective context. Inspection of Figures 5.1 and 5.2 shows, however, that the effect due to adjectives was limited to the case where the target occurred after the noun; there was no effect when the target was on the noun itself. One important implication of the main effects has to do with the mechanisms of monitoring (see Foss and Blank, 1980) and we will not discuss it further here. Let us concentrate on the RTs obtained when the target occurred after the noun (i.e. on the verb). Here the pattern of results is complex. In both Experiments 2 and 3, *post hoc* Neuman–Keuls tests showed that the RTs in sentences where the noun was preceded by an unrelated adjective were significantly longer than the RTs both for the no adjective sentences and for those in which the noun was preceded by a semantically related adjective. These latter two did not differ in either study. Thus, the rising and falling pattern shown in both Figures 5.1 and 5.2 for the verb targets was significant. This pattern was not expected; one main reason for conducting Experiment 3 was to see whether the effect replicated.

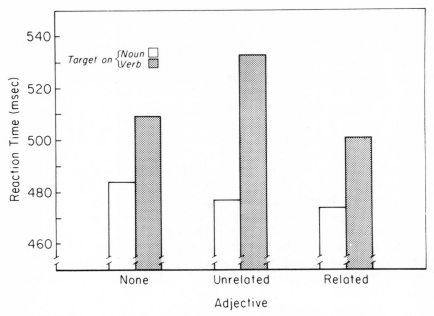

Figure 5.1   Mean reaction times to target phonemes, Experiment 2

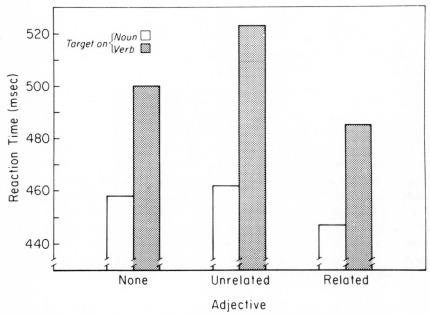

Figure 5.2   Mean reaction times to target phonemes, Experiment 3

Discussion: the integration hypothesis

The results of Experiments 2 and 3 are consistent with an integration interpretation of the effects of semantically related prior context. To make this argument we must first ask why the RTs increase when an unrelated adjective is presented prior to the noun of interest. There are a number of possible explanations for this increase. The one we wish to entertain here suggests that it is due to an increase in processing demands resulting from the requirement of combining the adjective and head noun into a semantically interpreted phrase. Since the adjective is not closely related to the noun, this semantic integration requires resources and time. In consequence, subjects cannot respond to the target phoneme in the next word as quickly as they can when no adjective is present. The next step in this line of reasoning is to suggest that semantic integration occurs more rapidly when the adjective and noun are closely related than when they are not. In consequence, listeners can more rapidly devote resources to the monitoring task and the resulting response will be rapid again.

It has not escaped our attention that we have proposed two neatly off-setting mechanisms in order to account for the three data points of interest here. Admittedly, this is not a terribly strong theoretical ploy. It was in recognition of that fact that the replication of Experiment 2 was carried out in the first place. It must be noted also that not all data gathered with the phoneme monitoring technique support the hypothesis that integration is more difficult and time consuming when phrases contain more lexical items. In particular, the Cutler and Foss (1974) study mentioned earlier did not find such an effect even though it manipulated the number of adjectives in a phrase (zero, one, and two adjectives were used). Indeed, Cutler and Foss found the longest RTs with zero adjectives. It is not clear what the important differences were between that study and the present ones.

There is, however, yet additional evidence on the side of an integration interpretation of Experiments 2 and 3. Pamela Holley-Wilcox carried out a phoneme monitoring experiment in the Texas laboratories in which subjects were presented sentences that varied the number and type of adjectives in a fashion similar to Experiments 2 and 3 (no adjective, unrelated adjective, relative adjective). In that study the noun of interest was an object noun and the target phoneme occurred immediately after it. In addition, however, Holley-Wilcox also manipulated the semantic relationship between the verb and the object noun: for half of the experimental sentences the verb was semantically neutral (not closely related to the noun), while for the other half of the sentences the verb was semantically related. Not surprisingly, she found that RTs were faster overall when the verb was semantically related to its object noun than when the verb was more neutral. Importantly, she found exactly the same pattern of results as did Experiments 2 and 3 when the adjectives were varied: RTs were longest when the adjective was unrelated to the noun and shorter (and approximately equal) when there was no adjective and when the adjective was semantically related to the noun. This pattern held across both the verb conditions (i.e. both when the verb was semantically neutral and when it was semantically related). Thus, this study essentially provides two additional replications of the adjective phenomenon shown in Figures 5.1 and 5.2.

To summarize, Experiments 2 and 3, along with the work carried out with Holley-Wilcox, are consistent with an explanation which says that phrases containing semantically related lexical items are more readily integrated into a higher level semantic interpretation. (This explanation requires the assumption that phoneme monitoring is, under some circumstances, sensitive to the integration process. Evidence consistent with this assumption exists, e.g. Foss and Lynch, 1969). Additionally, these data lend credence to the hypothesis that the results of Experiment 1 are due to speedier integration of a lexical item into the ongoing semantic interpretation when the lexical item is highly compatible with that interpretation than when it is not so compatible. Naturally, this view does not rule out an interpretation of Experiment 1 in which lexical access is speeded when the context is semantically compatible with the word. Indeed, the recent work of Swinney and his associates (e.g. Swinney, in press) would seem to force an access interpretation. This work merits more careful attention concerning its relation to LLA models than it has been given here (see Foss, forthcoming). The two alternatives, speedier access and speedier integration, are not mutually exclusive. It is likely, given the complexity of our field, that both may find a place in tomorrow's theory of comprehension. For the present we will note again that models based on LLA mechanisms appear inadequate to account for our data. It is important to investigate the properties of semantic facilitation within the framework of an integration hypothesis. The next section examines one such property.

THE TIME COURSE OF SEMANTIC FACILITATION

Recent research with both lists and sentences has examined aspects of the time course of facilitation and inhibition of lexical processing (e.g. Antos, 1979; Fischler and Bloom, 1979; Neely, 1977; Stanovich and West, 1979; Warren, 1977). Most of this research has been concerned with the rise time of facilitation and, stimulated by the Posner and Snyder two-factor theory (1975), with the temporal relationship between facilitation and inhibition. Here we will be concerned with the decay times of facilitation, asking how long such an effect lasts during comprehension.

According to the view expressed earlier, subjects rapidly compute a representation of the meaning of phrases and clauses, and it is this representation that determines the ease of processing (accessing or integrating) the next word in the sentence. We suggest that listeners keep in their processing memory a representation of the focused upon or foregrounded entities and their relationship with one another. Further, we propose that this information does *not* decay with time as long as the topic of conversation remains stable. In many ways this idea is similar to the 'leading edge' strategy suggested by Kintsch and Vipond (1979) for text processing, to the ideas discussed by Lesgold, Roth, and Curtis (1979) in their discussion of text processing, and to the work of Garrod and Sanford (chapter 8 of this volume).

It follows from the above conjecture that processing a later word will be speeded when the semantic interpretation of the earlier part of the passage is related to or obviously consistent with that word. This will remain true even if the distance between the critical word and earlier, semantically related words is very great—assuming, of course, that the intervening words are such that they do not bias the interpretation away from the earlier analysis. The listener need not continue 'attending' to earlier words; he or she only needs to comprehend the intervening material in a natural way. This case contrasts with a situation in which subjects are presented with lists of words, some of which are semantically related. The activation of semantically related words decays with intervening items (see, for example, Meyer and Schvaneveldt, 1971).

Our conjecture is, then, that the effects of semantic relationships among words will not decay with time in sentences, or even across sentences (assuming that the comprehender can continue to interpret the sentence in a way semantically consistent with the earlier words). Indeed, we will venture the strong hypothesis that there is no decrease in facilitation under such circumstances. On the other hand, the effects of semantic relationships among words in lists will only be subject to short-lived facilitation; such effects rapidly decay with intervening material. In order to test this conjecture, a series of studies was conducted; we will report one of them here.

Experiment 4[2]

There were three variables defining eight basic conditions in Experiment 4. The first variable was semantic context. Subjects were presented with a pair of context words that was either semantically related or semantically neutral with respect to a third critical word. As in Experiments 2 and 3, it is the processing of the critical word that will concern us. The second variable was the distance between the context words and the critical word. The pair of context words occurred either close to the critical one (an average of 1.5 words intervening) or they occurred considerably earlier (an average of 12 words intervening). These we will call the 'near' and 'far' cases, respectively. Finally, the words were embedded within sentences or within lists. When the words were in lists, exactly the same words appeared, but their order was scrambled. Examples of the eight conditions of the study are shown in (10)–(13).

(10) *Near sentence case*: The entire group examined the $\begin{Bmatrix} \text{gills} \\ \text{spots} \end{Bmatrix}$ and the $\begin{Bmatrix} \text{fins} \\ \text{stripes} \end{Bmatrix}$ of the fish caught in the Nile River.

(11) *Far sentence case*: The entire group examined the $\begin{Bmatrix} \text{gills} \\ \text{spots} \end{Bmatrix}$ and the $\begin{Bmatrix} \text{fins} \\ \text{stripes} \end{Bmatrix}$ with amazement. Everyone agreed that this was unlike any other fish caught in recent years.

(12) *Near list case*: Group the examined the entire $\begin{Bmatrix} \text{gills} \\ \text{spots} \end{Bmatrix}$ the and $\begin{Bmatrix} \text{fins} \\ \text{stripes} \end{Bmatrix}$ the of fish caught the Nile in River.

(13) *Far list case*: Group the examined the entire $\begin{Bmatrix} \text{gills} \\ \text{spots} \end{Bmatrix}$ the and $\begin{Bmatrix} \text{fins} \\ \text{stripes} \end{Bmatrix}$ any agreed. Unlike amazement this everyone other with that was fish caught years in recent.

Inspection will show that in lists and sentences exactly the same words intervened between *fish*, the critical word, and the earlier related or neutral context words.

According to the strong version of the present hypothesis, the processing of the critical word (e.g. *fish*) will be faster in both the near and far sentence cases when related words precede it (e.g. *gills* and *fins*) relative to when neutral words occur (e.g. *spots* and *stripes*). Further, the processing advantage will be of the same magnitude in the far case as it is in the near case. We also expect to observe an effect of semantic relatedness in the near list cases like (12), but not in the far list cases like (13).

Method

Forty basic experimental sentences were constructed. Each sentence had a pair of words that was either semantically related or semantically neutral with respect to a following critical noun. Within a sentence the two context words were always members of the same form class, but the form class varied across sentences; nouns, verbs, and adjectives were used. The sentences were constructed such that the word immediately following the critical noun began with a target phoneme. Time to respond to the target was used as a measure of relative processing difficulty of the critical noun. The beginning of each sentence was so constructed that a minimum of four words preceded the pair of related or unrelated words. Each sentence had four versions: the pair of context words was either semantically related or semantically more neutral relative to a following noun; and, crossed with this variable, the critical noun was either near to or far from the pair of words. In each far sentence case a full sentence stop intervened between the context words and the critical word, as in (13).

Four matching list conditions were derived from the sentences by quasi-randomizing the word order. Words preceding the related/neutral word pairs were randomized; the pair maintained the same left-to-right position as in the sentences. The words between the context words and the critical noun were randomized, but that noun and the word immediately after it (the target-bearing word) kept their same left-to-right position also. Finally, the remaining words in the sentence were randomized. This feature of the design is exemplified in (10)–(13).

The four sentence and four list conditions composed the eight material sets. The list vs sentence variable was between subjects, the other two variables were within subjects. Each material set contained the forty basic experimental items, ten each in the related near, neutral near, related far, and neutral far conditions. Across the eight material sets, each basic item occurred in all eight versions. Within any single material set, each basic item occurred but once.

Frequencies for the related and neutral word pairs were matched according to Kucera and Francis (1967) estimates so that within each material set the average frequency for the related word pair approximately matched the average frequency for the neutral pair. The number of syllables for both related and neutral words averaged approximately 2.5 syllables per word.

Forty filler items were included in each material set. Sixteen fillers were drawn from the sentences used by Blank and Foss (1978); eight contained related word pairs before a critical noun while eight had neutral words before the noun. All sixteen of the Blank and Foss filler items were similar to the near condition in the experiment proper. In those items, however, the noun always occurred immediately after the related/neutral word pairs; no words intervened. These filler sentences were approximately twelve words long, several words shorter than the experimental items. Fourteen additional filler items were constructed without a target phoneme; the remaining ten fillers varied the target position. Sentence fillers were included in the sentence material sets, and word-list fillers, derived from the filler sentences, were included in the list materials. The position of the forty filler items in the experiment was randomized, with each item occurring in the same position across the eight material sets.

The test materials were presented to subjects binaurally over headphones.

The lists were recorded at a rate approximating (and not significantly different from) the rate used for sentences. The lists were given an intonation contour similar to that for sentences.

Subjects in this experiment were 128 undergraduates from the University of Texas at Austin (16 in each of the 8 conditions). They were told to listen to materials and (in the case of sentences) to comprehend them. Subjects were asked to carry out the phoneme monitoring task. The target always occurred immediately after the critical word. In examples (7)–(10) the target is /k/ in *caught*.

Results and discussion

The mean RTs in the eight conditions are shown in Table 5.2. They may be summarized as follows: for sentences, the effect due to semantic relatedness was significant both by subjects $(F(1,80) = 71.55, p < 0.001)$ and by items $(F(1,36) = 40.10, p < 0.001)$. There was also a main effect for the distance variable (near vs far), with the times to respond to the near items taking longer $(F(1,80) = 67.51, p < 0.001,$ for subjects; $F(1,36) = 16.35, p < 0.001,$ for items). Importantly, the distance and semantic relatedness variables did not interact $(F(1,80) = 1.24, p = 0.27,$ for subjects; $F < 1,$ for items). In the case of lists, however, the results due to semantic relatedness were not clear. Overall, the relatedness variable did not reach significance $(F(1, 80) = 1.47$ for subjects). The distance effect was significant by subjects $(F(1,80) = 10.25, p < 0.005)$ but not quite by items $(F(1,36) = 3.23, p < 0.10)$. The predicted interaction between semantic relatedness and distance did not appear $(F < 1)$, although the mean RTs are consistent with the prediction.

The lack of an effect due to semantic relatedness in the near list case was surprising since earlier studies in our laboratory had observed it. It may be that the effect decays so rapidly in auditorily presented lists that the 1.5 words

Table 5.2   Mean phoneme monitoring reaction times (msec), Experiment 4

Materials	Relation between priming words and critical word	Distance between priming words and critical word	
		Near	Far
Lists	Related	603	578
	Unrelated	608	591
Sentences	Related	538	494
	Unrelated	588	534

Table 5.3   Mean phoneme monitoring reaction times
(msec), Experiment 4: Blank and Foss materials

Materials	Semantic relation	
	Related	Unrelated
Lists	591	627
Sentences	583	638

intervening between the context and critical word masked the effect. This interpretation gains support when we look at the RTs for the materials borrowed from Blank and Foss (1978). These RTs were collected and analysed; their means are shown in Table 5.3.

An overall analysis of variance resulted in a significant effect due to semantic relatedness $(F(1,164) = 29.59$, $p < 0.001$, for subjects; $F(1,28) = 19.17$, $p < 0.001$, by items), and importantly, no interaction between the list vs sentence variable and the semantic relatedness variable $(F < 1)$. Thus, there is evidence here for facilitation of processing in the near list case. As mentioned, such a result is consistent with many in the literature.

The results of Experiment 4 are clearly consistent with the hypothesis that in sentences (or in a series of related sentences) there is no decay of the semantic facilitation effect. This contrasts with the finding that the facilitation does decay with intervening material when presented in lists of words. The statement that there is *no* decay with intervening material in sentences is quite a strong one. It may turn out to be wrong in its strong form, but for the moment we will hold on to it. Actually, we suspect that the facilitation effect is going to vary with the 'importance' of the earlier material to the theme of the passage (i.e. this work will connect closely to work on text processing such as that carried out by Cirilo and Foss, 1980; Kintsch and van Dijk, 1978; Lesgold *et al.* 1979; and others). But that is another story.

Semantic facilitation was only marginal with the near list materials in the main part of Experiment 4. This finding suggests that the presence of even one unrelated intervening item may severely attenuate and even obviate the facilitation effect. Such an observation is consistent with the location shift model we cited above. This model, suggesting as it does that information on a topic is rapidly available (or integrated) only as long as the topic is not changed, is conceptually akin to the views cited in the previous paragraph.

SUMMARY AND CONCLUSIONS

Three issues have been raised in this chapter concerning the role of context during sentence processing. Let us state them in the form of hypotheses.

H1: The processing of a lexical item will invariably be speeded when that item is immediately preceded by a semantically related one.

In the first part of this paper we called models of language processing from which H1 may be derived lexical-lexical activation (LLA) models. We noted that the existing instantiations of most processing models are of the LLA type.

H2: The locus of the facilitation (of interference) effect on lexical processing is at the stage of lexical access.

H3: The facilitation effect from one lexical item to another decays rapidly with the time between the two items, lasting for a second or two at most.

We have presented here the results of experiments that bear more or less directly on these three hypotheses. We obtained evidence in Experiment 1 that H1 is incorrect. In that study we showed that facilitation of lexical processing does not always occur when the lexical item of interest is immediately preceded by a semantically related one. Thus, in that experimental paradigm, at least, it was not sufficient for facilitation of processing that two semantically related words occurred next to each other. We found evidence in Experiment 1 that it is the higher-level semantic interpretation that determines whether the processing of a subsequent word will be facilitated, not the semantic interpretation of the item immediately preceding that word. We recognize that evidence from this one experimental paradigm is not determinative on this matter, that other measures might find a short-lived priming effect, but it certainly does call H1 into question.

The work reported here is not clear enough to refute H2, though the results of Experiment 2 and 3 are consistent with an alternative. This alternative says that at least some of the effects due to semantic relatedness are due to speedier integration of related words into a higher level semantic interpretation. In these studies some evidence was found consistent with an integration interpretation; subjects apparently took longer to process phrases in which a neutral adjective occurred than they did to process phrases in which either no adjective or a semantically related adjective occurred. As noted, this work requires extension, but it at least calls the strong hypothesis, H2, into question. We believe that the issue—access vs integration—is an important and topical one, one that merits both conceptual clarification and empirical work. Of course, the two positions are not mutually exclusive.

It seems clear that the results of Experiment 4 refute H3. That study showed effects on lexical processing when the prior semantically related words occurred considerably in advance of the critical word of interest. Indeed, given our earlier arguments, we would now say that H3 is incorrectly stated since it presupposes that the correct interpretation of the facilitation effect is a member of the class of LLA models. Our view, which says that the facilitation effect is due to the higher level semantic nodes in the listener's ongoing interpretation of the input, makes the denial of H3 natural if not inevitable.

To conclude, then, our results from Experiments 1 and 4 suggest that *it is neither necessary nor sufficient that semantically related words occur near to each other for semantic facilitation to occur during sentence processing*. The results of the present studies are consistent with the view that subjects rapidly calculate a semantic representation for the higher-level nodes of input sentences and that it is these semantic representations that determine what additional words in the mental dictionary are rapidly processed (accessed or integrated). What remains now, of course, is to specify in more detail the semantic rules that are used in carrying out the calculations of higher-level semantic representations, and to specify how the accessibility functions operate. It is from this vantage point that we got our title: 'Great Expectations'.

NOTE

1. Experiments 2 and 3 were carried out in collaboration with Michelle A. Blank and David A. Harwood.
2. Further details appear in Foss (1982).

ACKNOWLEDGEMENTS

The work reported in this chapter was supported in part by a grant from the National Institute for Mental Health (MH 29891) to DJF, and in part by a training grant (MH 15744) supporting JRR. The authors wish to thank Susanne Doell who helped with many phases of the research.

REFERENCES

Antos, S. J. Processing facilitation in a lexical decision task. *Journal of Experimental Psychology: Human Perception and Performance*, 1979, **5**, 527–545.
Blank, M. A. Measuring lexical access during sentence processing. *Perception and Psychophysics*, 1980, **28**, 1–8.
Blank, M. A., and Foss, D. J. Semantic facilitation and lexical access during sentence processing. *Memory and Cognition*, 1978, **6**, 644–652.
Cirilo, R. K., and Foss, D. J. Text structure and reading time for sentences. *Journal of Verbal Learning and Verbal Behavior*, 1980, **19**, 96–109.
Cole, R. A., and Jakimik, J. Understanding speech. How words are heard. In G. Underwood (Ed.), *Strategies of Information Processing*. New York: Academic Press, 1979.
Collins, A. M., and Loftus, E. F. A spreading-activation theory of semantic processing. *Psychological Review*, 1975, **82**, 407–428.
Cutler, A., and Foss, D. J. Comprehension of ambiguous sentences: The locus of context effects. Paper presented at the Midwestern Psychological Association, Chicago, May 1974.

Fischler, I., and Bloom, P. A. Automatic and attentional processes in the effects of sentence contexts on word recognition. *Journal of Verbal Learning and Verbal Behavior*, 1979, **18**, 1–20.

Forster, K. I. Levels of processing and the structure of the language processor. In W. E. Cooper and E. C. T. Walker (Eds), *Sentence Processing: Psycholinguistic Studies Presented to Merrill Garrett*. Hillsdale, N.J.: Lawrence Erlbaum Associates, 1979.

Foss, D. J. A discourse in semantic priming. *Cognitive Psychology*, 1982, **14**, 590–607.

Foss, D. J., and Blank, M. A. Identifying the speech codes. *Cognitive Psychology*, 1980, **12**, 1–31.

Foss, D. J., Cirilo, R. K., and Blank, M. A. Semantic facilitation and lexical access during sentence processing: An investigation of individual differences. *Memory and Cognition*, 1979, **7**, 346–353.

Foss, D. J., and Harwood, D. A. Memory for sentences: Implications for human associative memory. *Journal of Verbal Learning and Verbal Behavior*, 1975, **14**, 1–16.

Foss, D. J., Harwood, D. A., and Blank, M. A. Deciphering decoding decisions: Data and devices. In R. A. Cole (Ed.), *Perception and Production of Fluent Speech*. Hillsdale, N.J.: Lawrence Erlbaum Associates, 1980.

Foss, D. J., and Lynch, R. H., Jr. Decision processes during sentence comprehension: Effects of surface structure on decision times. *Perception and Psychophysics*, 1969, **5**, 145–148.

Kintsch, W., and Vipond, D. Reading comprehension and readability in educational practice and psychological theory. In L. G. Nilsson (Ed.), *Perspectives on Memory Research*. Hillsdale, N. J.: Lawrence Erlbaum Associates, 1979.

Kintsch, W., and van Dijk, T. A. Toward a model of text comprehension and production. *Psychological Review*, 1978, **85**, 363–394.

Kucera, H., and Francis, W. N. *Computational Analysis of Present-day American English*. Providence, R.I.: Brown University Press, 1967.

Lesgold, A. M., Roth, S. F., and Curtis, M. E. Foregrounding effects in discourse comprehension. *Journal of Verbal Learning and Verbal Behavior*, 1979, **18**, 291–308.

Lewis, D. K. General semantics. In D. Davidson and G. H. Harmon (Eds), *Semantics of Natural Language*. Dordrecht: Reidel, 1972.

Marslen-Wilson, W. D., and Welsh, A. Processing interactions and lexical access during word recognition in continuous speech. *Cognitive Psychology*, 1978, **10**, 29–63.

Meyer, D., and Schvaneveldt, R. Facilitation in recognizing pairs of words: Evidence of a dependence between retrieval operations. *Journal of Experimental Psychology*, 1971, **90**, 227–234.

Neely, J. H. Semantic priming and retrieval from lexical memory: Roles of inhibitionless spreading activation and limited-capacity attention. *Journal of Experimental Psychology: General*, 1977, **106**, 226–254.

Posner, M. I., and Snyder, C. R. R. Attention and cognitive control. In R. L. Solso (Ed.), *Information Processing and Cognition: The Loyola Symposium*. Hillsdale, N.J.: Lawrence Erlbaum Associates, 1975.

Rubenstein, H., Lewis, S. S., and Rubenstein, M. A. Homographic entries in the internal lexicon: Effects of systematicity and relative frequency of meanings. *Journal of Verbal Learning and Verbal Behavior*, 1971, **10**, 57–62.

Stanovich, K. E., and West, R. F. Mechanisms of sentence context effects in reading: Automatic activation and conscious attention. *Memory and Cognition*, 1979, **7**, 77–85.

Swinney, D. Lexical processing during sentence comprehension: Effects of higher order constraints and implications for representation. In T. Myers, J. Laver, and J. Anderson (Eds), *The Cognitive Representation of Speech.* North Holland.

Swinney, D. A., Onifer, W., Prather, P., and Hirshkowitz, M. Semantic facilitation across sensory modalities in the processing of individual words and sentences. *Memory and Cognition*, 1979, **7**, 159–165.

Warren, R. E. Time and the spread of activation in memory. *Journal of Experimental Psychology: Human Perception and Performance*, 1977, **3**, 458–466.

The Process of Language Understanding
Edited by G. B. Flores d'Arcais and R. J. Jarvella
© 1983 John Wiley & Sons Ltd.

6

Comprehension Processes in Oral Reading

JOSEPH H. DANKS, LISA BOHN, and RAMONA FEARS
Kent State University, Kent, Ohio, U.S.A.

INTERACTIVE MODELS

Comprehension of language involves the transformation of speech or print into a mental representation of what the listener/reader thinks the speaker/writer intended. The representation arises from the interaction between the input and the knowledge base of the listener/reader. A major contemporary issue is how and when different types of information sources are used during comprehension. Many models of reading (e.g., Gough, 1972; LaBerge and Samuels, 1974; Massaro, 1975) have emphasized 'bottom-up' processing, in which different sorts of information are extracted in a strict serial order beginning with information closest to the physical input and ending with more abstract conceptual information.

Although a bottom-up orientation fits comfortably with our intuitive notions about comprehension, it has difficulty handling the robustness of human communication. Substantial distortions in the physical signal, for example, garbled speech or scrawled handwriting, commonly do not cause serious difficulty for listeners and readers. Listeners and readers rarely notice vague references and ambiguous phrasings. Apparently they interpret such constructions without realizing the presence of a potential problem. These causal observations of everyday phenomena have laboratory counterparts in which processing of lower-level information is facilitated by presentation in a larger context. Phonemes and letters are perceived better when presented in the context of a word or sentence (Reicher, 1969; Wheeler, 1970). Words are identified more accurately and rapidly in a grammatical, meaningful sentence than in ungrammatical or anomalous strings (Miller and Isard, 1963; Stevens and Rumelhart, 1975). Sentences that are vague and ambiguous out of context are readily interpreted in a story (Bransford and Johnson, 1973).

Finally, interpretation of paragraphs is aided when the listener or reader has sufficient knowledge to provide a scheme for interpretation (Dooling and Lachman, 1971; Kintsch and Green, 1978). These phenomena result from more abstract information influencing decisions at a lower level of abstraction. Any adequate model of comprehension must account for such 'top-down' effects.

The existence of top-down effects has been widely recognized (Danks and Glucksberg, 1980; Flores d'Arcais and Schreuder, Chapter 1 of this volume; Rumelhart, 1977; Wildman and Kling, 1978–79), but precisely what they portend for models of comprehension is not widely agreed. A pure top-down model in which information passes serially from a meaning representation to input is implausible, if for no other reason than that the input itself does exert considerable control over the listener/reader's interpretation. One response to demonstrations of top-down effects in language comprehension was to add feedback loops such that information from decisions at more abstract levels of processing was returned to lower levels of processing. However, top-down effects are spread across the entire range of processing levels. They are not restricted to a single level, or even a few levels, of processing. So the number of feedback loops needed to account for all of the top-down effects would result in the interconnection of virtually every level of processing. In such a model, the notion of directionality of processing loses much of its force.

Several investigators have proposed interactive models of language processing (Danks and Hill, 1981; Just and Carpenter, 1980; Marslen-Wilson, 1975; Rumelhart, 1977), but the details of the interactions are far from clear (cf. the papers in Lesgold and Perfetti, 1981). Interactive models diminish the importance of unidirectionality of processing as a salient property of comprehension models and allow a more open system of how information is transferred among components. Of necessity, some measure of directionality is retained because the listener/reader does start with a perceptual input and ends with a meaning representation. However, that directionality is not the overriding consideration. For example, a listener may impute meaning to a speaker's silence even though the listener has no input to process. So determining the directionality of information flow may not be as critical for building a model of language processing as had been assumed previously.

A problem with most interactive models is that they are too powerful; that is, they do not exlude any conceivable results. For example, most interactive models are capable of explaining both bottom-up and top-down effects separately or in combination. Any model, and an interactive one specifically, must be sufficiently precise that it can be falsified by some conceivable set of data. This requirement is complicated by the fact that language processing is extraordinarily flexible, so any model of language processing has to be very powerful. However, models cannot be allowed to grow too powerful or nothing is explained.

PROPERTIES OF INTERACTIVE MODELS

In this section, several general properties of interactive models are described. Not all interactive models accept all of these properties, but each property can be identified in one or another interactive model.

1. Results of processing at any level are immediately and simultaneously available to all other levels. A model incorporating the most powerful variant of this property was proposed by Rumelhart (1977), in which all information resulting from processing at each level is deposited in a message centre where it is available to all other processing levels. For example, as soon as a sequence of phonemes is identified, that information is available for use in lexical access. In some cases, a word might be identified before all its phonemes are identified (Marslen-Wilson and Welsh, 1978). For another example, information about the discourse topic may aid identification of specific words (Foss and Ross, Chapter 5 of this volume).

The power of interactive models can be limited either by restricting the availability of information or by restricting the types of information specific levels are capable of processing. For example, only phonetic information might be used in lexical access to activate candidates for identification, but then syntactic, semantic, and thematic information could be used to select among candidates (Marslen-Wilson and Welsh, 1978). A variation of this property that permits retention of some bottom-up characteristics is to allow intermediate results from one processing level to be available to other processing levels before the first level has finished processing is complete (cf. McClelland's cascade model, 1979; and Perfetti and Roth's reading model, 1981). Thus, more interaction among levels of processing is permitted than with a strictly serial, autonomous model.

2. Processing proceeds at all levels in parallel constrained only by the availability of information on which to operate (Just and Carpenter, 1980; Marslen-Wilson, 1975; Rumelhart, 1977). Any given level of processing does not necessarily wait until processing has been completed at any other level. Any level is potentially active at any point in time.

One constraint on this property is that sometimes processing at one level cannot proceed without information from some other level. For example, construction of sentence meaning cannot proceed without identification of at least some of the words in the sentence. Listeners and readers may have a good idea about what speakers and writers are going to say and write, but they do not enjoy perfect prescience. A second constraint results from differences in rates of processing among processing levels. Some processes occur automatically because they are so well practised. For example, it is very difficult to inhibit meaning access because determination of meaning is the primary goal of communication. In the Stroop task, the printed word interferes with naming the colour of the ink. Lexical access of common words is so automatic that it is impossible for skilled readers to inhibit it. Likewise, in an oral reading task, sentence meaning may be constructed even though only oral production is required because sentences are understood faster than the words can be spoken (Danks and Fears, 1979).

3. Interactive models posit processing flexibility as a function of individual differences among listeners and readers, as a function of the listener/reader's purpose or task, and as a function of properties of the text (Danks, 1978). Comprehension, in either the listening or reading mode, is not a fixed, invariant process, but adapts to the specific situation. This adaptability represents the normal mode of processing. It is not something that happens just when the processes have difficulty. Because there are so many things that can go wrong, the listener/reader never has the opportunity to develop one canonical process that can function effectively in most situations.

Some listeners/readers are more skilled than others at specific types of processing. For example, some readers have excellent word recognition skills, and others are more adept at determining the meaning of sentences (Perfetti and Roth, 1981). One obvious source of individual differences in processing skill is age. Children, in general, have different sorts of processing strategies than adults do (Bever, 1970), especially for reading (Schwartz, 1980). Skilled readers have developed some automatic processing strategies (LaBerge and Samuels, 1974). In contrast, children learning to read frequently have to attend more closely to each stage of processing.

Task differences are well recognized as contributing to differences in comprehension strategies (Aaronson and Scarborough, 1976; Danks, 1969; Frederiksen, 1975; Glucksberg, Trabasso, and Wald, 1973; Mistler-Lachman, 1972). Typically, one listens or reads with a purpose in mind. The purpose can direct attention to those processes that, when completed, will satisfy the task requirements. In addition, once task demands have been met at one level, processing at all levels may be terminated (Mistler-Lachman, 1972). However, there are limits to the amount of control that is possible because some processing levels proceed automatically or more rapidly than the processing at levels at which the task demands are met. For example, sentence comprehension usually proceeds more rapidly than does oral production in an oral reading task (Danks and Fears, 1979).

The type and structure of the discourse can alter processing strategies. With a difficult text, a reader may be more dependent on lower-level information being fed forward to higher levels of processing. With a simple text, in contrast, expectancies can be generated at abstract processing levels such that lower-level processing is facilitated or even short-circuited. In addition to variations due to text difficulty, processing changes according to the type of discourse. At a casual party, conversation may be processed only to the extent needed to make a polite reply, especially when the listener is more interested in a conversation across the room. With respect to print, reading a poem, a novel, a newspaper column, or a technical article yields different processing strategies, at least subjectively (Gibson and Levin, 1975). Most poetry keys on the sound properties of words, rhyme, rhythm, or word 'colour'. Hearing a poem in one's mind's ear is crucial for understanding the poet's message, but hearing a novel would get in the way of understanding its theme. Technical articles require considerable conceptual processing; how the text sounds is not nearly so important.

4. An interactive model may describe interactions among types of information or interactions among processing components. First, consider interactions among different types of information. A single processing component may have access to all types of information, but one type may be more useful than others. For example, perceptual information is more valuable for lexical access than is thematic information. In contrast, thematic information is more important for the construction of a story's macrostructure than any specific piece of perceptual information. If the information most typically used by a process has been distorted, violated, or is otherwise unavailable to the listener or reader, then another type of information may compensate for the deficiency (Stanovich, 1980). One reason for information unavailability is that something is wrong with the text. There may be physical distortions, or a story may be written in a vague, obscure, or metaphorical style (Bransford and Johnson, 1973). The lack of specific kinds of information can also be due to listener/reader factors. For example, children do not have as well developed story schemata as do adults (Poulsen, Kintsch, Kintsch and Premack, 1979) and thus depend on bottom-up information to understand stories. Some less-skilled readers have sufficiently poor word recognition skills that their ability to comprehend sentences and stories is impaired (Perfetti and Lesgold, 1977). So a poor reader is more dependent on contextual information than is a good reader who has well developed word recognition skills (Stanovich, 1980). This compensatory mechanism gives a processing component considerable flexibility since it is not dependent on a single source of information.

A second way to formulate interactive models is through interactions among processing components. When processes make use of information resulting from other processes, the information-generating process influences the information-receiving process. If the information comes from a more abstract process, then the influence is top-down; if the information comes from a less abstract process, then it is bottom-up. Interactions among processes may be complete or limited. If they are complete, then one process can influence another simply by generating information needed by the other. If interactions are limited, then there may be sectors of processing within which processes interact, but information transfer from one sector to another is restricted. For example, lexical access uses information from many levels of processing, but macroprocessing accepts information primarily from sentence comprehension.

An interactive model can be formulated in terms of what kinds of information interact in a single process or what kinds of processes influence other kinds of processes. These two types of formulations are complementary because different types of information are the result of different types of processing. So it is a question of whether the emphasis is on processing components or on types of information.

PROCESSING COMPONENTS

There are three major processing components in language comprehension: lexical access, sentence comprehension, and discourse understanding. *Lexical access* involves locating a lexical item in the mental dictionary and selecting an appropriate meaning. Bottom-up perceptual information, auditory and visual, is importantant for identifying a word; however, top-down contextual information, syntactic, semantic, textual, thematic, and factual, also influence lexical access. How lexical access might work in speech perception has been described by Marslen-Wilson and Welsh (1978). A cohort of potential words is activated by preliminary auditory analyses. In addition to continued processing of perceptual information, checks for consistency with contextual information are used to eliminate candidates from the cohort until a single item remains. Extending Marslen-Wilson and Welsh's model to lexical access in oral reading, Danks and Hill (1981) have suggested that top-down information may be used in the selection of the initial cohort as well as in eliminating candidates. Forster (1976) has proposed a more strictly bottom-up model, in which a word is first identified using only perceptual information and then is evaluated for contextual appropriateness. In interactive models, information from multiple sources converges in lexical access producing both bottom-up and top-down effects. Since lexical access provides the articulatory information that is needed to pronounce a word, any interaction among information sources will be reflected in oral-reading and speech-shadowing tasks.

In *sentence comprehension* the listener or reader integrates the word meanings into a representation for the entire sentence. Syntactic structure is available to guide the integration, but how active a role it plays is not clear. There are two primary hypotheses about how the sentence comprehension component works. The clausal processing hypothesis (Carroll and Bever, 1976; Carroll, Tanenhaus, and Bever, 1978) proposes three autonomous steps in its simplest version. First, the meanings of words are stored in a working memory buffer as they are accessed. When the end of the clause is reached, a representation is derived for the clause. Finally, the representation of the clause is integrated with the representations of prior clauses and with prior knowledge. The primary characterization of the clausal processing hypothesis is that it is serial, bottom-up, and autonomous. In contrast is the word-by-word processing hypothesis (Marslen-Wilson, Tyler, and Seidenberg, 1978; Marslen-Wilson and Tyler, 1980; Tyler and Marslen-Wilson, 1977). The listener/reader attempts to integrate each word's meaning into a comprehensive representation as soon as the word is accessed. If immediate integration fails, the word's meaning is held in a memory buffer until integration is possible. Frequently, the most appropriate point at which to re-attempt that integration is at the end of a clause. Interactive models imply a word-by-word comprehension strategy as opposed to a clausal processing strategy. Because processing proceeds in parallel at all levels, each word is processed immediately to the maximal extent possible. For the clausal level, that means attempting to integrate the word's meaning into the composite representation at the time that it is accessed.

In *discourse understanding*, listeners and readers organize the representations of individual sentences into discourse structures, for example, conversations, lectures, stories, and nonfiction prose. As sentences are comprehended, a discourse structure is constructed that is updated as additional information is received. At any point in time the representation is as complete as possible. One aspect of discourse understanding is to establish referential coherence for the discourse (Clark and Marshall, 1978). Listeners/readers tie together the sentences of a discourse into a coherent representation, or text base (Kintsch and van Dijk, 1978), making bridges and inferences as needed (Carpenter and Just, 1977; Crothers, 1979; Warren, Nicholas and Trabasso, 1979). In addition to local coherence, listeners/readers derive a macrostructure, a schematic representation of the main ideas or gist of the text (Kintsch and van Dijk, 1978). Interactive models permit considerable processing flexibility in discourse understanding. Listeners and readers are able to adapt the processing strategies and knowledge they have available to the wide variety of text that they encounter.

The emphasis in interactive models is on processes rather than on representations. In recent years, cognitive scientists generally have shifted away from attempting to specify representational structures to identifying the cognitive processes that produce those structures (Danks and Glucksberg, 1980). A change in the kinds of experimental tasks has attended this shift. Memory tasks provide information about mental structures and representations, but little information about processes. Hence investigators have developed other tasks, such as phoneme and word monitoring, speech shadowing, oral reading, and eye movement monitoring, that yield on-line measures of processing, dependent measures that are recorded concurrently with processing.

EXPERIMENTS ON ORAL READING COMPREHENSION

Although oral reading is used frequently in schools to evaluate reading (Durkin, 1978–79), its processing requirements are not fully understood

(Danks and Fears, 1979). In contrast to silent reading, the dominant task demand in oral reading is that each word be uttered in serial order. Oral reading yields a continuous on-line response that is roughly contemporaneous with the visual input and with comprehension. It is the reading counterpart to speech shadowing. The main difference is that in shadowing the listener does not control the order and rate of input as the reader does, but this difference corresponds to the difference between listening and reading generally.

The oral reader's primary task is oral production. To accomplish this task, each word is located in the mental dictionary and the articulatory information is used to pronounce it. A reader potentially could use lower-level information, such as grapheme–phoneme correspondences, spelling patterns, or syllabic structure, to pronounce a word without accessing it. However, since readers do not read pronounceable nonwords unhesitantly, dependence on lower-level information is unlikely. When oral reading is followed by a comprehension test, the reader also needs to understand the phrases, sentences, paragraphs, and main ideas of the text. Information from several levels must be integrated to construct a reasonable interpretation. During oral reading, the reader is attempting to satisfy both the verbal performance and the comprehension demands at the same time, but the press of the performance demand is greater. Analysis of oral reading performance provides an excellent opportunity to study lexical access, sentence comprehension, and discourse understanding in a relatively natural situation.

In the three experiments reported here, we investigated what kinds of information are used by the lexical access and sentence comprehension components. An oral reading task also permitted an estimation as to when the different types of information were being used. Specifically, the point in time when different types of information were processed in oral reading was assessed by violating each information type. If that information were normally used in oral production or in comprehension, then oral performance would be disrupted because the normal interplay among processing components would be modified to compensate for the violation. Furthermore, the disruption would be temporally close to when the violated information was needed by the reader. Our basic method was to change several critical words in a story, such that one or more types of information were violated. We then analysed readers' oral productions for disruptions near each critical word. The relative position of the disruptions resulting from the different violations indicated the order in which the information was typically used.

In three experiments, we manipulated various combinations of lexical, syntactic, semantic, and factual information. The first experiment established the basic pattern of results for syntactic, semantic, and factual (intersentential) information. The second experiment separated syntactic and semantic information types and replicated the results for factual information.

The third experiment tested lexical, syntactic, and semantic information and added a global text factor, namely the critical words were embedded in a difficult metaphorical story. The question raised by the text factor is whether information utilization changes when higher-level information is obscured. In particular, does the reader become more dependent on bottom-up processing strategies when top-down information is less available?

A bottom-up model predicts that disruptions resulting from having violated different types of information would be ordered from earliest to latest according to the level of abstraction of the violated information. The least abstract information, that was lexical information in our experiments, would produce the earliest disruption. Disruptions from syntactic and semantic violations would appear next, followed by disruptions from violating factual information, the most abstract in our experiments. Only lexical information is strictly necessary for oral production although a reader would need to determine the syntactic structure to read with appropriate prosody. So a lexical violation would produce a disruption near the critical word. Syntactic and semantic information would be used primarily at the end of the clause when the meaning of the clause is determined, so disruptions from these two violations would occur near the clause boundary. Violations of factual information would be important only after the meaning of the clause had been determined and the reader attempted to integrate the meaning of the clause with the representation of the preceding text.

Interactive models posit that several types of information are used in the same component and so their violation would produce similar disruption patterns. Such models also permit more than one component to operate at the same time, so that different information types might be used at the same time by different components. As discussed earlier, part of the difficulty with interactive models is sorting out these two types of interaction. Both types of interactive models predict that violations of different information types result in disruptions that occur at the same time. Other aspects of the data can be used to narrow the range of possible interactive models. For example, to the extent that the size and range of disruptions, as well as their timing, are similar, the involvement of only one processing component is more likely. The kinds of oral reading errors provide another source of evidence; for example, fluent restorations (cf. Experiment 2) reflect the operation of the lexical access component.

In general, interpretation of results depends on the relative positions of disruptions across violations, not on the absolute location of a disruption. So if violation of one information type produces a disruption before another violation type, utilization of the two information types is temporally ordered as well, regardless of the absolute positions of the disruptions. In some cases, however, the absolute position is interpretable; for example, disruptions that begin after a critical word has been uttered cannot reasonably involve lexical access. The absolute location of a disruption may reflect in part the eye–voice span, that is, the distance between where the eye is focused and the word being uttered (Levin, 1979). But the relative position of disruptions is not compromised because the size of the eye–voice span can be assumed to be relatively constant for all manipulations on average since all violations occurred equally often in each critical word segment. The size of the eye–voice span may vary systematically in other comparisons, such as in the results from different readers, for example, children at different levels of reading skill, or results from different texts, for example, the stories used in these experiments. In these cases, the effect of possible changes in the size of the eye–voice span must be considered.

Experiment 1

Method

A story about a high-school girl who was severely injured when a train hit her school bus was adapted from a popular magazine. The story was rewritten to eliminate all conversation and any difficult or infrequent words. The final story was 2171 words long and its readability was 7.8 (Fry, 1968). It was divided into four sections of approximately equal length. Four critical words were selected in each section, separated by an average of 129 words. The critical sentences for all experiments are contained in the Appendix.

There were four manipulations of the critical words—three types of violations plus a control condition. In the following sample segment, 'Her daughter had always been weak physically. Because of this, she even imagined her daughter being injured by the other children while trying to get out of the wrecked bus', the critical word was *injured*. In the control condition, there was no change in the critical word or in the surrounding text. To produce the syntactic and semantic violation, both syntactic and semantic information were distorted by replacing the critical word with a word that was the incorrect part of speech and that was semantically anomalous. The critical word *injured* was replaced with *iceberg*. To violate semantic information without disturbing lexical or syntactic information, the critical word was replaced with a word that was semantically anomalous, but which was the correct part of speech, for example, *planted* replaced *injured*. Readers can still determine the grammatical structure of the sentence, but the meaning of the sentence is distorted. At best, they have to imagine some very unusual circumstances in which the anomalous word could be interpreted metaphorically. Factual information is accumulated from the preceding text, so it was violated by introducing an inconsistency between the critical word and the preceding sentence. Unlike the other manipulations, neither the critical word nor the sentence containing it was altered. The sentence immediately preceding the sentence with the critical word was modified so that the critical word was factually inconsistent with the information of that sentence. In the example, the word *weak* in the preceding sentence was replaced with *strong*. The fact that her daughter was strong was inconsistent with the mother worrying about her being injured. There always existed a plausible substitution for the critical word; otherwise, the reader might sense something was amiss prior to reading it. For example, if the daughter were strong, the mother might imagine her being safe, unharmed, or helpful. All modifications were selected so that there was no plausible continuation following the critical word that would resolve the inconsistency.

Four versions of the story were constructed such that each violation occurred at each critical word segment in one version. There was one violation of each type in each section of the story. Each section of the story was typed starting on separate pages. Critical words did not occur in the top or bottom three lines on each page and were at least three words from the beginning and end of lines.

Subjects were 11 male and 29 female undergraduate students enrolled in general psychology courses at Kent State University. They received points toward their grades for their participation. All were native English speakers and were not screened for reading ability. Subjects for all experiments had not participated in any other oral reading experiment. Four experimental groups of 10 subjects were defined by the four versions of the story.

Subjects were tested individually. They were told that the purpose of the experiment was to examine the relationship between reading and comprehension. They were instructed to read each section aloud, and then to write a summary of it. They were given as much time as they needed to read and to summarize the story. The reading performances were tape recorded for later analysis. In order to provide some warm-up for the readers, the first critical word did not occur until the bottom of the first page.

Analyses

In fluent speech, each word is not spoken with clearly distinguished beginning and ending sounds as it would be spoken in isolation. Ending sounds of one word are blended with the beginning sounds of the next, making it difficult to mark precisely where one word ends and another begins. The result is that two words may be uttered as if they were one long word with no break separating them. At the other extreme, some words are pronounced with a break in the middle, depending on the particular configuration of phonemes. Because of these possibilities, the text surrounding each critical word was divided into word units in order to facilitate measurement of disruptions. Word units were specified by listening to several readers and dividing the text surrounding the critical words into groups that were pronounced as a unit.

The most consistent phraseology across readers was adopted. Word units typically consisted of one or two words, rarely three words, and averaged 1.54 words long. They did not necessarily follow the syntactic structure of the sentence. Five word units before and five word units after each critical word were identified and were numbered from -5 to $+5$.

The primary dependent variable was the production time for each word unit. These times were measured by slowing the tape recorder to half-speed. An experimenter then pressed a key at the end of each word unit. A laboratory computer monitored the key-presses and timed the latencies between them. Each interval included the production time for the word unit itself and any pause, hesitation, or filler words that preceded the word unit. Since the critical word was physically changed between the control, syntactic + semantic, and semantic conditions, the production times for the critical word itself were not comparable. An additional latency was measured from the end of word unit -2 to the beginning of the critical word. The production time for word unit -1 was subtracted from this additional latency. The difference corresponds to the time between the end of word unit -1 and the beginning of the critical word. This value was used as the production time for the critical word unit in all analyses.

It was impossible to have an experimenter who was blind to the experimental manipulations measure the production times because any English speaker would recognize the violations on hearing the taped protocols. In order to assess the extent of experimenter error in measuring the production times, inter- and intra-experimenter reliabilities were obtained. Seven randomly selected subjects' protocols were measured by a second experimenter. The latencies were correlated with those from the first experimenter, yielding an average correlation of 0.94. The same experimenter retimed four randomly selected subjects' protocols from Experiment 3 (reported below) about one month later. The average correlation between the two sets of measurements was 0.98. Finally, a spectrographic analysis of eight randomly selected subjects' protocols from Experiment 2 (reported below) was prepared. The relevant production times were measured from the sound spectrograms and correlated with the experimenter's timing; the average correlation was 0.91. Marking word boundaries on spectrograms is far from precise, but the source of the error is visual uncertainty, in contrast to the auditory uncertainty of the experimenter's timing. Thus, the procedure for measuring production times was reliable.

The production times were analysed with a mixed analysis of variance. Groups of readers, as defined by the four versions of the story, was a between-subjects factor. Type of violation, word-unit position around the critical word, and section of the story were within-subject factors. Versions, violations, and segments were mixed in a Latin-square design. This design permitted calculation of a quasi-F ratio (F'), in which both subjects (individual readers) and language materials (critical word segments) were random factors contributing to a single error term (Clark, 1973). All reported effects were significant with $p < 0.05$. The three experimental means were compared to the control mean at each word-unit position using individual planned comparisons (Winer, 1971), based on the quasi-F mean square error term. The planned comparisons comprised less than 4 per cent of the possible comparisons.

A second dependent variable was the probability of a major disruption at each word-unit position. Major disruptions were defined as pauses of at least one second duration, substitutions, omissions, reversals, stammerings, mispronunciations, repetitions, and regressions. In short, any deviation from fluent oral reading that indicated that the reader noticed a violation was scored as a major disruption. Only one disruption was tallied per word unit and the frequencies were converted to probabilities. The major disruption data were used to confirm the results of the production times and to provide qualitative information about the disruptions. In Experiment 3, the correlation between production time and major disruption means was 0.93. Production times were lengthened by the major disruptions, as well as by a general slowing of oral production. Yet there is no reason to attempt to separate these influences because both reflect a disruption of the underlying cognitive processes.

Results

The mean production times as a function of violation type and word-unit position are presented in Table 6.1. Since word units differed markedly in physical size, only the differences in production times between the experimental and control conditions were interpretable. These differences are depicted in Figure 6.1. The effect of primary interest was the significant interaction between violation type and word-unit position, $F'(30,240) = 5.029, p < 0.001$. A difference of 99 msec in mean production times was significant.

Both the syntactic + semantic and the semantic violations diverged from

Table 6.1   Experiment 1: Mean production times (msec)

Violation	\multicolumn{11}{c}{Word-unit position}										
	−5	−4	−3	−2	−1	0	+1	+2	+3	+4	+5
Control	596	430	501	578	355	146	454	511	509	405	477
Syntactic + semantic	549	449	489	609	621	586	791	700	636	448	553
Semantic	567	431	460	605	463	299	819	686	671	432	567
Factual	586	456	478	568	372	168	553	602	516	424	508

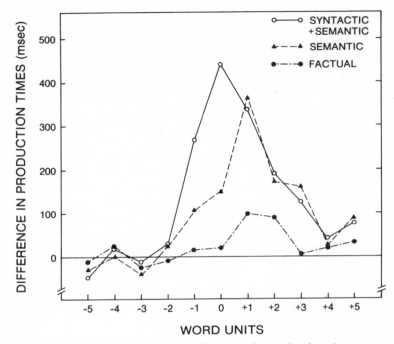

Figure 6.1   Experiment 1: Differences in production times

the control condition at word unit −1. The syntactic + semantic disruption peaked at the critical word, but the semantic disruption did not peak until word unit +1. Both disruptions continued to stay above the control through word unit +3. The factual inconsistency produced a much smaller effect, and was significantly different from the control only at word unit +1. The mean probabilities of a major disruption confirmed the results of the production time analyses in all respects.

Since both syntactic + semantic and semantic violations yielded lengthened oral production times before the critical word was uttered, both syntactic and semantic information evidently were being used in lexical access because words had to be accessed before they could be uttered. Both violations also were disruptive well after the critical word was produced indicating disruption of sentence comprehension. The factual inconsistency was disruptive only after the critical word had been uttered. So violation of factual information did not hinder lexical access, but it did affect sentence comprehension and story understanding.

The syntactic + semantic violation had a larger disruptive effect earlier than did the semantic, suggesting that the syntactic + semantic violation may have been a violation of two independent knowledge sources. If so, then confounding syntactic and semantic violations in a single manipulation can account for the greater disruption and the earlier peak of the syntactic + semantic violation relative to the purely semantic violation. If two independent information sources were violated, the likelihood that a violation would be noticed in one of them is greater than if only one information source were violated.

Experiment 2

Experiment 2 was similar to Experiment 1. The story and critical words were the same. The syntactic + semantic violation was replaced with a syntactic only violation and the semantic violation was retained. This change permitted a direct comparison of whether syntactic information was used at the same time as semantic information and whether they were independent sources of information.

Method

The story used in this experiment was identical to that used in Experiment 1 with the following exceptions. To violate syntactic information alone, the root morpheme of the critical word was retained, but the inflection was changed to that of a different part of speech. For example, the verb *injured* was changed to the noun *injury*. Although some semantic information is carried in syntactic categories, the reader could determine the intended meaning relatively easily. Several of the factual violations were rewritten so that the inconsistencies seemed more striking, at least to the intuitions of the investigators. Only four word units before the critical word were scored and the slightly altered word units averaged 1.60 words long.

The subjects were 17 male and 23 female undergraduate volunteers enrolled in general psychology courses at Kent State University. All were native English speakers, and were not screened for reading skill. The procedure was identical to that used in Experiment 1 with one exception. Instead of asking for summaries, multiple-choice questions were prepared for each section of the story. These questions tested literal, factual information that was unrelated to the critical word segments. Readers were very accurate on these questions (over 95 per cent correct) and there was no variation across sections or versions.

Results

The mean production times as a function of violation type and word-unit position are presented in Table 6.2. The differences in mean production times between the experimental and control conditions are shown in Figure 6.2. The

Table 6.2   Experiment 2: mean production times (msec)

Violation	\multicolumn{10}{c}{Word-unit position}									
	−4	−3	−2	−1	0	+1	+2	+3	+4	+5
Control	410	540	620	355	140	500	565	470	425	550
Syntactic	440	545	595	435	415	890	690	555	455	580
Semantic	425	540	630	460	405	850	750	620	480	580
Factual	415	530	660	415	175	655	650	585	415	515

critical interaction between violation type and word-unit position was significant $F'(27,216) = 2.891, p < 0.001$. A 112 msec difference in means was significant.

The syntactic and semantic violations both produced increased production times beginning at the critical word and continuing through word units +2 and +3, respectively. The curves followed each other almost exactly, peaking at word unit +1 (the same as the semantic disruption in Experiment 1), except that the syntactic disruption declined faster at word units +2 and +3. The pattern of results from the probability of a major disruption analysis confirmed the production time results. The syntactic violation produced a major disruption at the critical word a large percentage of the time relative to other violations—syntactic = 78 per cent, semantic = 44 per cent, and fac-

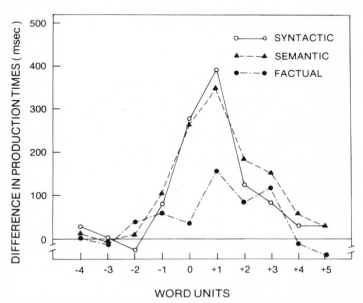

Figure 6.2   Experiment 2: Differences in production times

tual = 8 per cent. Half of these syntactic major disruptions were restorations of the correct form of the base word with the syntactically correct inflection. For example, 'injured' was uttered when *injury* was printed. Sixty-eight per cent of the restorations were fluent ones in that there was no pause or other disruption immediately before or during production of the restoration. If restorations are excluded from both the syntactic and semantic disruptions, the percentages of disruptions at the critical word were virtually identical—33 per cent for syntactic and 34 per cent for semantic. The restoration of the original critical word in the syntactic violation condition was a top-down effect. Apparently, readers were attempting to make sense of the text, so the original critical word was anticipated and restored. Readers substituted the original critical word in their productions because that was the word they were anticipating and the first several letters of the printed word confirmed those expectations. This restoration effect is the same as that obtained by Marslen-Wilson and Welsh (1978) in a speech-shadowing task.

The disruption from the factual inconsistency was larger although it still was not as large as that produced by the syntactic and semantic violations. In comparison with Experiment 1, the factual disruption was spread over three word units (+1 through +3 although it was not significant at +2) instead of two, and the peak was approximately 60 per cent higher. Even though the factual violations produced a larger effect than in the preceeding experiment, it still did not influence lexical access of the critical word. Its effect on sentence comprehension increased, but whether that effect occurred at the clause boundary or at an earlier point cannot be determined directly from these data.

Experiment 3

The story used in the preceding experiments was interesting and easy to understand in spite of the violations. It had good coherence among sentences and a macrostructure seemed easy to construct. How would processing change if the story were disjointed and if the events were strange and metaphorical? Many studies have shown that disordered and scrambled stories are difficult to understand and recall (Kintsch, Mandel, and Kozminsky, 1977; Mandler, 1978; Meyers and Boldrick, 1975; Stein and Nezworski, 1978). For this experiment, we selected unrelated paragraphs from a novel that described happenings that were difficult to understand, written in a highly metaphorical style. Because of this style, a reader would have difficulty constructing a coherent text base. In addition, it would be extremely difficult to construct a macrostructure incorporating all the paragraphs because they were not linked in the novel. So there would be less contextual information to aid lexical access and to guide sentence comprehension. In general, a reader would be more dependent on bottom-up processing to compensate for the reduced discourse information.

In addition to removing discourse information, we introduced a direct violation of lexical information by replacing the critical word with a pronounceable nonword. By definition, lexical access would be impossible because the nonword was not in the reader's mental dictionary. If the reader were using lexical information to pronounce the word, there would be a disruption in oral performance. But if the reader were relying solely on grapheme-phoneme correspondences to pronounce the word, there would be no disruption.

Method

Fifteen paragraphs with an average length of 124 words were selected from a contemporary novel. The passages were not contiguous in the novel, but the temporal sequence was maintained. The paragraphs seemed to the investigators to be much more vague, metaphorical, and difficult to follow than the story used in the first two experiments. However, the readability of these paragraphs was 6.0 (Fry, 1968), nearly two grade levels less than the story. This contrast reflects the fact that standard readability formulae do not measure discourse and conceptual properties of texts (Kintsch and Vipond, 1979). The first three paragraphs were used for practice. In each of the remaining 12 paragraphs, one critical word was identified that was not near the beginning or the end of the paragraph. Four nouns, four verbs, and four adjectives were selected as critical words. Each critical word was changed to obtain a lexical, syntactic + semantic, or semantic violation, or it was left unchanged as a control. For the lexical violation, the critical word was replaced with a pronounceable nonword that followed the rules of English orthographic structure. In the following example, the critical word *cool* was replaced with *brugen* (lexical), *flew* (syntactic + semantic), or *sharp* (semantic): 'When that was done, she pointed to his knee and removing the binding spread the cool paste thickly on the swollen flesh.'

There were four different versions of each paragraph representing each experimental manipulation. Critical words from other paragraphs were inserted to create the syntactic + semantic and the semantic violations. The occurrence of critical words was counterbalanced in such a way that no subject saw a specific critical word twice except in the control condition. The four versions of each paragraph were assembled into four presentation sets. Within each set, each manipulation occurred three times, once each as a noun, verb, and adjective. The sets were complementary so that each manipulation occurred once in each paragraph across versions. The paragraphs were typed on separate pages and arranged so that the critical words did not occur near the beginnings or ends of lines.

The subjects were 13 male and 27 female undergraduate volunteers from general psychology classes at Kent State University. All were native English speakers and were not screened for reading ability. The procedure was the same as that used in the first two experiments except that the reader orally summarized each paragraph after reading it. The production times before the critical word were measured initially in a slightly different way than in the two preceding experiments (cf. Fears, 1978). The times and analyses presented here have been adjusted to conform to the previously described pattern. Otherwise, the analyses were the same as in the first two experiments.

Results

The mean production times as a function of violation type and word-unit position are presented in Table 6.3. The differences between the production times of the experimental and control conditions are shown in Figure 6.3. The

Table 6.3   Experiment 3: mean production times (msec.)

Violation	Word-unit position										
	−5	−4	−3	−2	−1	0	+1	+2	+3	+4	+5
Control	520	520	485	535	405	267	450	640	495	460	435
Lexical	508	522	453	473	481	685	690	770	520	525	430
Syntactic + semantic	528	506	433	441	478	632	785	745	540	535	455
Semantic	538	479	546	465	436	318	595	695	525	485	430

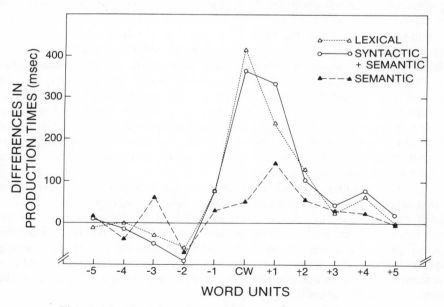

Figure 6.3   Experiment 3: Differences in production times

interaction between violation type and word-unit position was significant, $F'(27,160) = 3.899, p < 0.001$. A difference of 94 msec between means was significant.

Both lexical and syntactic + semantic violations lengthened production times beginning at the critical word. The disruptions peaked at the critical word and continued through word unit +2. Most of the disruptions from lexical violations were pauses as the readers balked before uttering the pronounceable nonword. Since the nonword was not in their mental dictionaries, they had difficulty pronouncing it solely on the basis of grapheme–phoneme correspondences. The curve for the syntactic + semantic disruption followed the curve for the lexical disruption almost perfectly, demonstrating that syntactic and/or semantic information was used in lexical access. By virtue of the way the lexical violation was constructed, it disrupted the lexical access component. Since the syntactic + semantic violation produced an identical pattern of disruption, syntactic and/or semantic information was being used by the same component. This result provides additional support for the conclusion from Experiments 1 and 2, that syntactic and semantic information was used in lexical access.

The disruption from the semantic violation did not occur until word unit +1 and was significantly smaller than the lexical and syntactic + semantic disruptions. In contrast to the first two experiments, the semantic violation did not produce a disruption until after the critical word had been uttered, so semantic information evidently was not being used for lexical access. The paragraphs were written in an abstract style using many figures of speech, so semantic violations were anomalies that easily could have been mistaken for metaphors intended by the author. Apparently, readers adopted the quite reasonable strategy of not giving high priority to semantic information for lexical access because it was not very informative. Lexical access used perceptual and syntactic information, which were not distorted by the difficulty and figurativeness of the story. The disruption produced by the semantic violation after the critical word was uttered indicates that semantic information was being used in sentence comprehension. Although semantic information may not have been useful for lexical access, it was essential for constructing a meaning for the sentence, so the semantic violation caused problems for the reader at that point.

In this experiment, the difficult text very likely shortened the eye–voice span relative to the first two experiments (Buswell, 1920; Morton, 1964). If such shortening occurred, the disruptions would have moved closer to the critical word, but their relative positions would not have been affected. Specifically, this shortening would not have changed the two primary results of this experiment, namely the simultaneity of the lexical and syntactic + semantic disruptions and the delay of the semantic disruptions until after the critical word was uttered.

DISCUSSION AND CONCLUSIONS

These experiments have provided information about how different kinds of information interact in the language processing components, particularly lexical access and sentence comprehension. Overall the results support an interactive model of language processing, but more importantly, they indicate something about the nature of the interactions.

Lexical access

Both bottom-up perceptual and top-down contextual information interact in lexical access. How violation of lexical information disrupted lexical access is evident: there was no mental dictionary entry for the nonword. According to Marslen-Wilson and Welsh's (1978) model of lexical access, a cohort of words would be activated corresponding to the initially processed portion of the nonword. For example, for the nonword *brugen* all known words beginning with *bru-* would be activated—*bruise, brunch, brunette, brunt, brush, brusque, brut, brutal,* and *brute.* Continuing perceptual analysis quickly would eliminate all the candidates because there is no common English word beginning with *brug-* or even *bru* + a letter with a descender (*g, j, p, q,* or *y*). A check with syntactic and semantic information for contextual appropriateness also would eliminate all members of the cohort. Hence, the lexical violation would be discovered very quickly.

Syntactic and semantic information also were involved in lexical access as demonstrated by the disruptive effects before the critical word was uttered. Furthermore, the pattern of disruption caused by the syntactic + semantic violation in Experiment 3 matched that from the lexical violation almost perfectly. If syntactic and semantic violations were disruptive of sentence comprehension only and were not involved in lexical access, the syntactic + semantic disruption would have been delayed at least slightly after the lexical disruption. Readers would not recognize that the syntactic–semantic information was inconsistent with the rest of the sentence until the critical word had been accessed and the information made available. But the lexical and syntactic + semantic disruption curves were virtually identical, suggesting that they affected either a common process, that process being lexical access, or processes operating at the same time.

The fluent restoration of the original critical word in the syntactic violation condition in Experiment 2 also supports the conclusion that syntactic information was involved in lexical access. The only way that the reader could have restored the original critical word was to have anticipated the part of speech from the preceding sentence context and then to have produced the syntactically appropriate ending for the critical word. Another piece of evidence for semantic involvement is the location of the semantic disruption in

Experiment 3 relative to the preceding experiments. In the paragraphs used in Experiment 3, semantic information was not useful for lexical access and so semantic constraints apparently were suspended, shifting the disruption until after the critical word was uttered. When semantic information was useful, as in Experiments 1 and 2, its violation was disruptive before the critical word was uttered. This shift in when semantic information was used as a function of its utility indicates a flexibility of processing at the lexical level, a property represented in interactive models.

Another instance of processing flexibility was obtained when these experiments were replicated in Polish (Kurkiewicz, Kurcz and Danks, 1981). Inflectional information varies in usefulness to Polish and English readers. In Polish *vis-à-vis* English, most syntactic information is carried in suffixes and very little in word order. Violation of syntactic information by altering inflections produced a larger disruptive effect earlier in Polish readers than in English readers. Polish readers used inflectional information to a greater degree in lexical access than did English readers.

Factual information was not used in lexical access because its violation was disruptive only after the critical word was accessed and uttered, and not before or at the critical word. Although in principle it could have influenced lexical access by supplementing syntactic and semantic contextual information, it did not. The finding that factual violations did not influence lexical access across clause or sentence boundaries suggests that lexical access was clausally autonomous. These results are in contrast to those reported by Foss and Ross (Chapter 5 of this volume). They found that information from a preceding sentence facilitated lexical access as measured by a phoneme-monitoring task. An explanation of the contrasting results of the two experiments probably lies in the quite different relations between the information in the preceding sentences and the target words and in the different experimental tasks.

Sentence comprehension

Syntactic, semantic, and factual information were involved in sentence comprehension: violations of all three produced disruptions for several word units after the critical word was uttered. However, the results do not differentiate between the clausal processing and word-by-word hypotheses because the location of the clause and sentence boundaries following the critical word were uncontrolled. In other experiments (Danks, Bohn, End, and Miller, 1980), we have both controlled and manipulated the location of the clause boundary following the critical word. The results have been quite clear. Both semantic and factual violations produce small, but significant, disruptions between the critical word and the end of the clause, followed by a much larger peak of disruption immediately after the clause boundary. The disruptions resulting from semantic and factual violations were the same size. The only difference was that the semantic violation produced an additional peak at the critical word, and the factual violation did not.

These more recent results support the word-by-word hypothesis of sentence comprehension. Violating either semantic or factual information produced a disruption while the clause was being read. As each word was accessed, the reader attempted to integrate its meaning into a larger representation of the text. This representation spanned more than just the immediate sentence because the factual violation, which involved the preceding sentence, produced a disruption as well. Since integration was not possible immediately, the reader held the words in a memory buffer until the end of the clause. At that time, the increasing memory load and processing demands required a final attempt at integration. The end of a clause or sentence is a natural point for readers to resolve any problems they have had in understanding a sentence. At the clause boundary, readers attempted to resolve the inconsistency, but given the nature of our violations, they were usually unsuccessful.

An interactive model of sentence comprehension provides the best account of these results. As words are accessed, each word's meaning is integrated into a global representation of the text to that point. The sentence comprehension component is not autonomous because the global representation spans more than the immediate sentence. Finally, sentence comprehension is a flexible process adapting to the difficulty of the text and the availability of information.

Discourse understanding

These experiments were not designed to evaluate discourse understanding, even though a story context was used and factual, intersentential information was violated. Most studies of discourse understanding have used memory tasks to assess whether the listener/reader has formed a coherent text base and a macrostructure representation (Kintsch, 1974; Meyer, 1975), but memory tasks do not provide much information about the process of story understanding. Several more recent studies have examined how this component operates using on-line measures, such as eye fixations and sentence reading times. Just and Carpenter (1980) monitored eye fixations and were able to attribute substantial amounts of gaze time to macroprocessing, as well as to lexical and sentential components. Cirilo and Foss (1980) and Cirilo (1981) found that discourse understanding, as measured by reading times, varied in predictable ways based on Kintsch and van Dijk's (1978) processing model. Reading times increased for sentences where the referential antecedent of nouns occurred much earlier in the story, thus increasing the difficulty of establishing referential coherence. Reading times also increased when the sentence was high in the macrostructure, a main idea of the story. When the reader's task was altered, readers were flexible in adapting their processing strategies at the discourse understanding level to meet the task demands. These results support an interactive model of discourse understanding. Macrostructure and referential coherence influenced gaze durations for individual words and reading times for individual sentences. Processing strategies shifted flexibly with changes in the demands on the discourse processing component.

In summary, the results of the experiments reported here and other studies supportive interactive-type models for all three major components of language processing—lexical access, sentence comprehension, and discourse understanding. Although we have considered the processing components separately for purposes of exposition, a comprehensive model will include all three components. We attempted to narrow the range of possible interactive models, but excessive explanatory power remains as their most salient fault.

ACKNOWLEDGEMENTS

We thank Richard Klich, Greg Hill and Jeff Hall for their assistance in conducting and analysing the experiments reported in this chapter. Experiment 3 was part of a Master's thesis submitted by Ramona Fears to Kent State University. The research and the preparation of this chapter was supported by Grant No. NIE-G-78-0223 from the National Institute of Education.

APPENDIX

The critical word segments for the three experiments are listed in the order in which they appeared in the story. The critical word is italicized. The manipulations introduced to produce the violations are indicated in parentheses: the factual change is in the sentence preceding the critical word (Experiments 1 and 2) and the lexical (Experiment 3), syntactic + semantic (Experiments 1 and 3), syntactic (Experiment 2), and semantic (Experiments 1, 2, and 3) violations follow the critical word. The slashes separate word units used in scoring the protocols.

Experiment 1

1. Everyone in the Scott family was in high spirits because on Saturday they planned to fly to Mexico for a vacation (. . . was depressed that morning because on Saturday they had to attend Mary Jane's grandmother's funeral). / No   one / in   the   entire / Scott / family / was   more / *excited* (pumpkin, smoked) / than / Mary Jane, / an intelligent / and pretty / girl. /

2. Her daughter had always been weak (strong) physically. Because / of

this, / she even / imagined / her daughter / being / *trampled* (iceberg, planted) / by other children / while / trying / to get / out of the wrecked bus. /

3. Sam Scott heard on the radio that morning (. . . went to work and did not know) that there had been a bus–train collision in / Lawrenceville. / Although / he was / relieved / that the / *accident* (subtract, delusion) / had not / occurred / in his / community / he felt / . . . .

4. There was enough time for the school bus to slow down and yet it did not (The bus stopped at the stop sign and waited until the entire train had safely passed). A loud sound like a powerful explosion / could be / heard / as the / train / and bus / *collided* (family, mailed). / The train / hit / the bus / at the / midpoint. /

5. One boy had his left leg severed below the knee (One boy who was not injured was screaming hysterically). She / applied / a large / tourniquet / to stop / his / *bleeding* (freeze, writing) / leg. / Within minutes, / several ambulances / were on the / scene. /

6. They were unconscious and few had (They were fully conscious and had) either / wallets / or purses. / Immediate / identification / was / *impossible* (phonograph, athletic). / Grabbing / a felt-tipped / pen, / Dr. Carr / inscribed / . . . .

7. Mary Jane's name was first on a list of survivors (deceased). / She was / at that / moment / being / prepared / for / *surgery* (summarize, trailer). / From time / to time / a doctor / would enter / the cafeteria / . . . .

8. The doctor told the Scotts that the leg may have to be amputated (. . . that their daughter's leg may be saved) as soon as a specialist could be found / to perform / the surgery. / Vera / and Sam / were / *saddened* (rapidly, polished) / by this / possibility. / Vera / collapsed / but Sam / . . . .

9. Once her vital signs stabilized, she was moved (In spite of the doctors' efforts, her vital signs did not stabilize which meant that she could not be moved) / from her / hospital / room. / Mary / was / *carried* (piano, printed) / in her / bed / from the / intensive / care / . . . .

10. She was not aware of anything (She was aware of everything) that happened to her / after / the collision / of the bus / and the train. / She was / *unconscious* (baseball, classical) / from a / blow / to the / back / of her / . . . .

11. Mr. Scott was shakened, but calm (. . . and dazed) after all / that had / happened / that day. / He had / clearly / *comprehended* (umbrella, transported) / all / that the / doctors / had said. / The Scotts / . . . .

12. On occasion, parts of her body would jerk uncontrollably (Her whole body was motionless) as she / lay / in the / bed. / Her arm / and leg / *shook* (money, spoke) / violently. / Her eyes / were closed / as though / she were / . . . .

13. The next day her temperature shot up over six degrees and

perspiration and dehydration accompanied her high fever (. . . returned to normal and the perspiration and dehydration accompanying her high fever were gone). As the hours / passed, / the nurses / continued / to change / her / *sweat-soaked* (accommodate, scuba-diving) / hospital / gowns. / For forty-eight / hours / her life / . . . .

14. Mary Jane became unusually more alert when she saw (Mary Jane rejected) / the special / drawing / board. / Immediately / she started / *copying* (divine, singing) / a picture / much / in the / style / of a / . . . .

15. She was allowed to have more visitors other than (Although Mary Jane was now feeling better she was only allowed to have visitors from) her immediate family. / Dozens / of her / classmates / came / to her / *bedside* (punish, teeth) / in the / evenings. / To the / Scotts, / who had / . . . .

16. Ever since Mary Jane had been conscious and alert, she had been without exercise of any kind (. . ., she was careful to exercise her muscles everyday) while in the hospital. / As a / result, / her muscles / started / to / *waste* (fork, rejoice) / away. / Now / with the / help / of three / . . . .

Experiment 2

1. Everyone in the Scott family was in high spirits that morning because on Saturday they planned to fly to Mexico for a vacation (Everyone in the entire Scott family was depressed that morning because on Saturday they had to attend Mary Jane's grandmother's funeral). No one / in the entire / Scott / family / was more / *excited* (smoked, excitement) / than / Mary Jane, / an intelligent / and pretty / girl. /

2. Her daughter had always been weak (strong) physically. Because of this / she even / imagined / her daughter / being / *injured* (injury, planted) / by other / children / while / trying / to get out / . . . .

3. Sam Scott heard on the radio that morning that there had been a bus–train collision in Lawrenceville (Sam Scott was not aware that there had been a terrible bus–train accident in Lawrenceville that morning). / Although / he was / relieved / that the / *collision* (collided, delusion) / had not / occurred / in his / community, / he felt / . . . .

4. There was enough time for the school bus to slow down and yet it did not stop (The bus driver saw the train just in time and miraculously stopped the bus) before / it reached / the tracks. / The bus / and train / *crashed* (crashing, mailed) / and a loud / sound / like a / powerful / explosion / . . . .

5. One boy had his left leg fractured below the knee (. . . was completely uninjured). She applied / a large / splint / to fix / his / *broken* (break, written) / leg. / Within minutes, / several / ambulances / were on / . . . .

6. Most of them were unconscious (conscious) and could not give (had given) their names to the / physician. / Immediate / identification / was

not / *possible*   (possibly,   athletic). / Grabbing / a   felt-tipped / pen, / Dr. Carr / inscribed / . . . .

7. Mary Jane's name was first on a list of survivors (deceased). She was at that / moment / being   prepared / for / *surgery*   (surgically,   trailer). / From time / to time, / a doctor / would enter / the cafeteria / . . . .

8. The doctor told the Scotts that the leg may have to be amputated (would be saved) as soon as a specialist could be found to perform / the surgery. / Vera / and   Sam / were / *depressed*   (depression,   polished) / by this / possibility. / Vera / collapsed, / but Sam / . . . .

9. Unfortunately (Fortunately), her vital signs did not (had) stabilized so it was impossible (possible) for the doctors and nurses / to move / her. / Mary Jane / was / *carried* (carrier, printed) / from the / intensive / care unit, / down the / corridor. /

10. After the collision of the bus and the train, she was not aware of anything (. . ., she was clearly aware of everything) / that had / happened / to her. / She was / *unconscious* (unconsciousness, classical) / from a / blow / to the / back / of her / . . . .

11. Mr. Scott was shakened but calm after all that had happened that day (. . . was so shakened and confused that he did not understand any of the medical explanations concerning his daughter's condition). All that the doctors / had told / him, / he had / clearly / *comprehended* (comprehension, transported). / The   Scotts / were / overwhelmed / with   grief. / They realized / . . . .

12. On occasion parts of her body would jerk uncontrollably (Her whole body was completely paralysed) as she / lay / in the bed. / Her arm / and leg / *shook*   (shaky,   spoke) / violently. / Her   eyes / were   closed / as though / she were / . . . .

13. The doctor then informed Mary Jane's parents that the leg would have to be removed (. . . that with more surgery, the leg would be able to be saved) / completely. / After / Mary Jane's / leg was / *amputated* (amputation, amplified), / she was / taken back / to her / room / in isolation / . . . .

14. Mary Jane became unusually more alert when she saw (Mary Jane rejected) the special / drawing / board. / Immediately, / she started / *copying* (copier, singing) / a picture / much / in the / style / of a / . . . .

15. She was allowed to have more visitors other than her immediate family (However, she still refused to have any visitors while she was bedridden). Dozens / of her / classmates / came / to her / *bedside* (bedridden, teeth) / in the / evenings. / To the Scotts / who had seen / her / . . . .

16. Ever since Mary Jane had been conscious and alert, she had been without exercise of any kind (. . ., she was careful to exercise her muscles everyday) while in the / hospital. / As a result, / her muscles / started to / *waste* (wasteful, rejoice) / away. / Now / with the / help / of three / . . . .

Experiment 3

1. . . . / down / the dark / aisles / and sat / on the / *moss* (glurck, school, killed) / beneath / the great / trees; / and again / his mind / . . . .

2. . . . / nostrils. / At first / the men / swore. / They / *struck* (brugen, flew, brilliant) / and prodded / the camels. / Then / they / too / . . . .

3. . . . / the   grinding, / the   screaming. / He / wriggled / in   the / *dry* (kaysen, brilliant, iron) / straw / stuffing / his mouth / with it / to keep / . . . .

4. . . . / crocodiles / were / shot / at, / the   storks / *flew*   (glurck, killed, streets) / into the air / in mass / panic. / The beat of / their wings / . . . .

5. . . . / to his / knee / and removing / the binding / spread the / *cool* (brugen, sharp, flew) / paste / thickly / on the / swollen / flesh. /

6. . . . / town / and / entered   it / and   walked / through   its / *streets* (kaysen, iron, sharp). / Faces / looked at / him / but he / did not / . . . .

7. . . . / struck / something / hard / and he / felt a / *sharp* (glurck, cool, streets) / pain. / When he / looked up / the train / was / . . . .

8. . . . / among / the dead. / Some of the / dead / had been / *killed* (kaysen, ran, school) / by / the fire / and lay / faceless / in the / . . . .

9. . . . / ships of / hard / fact, / of / hard / *iron* (brugen, moss, cool), / of coal, / machinery, / cargo / and / tonnage. /

10. . . . / behind, / a black / headland / notched / the / *brilliant* (glurck, dry, moss) / sky. / Far ahead, / barely / visible / in the / . . . .

11. . . . / from seven / to two / each / day / in the / *school* (brugen, streets, ran), / itself. / Later / they / went around / the town / . . . .

12. . . . / came, / in   wild / summer / thunderstorms. / The   rain / *ran* (kaysen,   struck,   dry) / down / his   clothing, / plastering, / the   dust / in streaks / . . . .

REFERENCES

Aaronson, D., and Scarborough, H. S. Performance theories for sentence coding: Some quantitative evidence. *Journal of Experimental Psychology: Human Perception and Performance*, 1976, **2**, 56–70.

Bever, T. G. The cognitive basis for linguistic structures. In J. R. Hayes (Ed.), *Cognition and the Development of Language.* New York: Wiley, 1970.

Bransford, J. D., and Johnson, M. K. Considerations of some problems of comprehension. In W. G. Chase (Ed.), *Visual Information Processing.* New York: Academic Press, 1973.

Buswell, G. T. An experimental study of the eye–voice span in reading. *Supplementary Educational Monographs*, 1920 (Whole n. 17).

Carpenter, P. A., and Just, M. A. Reading comprehension as eyes see it. In M. A. Just and P. A. Carpenter (Eds), *Cognitive Processes in Comprehension*. Hillsdale, N.J.: Lawrence Erlbaum Associates, 1977.

Carroll, J. M., and Bever, T. G. Sentence comprehension: A case study in the relation of knowledge to perception. In E. C. Carterette and M. P. Friedman (Eds), *Handbook of Perception: Language and Speech*, Vol. 7. New York: Academic Press, 1976.

Carroll, J. M., Tanenhaus, M. K., and Bever, T. G. The perception of relations: The interaction of structural, functional, and contextual factors in the segmentation of sentences. In W. J. M. Levelt and G. B. Flores d'Arcais (Eds), *Studies in the Perception of Language*. Chichester: Wiley, 1978.

Cirilo, R. K. Referential coherence and text structure in story comprehension. *Journal of Verbal Learning and Verbal Behavior*, 1981, **20**, 358–367.

Cirilo, R. K., and Foss, D. J. Text structure and reading times for sentences. *Journal of Verbal Learning and Verbal Behavior*, 1980, **19**, 96–109.

Clark, H. H. The language-as-fixed-effect fallacy: A critique of language statistics in psychological research. *Journal of Verbal Learning and Verbal Behavior*, 1973, **12**, 335–359.

Clark, H. H., and Marshall, C. Reference diaries. In D. L. Waltz (Ed.), *Theoretical Issues in Natural Language Processing*, Vol. 1. New York: Association for Computing Machinery, 1978.

Crothers, E. J. *Paragraph Structure Inference*. Norwood, N.J.: Ablex, 1979.

Danks, J. H. Grammaticalness and meaningfulness in the comprehension of sentences. *Journal of Verbal Learning and Verbal Behavior*, 1969, **8**, 687–696.

Danks, J. H. Models of language comprehension. *Polish Psychological Bulletin*, 1978, **9**, 183–192.

Danks, J. H., Bohn, L., End, L., and Miller, R. Integration of sentence meanings in stories. Meeting of the Psychonomic Society, St. Louis, 1980.

Danks, J. H., and Fears, R. Oral reading: Does it reflect decoding or comprehension? In L. B. Resnich and P. A. Weaver (Eds), *Theory and practice of early reading*, Vol. 3. Hillsdale, N.J.: Lawrence Erlbaum Associates, 1979.

Danks, J. H., and Glucksberg, S. Experimental psycholinguistics. *Annual Review of Psychology*, 1980, **31**, 391–417.

Danks, J. H., and Hill, G. O. An interactive analysis of oral reading. In A. M. Lesgold and C. A. Perfetti (Eds), *Interactive Processes in Reading*. Hillsdale, N.J.: Lawrence Erlbaum Associates, 1981.

Dooling, D. J., and Lachman, R. Effects of comprehension on retention of prose. *Journal of Experimental Psychology*, 1971, **88**, 216–222.

Durkin, D. What classroom observations reveal about reading comprehension instruction. *Reading Research Quarterly*, 1978-79, **14**, 481–533.

Fears, R. *Levels of processing in oral reading*. Unpublished master's thesis, Kent State University, 1978.

Forster, K. I. Accessing the mental lexicon. In R. J. Wales & E. Walker (Eds), *New Approaches to Language Mechanisms*. Amsterdam: North-Holland, 1976.

Frederiksen, C. H. Effects of context-induced processing operations on semantic information acquired from discourse. *Cognitive Psychology*, 1975, **7**, 139–166.

Fry, E. B. A readability formula that saves time. *Journal of Reading*, 1968, **11**, 513–516, 575–578.

Gibson, E. J., and Levin, H. *The Psychology of Reading*. Cambridge, Mass.: M.I.T. Press, 1975.

Glucksberg, S., Trabasso, T., and Wald, J. Linguistic structures and mental operations. *Cognitive Psychology*, 1973, **5**, 338–370.

Gough, P. B. One second of reading. In J. F. Kavanagh and I. G. Mattingly (Eds), *Language by Ear and by Eye*. Cambridge, Mass.: M.I.T. Press, 1972.

Just, M. A., and Carpenter, P. A. A theory of reading: From eye fixations to comprehension. *Psychological Review*, 1980, **87**, 329–354.

Kintsch, W. *The Representation of Meaning in Memory*. Hillsdale, N.J.: Lawrence Erlbaum Associates, 1974.

Kintsch, W., and Green, E. The role of culture-specific schemata in the comprehension and recall of stories. *Discourse Processes*, 1978, **1**, 1–13.

Kintsch, W., Mandel, T. S., and Kozminsky, E. Summarizing scrambled stories. *Memory and Cognition*, 1977, **5**, 547–552.

Kintsch, W., and van Dijk, T. A. Toward a model of text comprehension and production. *Psychological Review*, 1978, **85**, 363–394.

Kintsch, W., and Vipond, D. Reading comprehension and readability in educational practice and psychological theory. In L. G. Nilsson (Ed.), *Perspectives on Memory Research*. Hillsdale, N.J.: Lawrence Erlbaum Associates, 1979.

Kurkiewicz, D., Kurcz, I., and Danks, J. H. Reading comprehension processes in Polish and English. *Polish Psychological Bulletin*, 1981, **12**, 25–31.

LaBerge, D., and Samuels, S. J. Toward a theory of automatic information processing in reading. *Cognitive Psychology*, 1974. **6**, 293–323.

Lesgold, A. M., and Perfetti, C. A. (Eds) *Interactive Processes in Reading*. Hillsdale, N.J.:Lawrence Erlbaum Associates, 1981.

Levin, H. *The Eye–Voice Span*. Cambridge, Mass.:M.I.T. Press, 1979.

Mandler, J. M. A code in the node: The use of a story schema in retrieval. *Discourse Processes*, 1978, **1**, 14–35.

Marslen-Wilson, W. D. Sentence perception as an interactive parallel process. *Science*, 1975, **189**, 226–228.

Marslen-Wilson, W. D., and Tyler, L. K. The temporal structure of spoken language understanding. *Cognition*, 1980, **8**, 1–71.

Marslen-Wilson, W. D., Tyler, L. K., and Seidenberg, M. Sentence processing and the clause boundary. In W. J. M. Levelt and G. B. Flores d'Arcais (Eds), *Studies in the Perception of Language*. Chichester: Wiley, 1978.

Marslen-Wilson, W. D., and Welsh, A. Processing interactions and lexical access during word recognition in continuous speech. *Cognitive Psychology*, 1978, **10**, 29–63.

Massaro, D. W. Primary and secondary recognition in reading. In D. W. Massaro (Ed.), *Understanding Language*. New York: Academic Press, 1975.

McClelland, J. L. On the time relations of mental processes: An examination of systems of processes in cascade. *Psychological Review*, 1979, **86**, 287–330.

Meyer, B. J. F. *The Organization of Prose and its Effects on Memory*. Amsterdam: North-Holland, 1975.

Meyers, L. S., and Boldrik, D. Memory for meaningful connected discourse. *Journal of Experimental Psychology: Human Learning and Memory*, 1975, **1**, 584–591.

Miller, G. A., and Isard, S. Some perceptual consequences of linguistic rules. *Journal of Verbal Learning and Verbal Behavior*, 1963, **2**, 217–228.

Mistler-Lachman, J. L. Levels of comprehension in processing of normal and ambiguous sentences. *Journal of Verbal Learning and Verbal Behavior*, 1972, **11**, 615–623.

Morton, J. The effects of context upon speed of reading, eye movements, and eye–voice span. *Quarterly Journal of Experimental Psychology*, 1964, **16**, 340–354.

Perfetti, C. A., and Lesgold, A. M. Discourse comprehension and sources of individual differences. In M. A. Just and P. A. Carpenter (Eds), *Cognitive Processes in Comprehension*. Hillsdale, N.J.: Lawrence Erlbaum Associates, 1977.

Perfetti, C. A., and Roth, S. Some of interactive processes in reading and their role in reading skill. In A. M. Lesgold and C. A. Perfetti (Eds), *Interactive Processes in Reading*. Hillsdale, N. J.: Lawrence Erlbaum Associates, 1981.

Poulsen, D., Kintsch, E., Kintsch, W., and Premack, D. Children's comprehension and memory for stories. *Journal of Experimental Child Psychology*, 1979, **28**, 379–403.

Reicher, G. M. Perceptual recognition as a function of meaningfulness and stimulus material. *Journal of Experimental Psychology*, 1969, **81**, 275–310.

Rumelhart, D. E. Toward an interactive model of reading. In S. Dornic (Ed.), *Attention and Performance VI*. Hillsdale, N.J.: Lawrence Erlbaum Associates, 1977.

Schwartz, R. M. Levels of processing: The strategic demands of reading comprehension. *Reading Research Quarterly*, 1980, **15**, 433–450.

Stanovich, K. E. Toward an interactive-compensatory model of individual differences in the development of reading fluency. *Reading Research Quarterly*, 1980, **16**, 32–71.

Stein, N. L., and Nezworski, T. The effects of organization and instructional set on story memory. *Discourse Processes*, 1978, **1**, 177–193.

Stevens, A. L., and Rumelhart, D. E. Errors in reading: An analysis using an augmented transition network model of grammar. In D. A. Norman and D. E. Rumelhart (Eds), *Exploration in Cognition*. San Francisco: Freeman, 1975.

Tyler, L. K., and Marslen-Wilson, W. D. The on-line effects of semantic context on syntactic processing. *Journal of Verbal Learning and Verbal Behavior*, 1977, **16**, 683–692.

Warren, W. H., Nicholas, D. W., and Trabasso, T. Event chains and inferences in understanding narratives. In R. O. Freedle (Ed.), *Advances in Discourse Processing: New directions in discourse processing*, Vol. 2. Norwood, N.J.: Ablex, 1979.

Wheeler, D. Processing in word recognition. *Cognitive Psychology*, 1970, **1**, 59–85.

Wildman, D. M., and Kling, M. Semantic, syntactic, and spatial anticipation in reading. *Reading Research Quarterly*, 1978–79, **14**, 128–164.

Winer, B. J. *Statistical Principles in Experimental Design*. New York: McGraw-Hill, 1971 (2nd ed.).

The Process of Language Understanding
Edited by G. B. Flores d'Arcais and R. J. Jarvella
© 1983 John Wiley & Sons Ltd.

7

Pragmatic Influences in Producing and Perceiving Language: A Critical and Historical Perspective

ROBERT J. JARVELLA

*Max Planck Institut für Psycholinguistics, Nijmegen,
and N.I.A.S., Wassenaar, Netherlands*

and

JOHANNES ENGELKAMP

Universität des Saarlandes, Saabrücken, W. Germany

A word devoid of thought is a dead thing.
Vygotsky
Mysl' izrečennaja jest' lož'
Tyutchev

Psycholinguistics is concerned with the mental states and processes involved in language use as a whole. In the last fifteen years, workers in this field have become increasingly interested not only in how people represent and process language, but also, at least indirectly, in how we use it to communicate given messages. During that time, articles and papers concerned with the informativeness implied by using particular linguistic forms have appeared in some number, hypotheses have been put forward about how speakers may tailor their utterances to meet the needs of their addressees, and suggestions offered of how listeners may use context-specific knowledge to interpret what they hear. In the present chapter, we take a fresh look at some of this research, point to some of the conceptions which have given rise to it, and show how it has exploited, and sometimes misused, them. We will be particularly concerned with what, for want of a better term, we will call 'the given–new distinction'. However, other issues in the pragmatics of language use will also be taken up at least in passing, including the notion (cf. Grice,

225

1975; Allwood, 1976) that linguistic communication is basically a cooperative enterprise.

An adequate historical review of our topic would reach back as far as Aristotle, and, in a single paper focused around ideas and methods present in recent work, cannot be seriously attempted. However, notions (re-)emerging over about the last century will be introduced here with at least some historical perspective. One issue in linguistic pragmatics to be taken up thus extends a discussion in philosophy dating from Frege's (1892) *Über Sinn und Bedeutung* (e.g., Strawson, 1950; Searle, 1969). This is (roughly) that the use of certain referring expressions normally serves to locate or access knowledge relevant to interpreting utterances. Another, in some ways complementary, idea sometimes put forward is that there are conventional linguistic ways of conveying what it is that one judges to be worth saying with respect to that information, and thus of being understood by others. In general (e.g., Paul, 1886; Høffding, 1910; Bates and MacWhinney, 1979), authors have made a distinction between parts of utterances, largely intended to reflect this difference. However, it is confusing, and serves no very useful theoretical purpose, to associate this distinction with 'given' and 'new' information in utterances. In actual use, referential and predicative expressions may each display aspects of both.[1]

If the given–new distinction has any heuristic value, it is a distinction in need of greater precision. Consider some reasons why. As a first approximation, one might be led to propose that the given–new idea stands in close relation to the assumptions (or, perhaps better, the beliefs or expectations) which a language producer has in making an utterance about the existing knowledge, state of mind, etc., of a language understander.[2] Then, in actual cases it would have to do with the corresponding use of linguistic forms by the participants in a speech situation to convey and understand the contents of particular messages. What a speaker took for granted in this process he would somehow signal, and what he intended to be informative he would express so that this intention was perceived. Exploring how this process works, linguistically and psychologically, would in these terms be basic to understanding the relationship between utterances and their meanings. Thus, we might now expect that that part of what a speaker says which corresponds to something he takes to be already known (or readily accessible) to a listener, he will convey as 'old' information; what he believes will be unfamiliar to the addressee, he will tend to mark as *not* being old. In that case, there should be something about the utterances used—their prosody, word selection, syntax, etc.—which serves to reinforce this distinction. And for his part, the addressee might be thought of as using an utterance and its context to determine what is intended to be 'new' to him, and relate this via what is conveyed as being knowable to information he in fact is in possession of.

For practical reasons, and to serve as a link to previous ideas, the present chapter is written within such a conceptual framework, but also intended to challenge its basic foundations. One difficulty with the perspective described above becomes apparent when we ask more closely for whom or what information is to be counted as old or new. The hearer is clearly not the only candidate. Among other obvious candidates are the speaker himself and the speech episode in which the two are engaged. A too cooperative view of linguistic communication runs the risk of failing to recognize that many linguistic choices are probably dictated by states of the speaker's mind rather than the listener's, or out of consideration for the listener.[3] Independently of his desire to communicate anything, what a speaker says may be most strongly affected by his reaction to (jointly available) prior and just prior utterances which have occurred. Reference to the discourse being produced or to the perceptual surround will, of course, be supported by the hearer being co-present. In the wider sense of earlier contact and familiarity, context will also play a certain role in defining suitable topics for discussion. However, in general it seems unlikely that spontaneous speech reflects much deliberation over known-to-hearer and new-to-hearer information in advance. Except in quite special circumstances (such as when non-understanding is perceived, interest in topics or knowledge of referents brought up is checked explicitly, or in asking and answering questions), there may not be very much that a speaker says which can be attributed to an attempt to accommodate his words to the addressee alone.[4]

A second problem is that a single given–new distinction is difficult to apply without contradiction. Rather, what is relevant is a range of states of mind, of both conversational participants. This issue has been raised in an important and quite convincing fashion by Chafe (1976). Although Chafe defines givenness proper in a strict manner (as knowledge assumed to be directly in the listener's consciousness), the general tone of his appeal is for broad consideration of how mental states, representations, and use of linguistic forms may be interrelated. If one seeks out linguistic features of utterances with particular functions in reflecting and allowing access to, and the altering of, cognitive representations, a number of basic types might be found. These would include definiteness of reference used, prosodic prominence, word or constituent order, deixis, anaphora, and others. Linguistically, this set of possibilities extends well beyond 'a syntactic distinction the speaker is obliged to make between Given information and New Information'—Clark and Haviland's (1977) statement of what their 'given–new contract' is concerned with—and psychologically it reflects a set of states and conditions more diverse and finely graded than presence vs. absence of information in a speaker's or addressee's general memory. Here, we will concentrate mainly on the first phenomena cited, leaving deixis and most kinds of anaphora largely out of consideration. For a set of papers specifically concerned with the latter, see Jarvella and Klein (1982).

A third difficulty is the empirical basis upon which the given–new distinction rests. The majority of psychological experimentation making contact with this has been done under extremely artificial conditions, using no or only minimal context, from prepared written instead of spontaneous oral language, and with no more than a hypothetical human source or goal for messages sent and received. These kinds of limitations are fairly obvious simply from noting what was done in most cases; in our critical remarks, we will concentrate as much on the confusion evident in interpreting pragmatic properties of utterances as on the limits of extrapolating to real-life communication.

The chapter is organized as follows. The first main section contains a selective review of some lexical, syntactic, and prosodic features of sentences which have been taken to convey 'given' and 'new' information. It ends with a discussion of the independence of these features with respect to each other and prior utterances. In the second section, we take up the experimental literature and some hypotheses about how information expressed in using language originates and how it is represented and processed by an understander.

DESCRIBING THE FUNCTIONS OF LINGUISTIC CATEGORIES[5]

Speakers of English and similar languages seem to convey their presuppositions in utterances largely by means of linguistic contrasts. For example, we may choose to use a definite noun phrase rather than an indefinite one. Or we might employ a sentence construction which is non-basic in some way. Or we might express what is to be understood as not (or least) presupposed by producing it with prosodic emphasis. Usually, a combination of these (and other) features can be found in a single utterance, calling for an analysis which allows for, and even predicts, their combination.

Definiteness and indefiniteness

One of the functions of using both definite and indefinite articles with nouns is to refer. (For a useful review of previous linguistic approaches to determiners and reference, see Karmiloff-Smith, 1979, pp. 22–34.) In early modern analytic philosophy (e.g., Frege, 1892; Russell, 1905), use of particular noun phrases (especially proper names and definite NPs formed with count nouns) was recognized as implying the existence and uniqueness of their referents. Still more recent analyses have tended to conclude that when a speaker uses such a noun phrase referentially, he will also tend to presuppose some access to information on the part of an addressee. Thus, Strawson (1950) argues that use of *the* in an expression of the type 'the so-and-so' acts as a signal that a unique reference is being made, and that what follows *the*, together with context, should bring to light *what* unique reference is being made. Similarly, Halliday and Hasan (1976, p. 71) conclude that 'the definite article has no content (but) merely indicates that the item in question is specific and identifiable; that somewhere the information necessary for identifying it is recoverable.' Writing in a similar vein, Chafe (1976) reasons that if the speaker thinks the hearer can identify a particular referent he has in mind, he will give this item the status of being definite. Linell (1979), for example, points out that if an addressee is also witness to some event (e.g., a cat drinking some milk), the speaker can make the particular nominal references he uses to describe the event definite, since they will be obvious. In Clark and Haviland (1977, p. 3), the generalization is made that 'in most sentences, definite noun phrases carry Given information ... known to the hearer.' Hawkins (1978) points out that most such definitions are too general, but also adopts the view that the overall use of definite descriptions calls on a language understander to locate or match a referent from within a set of objects defined by the situation of utterance and other shared information.[6]

A number of authors have attempted to distinguish the case of indefinite reference from the one just discussed in terms of newness in some respect. A more conservative (and perhaps more defensible) position is taken by Hawkins (1978), who rather argues that the differences between referential expressions of the type 'the so-and-so' and 'a so-and-so' involves uniqueness. This seems to be consistent with Russell's (1905) observation that forms of the latter type may denote *ambiguously*. Hawkins suggests that simple indefinite descriptions do logically presuppose existence (cf. Keenan, 1976), but that it depends on how other conditions are satisfied whether a listener will be able to locate in memory an object referred to in this way. Unless the listener can narrow down the options and the sentence containing the reference permits a potentially locatable interpretation, an indefinite NP will, until it is re-mentioned in discourse as the object of that class already identified, remain just what its name implies.

Apparently stronger positions are taken by Chafe (1976, p. 42), who writes 'it may be valid to say that indefiniteness entails newness' (which he defines as what is *introduced* into consciousness), and by Clark and Haviland (1977, p. 13), who state that 'an indefinite noun phrase, because it presupposes the listener does not yet know its referent, has to be part of the New information.' Hawkins himself goes as far as to say that an expression of the form *a + singular count noun* cannot generally be used to refer to an object which is unique within the shared set defined for a speaker and hearer. For further discussion along these lines, see Engelkamp (1982).

There may be some difficulty with upholding this stronger view. More specifically, it seems to be possible to presuppose at least some familiarity with a noun referent whether one uses a definite article with it or an indefinite article. Suppose a speaker utters (1).

(1) At the anti-war march in Brussels, a mounted policeman struck and killed a demonstrator. The policeman who killed $\begin{pmatrix} a \\ the \end{pmatrix}$ demonstrator was not even suspended.

Though the presence of other demonstrators is implied in (1), the acceptability of repeating *a demonstrator* there shows that an indefinite NP can be used for a referent already introduced. In the second sentence, this NP fulfils Chafe's definition of givenness—as the last mentioned thing, it must be in the understander's consciousness—and therefore can hardly entail newness. This use does not seem to presuppose that the hearer, in the discourse context, is unfamiliar with its referent, namely which demonstrator is intended.[7] When re-mentioned, *a demonstrator* in (1) is not part of the 'New' information. We will return to this kind of issue in discussing the independence of pragmatic features in section 1.4.

There are also other uses of *a* and *the* in conversation and writing which are not referential in the particular ways mentioned. The existence presupposition, which Keenan (1976) labels *absolute* reference, may vary for different indefinite NPs entering into a predication. It seems strongest for basic subjects (or agents). Thus, if a certain book editor truthfully utters the sentence 'A contributor still owes me a paper', the existence of someone satisfying the description *contributor* is implied, but not that of something having the feature *paper*. Similarly, the condition on recoverability for definite descriptions often will not be satisfied by prior context or knowledge. Immediate prior mention (a primary source of givenness according to Chafe) is not required for using definite NPs in expressions like 'After a big freeze, they had to call the plumber to fix the boiler.' And a listener need have no previous knowledge of the person mentioned first in 'The girl I went out with last week . . .' or in many cataphoric uses.[8]

Finally, it may be pointed out that many languages fail to exhibit definite and indefinite articles on the pattern found in those we are often most familiar with. Ancient Indo-European and modern Slavic languages (except Bulgarian) are among these. Classical Greek had definite articles but Latin did not. Even Gothic did not have them. In some languages, definiteness (or situational givenness) can be conveyed by positional phenomena. In Mandarin (Mark Hansell, personal communication), which also has no direct equivalents of English *the* or *a*,[9] this is possible by inverting word order, such that when a noun is fronted it is made more definite, when it is postponed, less definite. Thus one would say *kè lái lĕ* (guest-come-ASP) for 'The guest (who we were expecting) is coming' but *lái kè lĕ* (come-guest-ASP) for 'A guest (don't know who) is coming'. Similarly, one would say *sĭ lĕ liăng gĕ rén* (die-ASP-two-CLASS-person) for 'Two people died', where the persons concerned are not known or their identity not relevant, but *liăng gŏ rén sĭ lĕ* (two-CLASS-person-die-ASP) for 'The two people died' or 'They both died'. (The examples cited come from Chao, 1968.)

Word and constituent order

The interpretation of word order in terms of where 'given' and 'new' information falls in utterances, and what in them is talked about and what is said, has roots going back well into the last century.[10] Here, we provide a kind of summary review before taking up more recent work or suggesting conclusions. Weil's work *De l'ordre des mots dans les langues anciennes comparées aux langues modernes* (1844; English translation 1887) has been thought of as a pioneering effort on this topic, although influenced by ideas from the French Enlightenment (especially Condillac's notion of a *liaison des idées*) and German linguistics of the time (cf. Scaglione, 1972). With respect to a *marche des idées* underlying speech, Weil argues that the progression in a sentence from an initial notion, or point of departure, towards a goal, or the information imparted to a hearer, reflects the subjective movement of the mind itself (*la marche de l'esprit même*). With respect to the communication of ideas which are not grounded in immediate perception (of what the hearer does not, or is supposed not, to know), Weil writes (p. 20) that the initial notion establishes a common ground by the speaker seizing on something the hearer does know, and (normally) precedes the part of the discourse which forms the statement proper:

> il fallait s'appuyer sur quelque chose de présent et de connu, pour arriver à quelque chose de moins présent, de plus nouveau ou d'inconnu. Il y a donc un *point de départ, une notion initiale*, qui est également présente et à celui qui parle et à celui qui écoute, qui forme comme le lieu où les deux intelligences se rencontrent; et une autre partie du discours, qui forme *l'énonciation* proprement dite. Cette division se trouve dans presque tout ce que nous disons.

Though Weil's influence on other German linguists (he himself had become French) is difficult to estimate, a similar conception was advanced later in the century, usually by distinguishing between a 'psychological' subject and predicate. Just what these terms meant, and how their substance was conveyed, was evidently never a matter of complete agreement.

In hypothesizing how a speaker may first direct a listener's attention to something, and then say something about it, von der Gabelentz (1869, p. 378) defines the psychological subject quite teleologically, as 'das, woran, worüber ich den Angeredeten denken lassen will' (that about which I *wish* to have the addressee think), and the psychological predicate as 'das, was er darüber denken soll' (that which he *should* think about it). He claims further that these activities occur universally (in all languages) in the same order, an argument he later repeated (1887, p. 103):

Die mitteilende Rede zerfällt in (1) den Gegenstand, von dem ich rede, und (2) das was ich davon aussage. Jene Gegenstand nenne ich das *psychologische* Subjekt, jene Aussage das *psychologische* Prädikat, und das psychologische Subjekt steht zuerst, das psychologische Prädikat zu zweit.

(Informative utterances can be divided into (1) the thing about which I am talking, and (2) what I state about it. That thing I call the *psychological* subject, and that statement the *psychological* predicate. The psychological subject stands first, the psychological predicate second.)

Paul (1886), on the other hand, describes a psychological predicate as 'das wichtigste, dessen mitteilung der endzweck des satzes ist' (p. 236); 'das bedeutsamer, das neu hinztretende' (p. 101) (what is most important, whose communication is the primary goal of the sentence; what is more meaningful, coming in in addition). But this can consequently be further identified, he argues, as the phonetically most prominent part ('das stärker betonte element'; 'auf was daher der stärkste ton fällt'). [The orthography in these citations is Paul's.] In his major work, *Sprachwissenschaft* (1891), von der Gabelentz himself rejects this association, and suggests that accent serves instead principally to mark contrast (see section 1.3). He also argues there (pp. 353–4) that the psychological subject–predicate distinction originates in the stimulation of a speaker's thought, though it can be described more precisely by the corresponding process it gives rise to in the mind of the addressee. He further proposes that each successive part of a sentence produced and perceived becomes in turn the psychological predicate of a psychological subject defined by what has already been said and heard.

Høffding (1910, p. 84), in discussing what he calls the 'logical' subject and predicate, writes that the latter

er det vigtigste Led in Dommen. Det betegner det Nye . . . Subjektet er stedse forudsat. Alle Ord begynder derfor som Prædikater, og det er først senere, de bruges til at udtrykke Subjekter.

(is the most important member of the judgment. It marks the new . . . The subject is always taken for granted [literally, 'set out before']. All words thus begin as predicates, and it is only later that they are used to express subjects.)

The perspective taken here seems to combine some of the ideas of von der Gabelentz and Paul (see also below). Høffding's view of thinking and talking also stands in interesting relation to some of Vygotsky's (1934) later ideas, for example, that *inner* speech becomes largely predicative and, omitting mention of what is obvious to the 'speaker', incomprehensible out of context. The omission of psychological subjects through 'ellipsis' was itself discussed by von der Gabelentz as early as 1869.

In more recent times, a theme–rheme distinction often related to word order has been put foward largely on the basis of arguments emanating from the Prague school. Mathesius (1939) defined the 'starting point of the utterance' (*východisko*) as 'that which is known or at least obvious in the given situation, and from which the speaker proceeds', and the core of the utterance (*jádro*) as 'that which the speaker states about, or in regard to the starting point of the utterance'. In 1942, he further defined the foundation (or the theme) of the utterance (*základ, téma*) as something 'that is being spoken about in the sentence' and the core (*jádro*) as 'what the speaker says about this theme'. (For further discussion, see Firbas, 1964, 1974; Daneš, 1974.) A third distinction, degree of 'communicative dynamism', was introduced by Firbas (1964) to reflect the extent to which various parts of an utterance contribute to a communication, and move it forward. Together, these notions seem to make reference to how an utterance relates to context, what it is about, and what is informative in it. There have also been further refinements suggested. Thus, Beneš (1959) argues that the opening or 'basis' of a sentence, which links an utterance to context and from which it unfolds, be distinguished from its 'theme', while Trávníček (1962) argues that the theme opens the sentence, is linked directly with the object of thought (but not given contextual information), and proceeds from it. Mathesius himself had suggested that thematic and rhematic elements may be interlaced; it seems to be a current position of Czechoslovakian linguists that both can also vary internally in informativeness (cf. Firbas, 1979; Svoboda, 1980).

As adopted by Halliday (1967), the theme–rheme distinction and the given–new one, though not considered to be statistically independent, are treated as being in principle largely orthogonal. To capture the difference between 'theme' and 'given', Halliday writes (p. 212) 'it can perhaps best be summarized by the observation that, while "given" means "what you were talking about" (or "what I was talking about before"), "theme" means "what I am talking about" (or "what I am talking about now")'. Following Trávníček, in Halliday's system 'theme' (and consequently 'rheme') is defined by order of appearance (each English clause beginning with its theme and ending with its rheme), whereas 'given' and 'new' are marked by intonation.

Wundt (1900, Part 2, pp. 363–364) took word order to reflect the order of importance of information expressed in sentences. In *Die Sprache*, he argues namely for a principle based on descending importance, whereby words occur in *decreasing* order of their conceptual emphasis, if grammatical factors allow freedom of expression:

> Nun ruht die stärkste Betonung naturgemäss stets auf derjenigen Vorstellung, die den Hauptinhalt der Aussage ausmacht: sie steht auch im Satze voran.

> (Now, the strongest accent always rests by its very nature on that idea which makes up the primary content of the message: this comes at the beginning of the sentence.)

This idea, probably originating before Wundt, could reflect some feeling about thematization in German brought about by fronting, e.g., object NPs (see section 1.4), but may also have come partly from Latin and Greek grammars of the time, in which the notion was put forward (especially for marked sentence orders) that the more important some idea, the more stressed it should be, and the more it should move towards the beginning. Von der Gabelentz (1891) himself pointed out but rejected the assertion. The context of Wundt's remark itself follows a discussion of the various ways one can say 'Romulus founded Rome' in Latin, an example also used by Weil to demonstrate that different word orders would be used in different contexts. The contexts Wundt imagines are *questions* to which sentences like *Romulus Romam condidit* are answers.

Von der Gabelentz did acknowledge that the 'thematic' constituent in an utterance carries a certain emphasis (1891, p. 357):

> Denn erstens ruht natürlich ein gewisser Nachdruck auf demjenigen Teile der Rede, der als ihr Thema vorangestellt wird, also auf dem psychologischen Subjekte.
>
> (For first there does rest a certain emphasis on that part of the speech which is placed in front as its theme, thus on the psychological subject.)

And he points out that in some utterances the main accent does occur at the beginning. But his general position is carefully to distinguish such accent from word-order phenomena, and to argue for the theme–rheme type of notion being reflected not by the former but the latter.

Finally, a position nearly opposite to that expressed by Wundt seems to have been taken by Paul: namely that the relative prominence of constituents across a sentence normally *increases* (1886, p. 236; see also below). Paul was interested in arguing, however, that the *current* predicate is most perceptually pronounced, as well as in maintaining that a psychological predicate can be known from its accent. (The former argument von der Gabelentz would not have denied. As already noted, he also clearly recognized cases in which only the psychological 'predicate' is expressed, e.g., in the exchange 'Was! Schon wieder da?' 'Ja, und alles besorgt'.) Paul's idea of graded increasing stress was also somewhat tempered. In making his argument for final phonetic prominence in the example *Karl fährt morgen nach Berlin*, he was careful to qualify that this should hold primarily when all parts of the sentence can be thought of as being *equally* informative (1886, p. 236):

> wenn er [the sentence] ohne irgend welche vorbereitung des hörers ausgesprochen ist, so das diesem die verschiedenen bestandteile desselben gleich neu sind.

Wundt, on the other hand, may have intended his remarks to hold mainly for written language. Following a similar conclusion elsewhere, he does note how speech prosody can function to extend the range of meanings that utterances convey.

In the passages mentioned, neither Paul nor Wundt specifically does consider the kind of topicalization in German whereby a phrase which is not a subject comes to occupy main clause-initial position (before the finite verb), such as 'Das Goethehaus findest du in der Frankfurter Altstadt'. Von der Gabelentz himself discusses the psychological subject–predicate distinction primarily for sentences whose subject is indeterminate (e.g., 'Heute ist mein Geburtstag'). He does mention non-subject voices in Philippine languages, in which place and instrument functions as well as objects can become subjects (1869, p. 378), but may well be referring there to phenomena modern linguists have described in terms of topic markers (Schachter, 1976; see, however, also Dik, 1978). Høffding (1910, p. 88) gives examples of a phrase being placed sentence initially for emphasis in Danish, and implies a corresponding difference in intonation. But given this variety of observations and opinions in the absence of more systematic data, we might most generally conclude from work of Weil to the present that sentence–initial thematization can and does occur with special (e.g., emphatic) stress *and* without it; besides the theme function, there are others which can co-occur there. This conclusion, though tentative, seems supported in at least one language we are fairly confident about, namely German (see 1.4 below).

In English, the constraints on utterance–initial thematization may be somewhat greater than in other familiar languages. Perhaps this is one reason why so many studies have been done of subject rather than topic selection. (See also Firbas, 1974, pp. 12–13.) As Lyons (1977) points out, early English-speaking linguists often seemed to view the subject of a sentence as identifying what a speaker wished to talk about, and its predicate as commenting on this (cf. Sapir, 1921, p. 119). German authors have usually taken another standpoint. Thus, Frege (1879), while writing that 'the place occupied by the subject in the word-order . . . is where we want the hearer to attend to specially' (Geach and Black, 1952, p. 3), also argues that propositional judgements are only mainly concerned with their subject concepts, and that in conceptual content, propositions whose only difference lies in what is chosen as subject in a sentence have the same conceptual content, and nearly the same sense.[11] Wundt (1900, Part 2, pp. 269–270) himself treats the convergence of theme and subject functions as a special case, and argues that it is misleading to call what the speaker wishes to attract attention to a 'subject' at all, sentences already having a logical one (in the modern sense) and a superficial grammatical one. Largely the same point has been remade in standard generative grammar. On the one hand, the grammatical subject of a sentence not need be its agent, as in passive (and generally non-subject voice) constructions. And, on the other hand, the theme of a sentence need not be its grammatical subject, *or* its agent as in (2).

(2) This book of Flann O'Brien's I was given by Celia.

(For further examples, see Jesperson, 1949, pp. 68–72). Chomsky (1965) suggests that topic–comment structure may be only a surface phenomenon, though often corresponding to a deep subject–predicate distinction. Dahl (1969, 1974), on the other hand, has argued that it further reflects fundamental aspects of the semantic representation or logical form of sentences.

In 'The case for case', Fillmore (1968) suggests that subject assignment does have a topicalization function (which he calls 'primary'), perhaps to be differentiated from the consequences of 'late' word order changes, stress placement, clefting, and so on (which he refers to as examples of 'secondary' topicalization). It is an interesting question in which of Fillmore's senses *passivization* in English counts as a thematizing device. One possible answer seems to be in both senses. Thus, Halliday (1967, p. 216) writes about sentence (3) produced as a single intonation unit with final phonetic prominence:

(3) These houses were built by my grandfather,

that 'the actor is focal and the goal thematic and the effect is to "emphasize" the actor as the point of new information and also to "emphasize" the goal as what the message is about'. In Halliday's (and Mathesius') view, it is the making of *these houses* in (3) into the subject which gives the sentence a marked pattern: 'the passive has precisely the function of dissociating the actor from this complex [the thematic subject], so that it can either be put into focal position at the end or, more frequently, omitted' (1970a, p. 161). We return to this latter notion of focus in the following section.

The discussion above suggests that, except in the sense that there is always some forward movement in discourse, word order may generally not be counted on to express what it is in some part of an utterance that counts as given and what as new. It is then more an empirical question whether there is a tendency within speakers' utterances for 'given' information to precede 'new' information. This has been hypothesized by Halliday, Clark and Haviland, and others, but convincing empirical evidence for this hypothesis is still to be forthcoming. Given–new 'order' in speech might best be regarded as a convenient strategy for speaking, independently of how it may direct a listener's attention.

One can all too easily be misled by examples, moreover. Chafe (1976) points out that it has often been the case that examples used to support a 'given–new' distinction actually seem to reflect some other process in speaking. This also may hold for the question of preferred given–new 'order'. Linell (1977) suggests, for instance, that we imagine a setting in which a boy named John gives a girl a certain book, and only the girl is unknown and has not previously been mentioned. In describing this event, Linell argues, one would normally say 'John gave the book to a girl' rather than 'A girl got the book from John'. This seems intuitively reasonable, but the impression may be due to the perspective given in the context as well as to which referents are supposed known or unknown. If one imagines the situation as one in which a girl is given (gets, receives) a book from a boy with otherwise the same given–new assumptions, it seems as natural, or even more so, to say 'A girl got the book from John', without contrastive stress on 'girl'.

Factors other than givenness, and newness themselves may often motivate the selection of a topic and comment, their order of expression, whether they are partly nested, and so on (cf. Bates and Macwhinney, 1979). There is a large number of cases, moreover, where a 'given, then new' strategy could be applied only with difficulty or not at all, even if this were a speaker's desire. Thus, contrastive stress is often produced in combination with marked word orders which bring a to be emphasized concept forward in a sentence. Similarly, what is new in what a speaker expresses will often be the relation between information already presumed known.

What about given–new word order from the side of the perceiver? We would suggest that where 'given' information within some utterance is not presented first, the process of understanding need not be very different from that where it is presented first. Clark and Haviland (1977), on the other hand, describe a procedure whereby the listener is postulated to begin by identifying given information, then look for antecedents to this, and finally attribute new information identified to the antecedents found. Thereby, they argue, in 'reversed-order' cases, the listener would need to hold new information perceived in abeyance; this would burden his immediate memory, prevent him optimizing speed of comprehension, and the like. This set of conclusions seems to us to be largely unwarranted. Information perceived early on in an utterance cannot be counted upon directly or indirectly to reference the contents of consciousness or particular memory structures. As Jesperson pointed out (1924, p. 148), 'what is new to the hearer in any piece of communication may be found according to circumstances in any part of the sentence'. Also, it is not evident that superficial linguistic analysis alone (e.g., recognition of definite NPs, sentence subjects, deaccenting of constituents, etc.) would form a sufficient or natural basis for locating information a speaker may take to be recoverable. That is, the crucial process in Clark and Haviland's model would seem to be the partitioning of information into two kinds, given and new; it is difficult to see why this process should be retarded by recognizing new information, or, indeed, how it should succeed without doing this. Finally, a rather obvious qualification is needed to distinguish a model for understanding some utterance, and one motivating storage of the new information perceived together with any antecedent(s) identified in memory. Understanding needs to be relativized to very limited contexts. To evaluate the significance of what someone tells us, we need to take this context into account (there may be no need for integration into more permanent knowledge structures), as well as the speaker's general credibility, apparent degree of well-informedness, motives, and so on. Much of what we are told may quickly become inaccessible, indistinguishable from other knowledge, or be retained hardly longer than the time that is needed to understand it in the first place. We are not the first to make this point (see, e.g., Chafe, 1974).

Stress and contrast

In what way might the given–new distinction be reflected in, or marked by, sentence accent? That tonal modulation and relative perceptual prominence of sentence parts serves as some kind of pragmatic cue in speech was recognized early on by von der Gabelentz, Paul, Høffding, Wundt, and others. Generally speaking, such writers have hypothesized that, largely apart from the effects of left-to-right order and grammatical function, accent can be used by speakers for emphasis or contrast, or to set off what they consider new or important. About such accent (*Betonung*), von der Gabelentz (1887, p. 105; 1891, p. 375) thus writes

> Immer nämlich drückt sie einen Gegenstand aus . . .: *heute*—nicht 'gestern' oder 'morgen'; *ist*—nicht 'wird sein' oder 'war' u.s.w.'

> (it namely always expresses some opposition . . .: *today*—not 'yesterday' or 'tomorrow', *is*—not 'will be' or 'was', etc.)

In this view, one concept is emphasized over some other(s) *not* expressed (and in the cases shown, probably *one* of the temporal oppositions mentioned rather than both). The other question, of what is considered new *within* the scope of an utterance, found expression in Paul and Høffding. Paul (1886, p. 236) writes concerning his example *Karl fährt morgen nach Berlin* that, against the tendency for later stresses to be perceived as most prominent (see also below),

> bei bestimmter, dem sprechenden bekannter dispositionen des angeredeten kann jedes der vier glieder scharf abgehobenes prädikat werden.

> (when certain dispositions of the person being addressed are known to the person speaking, any of the four parts can become the most sharply inflected predicate.)

Similarly, Høffding (1910, p. 88) writes the following about the (psycho)logical predicate, the element in a predication he takes to be new:

> Man vil stedse kunne kende det logiske Prædikat paa Betoningen, hvilken Plads det saa ellers indtager i grammatisk Henseende.

> (One will always be able to recognize the logical predicate from the accent [which it bears], whatever place it happens to have from a grammatical point of view.)

Similarly, Chafe (1974, p. 112), for example, writes that a speaker typically 'will attenuate the given material in one way or another, e.g., by pronouncing the items that convey such material with lower pitch and weaker stress'.

Halliday (1967; for examples, see also 1970b, pp. 40–43) has proposed a theory of information structure in speech the basic unit in which is the 'tone group'. Each such tone group is taken to correspond to a block of information in a speaker's message, and represents a different kind of organization from its major (deep or surface) syntactic structure. Central to any tone group is a segment which carries the pitch contour of the primary tone—the main or tonic accent—and whose function it is to express the speaker's main point, i.e. the focus of the information expressed. Information which a speaker takes as not already being available to a hearer Halliday labels as 'new', and considers obligatory in a tone group. What a speaker treats as known or assumed, the 'given' information, is optional. New information according to this theory may fall anywhere in a tone group, and may also make up the whole of it.

To illustrate the difference and 'interaction' between the concepts of given and new and theme and rheme, Halliday (1970a, p. 163) cites sentence (4).[12] (The double splashes indicate the boundaries of information units, the italics phonetic prominence, and the numbers 4 and 1 stand for a falling-rising and a falling tone respectively.)

(4) //4 *this* gazebo //1 *can't* have been built by Wren//

Halliday paraphrases sentence (4) to mean 'I am talking (theme), specifically, (new) about this gazebo: the fact is (rheme) that your suggestion (given) that Wren built it is actually (new) quite impossible'. For Halliday, 'new' information need not be something not already mentioned, but may also, for example, be unexpected or contrary to what has been implied (1967, pp. 205–6). As Chafe (1976, p. 38) points out, this seems to be very much the case in (4), which he argues is a better example of a double *contrast*.[13] The addressee here is implied to have made a claim about the same gazebo, which otherwise would make it recoverable; the first contrast is then apparently to other gazebos (mentioned or not), which Wren *did* build. The second contrast then seems to be a denial of the addressee's assumed claim that Wren could have or did build the gazebo now referred to. If one were to define 'given' and 'new' more narrowly here, the example would no longer be very sensible. But an analysis of this abstractness nevertheless seems needed to address adequately the problem of determining what information a speaker actually wishes to emphasize. We further consider this kind of analysis as suggested by Chafe, Jackendoff, and others below.

Final stress

It has been rather widely argued that the end of an utterance (or of some subsection of it) is the unmarked or default position for phonetic prominence. This kind of argument has been suggested for German as well as for English. Thus, Paul (1886, p. 236) writes about an example already mentioned in passing (*Karl fährt morgen nach Berlin*) that the final constituent will tend to be emphasized slightly above the others when no single part of the sentence can be taken a priori to be the most informative to a hearer:

Hierbei wird zwar naturgemäss die letzte bestimmung etwas stärker hervorgeheben als die übrigen, aber doch nur um ein geringes.[14]

For English, it has been noticed by linguists as early as Sweet (cf. Western, 1908) that 'sentence-final stress' is often just a function of the last in a series of potentially accentable forms in some structural or prosodic unit receiving greater prominence (see Cutler and Isard, 1980, for further discussion). As Bolinger (1972) put it, the English speaker will tend to place the main accent in his utterance as far to the right as he *dares*.

The observation has also been made that accents of this kind tend to underspecify the scope of 'new' information presented in utterances. This is clearly related to the point just raised. Thus, Halliday (1967; 1970b) notes that when there are several new items within a tone group in English, the tonic (main) accent will be placed on the last item which is new. Chafe (1974, p. 118) similarly argues that if both *Matthew* and *book* convey new information in 'I bought Matthew a book', a high pitch on Matthew will be sustained through to the end. For a sentence spoken in isolation, or one initiating a conversation, Halliday considers the 'neutral' place for the tonic to be the most prominent syllable of the last content word.[15] According to this view (and a somewhat more syntactic version of it), any portion of the tone group (or of the sentence which is a constituent) from that point backwards may represent new information. Thus, the final noun or prepositional phrase in a simple sentence produced as a single prosodic unit with final 'stress' can represent only part of the information a speaker presents as not being recoverable. Clark and Clark (1977, pp. 93–4), for example, suggest that, according to circumstances, such a full English sentence, its verb phrase, or just its final constituent might provide information asked for by a hearer, and thus count as being 'new'.

A pair of related observations might finally be made about 'normal' final stress and its interpretation. One is that it seems misleading to refer to, for example, the last NP in sentences like simple passives as occupying *the* focal position, even when the sentences are not spoken. The other is that final stress of the kind discussed can easily be falsely interpreted from contexts in which test subjects are asked in a forced-choice situation *which* NP, the first *or* the last, is 'new', which is 'given', which one the sentence is about, which it emphasizes, and so on. Besides inviting subjects to perceive or produce contrastive stress, such tasks unnaturally limit the number of alternatives which would otherwise be entertained. Removed from context, simple sentences are likely to elicit diverse and rather fortuitous judgements (though not random responses) about what a person who uses such a sentence would assume a hearer to whom he addressed it would already know and not know. In context, on the other hand, what counts as given and new information may typically be quite evident. If 'Ronald made some *ham*burgers' is used to answer 'What did Ronald make?', 'some hamburgers' is clearly the information presented as not being recoverable, just as '*Ron*ald' would be if the question asked were 'Who made the hamburgers?' and the answer given was '*Ron*ald did'. Such examples are consistent with Høffding's observation that questions demand a stressed predicate, or bearer of new information, as well as with Halliday's conception of phonetic prominence and focus of information. It can also be noted that 'newness' in this sense does not imply that the relevant information has not previously been mentioned, nor even that the appropriate referent is absent from the hearer's consciousness.

Focus-presupposition and contrastiveness

As the preceding discussion perhaps suggests, to relate even relatively simple cases like the above question–answer sequences to a listener's presumed state of mind, it may be necessary to go beyond the given–new distinction, and make further orthogonal oppositions between referent familiarity and the assumptions conveyed about propositional knowledge in sentences. One might, for example, take various kinds of NP reference to correspond to concepts of individuals mentioned, and certain prosodic and structural phenomena to mark assertions and presuppositions made about their behaviour or interrelation (Engelkamp, 1982).

Two interpretations in linguistics of prosodic prominence in sentences which go beyond a superficial partitioning of information into given and new are those of Chomsky (1971) and Chafe (1976). We will briefly consider both.

Chomsky (1971; see also Jackendoff, 1972; Akmajian, 1973) proposes a distinction between 'focus' and 'presupposition' in sentences. The focus of a sentence he defines as 'the phrase containing the intonation center' (the point of greatest phonetic prominence) and the presupposition as 'an expression derived by replacing the focus with a variable' (1971, p. 205). This idea of focus is consistent with more than the final NP in a sentence with final stress being the domain of the 'new' information. Suppose that sentence (6) is uttered as an answer to question (5).

(5) Who did Reagan urge to invade Nicaragua?
(6) Reagan urged *Haig* to invade Nicaragua.

The focus of (6) would be 'Haig' and the presupposition would be 'Reagan urged x to invade Nicaragua'. As elaborated by Jackendoff (1972) and Akmajian (1973), we should take the assertion of a sentence like (6) to be that the focus *satisfies* the presupposition. Phrased in terms of given and new information, Akmajian further argues that the presupposition corresponds to information assumed to be shared by a speaker and hearer; the focus corresponds to information which the speaker assumes to be novel to the hearer. The latter statement he qualifies, however, remarking that the focused constituent is novel 'because the semantic relation which the constituent enters into is novel with respect to a given universe of discourse' and 'not because the constituent itself is necessarily novel' (1973, p. 218). Thus, Haig could have been mentioned repeatedly in the conversation prior to sentences (5) and (6).

Chafe (1976, especially pp. 33–8) makes a somewhat similar appeal to distinguish new information conveyed in contrastive sentences from their focus of contrast. Basically, he argues that three general factors are involved when a speaker constrastively uses a sentence like (7):

(7) *Lily* made the bouillabaisse.

First, the speaker takes for granted some common awareness, or background knowledge, on the part of the addressee. In (7), this awareness would be knowing that someone made the bouillabaisse mentioned, and according to Chafe, should be given (in the listener's consciousness at the time of utterance) or 'quasi-given' (in which case the speaker only pretends it is in the hearer's consciousness). The second condition is that there be a set of, rather than one possible candidate. That is, the speaker implies that the listener would entertain at least one other individual than the one he mentions for the role of 'cook'. Not all members of this set need be in the hearer's immediate consciousness; thus, some could be considered as not given. Third, Chafe argues that the work performed by a constrastive sentence is an assertion made that one candidate, the focus of the contrast, is the correct one. In this case, that would be Lily. The focus of contrast need not introduce a referent into consciousness and thus may itself represent given or new information. Asserting that one candidate is correct rather than others, Chafe observes, can serve a different communicative function than bringing a new referent to mind.

Distinguishing contrastiveness from focus and presupposition in declarative sentences may be largely self-defeating. In some sense, any answer given to a question implies contrast. Thus, one alternative rejected in most assertions answering yes/no questions is that their negation is true. If we could read the minds of two speakers engaged in casual conversation rather than simply observing their utterances, it might be possible to tell from what they are thinking how the questions asked and answers offered reflected consciously considered alternatives and contrasts. Perhaps there is a possibility of investigating this kind of issue by asking speakers what they were thinking. Normally however, the amount of contrast implied in an utterance will be imprecise. Prosodic prominence, and perhaps some features of syntax, seem to have the function of providing (or eliciting) information given in relation to some background, and only optionally do speakers specify alternatives being considered. At the same time, higher pitch and stress may only signal that information is *not* being treated as being given (cf. Chafe, 1974).

What sentences are explicitly contrastive? It is perhaps significant that

Chomsky (1971) discusses cleft sentence sequences such as (8) and (9):

(8) Is it *John* who writes poetry?
(9) No, it is *Bill* who writes poetry,

without making particular note of their contrastiveness (or the latter's corrective character), whereas Chafe (1976) maintains that cleft sentences provide 'an additional way in which contrastiveness may be expressed' (p. 37), criticizes Clark and Haviland (1977; but then in press) for beginning their discussion of the given–new distinction with a cleft sentence example, and cites Jesperson (1949, pp. 147–8) in support of his interpretation:

> A cleaving of a sentence by means of *it is* (often followed by a relative pronoun or connective) serves to single out one particular element in the sentence and very often, by directing attention to it and bringing it, as it were, into focus, to mark a contrast.[16]

Paul (1886) gives examples of pseudo-cleft type sentences (in which presupposed comes before focused information) as providing a frame for saying something new in a context of what is already known or has been mentioned. The following illustrations are given there as variants of the example *Karl fährt morgen nach Berlin*, when only the goal, time, or person involved respectively are unknown to the hearer:

(10) Das Ziel der Reise, die Karl morgen macht, ist Berlin.
(11) Die Fahrt Karls nach Berlin findet morgen statt.
(12) Derjenige, der morgen nach Berlin fährt, ist Karl.

In German, cleft sentences can sound somewhat peculiar, however. Usually, one would say 'Herr *Meyer* hat seine Frau umgebracht' and not 'Es war Herr *Mey*er, der seine Frau umgebracht hat.' Or a slightly different sentence form with initial stress may be used, as in '*Er* war das, der seine Frau umgebracht hat?' Cleft constructions in German, moreover, imply rather direct contrast, i.e., as in (9), one would (or could) begin them with a denial, use them to express incredulity, and so forth.

In general, contrastive and non-contrastive uses of sentences may substantially overlap. In some instances, such as in (9) and in other cases where there is clear rejection of alternatives, contrast is explicit. (Legitimate contrast seems to be a function of actual knowledge, either general or specific—see the discussion below of Jarvella and Nelson, 1982.) Where contrast is more implicit, especially if it coincides with new information, it will be less easy to infer. From an English sentence like (13):

(13) The intellectual felt menaced by the *bur*eaucrat,

it may often be impossible to tell whether contrast is intended, whereas in cases like (14),

(14) The bather felt menaced by the *poi*sonous *cor*al,

failure to sustain high pitch across the elements stressed may be a cue to their essential contrastiveness (see Chafe, 1974, pp. 118–9; 1976, pp. 35–6). The alternative here may have been a playful mantaray, for example. And just as for new information in sentences, the scope of a contrast may range from the very small (e.g., a phoneme in 'No, John went into the bushes to *see*') upwards with no apparent limit (e.g., 'No, what pleased Mary most of all was *dining on tortelli over a bottle of pinot grigio under Rialto at midnight in a gondola filled with red roses to the music of Rossini*, etc.-)

The relative independence of linguistic–pragmatic features

The kinds of distinctions considered above may be largely thought of as binary features. Before going on to discuss psycholinguistic studies which have been aimed at defining pragmatic concepts, we wish to point out that those features defined by givenness (in Chafe's sense), definiteness, focus (of contrast) and presupposition, and topicalisation are also largely orthogonal. That is, not only can they be motivated in terms of particular (partial) states of mind, but they also rather freely combine.[17] This may already seem implicit, for example, from Chafe's (1974; 1976) analysis. But, as noted above, Chafe himself did not seem fully to appreciate this implication. Not only did he suggest that indefiniteness entails that NP referents are not already in consciousness, but that introducing these into consciousness is not acceptable in the *non*-focused part of contrastive sentences. The latter claim apparently must also be weakened. Below, we show using examples that either a more extensive definition of givenness is in fact needed, or recognition of the fact that what is presented as presupposed need bear only partly upon, or include indirect reference to, what is presumably already in an addressee's mind.

To make clear that the full range of cases is not restricted to a single language, we will present German examples, supplemented by rough English equivalents. Moreover, to keep things simple (and at the possible cost of complete naturalness in German), in each case we will resort to using cleft-'sounding' construction in both languages. Following Chafe (1976), and even stronger claims about universality by Harries-Delisle (1978) that cleft sentences involve contrastive emphasis, we will give such contexts explicitly. First, we will consider the three potential polarities, focus of contrast vs. presupposition (of shared awareness), definiteness vs. indefiniteness, and information already in consciousness vs. newly introduced. We will then illustrate the independence of topic and focus even with marked word orders. The labeling used in the following is always in reference to some NP(s) mentioned in an example.

In consciousness, definite, in focus

Imagine a case in which a pair of delinquent adolescents are brought before a high school principal by the truant officer. After the parties exchange glances, the latter says:

(15) Es ist das *Mäd*chen, das die Schule angezündet hat.
     Der *Jun*ge hat geplannt, Sie zu vergiften.
     (The *girl* is the one who set the school on fire.
     The *boy* planned to poison you.)

In consciousness, indefinite, in focus

In token of being promoted to president of an aerospace company, a former French general is given a solid gold model airplane. Inviting a German colleague into his office, he asks his guest, with an appropriate gesture, how he likes the new Concorde he has been given to fly around in. The German replies:

(16) Neine, das ist ein *Mess*erschmidt, die auf Ihrem Schreibtisch steht.
     (No, what you have on your desk is a *Mes*serschmidt.)

In consciousness, definite, presupposed

After a heavy morning dew, a man is seen picking up a passing earthworm and swallowing it. A stranger who asks an onlooker who the first man was, is told (17) by way of reply:

(17) Es war *Schu*macher, der den Regenwurm gegessen hat.
     (It was *Schu*macher who ate the worm.)

In consciousness, indefinite, presupposed

Sentence (17) can serve equally well in the context when changed so that *den* is replaced by *einen*, and *the* by *a*:

(18) Es war *Schu*macher, der einen Regenwurm gegessen hat.
     (It was *Schu*macher who ate a worm.)

By any reasonable standard, the worm in (17) and (18) remains the same.

Not (already) in consciousness, definite, in focus

A small group is mourning the unhappy state of the world. One of them laments offhand:

(19) Ja, ja, es war mal wieder der Ameri*kan*er, der den Krieg
     angegangen hat.
     (Yes, well, once again it was the Ameri*can*(s) who started the war.)

In this case, 'American' happens to be used in a generic rather than specific ·

sense. A better example is perhaps (20), said by a host to his guest as they look onto the former's ravaged garden:

(20) Es war der *Sturm*, der alles kaputt gemacht hat.
(It was the *storm* that destroyed everything.)

Not in consciousness, indefinite, in focus

Two cleaning ladies working in a clinic for marriage problems stand amidst the wreckage in a room used for therapy. The first suggests that only a man could have been responsible. The other replies with (21):

(21) Nein, ich habe gehört, es war eine *Frau*, die diese Tobsuchtsanfälle bekommen hat.
(No, I heard it was a *woman* who had this fit of rage.)

Not in consciousness, definite and indefinite, presupposed

The final two possibilities might be expected to present the greatest problem. In these cases, new referents, perhaps even ones fully unknown to an addressee, would be mentioned within the part of a sentence which Chomsky (1971) labels its presupposition, Akmajian (1973) argues consists of knowledge shared by the hearer, and Chafe (1976) supposes is at least presumed to be in consciousness. We will therefore give more than a single kind of illustration.

At least two kinds of instances seem to occur in which a referent mentioned for the first time can be presupposed. Consider first sentence (22) used in a context in which the addressee has just maintained that Mr Meyer's vacation this year was not a success:

(22) Neine, es war Herr *Schmidt*, der $\left\{ \begin{array}{c} \text{einen} \\ \text{den} \end{array} \right\}$ schlechten Urlaub verbracht hat.

No, it was Mr *Schmidt* who had $\left\{ \begin{array}{c} \text{a} \\ \text{the} \end{array} \right\}$ bad vacation.

The vacation mentioned in (22), namely Schmidt's, is clearly a different vacation here than that mentioned in the utterance we suppose provoked (22), namely Meyer's; this is true whether the article used is definite or indefinite. It might be argued, of course, that since (22) involves reference to the *respective* vacation of Schmidt, it actually conceals a second, implicit reference to him (e.g., a possessive), which also needs to be replaced by a variable (following Chomsky) to define the presupposition. Other examples, however, suggest that this analysis is not far-reaching enough to handle all focus-linked changes in reference. Consider the case where someone has smashed his thumb while hanging a picture; the addressee in (23) has suggested that this person was a certain Wagner:

(23) Nein, es war Herr *Strauss*, der sich beim Schlagen eines Nagels in die Wand die Hand verletzt hat.
(No, it was Mr *Strauss* who hurt his hand pounding a nail into the wall.)

The proposal to substitute the same variable for repeated references seems to work here for both *sich* ('himself') and *die Hand* ('his hand'). But example (23) contains two further references—one definite (*die Wand*) and one indefinite (*eines Nagels*)—which would still count as new information in a particular sense. Even if the addressee had included a wall and a nail in his representation of the scene, the nail and wall used by Strauss, and those used by Wagner, would almost invariably be different. And thus so would the referents in (23) be different from any in the addressee's mind.

A second set of cases in which new referents can be presupposed involves substituting or augmenting information, in contrast to use of the same words to refer to different things. Consider first the exchange given in (24).

(24) A: Ich hörte, Herr Diebels ist erkrankt.
B: (I heard Mr Diebels has fallen ill.)
B: Nein, es ist Herr *Hannen*, der die Pest gekriegt hat.
(No, it was Mr *Hannen* who's caught the plague.[18])

In this case, catching the plague might be regarded as elaborating the concept of becoming ill. But *die Pest* nevertheless introduces a new referent into the exchange.

A final example can illustrate that the amount of elaboration in such cases is in principle unlimited. Consider three responses speaker B might give in the context of (25).

(25) A: Ich hörte, Herr Dupont hat sich verletzt.
(I heard Mr Dupont injured himself.)
B: Nein, es ist Herr *Schultze,* der sich verletzt hat.
(No, it's Mr *Schultze* who injured himself.)
B': Nein, es ist Herr *Schultze*, der sich beim Holzhacken verletzt hat.
(No, it's Mr *Schultze* who injured himself chopping wood.)
B'': Nein, es ist Herr *Schultze*, der sich beim Holzhacken während seines zweiwöchigen Urlaubs in den südlichen, dauernd von Erdbeben heimgesuchten und von der Mafia beherrschten Gebieten Italien's zu meinem grössten Vergnügen, was, wie ich weiss, für meinen schlechten Charakter zeugt, etc. etc., verletzt hat.
(No, it's Mr *Schultze* who injured himself chopping wood in

Mafia-controlled, earthquake-threatened southern Italy, to my
great pleasure, which, as I know, testifies to my bad character,
etc. etc.)

From such examples, it is clear that new referents in presuppositions may be
introduced into consciousness at will. Such referents might be taken as being
otherwise recoverable, for example, as part of common knowledge, inferrable
using common sense, and so on. Absolute recoverability does not seem to be
required, however. If Schultze in example (25) is placed among the msulula
trees in the Gombe National Park (which to most non-students of primate
behaviour may represent unknown referents), several things can still happen.
Clarification is thus always possible *a posteriori*, and the conventions on when
it is used may differ from situation to situation. Secondly, not all such
referents need be signalled by definite NPs, of course (e.g., one could as easily
say 'under a msulula tree'). Perhaps most importantly, however, to
substantiate any general claim for mutual or common knowledge and how it
relates to the uses of definite reference, the relevant knowledge types must be
themselves better defined (cf. Hawkins, 1978; Clark and Marshall, 1982).

The eight kinds of examples we have given together seem to substantiate
the claim that prior knowledge (and especially consciousness of linguistic
context) may be relatively independent of what information in sentences is
brought into focus or structurally presupposed, and from definiteness. There
is, however, another issue which we should take up, and which may serve to
reinforce the conclusion that 'given' and 'new' information often cannot be
inferred from a single parameter, or sometimes even from some cluster or
configuration of linguistic features. This is the fact that there seems to be no
one-to-one correspondence between such features and given pragmatic or
functional categories. In some respect, this could already be seen from our
first example chosen. In *The policeman who killed a demonstrator* . . . , there
is evidently some interaction in deciding givenness between the clause
hierarchy and definiteness. Chafe's discussion of newness and contrastiveness
as expressed by sentence accent in English may be another relevant case.

In our discussion of word order and sentence accent, we suggested that the
latter was more decisive in reflecting emphasis. It has, however, been argued
that the focus function in languages like German and English is displayed by
'marked' word order as well as (rather than just in combination with)
prosodic prominence. Thus, Harries-Delisle (1978) points out that special
word orders are used with emphatic effect in languages in general, and that, in
English, for object emphasis OVS order is used. In German, fronting an
object often has a corresponding effect. This was recognized by Paul (1886, p.
237), who notes that for some but not all word orders, the beginning of a
sentence tends to become most heavily accented. This view was evidently not

shared by Wundt, who argued that emphasis will be initial irrespective of word order. However, it appears that for many sentences in German, the critical accent may rather than must fall at their beginning. It does not fall there for SVO sentences in which the subject is not specially stressed. Paul argues that it does not fall there if the logical subject is first but not the grammatical subject. And it usually does not appear to fall there when adverbial constituents are fronted.

In fact, it might be argued that there are *no* word orders in German where the constituent preceding the verb *must* receive an emphatic interpretation. This is not even so for marked, object-first word order, as the following example (suggested by Claus Heeschen) demonstrates:

(26) A: Was für ein Wetter! Da mag man ja keinen Hund vor die Tür jagen.
(What weather! In that you can't even put a dog out.)

B: Apropos Hund, $\left\{ \begin{array}{l} \text{'ne} \\ \text{die} \end{array} \right\}$ Wurst für den Hund muss ich aber doch schon *heute* kaufen.

(Speaking of dogs, I have to buy $\left\{ \begin{array}{l} \text{some} \\ \text{the} \end{array} \right\}$ sausage (meat) *today* for the dog anyway (despite the bad weather).)

In the second utterance in (26), different constituents carry the various pragmatic functions conveyed. From the statement made by speaker A, one might infer that it is no day for going shopping. The reference to a dog there is simply idiomatic. Speaker B, however, seizes on this reference to emphasize his need to buy dogfood. The *discourse* topic—the bad weather mentioned—may be largely maintained (see Keenan and Schieffelin, 1976). But the left dislocation, *apropos Hund*, does change the *topic* largely in the sense of topic discussed by Chafe (1976) and Li and Thompson (1976). It follows from the marked word order that the preposed object phrase is the sentence's (or comment's) *theme*. This phrase may be used either with a definite or indefinite article, and though unlikely to be already in the hearer's consciousness, need not be phonetically accentuated. Finally, the sentence's *focus*, exhibited by contrastive stress on *heute*, emphasizes that buying the dog's food cannot wait until another day. No more than the theme function in the Trávníček–Halliday sense seems necessarily to be held by the constituent in preverb-position, even when word order is marked. But other functions can coincide with this one in this position. Cases like (26) simply indicate that there is no need for them to do this, and again that they are functions which are largely independent of givenness as defined by previous mention, and largely also from definiteness.

EXPERIMENTAL FINDINGS AND THEIR SIGNIFICANCE

We now turn briefly to some of the psychological literature concerned with informativeness in language use in light of the pragmatic distinctions (re-)raised above. In choosing to highlight individual studies, our purpose will be less to show the validity or generality of these concepts than to illustrate how obliquely and narrowly pragmatic issues have been approached, and argue for the refinement and use of more flexible and natural methods. In fact, our understanding of the principal distinctions raised can perhaps best be deepened from new research of a different kind. If so, the direction in which progress should be made can be defined by movement away from what has already been done.

Previous research cannot by and large be described as having investigated language processing in context, i.e., in reference to actual or potential situations, except in passive understanding, where the scope of pragmatic variables is considerably reduced. It has rarely been the case that a task used has involved give-and-take between two or more speech partners, i.e., people functioning as *speakers–hearers*. Secondly, even in most studies of understanding, printed rather than spoken language has been the main object of inquiry, without serious account taken of the difference between them. This holds, for example, for many studies of listening to (recorded) printed texts. The structure of spoken language and normal speech prosody are but two of the relevant factors usually not taken into consideration (see also Linell, 1982).

What is a sentence about?

Language psychologists *have* debated at some length the question of how particular linguistic features of sentences, such as voice or determiners used, relate to messages which could be intended or conveyed if the sentences were used. The data they have collected and based arguments upon, however, may in a large number of cases be of very limited generality. For one thing, resort has hardly even been made to check the validity of some hypothesis or conclusion drawn, or its freedom from other natural factors, by examining the relevant distribution of instances available from a corpus of speech. Secondly, experiments manipulating such features have usually been done with no supporting context. One fairly common strategy seems to have been to determine what subjects treat as being most important, immutable, novel, or contrastive about sentences they are presented *in vacuo*. To determine this, subjects have been rarely asked to do anything relevant to communication with the sentences: almost never to respond to or use them as messages, and frequently not even to produce or understand them.

In such circumstances, it is unlikely that pragmatic features associated with using utterances will be discovered; those which we already know something about may be mis-characterized, falsely inferred or declared to have not been manifested in data collected, passed over as insignificant, or simply ignored. In null contexts these objections will hold most obviously with respect to *available* information (i.e., to concepts like 'in consciousness', 'recoverable', and 'presumably already known'), but they may extend as well to those aspects of utterances which contribute most to their informativeness. Moreover, in limited experimental settings, at most a few pragmatic factors can be dealt with at a time, and hence thought of as potentially orthogonal. An unfortunate consequence is that a task which may rely, for example, on implicit or explicit contrastiveness, might be interpreted to substantiate some notion of topichood.

Consider the following example. Grieve and Wales (1973) asked subjects to regard printed English active and passive sentences as if they were *answers*, and to supply *questions* for them. They then analyzed the co-references between the answers and questions to try to decide what the subjects had thought the sentences were about: their most 'important' entity, 'topic', or 'the person, object, or event about which something is said' (1973, p. 175). The noun phrases in the sentence 'answers' had been count nouns used with definite or indefinite articles. The main findings were that, independently of sentence voice: (a) if only one of the nouns occurred with a definite article, subjects who behaved consistently on two-thirds of the relevant trials tended to re-use this noun (or a non wh-pronominal form of it) *alone* in their 'question'; (b) when both NPs were indefinite, subjects tended to re-use neither noun; and (c) when both NPs were definite, subjects tended to re-mention just the logical object from the sentence. Only the first result really was interpreted by Grieve and Wales, to mean that the definitely determined noun was the sentence's *topic*, seeming to require presupposition of previous knowledge. This noun, in the context of the questions usually supplied, would be given both in Chafe's and in Halliday's sense of the word. If one equates this given information with the notion of topic, then it follows that the noun following *the* in the relevant sentences was what they were about. Or does it?

There are several rather subtle problems with this analysis. To see them, we need an example. In (27), the two questions mention in the sense discussed the definitely and indefinitely marked nouns in the answer:

(27) Question (a): What did a girl/the girl/she do?
     Question (b): What happened to a boy/the boy/him?
     Answer: A boy was hit by the girl.

The question we want to ask is why the results came out as they did. One problem is that the (b) sequences do not work very well. In fact, two of them— those with 'the boy' and 'him'—are obviously unacceptable: in these contexts, 'a boy' in the answer *cannot* refer to the same person. This is a case where

Chafe's analysis of indefiniteness is roughly correct, and indefiniteness entails non-givenness. The remaining (b) sequence—with 'a boy'—is only understandable if the questioner cannot identify and is not interested in which boy was involved, i.e., where there is a set of boys involved, to one of which something occurred. Thus, it is hardly surprising that (b)-type questions were not often supplied. In two of the cases, the question could not be used with the same referent, and in the third case specific reference is never made at all.

What about the (a) sequences? Are they then predicted? One answer to this question might be 'Yes, by default—if one referent is (re)-mentioned, it must be the girl.' And superficially, the (a) sequences all look acceptable. If one reads them aloud, however, it is clear that the 'answer' could not be produced as it is written, with unmarked stress. In Halliday's sense of information structure, what we have here (and in other relevant question–stimulus pairings) is *new–given* order: the tonic accent following such questions in English would normally fall on the stressed syllable of the last content word of the new information, in this case on the verb 'hit', rather than sentence-finally. This point would move back still farther to the subject NP if the question formulated were 'Who did the girl hit?'

These details bring Grieve and Wales' interpretation into doubt, even with such minimal context. Leaving further particulars aside, what they have largely done is to associate (equate) 'given' with the notion of 'topic' and 'new' with the notion of 'comment'. This association, as Halliday pointed out, has existed for a long time, but here it is particularly confusing, since in (27) it leads to a comment followed by topic order against other traditional expectations, and a peculiar relational concept of topic in addition. It is also really not satisfactory to retreat from a topic-comment notion to the concept of 'most important entity' to describe what it was to which subjects most often co-referred in their questions. In the first place, this term is exceptionally vague, and in the second, the information Grieve and Wales refer to by it would *not* have been phonetically prominent, and in real answers to real questions is often omitted (e.g., Question: What are we having for dinner tonight? Answer: *Fish*). A more natural interpretation of Grieve and Wales' task and the data obtained in it is that subjects usually treated definite NPs as if they were given information, they sometimes treated the verbs in sentences as given and other times as new, and they treated indefinite NPs as new. This would also explain why they tended to mention neither noun in their questions about sentences containing two indefinites. What subjects didn't, or couldn't do, was check or mark the corresponding intonation needed.

A somewhat different kind of judgement of the relation between sentences and their possible contexts was obtained by Hornby (1972) in a paper intriguingly called 'The psychological subject and predicate'. Hornby presented a single kind of spoken English sentence to a group of subjects, and for each sentence, asked the subjects to decide which of a pair of pictures they thought the sentence heard was about. The pictures were constructed so that neither one was accurately described in the corresponding sentence, but that either one might have been produced *incorrectly* as a description. For example, for sentence (28):

(28) The Indian is building the igloo,

the two pictures showed an Eskimo building an igloo and an Indian building a teepee. Although evidently aware of von der Gabelentz, Hornby appears to have been primarily interested in finding psychological evidence for the notions of the Prague school of topic and comment, which he paraphrases as being parts of an utterance which refer to information which may be taken for granted and contain actual new information, respectively. The sentence types Hornby studied were clefts and pseudo-clefts in which the focused constituent was either their logical subject or object, simple active and passives, and simple active sentences with extra stress on their subject. The main finding was that subjects usually (about 60 to 80 per cent of the time) chose as the picture being described (however wrongly) the one whose actor or object was *not* phonetically prominent in the sentence heard. Across the group of sentence structures studied, there were no exceptions to this tendency. Because the surface and deep grammatical functions of these referents, and also their position, varied across these structures, this is also the only consistent description of what happened. Hornby's conclusion missed this generalization. Rather, he took the 'psychological' subject and predicate to be determined by a set of features in English (which may, of course, be true, though not to Paul or von der Gabelentz).

Why did the results come out the way they did here? Again, we can offer only a plausible conjecture. To make their judgements, the subjects Hornby tested may have somehow tried to decide what was right and what was wrong with the sentence they heard as a description. In a sense, they could have asked themselves (and they had 10 sec of viewing time to respond) 'What is it? The sentence is false, it shouldn't have been this way, but that way instead.' Now, there are two related reasons why they should have usually decided that the more phonetically prominent NP in the sentence was the incorrect one. (Since only the actor and object were varied in the pictures, the verb is already excluded.) One is that phonetic prominence in English is used to signal contrast, and the task implicitly called for drawing one, as already suggested. And the other is that the presuppositions of sentences are oblivious to negation (cf. Strawson, 1952; Langendoen and Savin, 1971), and in this task the sentences were *offered* as being false. Whether one takes Chomsky's notion of focus and presupposition or Chafe's notion of focus of contrast and background knowledge, the information not focused in a sentence is conveyed as *assumed* to be correct.

All of the sentence types examined by Hornby (1972), except the normally stressed simple actives and passives, namely can be argued to have clear presuppositions, to make the assertion that, in Chomsky's sense, these are satisfied by their focused NPs, and to imply, in Chafe's sense, that at least one other candidate is worth considering. In the experimental context, such an alternative was given explicitly, and subjects may often have made their decisions to select this picture after noticing this and concluding that the asserted candidate was *not* correct (i.e., by elimination). For the simple sentences with sentence-*final* stress, a contrastive interpretation is also possible. In the test context, such 'normal' stress might be perceived as meaning that just the final NP in these sentences was their focus. Because the stress *was* final, the initial NP could *not* have this function. Since not all of the information in sentences was to be considered false, and their verb was non-distinctive, the final NP might have been rejected as being correct either because it was taken to be focused, or simply because it was final (e.g., in Halliday's 'rheme'). Evidence that the final NP in (especially passive) *printed* simple sentences is more often perceived as what is negated when the sentences are implicitly or explicitly denied has been obtained by Klenbort and Anisfeld (1974) and Hupet and Le Bouedec (1975), for English and French respectively. One would expect similar results for German, where in passives (and many other sentences) the final noun is usually stressed rather than the following main verb.

A third kind of experimental finding which may have some bearing on the notion of sentence topics being 'given' is a tendency for subjects in the absence of contextual constraints to prefer definite articles at the beginning of simple sentences and in the presupposed part of cleft sentences based on them, but for indefinite NPs to be more acceptable at the ends of passive constructions and in the focused part of simple clefts. This tendency for active and passive sentences has been demonstrated for British and American English by Wright and Glucksberg (1976) in a sentence fill-in task (e.g., using frames like —— *dog bit* —— *postman*), and for cleft and simple sentences for German by Engelkamp (1982) in a task where subjects were asked to rank sentences differing only in the articles present (e.g., *Es ist der Offizier den der Zivilist gelobt hat*) for relative acceptability. What the 'real life' source of these effects is seems uncertain. One possibility is that they simply reflect a statistical association between definiteness and subject or theme in utterances generally, which is a consequence of the given–new contract as envisaged by Clark and Haviland (1977). Another possibility is that they represent a text-cohesion phenomenon between utterances or sentences, that is, a kind of referent elaboration via anaphora, or script elaboration via bridging inferences. Thus, we know from the discussion of Grieve and Wales (1973) above that *a boy* doesn't work very well sentence-initially in at least the first respect, while *the waiter* (cf. Schank and Abelson, 1977) does in the second. Informal examination of written language sources ranging from scientific writing to novels in several European languages leaves one with the impression that directly anaphoric expressions using definite articles are fairly rare, compared with anaphoric pronouns and indirect references, and great variance across sources in the use of indefinite references. Perhaps most strikingly, however, there are clear differences in the *way* articles are used between English and German, between both together and the major Romance languages, and so on.[19]

The effects of focus and clefting

Much psychological research concerned with the given–new distinction reflects an assumption, often made explicitly, that the function of language understanding is to increase a listener's or reader's knowledge, and that this is accomplished most efficiently by storing new information conveyed at appropriate addresses in memory. Thus, to this end, Clark and Haviland (1977) suggest that speakers will mould their utterances in a way which allows their addressees to discover links to what they know and update this information. We would like to suggest here that such a 'text integrative' viewpoint on communication places emphasis on the wrong process (namely learning), although it has face validity in text contexts in which texts are given to subjects such as college students to read and understand. But, even there, the 'given' information in sentences functions first of all to allow retrieval or plausible re-construction of referents so that sentences can be understood. There are, moreover, many speech situations in which expressing or understanding 'given' information in an utterance is superfluous, either because no clear antecedents are required or because they are clearly *already* in consciousness, as in the answers in sequence like (29) and (30).

    (29) Question: Who did you say was a blooming genius?
           Answer: Monte Python.
    (30) Question: Did the penguins re-occupy Port Stanley after the war?
           Answer: What do *you* think?

And in most situations, new information conveyed must at least be evaluated before it is assumed true or worth remembering.

    In the present section we would like to consider briefly what the perceptual consequences are of listening to or reading cleft and pseudo-cleft sentences. (For a useful cross-linguistic discussion of focus constructions, see Harries-Delisle, 1978.) We will argue here that it is the drawing of attention to the focused phrase in such sentences, both structurally and in relation to their presuppositions and some notion of contrast conveyed, which makes them informative and is psychologically most crucial to their interpretation. First, however, we wish to show that a given–new 'partition' of cleft sentences does not lead to a unique address in memory at which the new information they convey might be stored, and note that understanding the presuppositions of sentences often may require having understood their assertions.

Clark and Haviland (1977) give the following example in discussing why a cleft sentence cannot simply be divided into two parts, one which is given and the other new:

(31) It was the *judge* who took the bribe.

Clark and Haviland (p. 12) state that what is (conveyed as being) new in (31) is the identification of the judge as the person taking the bribe. Because Clark and Haviland treat definite NPs as usually conveying given information, the given information in (31) includes the focused phrase *the judge* (call him X) as well as *the bribe* (Y) and the presupposition that someone (Z) took the bribe. In these terms, the assertion made is that $X = Z$. Now, to add to our knowledge, it is of course necessary to have some referents for the things marked as available, and recover (or imagine) what these are. But where does one 'attach' the new information conveyed in (31) in memory? To our prior knowledge of only one of the referents accessed, to our memory file of asserted cases of bribery, to our list of examples of psycholinguistic interest, or what? Or is it important enough to remember, or even convincing? Many such questions can be asked and there seems to be no simple answer to them, other than to say that the information recovered helps to understand the sentence. Presumably, this will be used as it becomes available, but there are cases, for example, where it is plausible that the presuppositions of sentences may not be interpreted except in relation to their assertions (see e.g., the discussion of subordination in Townsend and Bever, 1978; Townsend, Ottaviano, and Bever, 1979).

For several reasons, the above description is not satisfying. One is that, to the extent that cleft sentences are used *correctively*, or to further specify information, subjects should not use a given–new strategy which stops short of at least evaluating the correction or further specification. Secondly, if the argument presented earlier is valid, the psychological consequences of hearing or reading a cleft sentence should extend well beyond perceiving what a speaker or writer intends as given information, and what as new. What are these other effects, and how might one describe them in terms of what the perceiver does? Here, we will try to make just two fairly obvious points. One is that Jesperson's (1949) idea of clefting as an attention-directing or focusing device is empirically demonstrable. The other is that, as Jackendoff (1972) and Chafe (1976) suggest, the perceiver may be expected to treat the focused element in such constructions as being *contrastive* in context rather than simply noting that it is put forward as satisfying their presupposition. Although the evidence which can be cited for the two claims intersects, we will try to mention several results of interest for each.

Hornby (1974) reported on some studies of sentence–picture verification using cleft and pseudo-cleft sentences in English. In one of his studies, spoken sentences in which the agent or patient was clefted were presented before a picture in which one of the nominal concepts was sometimes falsified. Two kinds of negative instances were of interest, as illustrated in (32) and (33) in relation to a picture showing a girl petting a cat.

(32) It is the boy that is petting the cat.
(33) It is the girl that is petting the dog.

The pictures were exposed for only 50 msec and subjects had insufficient viewing time to perform the task very accurately. The main result found was that, when the disconfirming piece of evidence related to the sentence's presupposition, as in (33), there were more errors made than when it related to the focus, as in (32). This result might be explained on the grounds that presupposed information ordinarily can be assumed correct; that it is not subject to negation or questioning in the same way as what is asserted, and led therefore to fewer correct 'false' responses. However, there is another converging interpretation. As Hornby writes, 'it is impossible to determine whether a person failed to notice a discrepancy between the presupposition and picture because he took it (the presupposition) for granted, or because his attention was drawn to the other part of the picture (the focus), and he simply failed to notice the discrepancy' (1974, p. 357). One thing that is clear, however, is that subjects could not have followed a given–(then) new strategy in their pattern of visual search. If they had, the results should have gone in the opposite direction.

A second kind of evidence that the focused constituent in cleft sentences may become the main target of attention for an understander comes from a series of experiments done in German by Zimmer and Engelkamp (1981). Zimmer and Engelkamp used picture *inspection* time as an index of this effect. It is known from experiments on visual processing that subjects will look longer at those parts of a picture which can be described as more informative or important (e.g., Mackworth and Morandi, 1967; Loftus, 1972), or which are unexpected (Loftus and Mackworth, 1978). To provide a somewhat plausible context for using cleft sentences (i.e., one which is potentially contrastive), Zimmer and Engelkamp first presented their subjects with a picture of, for example, three individuals and a sentence in which one of them was mentioned and it was left open who else was involved (e.g., *Der Motorradfahrer sucht jemanden* with a picture of a motorcyclist, a boy, and a girl). Then an active or passive cleft sentence was presented such as (34).

(34) Es ist das Mädchen, das der Motorradfahrer sucht.
(It is the girl the motorcyclist is looking for.)

Finally, subjects were asked to inspect new pictures of the two individuals mentioned in this sentence. It was found that the picture corresponding to the cleft portion, whether this was the agent or the patient in the action described, was inspected significantly longer. Zimmer and Engelkamp interpreted this to mean that clefting indeed sets up a focus of attention in the sentence's representation, and that this prolonged the visual inspection time observed for the cleft-related pictures (cf. also Engelkamp and Zimmer, 1982).

Third, studies of question-answering and target monitoring for spoken sentences seem to suggest greater perceptual salience for words which are brought into focus. For such effects to occur, however, neither clefting nor particular phonetic prominence appear necessary if a contrast is suggested with respect to some context. In one series of studies, Cutler (1976; Cutler and Fodor, 1979) thus was able to show that reaction time in phoneme monitoring was faster if the word in a sentence containing the target phoneme was a focus of contrast. In a sentence such as 'The woman with the bag went into the dentist's office', subjects' latencies to detect the /b/ in *bag* were faster if they had been asked the question 'Which woman went into the office?' than the question 'Which office did the woman go into?' Similarly, Jarvella and Nelson (1982) found that when listeners falsely answer wh- questions about cleft sentences, they tend to answer with the sentences' focused phrase. This result suggests that presuppositions needed to fully understand their assertions sometimes went unanalysed, though the focus–presupposition distinction itself was superficially perceived. To summarize, it appears that sentences are interpreted as if they have a perceptual focus, this corresponds to what has been called their focus by linguists, and it can be conveyed by prosodic and (as in cleft sentences) structural prominence, by (implicit or explicit) contrast, or, as is perhaps most often the case, by both together.

We would like to further justify the claim that understanders entertain the possibility of contrast in a focus in cleft sentences, and that this has observable consequences. While the results just mentioned, and especially those of Zimmer and Engelkamp (1981) and Cutler, are not irrelevant to this hypothesis, nor are, for example, those of Hornby (1972) discussed earlier, the point can perhaps be strengthened by considering two additional examples.

Carpenter and Just (1977a, 1977b) performed a reading experiment with cleft and pseudo-cleft sentences in English in which college students were asked to judge whether each successive sentence in paragraphs they were shown was consistent or contradictory with the previous context. In these paragraphs, the introductory sentence always dealt with how one person interacted with a unspecified member of some group, and a critical later target sentence identified this member of the group. For example, in the illustration paragraph cited by Carpenter and Just, the introductory sentence was (35).

(35) The ballerina captivated a musician in the orchestra during her performance.

In this case, the later target sentence of interest might have been either (36) or (37):

  (36) The one who the ballerina captivated was the trombonist.
  (37) The one who captivated the trombonist was the ballerina.

It was found that sentences like (36), which were taken to match the given–new structure of the context, were accepted faster than sentences like (37), for which a mismatch in the information structure was hypothesized. Subjects were also found by eye-fixation measurements to have gazed at the second kind of target substantially longer than at the first kind. The results were taken to be consistent with Carpenter and Just's main hypothesis: that comprehension would be facilitated when information marked as being 'old' in a target sentence actually could be known from the introductory sentence. This is, of course, descriptively correct: the proposition that the ballerina captivated someone is entailed by (35), whereas the proposition that the trombonist was captivated by someone is not. In (35), which musician the ballerina captivated is not stated. As an explanation, however—that comprehension was facilitated *because* the information in (36) conveyed as being given was known—Carpenter and Just's conclusion is more open to doubt. Let us consider why. To do so, we need to present a few more details, insofar as these can be inferred from the published accounts of the experiment.

It should be noticed first of all, however, that, whatever one's hypothesis, there is clearly something wrong or unnatural about (37), particularly when it immediately follows (35), whereas (36) is especially good when it closely follows (35). This impression is confirmed by Carpenter and Just's results: the 'immediate' effect (with no intervening sentences and where subjects were not allowed to look back) was by far the greatest (1444 msec per sentence judged vs. 991 msec overall). The question, however, remains what is it that makes (37) seem less consistent, or even contradictory, with (35). One answer is that it is not possible to draw the inference from (37) that the musician mentioned in (35) was the trombonist, unless one first recognizes that the ballerina mentioned may have been the same person, and that no contradiction may be implied. In the context of the experiment, this difficulty may have been enhanced, since the remaining repeated definite references appear to have involved contradiction (e.g., 'It was the stagehand who arranged the choreography' followed by 'The one who arranged the choreography was the conductor') in the contrast being asserted (cf. *the ballerina* in (37)). Because they were only thematically related to the introductory sentence, inconsistencies of this type were *excluded* from appearing in the position immediately following it.

We would argue that (37) invites the perception of constradiction with respect to (35). Not only can we not tell in (37) that the trombonist is the musician who was captivated, but the focal phrase is redundant under this reading: the sentence can as well end 'was the *male* soloist, however'. In contrast, in (36) once the relative clause is read, the person identified as the ballerina must be the same dancer mentioned in the context; the trombonist is a legitimate focus of contrast, because we know that there was an orchestra present taken to be a group.

For neither (36) or (37) does it seem sufficient to argue that comprehension is helped or hindered just because what is conveyed as given is known or unknown. On the one hand, other conditions may need to be met (example (36) works less well if 'was the trombonist' is replaced by 'was a butcher in his spare time' or 'danced Romeo after the intermission'). And, on the other hand, what is conveyed as 'given' in many circumstances (including Carpenter and Just's experiment) actually may not need be known at all. Thus, one of the presuppositions of (38):

(38) Who really floored him was Nureyev, however,

in the context being considered would be that someone besides the ballerina impressed the musician. This information, as in some of the other examples given in section 1.4, is not part of, nor can it be inferred from, the previous discourse. Perhaps the more critical condition for focus constructions to be understood is that of plausible contrast. A second way of viewing the results of Carpenter and Just's experiment is to say that the assertion in cleft-type sentences should be informative, and this depends on, as Chafe (1976) suggested, a legitimate contrast being made and perceived.

Some further, indirect evidence for the view just expressed comes from a study, already mentioned, by Jarvella and Nelson (1982). If the function of cleft sentences is largely to assert which of several possible candidates is correct with respect to some information taken for granted (or considered as background knowledge), then the candidates asserted should not only not be known to be correct, but sometimes should represent a non-preferred alternative (as in the case of corrections). Perhaps one could say that they should not be *too* expected. How one should define expectation in this sense might vary, but one thing that is clear is that, if the propositional information in a sentence is considered as a whole, what is made its focus should be its most informative (or unexpected) part. If what is then presupposed in such a sentence is known or might be inferred, this should be true to a lesser degree or not at all for what is *not* presupposed.

In the experiment in question, Jarvella and Nelson presented subjects with cleft-type English sentences which were made difficult to hear by white noise. The subjects' task was to listen to the sentences, and answer one question asked about each of them. Questions were of the constituent (wh-)type and randomly probed either a noun mentioned in the heard sentence's presupposition, or its focus. The materials were designed so that, before clefting, the two nouns and verb in each sentence described a highly stereotypic human activity (such as a clerk selling goods) or an activity or event without such associations (e.g., a boy burning a house). (The same lexical items were used in the two conditions in different combinations.) An example of a test sentence of the former sort is the following:

(39) The person who sold the merchandise was the clerk.

It was found in this study that the number of perceptual errors made by subjects in the two plausibility conditions varied as a function of whether the question asked probed the focused or presupposed information. For stereotypic content, there were more than twice as many lexical intrusions (e.g., *client* in (39)) and failures to respond when focused information was probed. For the non-stereotypic content, these trends went in the opposite direction; more errors were made when the information presupposed was probed. From both the Carpenter and Just, and Jarvella and Nelson studies, one might infer that the focused phrase in sentences is perceptually most prominent. But if this focus fails to provide an informative contrast with respect to the sentence's presuppositions and background knowledge, a reader or listener may tend to misperceive it. When this happens, the representation which is assigned (and whether this is referential or lexical) will tend to be more contrastive. In the second case cited, it is somewhat as if expecting the unexpected on the basis of structural information inhibits or modulates the use of other, general pragmatic knowledge in recognizing the speech signal.

One final matter might be touched on here. Weil (1844) was perhaps the first modern student of text structure to recognize that the theme (or topic) of one sentence in discourse may be related on several dimensions to the previous sentence and context. He characterizes two of these in particular. A topic may have the relation of identity (*égalité*) or opposition to something already said, and it can relate to the previous point of departure in the discourse, somehow reflecting a parallel development in it, or be linked to the previous goal and be thought of more as a progression. Weil suggests that the identity relation is more particular to such progressive movement, and that of opposition to parallelism.

A certain amount of psycholinguistic work not already reviewed seems to be consistent with Weil's type of analysis. Thus, there appears to be a tendency in both language production and (accordingly) understanding for what is presented and perceived as being in focus in one utterance or sentence becoming the theme (and topic) of the sentence following it, whereas contrasts often are made in parallel contexts. Outside of these, it may be that the focus of attention at one point (and at one level) in discourse may serve as the major potential antecedent, or subject, of further discussion. For speech production, this is perhaps most clear in the choice of sentence subjects (e.g. Engelkamp, 1982; Ertel, 1977; Flores d'Arcais, 1975; Tannenbaum and

Williams, 1968); contextual focus may be one of the reasons why Wundt (1900) preferred to think of the dominant idea ('dominierende Vorstellung') in a sentence coming early. Its presumed effect in perception can perhaps be most easily appreciated by looking at (or doing) studies of text cohesion, though the identity relation most often treated there has probably involved topical parallelism rather than the interaction predicted (cf. Halliday and Hasan, 1976). Other investigators have argued that indefinite NPs and grammatical objects are perceived as being focal in written French and English, and definite NPs and sentence subjects as presuppositional (e.g., Hupet and Le Bouedec, 1975; Yekovich, Walker, and Blackman, 1979). In the framework of the present paper, this kind of labelling fails to recognize the multidimensionality of pragmatic factors. However, such studies' data may reflect aspects of the association among such factors which exist statistically in these languages, and strategies for dealing with them as a whole.

Further problems

Psycholinguistic experiments in pragmatics provide an interesting framework for thinking about certain aspects of discourse processing and speech communication. Since the kinds of distinctions which have so far been investigated in such studies were largely put forward by linguists and philosophers as being psychologically valid with respect to language use (*la parole*), perhaps more than in some branches of language studies, this is one in which psychologists may properly feel at home. That the studies which we have talked about here seem in retrospect to raise more questions than they answer is not reason to dismiss their findings. In fact, the discussion presented here is only intended to raise hope that we can more properly understand them as a reflection of the various influences which do operate in language use. What does seem obvious is that it is already beyond the time when it was useful to talk in an undifferentiated way about given and new information and related distinctions. Experimental work must go beyond such dichotomies to study the interactions between the dimensions that linguists such as Halliday and Chafe have pointed to, and should be guided or complemented by investigations done on real speech corpora, is possible in a way which preserves the basic characteristics of linguistic communication. A final point is that much more needs to be done in languages other than English. Without comparative results, the real value of much work which is done will remain unclear.[20]

NOTES

Title note: This chapter originated as a symposium paper delivered by Johannes Engelkamp on given and new information at the 22nd International Congress of

Psychology, Leipzig, July 1980. In the present draft, the authors have attempted to consider some historical roots of this distinction, as well as their wider implications for research on speech communication. A number of additional issues in linguistic pragmatics are therefore taken up. For a more focused discussion, the reader is referred to Engelkamp (1982).

1. The point here is that in real utterances, what information is treated as given and new is not specifically a function of which expressions are used referentially and which predicatively, nor is the reverse necessarily the case. It is also true that linguistic expressions are sometimes (if not usually) used in both senses at once. Engelkamp (1982) proposes a distinction the consequence of which is that NPs which enter into the relational presuppositions of an utterance cannot be (interpreted as being) conceptually new.

2. The usefulness of analysing this process in terms of further primes, and limited recursion, has recently been discussed by Clark and Marshall (1982) for how speakers may expect their addressees to infer what referents they intend, and by Perrault and Allen (1980) for indirect speech acts.

3. There is a sense in which many utterances speakers use count as a kind of assault on addressees' (and overhearers': see Clark and Carlson, 1982) general attention. In this sense, in talking, a speaker will be asserting something like 'I think what should be interesting (to you) is *this*'. The means which he or she may use to convey this vary, and are one of the main topics we consider here. However, what the information of interest in an utterance should be taken to be is not always obvious, especially, for example, at conversation openings. (See also Dore and McDermott, 1982, for a relevant discussion of indeterminacy in speech.) It can then be the listener's right to respond conveying his *non*-interest, or lack of interest (or perhaps understanding), by saying 'So?' or 'So what?' in English, or 'Na und?' in German. Such responses also need not be seen as particularly cooperative, though their effect may be to lead the original speaker to explain why, or *what* in what he said should be worthy of attention. Not frequently, these kinds of behavior extend to wilful obscurity in speaking or writing, or to intentional misunderstanding. Sometimes, they even become institutionalized. Thus, some Germans seem to have been *taught* that using language too transparently is not necessarily a virtue; there is sometimes a value in exceeding an audience's ability to understand. Bureaucratic writing seems to have developed much the same function.

4. Sometimes a speaker will not only appear to falsely assume his addressee knows something he does not, but give the impression that he himself knows something (even about the addressee) he does not. Thus, if X asks a former girlfriend 'Ist das der neue Freund?' in reference to some acquaintance brought up, X's utterance might be interpreted as being provocative, since it presupposes that the woman concerned has started a new relationship she may not have. Often, addressees are forced to play along in such 'When did you stop beating your wife' type contexts.

5. We are interested here primarily in making psychological rather than linguistic distinctions. An alternative approach might have been to first summarize linguistic means and communicative causes and effects, whereby more emphasis could be placed on how different means may serve the same or similar ends (cf. Bates and MacWhinney, 1979). Since there seem to be primarily different pragmatic functions associated with the different linguistic means taken up, however, the alternative approach runs the risk of being overly reductionistic.

6. As Stenning (1977) points out, claims made that words like the articles mark psychological distinctions between speakers' and hearers' ability to identify referents 'must explain how we are so good at talking about things we cannot recognize'.

7. To be sure, the context does not provide the hearer (or reader) with further information concerning the identity of the demonstrator; though we know that this person is the one who was struck and killed, we do not know the demonstrator's name or some other property which would (also) uniquely identify him. On the other hand, we know from the context sentence essentially no more about the mounted policeman. Thus, if there is a presupposition of familiary or unfamiliarity associated with definiteness here, it does not seem to involve recoverability *per se*. One could also say 'The demonstrator who a policeman killed is being hailed as a martyr', in which the articles used are reversed. Interestingly, in both cases, the indefinite article cannot be used with the same reference outside the relative clause, however.

8. One use of the definite article in German tends to convey reduced rather than increased familiarity, namely its use together with proper names. Thus, if I ask a friend, 'Wo warst du am Wochenende?' and he answers 'Ich war beim Manfred', his answer can be understood to imply less familiarity on my part with the Manfred mentioned than 'Ich war bei Manfred' would. Or, if a person is asked 'Hast du den Erhard gekannt?' and replies 'Nein', from his answer one could not say that he knew even of the existence of someone named Erhard before. On the other hand, if asked 'Hast du Kennedy gekannt', an addressee would be expected to answer 'Ja', or 'Nein, nicht persönlich', both of which would imply knowledge of the existence of Kennedy. There are similar phenomena in colloquial English involving demonstratives: 'Well, this Johnny comes along and . . .', 'That Billy Carter could really brag', etc.

9. There do exist definite and indefinite demonstratives in Chinese comparable to English *this* and *that*.

10. As pointed out at the paper's outset, one could trace some such ideas back for millenia. Such a historical review with special reference to English, French, and Italian can be found in Scaglione (1972). With respect to German, Jellinek (1913–14) appears, according to Firbas (1979), to be a useful reference.

11. Frege's further speculation on the function of the subject position is also interesting enough to quote. He writes

> This may, e.g., have the purpose of indicating a relation between this judgment and others, and thus making it easier for the hearer to grasp the whole sequence of thought. All such aspects of language are merely results of the reciprocal action of speaker and hearer: e.g. the speaker takes account of what the hearer expects, and tries to set him upon the right track before actually uttering the judgment (Geach and Black, 1952, p. 3).

12. We assume that, when Halliday (1970a, p. 163) writes that 'the function "given" means "treated by the speaker as non-recoverable information" ', he clearly means to say 'new' rather than 'given', or 'recoverable' rather than 'non-recoverable'.

13. The examples Høffding chose to illustrate how one might determine a logical predicate from its accent—'Kongen kommer *ikke*' ('The King is *not* coming) and 'Han *er* gaaet' ('He *has* left') are also clearly emphatic, or contrastive in nature.

14. Besides Paul's earlier mentioned qualification of what can happen when the speaker includes some 'known' information in his utterance, this example does not give the clearest picture of the pattern of accents in German generally. Usually, the main verb at the end of independent clauses in German does not receive the main accent, but rather the constituent preceding it; when a constituent follows this verb (e.g., a prepositional phrase), the pattern might be considered marked. Thus, we have 'Ich habe mein Auto nach Schweden

mitgenommen' and 'Ich muss unbedingt mein Auto mitnehmen nach Schweden' (In both cases, *Schweden* is accented.) It is also somewhat unclear whether there is in fact a heavier accent on the last such constituent, or that this is perceived *because* it is last. The most useful treatment of accent in German is probably that of Bierwisch (1966).

15. Neutral intonation is not an uncontroversial topic. Thus, Schmerling (1974) points out that the final stress in 'John was killed by himself', which she argues is contrastive and mandatory, has no neutral counterpart. Chomsky (1971, p. 205), on the other hand, appears to argue that extra emphasis can be placed, or superimposed, on an already stressed word.

16. The notion of contrast was also elaborated in Jackendoff's (1972) work on semantic interpretation in generative grammar. There, he writes, for example:

> In accordance with the definition of presupposition given above, the variable must be chosen in such a way that it defines a coherent class of possible contrasts with the focus, pieces of semantic information that could equally well have taken the place of the focus in the sentence, within bounds established by the language, the discourse, and the external situation. The class of possible contrasts represents the range of information over which either the speaker or the hearer is uncertain (depending on whether the sentence is interrogative or declarative) (p. 243).

Though it may be most parsimonious to argue that focus can occur with contrast or without it, German, for example, seems to accept cleft sentences only when there is contrast (and usually correction) intended. Harries-Delisle (1978) argues that cleft sentences, and ones derived from them, universally have contrastive emphasis.

17. To make this claim more worthy of note, several things are needed which we are unable to do here. On the one hand, examples need to be worked out which test the limits on independence among not only the dimensions considered below, but even ones not even mentioned here. On the other hand, empirical evidence of a quite different kind—some kind of actual text/conversation based analysis—is necessary to confirm the presence of possible statistical association among these factors. In expanding the enterprise, it might turn out that the kind of autonomy suggested here in particular cases is not worth defending, because significant psychological generalizations about the means/ends relationship are overlooked (see also Engelkamp and Zimmer, 1982).

18. One difference between the two sets of cases besides the semantic one just mentioned is that the present one seems to allow for both restrictive and unrestrictive interpretations of the relative clauses involved.

19. As Stenning (1977) suggests for English, a general analysis of what these words are used to mean should include examination of plural indefinites (such as French *des* and the corresponding Italian contractions), phrases within the scope of other quantifiers, etc.

20. Just as the grammars written for languages were for a period of history influenced by a different, irrelevant language (namely Latin), there seems to be a danger that psycholinguistic studies in English will have a pervasive and undue effect on how other languages are investigated, and even on what is found and concluded from such studies in these languages. While parallels can be sought, they clearly must not be the main motivation for the conduct of research. Or they must be closer to universal parallels. Of course, one great advantage of having such a great diversity of languages available to work in is that one can be surer of discovering general properties of human language use. But another, equally great advantage is that

questions can be asked and answered about language production *and* perception, which never come up, or are not investigable, in any particular language one chooses to study.

ACKNOWLEDGMENTS

This chapter owes much to Claus Heeschen, who on many points shared both examples and insights with us, and thoroughly criticized our manuscript. Ino d'Arcais was also kind in pointing out some of the more serious shortcomings of previous drafts, and some of the ideas expressed were further stimulated by discussions with Jens Allwood, Elisabet Engdahl, Charles Fillmore, and Susan Fischer and Yuki Kuroda. This paper nevertheless should be seen largely as a preliminary to further work still to be done, backed up by relevant empirical evidence.

REFERENCES

Akmajian, A. The role of focus in the interpretation of anaphoric expressions. In S.R. Anderson and P. Kiparsky (Eds), *A Festschrift for Morris Halle*. New York: Holt, 1973.

Allwood, J. *Linguistic Communication as Action and Cooperation.* Gothenberg Monographs in Linguistics, 2. Göteborg: Gothenberg University Department of Linguistics, 1976.

Bates, E., and MacWhinney, B. A functionalist approach to the acquisition of grammar. In E. Ochs and B. B. Schieffelin (Eds), *Developmental Pragmatics.* New York: Academic Press, 1979.

Beneš, E. Začátek německé věty z hlediska aktuálního členění věného. *Časopis pro moderní filologii*, 1959, **41**, 205–217.

Bierwisch, M. Regeln für die Intonation deutscher Sätze. *Studia Grammatica*, 1966, **7**, 99–201.

Bolinger, D. Accent is predictable (if you're a mind reader). *Language*, 1972, **48**, 633–644.

Carpenter, P. A., and Just, M. A. Reading comprehension as eyes see it. In M. A. Just and P. A. Carpenter (Eds), *Cognitive Processes in Comprehension*. Hillsdale, N.J.: Lawrence Erlbaum Associates, 1977(a).

Carpenter, P. A., and Just, M. A. Integrative processes in comprehension. In D. Laberge and S. J. Samuels (Eds), *Basic Processes in Reading: Perception and Comprehension*. Hillsdale, N.J.: Lawrence Erlbaum Associates, 1977(b).

Chafe, W. L. Language and consciousness. *Language,* 1974, **50**, 111–133.

Chafe, W. L. Givenness, contrastiveness, definiteness, subjects, topics, and point of view. In C. N. Li (Ed.), *Subject and Topic*. New York: Academic Press, 1976.

Chao, Y. R. *A Grammar of Spoken Chinese*. Berkeley: University of California Press, 1968.

Chomsky, N. *Aspects of the Theory of Syntax*. Cambridge, Mass.: M.I.T. Press, 1965.

Chomsky, N. Deep structure, surface structure, and semantic interpretation. In D. D. Steinberg and L. A. Jakobovits (Eds), *Semantics: An Interdisciplinary Reader in Philosophy, Linguistics and Anthropology*. Cambridge: Cambridge University Press, 1971.

Clark, H. H., and Carlson, T. B. Hearers and speech acts. *Language*, 1982, **58**, 332–373.

Clark, H. H., and Clark, E. V. *Psychology and Language*. New York: Harcourt Brace Jovanovich, 1977.

Clark, H. H., and Haviland, S. Comprehension and the given–new contract. In R. O. Freedle (Ed.), *Discourse Production and Comprehension*. Norwood, N.J.: Ablex, 1977.

Clark, H. H., and Marshall, C. R. Definite reference and mutual knowledge. In A. Joshi, B. L. Webber, and I. Sag (Eds), *Elements of Discourse Processing*. Cambridge: Cambridge University Press, 1982.

Cutler, A. Beyond parsing and lexical look-up: An enriched description of auditory sentence comprehension. In R. J. Wales and E. Walker (Eds), *New Approaches to Language Mechanisms*. Amsterdam: North-Holland, 1976.

Cutler, A., and Fodor, J. A. Semantic focus and sentence comprehension. *Cognition*, 1979, **7**, 49–59.

Cutler, A., and Isard, S. The production of prosody. In B. Butterworth (Ed.), *Language Production*. New York: Academic Press, 1980.

Dahl, Ö. *Topic and comment. A study in Russian and general transformational grammar*. Slavica Gothoburgensia 4. Acta Universitatis Gothoburgensis, Stockholm: Almkvist and Wiksell, 1969.

Dahl, Ö. Topic–comment structure in a generative grammar with a semantic base. In F. Daneš (Ed.), *Papers on Functional Sentence Perspective*. The Hague: Mouton, 1974.

Daneš, F. Functional sentence perspective and the organization of the text. In F. Daneš (Ed.), *Papers on Functional Sentence Perspective*. The Hague: Mouton, 1974.

Dik, S. *Functional Grammar*. Amsterdam: North-Holland, 1978.

Dore, J., and McDermott, R. P. Linguistic indeterminancy and social context. *Language*, 1982, **58**, 374–398.

Engelkamp, J. Given and new information: Theoretical positions and empirical evidence. *Arbeiten der Fachrichtung Psychologie der Universität des Saarlandes*, No. 79. Saarbrücken, 1982.

Engelkamp, J., and Zimmer, H. D. The interaction of subjectization and concept placement in the processing of cleft sentences, *Quarterly Journal of Experimental Psychology*, 1982, **34**, 463–478.

Ertel, S. Where do the subjects of sentences come from? In S. Rosenberg (Ed.), *Sentence Production*. Hillsdale, N.J.: Lawrence Erlbaum Associates, 1977.

Fillmore, C. J. The case for case. In E. Bach and R. T. Harms (Eds), *Universals in Linguistic Theory*. New York: Holt, Rinehart and Winston, 1968.

Firbas, J. On defining the theme in functional sentence analysis. *Travaux Linguistiques de Prague*, 1964, **1**, 267–280.

Firbas, J. Some aspects of the Czechoslovak approach to problems of functional sentence perpective. In F. Daneš (Ed.), *Papers on Functional Sentence Perspective*. The Hague: Mouton, 1974.

Firbas, J. A functional view of 'ordo naturalis'. *Brno Studies in English*, 1979, **13**, 9–22.

Flores d'Arcais, G. B. Some perceptual determinants of sentence constructions. In G. B. Flores d'Arcais (Ed.), *Studies in Perception*. Milano: Martello-Giunti, 1975.

Frege, G. *Begriffschrift, eine der arithmetischen nachgebildete Formelsprache des reinen Denkens*. Halle, 1879. English translation of Chapter 1 in Geach and Black, 1952.

Frege, G. Über Sinn und Bedeutung. *Zeitschrift für Philosophie und philosophische Kritik*, 1892, **100**, 25–50.

Gabelentz, G. von der. Ideen zu einer vergleichenden Syntax. Wort- und Satzstellung. *Zeitschrift für Völkerpsychologie und Sprachwissenschaft*, 1869, **6**, 376–384.

Gabelentz, G. von der. Zur chinesischen Sprache und zur allgemeinen Grammatik. *Internationale Zeitschrift für allgemeine Sprachwissenschaft*, 1887, **3**, 93–109.

Gabelentz, G. von der. *Die Sprachwissenschaft*. Leipzig: Weigel, 1891.

Geach, P. and Black, M. (Eds). *Translations from Philosophical Writings of Gottlob Frege*. Oxford: Blackwell, 1952.

Grice, H. P. Logic and conversation. In P. Cole and J. L. Morgan (Eds), *Syntax and Semantics*, Vol. 3. *Speech Act*. New York: Academic Press, 1975.

Grieve, R., and Wales, R. J. Passives and topicalization. *British Journal of Psychology*, 1973, **64**, 173–182.

Halliday, M. A. K. Notes on transitivity and theme in English, Part 2. *Journal of Linguistics*, 1967, **3**, 199–244.

Halliday, M. A. K. Language structure and language function. In J. Lyons (Ed.), *New Horizons in Linguistics*. Harmondsworth: Penguin, 1970(a).

Halliday, M. A. K. *A Course in Spoken English: Intonation*. Oxford: Oxford University Press, 1970(b).

Halliday, M. A. K., and Hasan, R. *Cohesion in English*. London: Longman, 1976.

Harries-Delisle, H. Contrastive emphasis and cleft sentences. In J. H. Greenberg (Ed.), *Universals of Human Language*, Vol. 4. Stanford: Stanford University Press, 1978.

Hawkins, J. A. *Definiteness and Indefiniteness*. London: Croom Helm, 1978.

Hornby, P. A. The psychological subject and predicate. *Cognitive Psychology*, 1972, **3**, 643–654.

Hornby, P. A. Surface structure and presupposition. *Journal of Verbal Learning and Verbal Behavior*, 1974, **13**, 530–538.

Høffding, H. *Den menneskelige tanke. Dens former og dens opgaver*. Copenhagen: Nordisk, 1910. (Also translated into French as *La pensée humaine*, Paris: Félix Alcon, 1911).

Hupet, M., and Le Bouedec, B. Definiteness and voice in the interpretation of active and passive sentences. *Quarterly Journal of Experimental Psychology*, 1975, **27**, 323–330.

Jackendoff, R. S. *Semantic Interpretation in Generative Grammar*. Cambridge, Mass.: M.I.T. Press, 1972.

Jarvella, R. J., and Klein, W. (Eds). *Speech, Place and Action: Studies in Deixis and Related Topics*. Chichester and New York: Wiley, 1982.

Jarvella, R. J., and Nelson, T. R. Focus of information and general knowledge in language understanding. In J.-F. Le Ny and W. Kintsch (Eds), *Language and Comprehension*. Amsterdam: North-Holland, 1982.

Jellinek, H. M. *Geschichte der neuhochdeutschen Grammatik von den Anfangen bis auf Adelung*. Heidelberg, 1913–1914.

Jesperson, O. *The Philosophy of Grammar*. London: Allen and Unwin, 1924.

Jesperson, O. *A Modern English Grammar on Historical Principles*, Part 7: *Syntax*. Copenhagen: Ejnar Munksgaard, 1949.

Karmiloff-Smith, A. *A Functional Approach to Child Language*. Cambridge: Cambridge University Press, 1979.

Keenan, E. L. Towards a universal definition of subject. In C. N. Li (Ed.), *Subject and Topic*. New York: Academic Press, 1976.

Keenan, E. L., and Schieffelin, B. B. Topic as a discourse notion: A study of topic in the conversations of children and adults. In C. N. Li (Ed.), *Subject and Topic*. New York: Academic Press, 1976.

Klenbort, I., and Anisfeld, M. Markedness and perspective in the interpretation of the active and passive voice. *Quarterly Journal of Experimental Psychology*, 1974, **26**, 189–195.

Langendoen, D. T., and Savin, H. B. The projection problem for presuppositions. In

C. J. Fillmore and D. T. Langendoen (Eds), *Studies in Linguistic Semantics*. New York: Holt, Rinehart and Winston, 1971.

Li, C. N., and Thompson, S. A. Subject and topic: A new typology of language. In C. N. Li (Ed.), *Subject and Topic*. New York: Academic Press, 1976.

Linell, P., *Människans Språl* Lund: LiberLäromedel, 1977.

Linell, P. *Psychological Reality in Phonology*. Cambridge: Cambridge University Press, 1979.

Linell, P. *The Written Language Bias in Linguistics*. Studies in Communication, 2. Linköping: University of Linköping, 1982.

Loftus, G. R. Eye fixations and recognition memory for pictures. *Cognitive Psychology*, 1972, **3**, 525–551.

Loftus, G. R., and Mackworth, N. H. Cognitive determinants of fixation location during picture viewing. *Journal of Experimental Psychology: Human Perception and Performance*, 1978, **4**, 565–572.

Lyons, J. *Semantics*. Cambridge: Cambridge University Press, 1977.

Mackworth, N. H., and Morandi, A. J. The gaze selects informative details within pictures. *Perception and Psychophysics*, 1967, **2**, 547–552.

Mathesius, V. O tak zvaném aktuálním členění větném. *Slovo a slovesnost*, 1939, **5**, 171–174. Reprinted in V. Mathesius, *Čeština a obecný jazykozpyt*, Prague, 1947.

Mathesius, V. Řec a sloh. In *Čtene o jazyce a poetzii*. Prague, 1942.

Paul, H. *Prinzipien der Sprachgeschichte*, 2nd edition. Halle: Niemeyer, 1886.

Perrault, C. R., and Allen, J. F. A plan-based analysis of indirect speech acts. *American Journal of Computational Linguistics*, 1980, **6**, 167–182.

Russell, B. On denoting. *Mind*, 1905, **14**, 479–493.

Sapir, E. *Language*. New York: Harcourt, Brace and World, 1921.

Scaglione, A. *The Classical Theory of Composition, from its Origins to the Present: A Historical Survey*. Chapel Hill: University of North Carolina Press, 1972.

Schachter, P. The subject in Philippine languages: Topic, actor, actor-topic, or none of the above. In C. N. Li (Ed.), *Subject and Topic*. New York: Academic Press, 1976.

Schank, R. C., and Abelson, R. P. *Scripts, Plans, Goals, and Understanding: An Inquiry into some Knowledge Structures*. Hillsdale, N.J.: Lawrence Erlbaum Associates, 1977.

Schmerling, S. F. A re-examination of normal stress. *Language*, 1974, **50**, 66–73.

Searle, J. R. *Speech Acts*. London: Cambridge University Press, 1969.

Stenning, K. Articles, quantifiers, and their encoding in text comprehension. In R. O. Freedle (Ed.), *Discourse Production and Comprehension*. Norwood, N.J.: Ablex, 1977.

Strawson, P. F. On referring. *Mind*. 1950, **59**, 320–344.

Strawson, P. F. *Introduction to Logical Theory*. London: Methuen, 1952.

Svoboda, A. *Diatheme*. Brno: Univerzita J. E. Purkyně, 1980.

Tannenbaum, P. H., and Williams, F. Generation of active and passive sentences as a function of subject and object focus. *Journal of Verbal Learning and Verbal Behavior*, 1968, **7**, 246–256.

Townsend, D. J., and Bever, T. G. Interclause relations and clausal processing. *Journal of Verbal Learning and Verbal Behavior*, 1978, **17**, 509–521.

Townsend, D. J., Ottaviano, D., and Bever, T. G. Immediate memory for words from main and subordinate clauses at different age levels. *Journal of Psycholinguistic Research*, 1979, **8**, 83–101.

Trávníček, F. O tak zvaném aktuálním členěni větném. *Slovo a slovenost*, 1962, **22**, 163–171.

Vygotsky, L. S. *Thought and Language*, 1934. Edited and translated by E. Hanfmann and G. Vakar. Cambridge, Mass.: M.I.T. Press, 1962.

Weil, H. *De l'ordre des mots dans les langues anciennes comparées aux langues modernes*, 1844. Translated by C. W. Super as *The Order of Words in the Ancient Languages Compared with that of the Modern Languages.* Boston: Ginn, 1887. Reprinted 1978 by Benjamins, Amsterdam.

Western, A. On sentence-rhythm and word-order in modern English. *Videnskabs-Selskabets Skrifter.* Cristiana: Fridtjof Nansens Fond, 1908.

Wright, P., and Glucksberg, S. Choice of definite versus indefinite article as a function of sentence voice and reversibility. *Quarterly Journal of Experimental Psychology*, 1976, **28**, 561–570.

Wundt, W. *Die Sprache*, Leipzig: Engelmann, 1900. (Citations from 3rd edition, 1912).

Yekovich, F. R., Walker, C. H., and Blackman, H. S. The role of presupposed and focal information in integrating sentences. *Journal of Verbal Learning and Verbal Behavior*, 1979, **18**, 535–548.

Zimmer, H. D., and Engelkamp, J. The given–new structure of cleft sentences and their influence on picture viewing. *Psychological Research*, 1981, **43**, 375–389.

The Process of Language Understanding
Edited by G. B. Flores d'Arcais and R. J. Jarvella
© 1983 John Wiley & Sons Ltd.

8

Topic Dependent Effects in Language Processing

SIMON GARROD and ANTHONY SANFORD

University of Glasgow, UK

INTRODUCTION

Throughout the brief history of psycholinguistics there has been a strong tendency to produce fragmentary accounts of sentence comprehension in which the comprehension process is partitioned off into distinct domains corresponding to those found in the linguistic description of the sentence. For instance, until quite recently it was common to see what might be termed translation models, which identify a sequence of processing stages aimed at translating the input into increasingly abstract levels of linguistic description. Thus comprehension was viewed as starting with a phonological analysis, going on to syntactic analysis, and on the basis of this to semantic and pragmatic analysis of the sentence. More recently, this radical stage approach to sentence comprehension has been questioned, and a number of theorists have argued for sentence processing systems which incorporate the syntactic and semantic analysis into one domain. For instance, Marslen-Wilson (1975) has proposed an interactive parallel process for sentence perception in which the stage analysis is essentially discarded. Furthermore, in many recent computer-based models of language understanding, it is difficult to winkle out the semantic part of the process from the syntactic (e.g. Winograd, 1972; Rumelhart, 1977).

However, when one turns to accounts which include pragmatic analysis, many theorists still tacitly assume a processing partition. At the risk of grossly oversimplifying the picture, two stages of analysis emerge. The first might be characterized as a process aimed at extracting the literal meaning of the sentence via a sequential parsing system, while the second process determines the significance of this analysed meaning in terms of the context in which the sentence was encountered. To take two recent examples, Foss and Hakes (1978) in an introductory book on psycholinguistics suggest that 'the hearer arrives at the sentence's literal meaning and then evaluates that meaning in terms of the situation in which it occurred' (p. 60). Similarly, Cutler (1976), in a somewhat different context, has argued for a two-stage model of sentence comprehension in which there is 'a processing stage subsequent to the estab-lishment of the literal meaning of a sentence in which this meaning may be revised', on the basis of paralinguistic cues such as stress assignment. Implicit in both these statements is the idea that establishing the literal meaning of a sentence is in some way independent of, and from a processing point of view, prior to establishing its significance. This idea is intimately connected with the view that deriving the propositional content of a sentence represents the major milestone in its interpretation and something which will yield the ling-uistic basis on which subsequent pragmatic processes may operate.

In this chapter, we intend to examine the value of such a processing distinc-tion, both in terms of sentence comprehension in general, and as it relates to the difference between syntactic or semantic analysis on the one hand and pragmatic analysis on the other. However, before considering the rôle of pragmatics in a language processing system, it may be helpful to establish the difference between the literal meaning of a sentence and its significance.

In the past this distinction has most commonly been drawn in the context of indirect speech acts (Searle, 1975). If a person asks a question such as (1) below, in most circumstances the listener will interpret this not in terms of its literal meaning but rather as a request for the interlocutor to provide the speaker with information about the current time.

(1) Do you know the time?

Hence if one responds to the literal meaning by answering 'Yes', this would in most cases be taken as a breach of conversational etiquette. Despite the fact that indirect speech acts of this sort have received considerable attention, it is not with these rather special examples which we will be concerned.

Let us instead consider a pair of statements such as (2) and (3) below:

(2) The policeman help up his hand and stopped the bus.
(3) The goal-keeper held up his hand and stopped the ball.

The literal meaning of these two statements might be represented according to some formula as: 'A person held up that person's hand and that person stopped an object (bus or ball)'. To this extent the two sentences may be said to be quite similar in their literal meanings. However, to the average reader the two sentences 'mean' something quite different. Sentence (2) describes an event where a policeman raised his hand in a conventional gesture which results in the driver of the bus putting his foot on the brake and bringing the bus to a halt. Sentence (3), on the other hand, describes an event in a game of football where a goal-keeper puts up his hand to stop a football which was probably kicked by a member of the opposing team towards his goal.

It is because these two sentences refer to such recognizably different events that their significance is so different, so much so that the verb 'stop' seems to take on a completely different 'meaning' in the two cases, although it is unlikely that a lexicographer would want to write separate semantic entries in his dictionary for the two uses of the word. These two sentences illustrate the difference between the significance of a statement and its literal meaning, and as Johnson-Laird (1977) has pointed out, this is largely a matter of reference. In terms of the description of a language processing system, the problem is whether the reader or listener is able to get at the significance of the sentence while parsing it, or whether he has to wait until he has carried out a preliminary syntactic and semantic analysis of the complete sentence, as Foss and Hakes (1978), among others, seem to be suggesting.

In this paper, we will argue that while it may indeed be useful to think of sentence processing in terms of a primary stage occurring at the time of parsing the sentence and a secondary stage occurring only after an initial interpretation has been made, these two stages should not be identified with distinct levels of description of the sentence. In contrast we will suggest, along with such theorists as Johnson-Laird (1977) that it may be more fruitful to consider comprehension as a unified process whose primary goal is to relate incoming sentences directly to some mental model of what the text, of which the sentence is part, is about. In this way pragmatic operations such as determining the significance of a sentence in its context may be seen as an integral part of understanding that sentence. These operations should enter into the process at the time of parsing, whenever this is possible. Nevertheless, it may still be necessary to recognize a distinction between an immediate primary level of analysis which operates within the constraints of the current global topic of discourse, and a secondary level which operates outside these constraints and is responsible for registering shifts in discourse topic.

However, before we can directly confront the processing issue we will need a brief discussion of the notion of topic, both as it relates to individual sentences and discourse as a whole. It should not be surprising that 'topic', which is usually taken to indicate what a sentence or larger piece of discourse is about, should have some bearing on determination of sentential significance in the sense which we have used the term here. In fact we will go on to demonstrate that the ease with which a reader may comprehend a sentence seems to depend upon the nature of the discourse topic at the time when the sentence is encountered.

DISCOURSE TOPIC AND REFERENCE RESOLUTION

Several linguists have drawn a distinction between the *topic* of a sentence and its *comment*, a long-standing distinction formalized by Hockett (1958).

According to its notional definition the term 'topic' is used to describe that person, thing or event which the sentence is *about*, whereas the term 'comment' describes the new information asserted of this topic. In attempting to formalize the distinction, Hockett suggested that since speakers tend to first announce a topic and then say something about it, the topic usually coincides with the grammatical subject of a sentence, whereas the comment corresponds to its predicate. Thus for a sentence such as (4) most readers would take 'John' to be the topic and 'ran away' the comment:

(4) John ran away.

However, in more recent analyses (see for instance Lyons, 1968), it has been pointed out that the topic of a sentence in its original sense can only be established by reference to the context in which that sentence occurs, be that context specifically stated or unstated. Thus Halliday (1967) introduced the terms *given* and *new* to throw more light on the matter. According to this analysis the topic of a sentence is usually *given*, in that the thing to which it refers should already be known to the reader/listener; by contrast, the comment is usually *new* in that it conveys hitherto unknown information pertaining to that topic. This distinction can be made clearer by considering sentence (4) as an answer to various questions:

(5) Q: Who ran away?
   A: John ran away.

In this case, *John* was the unknown factor, and so constitutes new information, and may be considered the comment. By contrast, that someone ran away is taken as given and thus the 'running away' may be considered the topic. This example contrasts well with:

(6) Q: What did John do?
   A: John ran away.

Here, *John*, is known or given, and so may be identified with the topic, while what he did is not known, is therefore new in the answer, and may be identified with the comment.

To a certain extent the contrast between two views of topic, namely, the purely sentential view, and the predominantly contextual one, may be resolved by drawing a distinction between the 'global topic' of discourse as opposed to the 'local topic' of various elements in it (see Hirst, 1979). According to such a formulation, 'local topic' is used to refer to what a *sentence* is about, whereas 'global topic' refers to what the *discourse* is about at any given time, and what seems to be important here is that 'local topic' relates to something represented in the 'global topic' of discourse at that time.[1]

Even this oversimplified account of topic serves to illustrate one important thing: any notion of topic along the lines of 'what the sentence is about' should be considered in terms of what the reader/listener already knows. With reading a connected piece of discourse, the processing problem is one of deciding (a) what kind of knowledge the reader has at any point in processing, and (b) how linguistic cues in a new sentence serve to integrate this sentence into the old knowledge structure. The complication comes in when it is appreciated that the knowledge the reader has available during processing may exceed that of the propositional content of the text itself, as the introductory discussion suggested it must. Let us illustrate this complication by way of two further examples, and then suggest a possible resolution through a third.

The pair of sentences below illustrate a coherent if uninteresting piece of discourse.

(7) Harry fell several times in the snow.
(7′) The snow was cold and wet.

This text is coherent because the local topic of the second sentence 'the snow' is also a simple anaphoric expression with a (given) antecedent in the first sentence. To this extent the local topic of (7′) identifies an element of the global topic of the discourse up to that point. However, once this antecedent is removed from the text as with (8) and (8′) below, determining what the sentence is about becomes less straightforward.

(8) Harry fell several times.
(8′) The snow was cold and wet.

To determine the significance of (8′) in the context of (8), insofar as this is possible, one would need to draw a bridging inference (Clark, 1975) which requires a certain amount of additional pragmatic analysis. One must conclude that it had been snowing, and that Harry fell in the snow. That forming such bridges takes up considerable processing time was demonstrated by Haviland and Clark (1974). They used reading time as an index of processing load and demonstrated that when sentences contained indirect references with no stated antecedent such as in (8′) above, this gave rise to a substantial increase in overall comprehension time. In Clark's original account, the processing difficulty was identified solely with the problem of discovering some relationship between anaphoric expressions and potential antecedents, and consequently when no antecedent is explicitly mentioned in the context it was argued that there should be considerable processing difficulty. But does this account give a complete explanation of what is going on when a reader encounters (8) and (8′)? After all, according to our analysis of this example, sentence (8′) seems to introduce a radical change of topic. There is no component of (8′) which may be identified as present or implicit in (8), and so it can be argued that (8) specifies no appropriate 'global topic' with which the 'local topic' of (8′) may be readily identified. To illustrate what we are getting at, consider (8) and (8′) embedded within a slightly longer text, entitled 'Learning to ski':

> *Learning to ski*
> Harry fell several times.
> He didn't like skiing at all.
> *The snow* was cold and wet.

In this case, the sentence does not seem awkward at all, and follows quite naturally from the prior text, although 'snow' is not directly mentioned at any point until the critical sentence is encountered.

In order to explain this, an extension and elaboration of the concept of the topic is called for. The text as a whole is about learning to ski, and this could properly be called the 'global topic' of the discourse. As long as the entire episode being recounted is about learning to ski, this constitutes given information. However, what is given is not simply that 'Harry is learning to ski', but seems to carry with it at least some of the things which typically act as props in such a situation, such as the presence of snow. So the presence of snow is also given, at least in the sense of being presupposed. One way of thinking of this is that for a text with a well defined global topic such as 'Learning to ski', a mental model is evoked in the reader which consists in part of a representation of things, and perhaps events, which are a normal part of our knowledge of learning to ski.

Thus the total representation available (given) may extend beyond that which is explicit in the text, and include representations of implicit referents. According to this view, a 'given' element for a newly encountered sentence will be anything which has either been explicitly mentioned, or which has been called forth as part of the implicit representation built up on the *basis* of explicitly mentioned material. The two aspects of the given element comprise an extended domain of potential reference, and it is this which corresponds to the global topic of the discourse at any time.

AN EXPERIMENTAL DEMONSTRATION OF SITUATION-DEPENDENT REFERENCE RESOLUTION

Up to now our arguments have relied on the reader's intuitions regarding example passages. Let us now turn to an experiment which tests the difficulty associated with understanding sentences containing indirect references in the context of either appropriate or inappropriate discourse topics. The study uses self-paced reading time as an index of the ease of comprehension, a procedure described in detail elsewhere (Garrod and Sanford, 1977; Sanford and Garrod, 1980). With this procedure the text is presented to the subject one sentence at a time and the subject presses a key when he is ready to go on to the next sentence in the sequence. It is thus possible to obtain an estimate

Table 8.1

APPROPRIATE TOPIC PASSAGE

Title	*Learning to ski*
Context sentence:	Harry fell several times (*in the snow*)
Filler sentence:	He didn't like skiing at all
Target sentence:	*The snow* was wet and cold.

INAPPROPRIATE TOPIC PASSAGE

Title	*Cross-country running*
Context sentence:	Harry fell several times (*in the snow*)
Filler sentence:	He hated running in winter
Target sentence:	*The snow* was wet and cold.

---

of the comprehension time associated with each sentence in a connected piece of discourse. In order to manipulate the 'global topic' of the passages containing the critical references, alternative titles were used. The general design of the material can be illustrated by reference to Table 8.1, which gives an example similar to the one shown above.

Twenty sets of three-sentence passages were generated of the sort shown in Table 8.1. In each case a pair of titles indicated an appropriate or an inappropriate topic with respect to the target sentence. There was also an option in the initial context sentence, which could either contain a mention of the critical reference or not. Thus each passage could be presented in either the appropriate or inappropriate topic condition and either with or without the stated antecedent. In order to ensure that the title manipulation was appropriate the set of titles and target items were first shown to 20 judges who were asked to judge on what proportion of times they would expect the target entity to be associated with the event described by the title (in effect be given as part of that topic). For the appropriate titles, this yielded a mean proportion of 90 per cent while for the inappropriate the proportion was only 34 per cent. There was no overlap in the two distributions.

Two groups of 30 subjects each were then tested, with one group reading 20 appropriate title materials and the other the matching inappropriate title materials. Each group was exposed to half the materials in the stated antecedent condition and half in the unstated, with this factor counterbalanced across subjects. By using the self-paced reading time procedure it is possible to measure the amount of time each subject chooses to spend reading each sentence in the text, since the text is presented one sentence at a time and the subject controls the rate of presentation.

From the point of view of the present discussion it is the relative reading time for the target sentence which is of interest, and for this the mean times are shown in Figure 8.1. Analyses of variance were carried out on these times

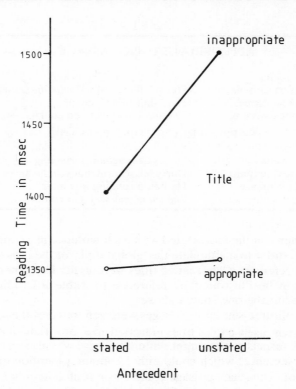

Figure 8.1   Sentence reading times for the target
sentence after appropriate or inappropriate title and
with either stated or unstated antecedent

both by subjects and materials. From the figure it can be seen that there is a
main effect for the stated versus unstated antecedent conditions of 62 msec.
This is reliable both by subjects ($F_1(1,58)$ = 6.58, p < 0.05) and materials
($F_2(1,19)$ = 7.25, p < 0.05). The figure also indicates a difference of 98 msec
between appropriate and inappropriate topic conditions. This is highly reliable by materials, with $F_2(1,19)$ = 12.46 p < 0.005 (s.e. = 27 msec), but not
by subjects, with $F_1(1,58)$ = 1.195 (s.e. = 64 msec). The discrepancy is due
to the fact that the material analysis relies on a *within-subjects* design, and the
subject analysis on a *between-subjects* design. There is considerable variability
between subjects, and so the analysis by subjects is essentially insensitive. This
is borne out by a comparison of the standard errors on the mean by subjects
and materials.
    The crucial comparison in terms of our predictions here is that between
stated and unstated antecedents under appropriate or inappropriate topic

conditions. As can be seen from Figure 8.1, under the appropriate topic condition there is only a small reading time difference of 21 msec in favour of the stated antecedent, whereas under the inappropriate condition the corresponding difference is 104 msec. By the analysis of variance, the interaction is marginally reliable both by subjects ($F_1(1,58) = 2.967$, $p < 0.08$) and by materials ($F_2(1,19) = 3.275$, $p < 0.08$).

However, the presence of a true interaction cannot be rejected by these results, because of the insensitivity of the between-subjects component. In terms of the predictions made above, it is the performance *within* each group which is important, and thus a simple effect analysis was also carried out (Winer, 1971). Looking first at the effect of stated versus unstated antecedent under the inappropriate topic condition, by materials a value of $F_2(1,38) = 10.135$, $p < 0.005$ was obtained, and by subjects, $F_1(1,116) = 9.189$, $p < 0.005$. Thus the substantial reading time difference here can be seen to be highly reliable statistically (min $F'(1,108) = 4.819$, $p < 0.05$). Under the appropriate topic condition, on the other hand, there is no reliable effect (by subjects, $F_1(1,116) = 0.18$, and by materials, $F_2(1,38) = 0.394$. For the most sensitive test the standard error of the effect was only 12 msec and so it is reasonable to conclude that there is indeed no effect.

The results of this experiment confirm our intuitions about the importance of discourse topic in the resolution of reference, and consequently in determining the significance of a sentence. Provided a representation of an entity is part of the mental model set up by the discourse, it is given, and a reference to the entity can be resolved equally easily whether it has been mentioned explicitly or whether it is represented as an implicit component of the global discourse topic.

THE EXTENDED DOMAIN OF REFERENCE AND SENTENTIAL PROCESSING

In the introduction to this paper we suggested that the traditional distinction between processes aimed at extracting literal meaning and those aimed at establishing significance could perhaps be replaced by a distinction between primary and secondary semantic processes, where primary processes are identified as processes operating within the constraints of discourse topic and secondary processes as those operating outside these constraints. The study described above serves to illustrate such a distinction. The results for the appropriate topic condition indicate that the direct resolution of reference is possible not just within the set of entities mentioned explicitly in the prior text, nor is it necessary to have recourse to time-consuming 'bridging' processes which call upon general knowledge. Rather, references may be resolved directly by searching a topic-defined set of representations, reflecting both explicitly mentioned entities and those implied by the current discourse topic.

The resolution of reference within this set reflects what we have called primary processing. Thus in the example given above, 'Learning to ski' entails the presence of 'snow', and so whether or not snow is mentioned explicitly in the antecedent material, subsequent reference to it will succeed on the basis of the extended topic representation. On the other hand, the results from the inappropriate topic condition suggest that when reference is made to something which is not represented as part of the global topic of discourse, then the natural flow of comprehension is interrupted and the reader needs recourse to time-consuming 'bridging' processes in order to identify a link between the current sentence and the prior discourse. This type of resolution, we would suggest, comes about through a secondary semantic process which is not so intimately linked to the on-line analysis of the sentence as are processes at the primary level, and is only instigated when there is a recognized failure of the primary process.

The notion of primary processing sketched above carries with it several implications and problems. At the most fundamental level it implies a picture of comprehension in which the main goal is to link incoming information into the current topic of discourse, using 'topic' in the sense discussed above. The motivation behind the processing distinction is that ultimately all processes used in language understanding should be geared towards this goal. Consequently, the assumption that sentential semantic and syntactic analysis precede determination of significance, and thereby represent the only kind of primary process must be questioned. This we shall do a little later. For the moment let us consider some of the other implications of this account.

Limits on the scope of a topic-based mental representation

The argument to this point is that the reader uses his interpretation of a text as the basis for isolating a mental representation corresponding to the global topic of discourse. This mental representation may then be used as a setting in terms of which subsequent sentences in the text can be directly interpreted. We will refer to such representations as *scenarios*, following Sanford and Garrod (1981).

In the example described above, the claim was made that some representation of 'snow' was part of the scenario for 'learning to ski'. One might also expect representations of other entities to be part of the scenario, such as 'skis', 'sloping ground', 'piste', 'instructor', etc. Clearly, there is a problem here-where does the scenario representation end? How is it possible to decide what is in a scenario? And, more generally, how are entities and actions to be represented in a scenario? These questions relate to the static limitations of scenarios. Another issue concerns *dynamic limitations*. Any scenario-based account of comprehension must specify some mechanism whereby interpretive scenarios are replaced as the text unfolds. The problem here is to specify those cues in a text which bring about such a change. Let us examine static and dynamic limitations in turn.

Static limitations of scenarios

It is likely that a scenario, as a minimum will consist of elements necessary to the situation that the scenario represents. As an illustration of this idea, consider the situation depicted by sentence (9):

(9) Mary was dressing the baby.

In this case, it may be argued that the verb phrase *was dressing* entails that 'clothes' were transferred. Indeed, some concept of transfer of clothes is a necessary part of the meaning of the verb. Garrod and Sanford (1980) have argued that it is also part of the working representation (equivalent to a scenario) associated with the verb. They demonstrated that subsequent references to 'the clothes' are handled just as quickly after (9) as after a sentence in which clothes were explicitly introduced, paralleling the experiment described earlier. However, as an independent check on the necessary nature of 'transfer of clothes' for 'was dressing', sentences were made up in which the verb and the implied entity were both mentioned, for instance:

(10) Mary dressed the baby *with clothes*.
(11) Keith drove to London *by vehicle*.

Such sentences have a curious ring about them—they are pleonastic, in that the verb implies the entities so strongly that to mention the entities explicitly is quite unnecessary. We would argue that the difficulty with these pleonasms arises from the verb 'dressed' eliciting a representation including 'clothes' (for instance), and so to say *with clothes* is redundant. How such implied items may be best represented is a difficult problem; however, Garrod and Sanford (1980) have suggested that they might be thought of as variables which specify the range of possible instantiations in this working representation. Thus with the verb 'dress' there might be a variable (*clothes*) which will accept anything which qualifies as an instance of clothing as a value. The degree of specification on the variable will, of course, have implications for whether or not a sentence containing mention of the entity is seen as pleonastic. Thus while (11) is pleonastic, a sentence such as 'Keith drove to London by bus' is not. Presumably 'bus' further specifies the variable (*vehicle*). A more complete discussion of this problem is given in Garrod and Sanford (1980), where it is also argued that mental representations for entities that have been explicitly mentioned must differ in certain ways from scenario-based representation of variables. From the point of view of the present discussion it is simply worth noting that considerations such as these may provide one means of coming to grips with the problem of scope of scenarios.

Leaving the rather sparse empirical evidence behind, let us turn briefly to the considerations of representations which have emerged from research on natural language processing in artificial intelligence. The idea that machine comprehension requires situation-specific data structures has been given a popular status by Minsky (1975) and his students (e.g. Charniak, 1972), and has been implemented to some extent by Schank and his colleagues (see Schank and Abelson, 1977, for a review). Schank and Abelson refer to such data structures as *scripts*, and give as an example a script for the situation of 'a restaurant from a customer's point of view'. The script is simply a plan of what happens at a restaurant (knowledge we all possess), and of course necessarily contains representations of characters (waiters, cashiers, customers), props (tables, food, etc.), as well as descriptions of the actions linking characters and props (being shown to a table, ordering, eating, etc.).

In a script-based comprehension program, the script serves to integrate explicitly mentioned events within a common (pre-established) framework. Thus a script parallels our notion of a scenario as a potential global discourse topic. While Schank's work with scripts is purely within the domain of artificial intelligence, it does provide some useful guidelines for thinking about how people may represent episodes (see, for instance, Bower, Black, and Turner, 1979).

Although the static limitations on scenarios (or scripts) are so difficult to establish empirically, we believe that this does not destroy the utility of the concept. In the next section we shall examine some of the dynamic aspects of a scenario-based theory of comprehension, which we have found more tractable.

Dynamic aspects of scenarios

Just as a scenario must be bounded in content, so the lifespan of a scenario as a useful topic must be limited. After all, as a text unfolds there are shifts in what the text is about. The simplest case of a discourse topic shift occurs when there is a clear indication that a principal actor in a narrative moves from one setting or situation to another. For example:

(12)   John went to have a haircut.
(12')   He received excellent and rapid treatment.
(12")   After that, he went to the cinema with his girlfriend.

It is fair to claim that there are two major settings in this text—'having a haircut' and being at a 'cinema'. In sentence (12"), both the expression 'After that' and the action which follows signal the end of the 'barber shop' scenario as an extended domain of reference. Among other expressions which might indicate an imminent change of setting are '(sometime) later', and 'when X had finished', etc.

Furthermore, since many stereotypic situations seem to have time or space boundaries associated with them (see Grimes, 1975), certain temporal or spacial references should also influence the utility of a scenario as a reference topic. For instance, take the pair:

(13)   John was having a haircut.
(13′)   Three yards away, someone had his throat cut.

According to the primary processing principle, (13′) should be interpreted in terms of a barbershop scenario. Sentence (13′) will cohere with (13) because the person whose throat was cut should be construed as being in the barbershop too, putting a severe constraint on the possible worlds which might be associated with (13′). Now compare:

(14)   John was having his haircut.
(14′)   Three miles away, someone had his throat cut.

In this case, the expression *three miles away* makes it impossible to interpret the following event-description in terms of the barbershop scenario. Primary processing fails, and the significance of (14′) with respect to the text cannot be interpreted in terms of the barbershop scenario at all. The reader must await some new link, since there has been a radical change in topic. Similar considerations apply to time. In the context of getting a haircut, 'twelve hours later' should signal that the barber shop scenario is no longer to be directly relevant.

These examples are certainly compatible with the view that, from point to point in a text, the scenario which will be used in order to produce coherence will change. Let us say that there is a change in *focus*, and that the primary processing of referential expressions is restricted to the *scenario currently in focus*. Such a formulation may be examined in a variety of ways, three of which are discussed in the next section. The argument in common to each study is that when a scenario is signalled as no longer being relevant, it will not be kept in focus, and so will not be available as an extended domain of reference. Consequently, any incoming reference to an entity which was part of that scenario will be difficult (slow) to resolve. The following passage appeals to the reader's intuitions on this point; shortly we shall describe direct empirical evidence:

(15a)   John Brown went into town for a meal.
(15b)   He enjoyed his trout very much.
(15c)   Because he had time to spare, he later went to the cinema.
(15d)   The film was a rather poor western.
(15e)   The sheriff looked just like the waiter.

In (15e), a reference to *the waiter* is encountered. But according to our argument up to now, (15c) should have caused the 'restaurant' scenario to be shifted out of focus in favour of the 'cinema' scenario. Our claim is that *the waiter* should be relatively difficult to interpret in relation to the text as a whole. This assertion is examined in the next section.

EXPERIMENTAL STUDIES OF SHIFTS IN FOCUS

Direct focus shift

This study (Sanford, Garrod and Henderson, 1980) investigated the ease of resolving references made to entities either mentioned explicitly as an antecedent, or assumed to be implied by some antecedent event, as in the study described earlier. However, an additional manipulation was employed. Either the text was written so that a single scenario was maintained, or else it was written so that a complete shift in setting was indicated, a manipulation which should force the initial scenario out of focus. An example of the materials employed is given in Table 8.2.

In the first sentence, either a verb implying an entity (e.g. dressing: clothes) or a direct reference so that entity was made (implicit versus explicit contrast). In the second sentence, either a statement compatible with the first event was added, or else a progression to a new event was introduced. Progress to a new event was signalled by a phrase signifying end of event, and by the introduction of a new event description. Finally, the third sentence introduced a reference to the critical entity which was implied or stated in the first sentence. The prediction was that resolution of the reference to the critical entity should be made more difficult after a shift in focus had taken place.

The mean reading times for the third sentence shown in Figure 8.2 bears out this prediction. Whether or not the critical entity was mentioned explicitly, a shift in focus does result in a reliable increase in reading time. That this increase might result from a general difficulty associated with read-

Table 8.2

CONTEXT	Explicit antecedent	: 'Mary was putting the clothes on the baby'
SENTENCE	Implicit antecedent	: 'Mary was dressing the baby'
SHIFT SENTENCE	Topic maintained	: 'She always had trouble doing this'
	Topic shifted	: 'When she had finished she went to the shops'
TARGET SENTENCE	Topic reference	: The clothes were made of pink wool'
	Central character reference	: 'Then Mary took the baby to the nursery'

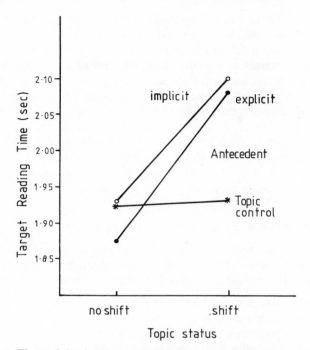

Figure 8.2   Sentence reading times for the target sentence after either a topic shift or no shift in topic, and with either implicit or explicit antecedent. The reading times for the topic reference control are also shown

ing any sentence after a shift was ruled out by employing a control procedure in which the target sentence itself constituted another new event, and referred back to the principal actor in the materials (*Mary*, in our example). An example control sentence is 'Then Mary took the baby to the nursery'.

These results show a number of things. First, they confirm our intuitions about the difficulties of resolving a reference based on an implicit representation when such a representation is no longer in focus. Second, they show a similar change in the ease of referring to an *explicitly* mentioned entity. This forces us into a position of supposing that the representations of explicitly mentioned entities are also subject to changes in focus, a position upon which we shall elaborate shortly. Finally, there is a small (but not significant) difference between target reading times for implicit and explicit antecedents, albeit very small compared to the effects of focus shift. This may reflect no more than statistical noise, but it may be equally due to the criteria by which the entities implied by the verbs were selected.[2]

One noteworthy feature of this study is that the critical entities of interest are *scenario-dependent*; that is to say, they only have significance *because* of the position in a scenario. For example, the 'clothes' are not just any clothes, or clothes in general, but are 'the clothes Mary used to dress the baby'. By contrast, 'Mary' is not scenario-dependent. Indeed, it could be argued that the events are only related to one another because 'Mary' plays a principal-actress role in each of them. If this view has any force, it should mean that as scenarios go out of focus, along with the representations of scenario-dependent entities, the representation of a principal actor is not affected, even if the actor is not mentioned in the focus shift sentence. In the next pair of studies, this proposal was tested, and, simultaneously, a test was made of the efficacy of temporal cues as focus-shifters.

Indirect shifts through changes of temporal setting

In this study (Anderson, Garrod, and Sanford, in press) temporal setting statements were used in an effort to manipulate the relevance of an established scenario. Consider the following brief passage:

> *At the cinema*
> Jenny found the film rather boring.
> The projectionist had to keep changing reels.
> It was supposed to be a silent classic.
> Seven hours ⎫
> Ten minutes ⎬ Later the film was forgotten.
> He ⎫
> She ⎬ had fallen asleep and was dreaming.

This passage is about someone going to the cinema to see a film. Such an event has associated with it a time interval of about two hours. However, in the fourth sentence a shift in temporal setting is indicated, which may either be well within these bounds ('ten minutes later') or beyond them ('seven hours later'). According to the argument given above, one might expect a shift in temporal setting which is in violation of the normal time boundary to have the effect of shifting the topic away from the event. What effect should this have on the extended domain of reference associated with this previous topic of discourse? If the suggestions made above are correct it should have the effect of reducing the reference domain to exclude those things associated with that topic scenario, and thus make them more difficult to refer to.

This can be illustrated by reference to the passage shown above. This passage contains mention of two characters, 'Jenny' and 'the projectionist'. However, only one of these characters, 'the projectionist', is bound to the cinema scenario in that his role is entirely dependent upon it. Thus in this case we would expect a shift in topic to have a differential effect on the subsequent accessibility of the two characters, with the central character being unaffected and the scenario-dependent character becoming less accessible for reference. This is testable with passages containing target sentences which either refer to one character or the other after appropriate changes in temporal setting. An example is provided in the final sentence of the passage used above.

As a preliminary to doing any such experiment, it is necessary to establish the time boundary associated with any scenario on a normative basis. This was done here by presenting a number of subjects with the set of titles to be used in the experiment and simply asking them to indicate the range in time over which they would expect such an event or episode to occur. These results were then used to establish limits on the normal time range associated with the events. We will mention two experiments which employed these materials.

The first experiment was designed to check whether time changes would in fact have the effect of differentially shifting global topic. The rationale behind this study was simple. If one presents subjects with passages like that shown in the 'cinema' example above, but only with material up to and including the time change sentence, and one then asks the subjects to write a continuation sentence which seems to follow, an independent check can be made of perceived topic. Incidence of mention of either the central character or topic-bound character following the different time changes should yield an estimate of their current state of topicalization.

Twenty materials of the sort illustrated above were used, and the incidence of mention of either character following the two types of time-change sentence was recorded. The results from 40 subjects are shown in Figure 8.3. As can be seen from the figure, the nature of the time change has the expected differential effects on probability of mention.

A number of results emerge from the continuation data. First, it is apparent that there is a greater tendency to mention the central character than the topic-dependent one. Furthermore, there is higher likelihood of using a pronoun for such mentions. But in terms of differential effects of topic shift with temporal statements it is the interaction of time change with type of character which is of interest. The reliable presence of this interaction suggests that the time changes do have the effect of shifting the global topic away from the event whose temporal boundaries have been violated.

The second experiment was designed to determine effects of time change on the comprehension time for sentences referring to either of the characters. This was done by using the self-paced reading time procedure with the same passages as were used for the continuation study but including two forms of subsequent reference. Immediately after the time-change sentence there was a target sentence which contained a pronominal reference either to the central character or to the topic dependent one. We would expect to find a differential effect on the reading time for the topic-dependent character fol-

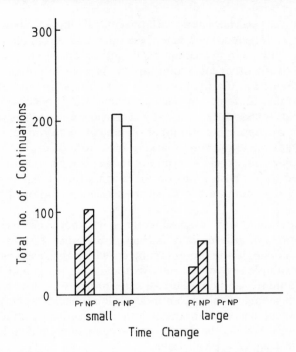

Figure 8.3 Number of mentions using either pronouns (Pr) or noun phrase (NP) for topic-dependent character (hatched) or central character (plain) following small or large time shifts

lowing the two types of time change but not for the central one. A further reference was also included in the two questions which followed each passage. The first question contained a definite nominal reference to the central character and the second contained a similar reference to the scenario-dependent character. In this way the question answering times may also be used to discover topic shift effects.

Using 20 materials (based on those used in the continuation study) in a self-paced reading time study with 40 subjects, it was possible to get estimates of comprehension difficulty for both the sentences and the questions. The mean question-answering and reading times are shown in Figure 8.4. Looking first at the question-answering times, it can be seen that there is an interaction between the time change and question referring to the central versus topic-dependent character. Answering questions about the topic-dependent character after time changes in violation of the boundaries on the initial topic scenario takes longer than after time changes which do not violate this boundary. This is not the case for questions referring to the central character.

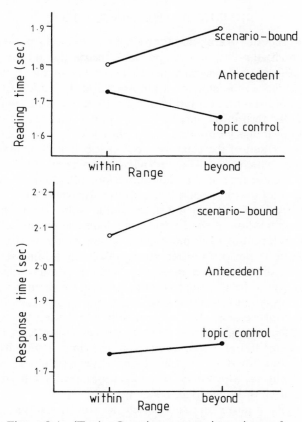

Figure 8.4 (Top) Question answering times for questions referring to the topic-dependent character or central character following time changes within or beyond the topic boundary. (Bottom) Matching reading times for the sentences containing references to these two characters

Turning now to the sentence reading times, a similar interaction appears. However, in this case it is not statistically reliable.[3]

If one ignores the problem of the pronoun sentences, these two experiments serve to demonstrate that readers are sensitive to indicators of imminent shifts in discourse topic, and this seems to have quite striking effects on their ability to resolve reference to entities bound to the discourse topic. The continuation study suggests that indirect shifts in topic serve to reduce the domain of reference by removing entities dependent on the previous topic; the question-answering results suggest that these entities are made less accessible for subsequent processing.

SUMMARY AND DISCUSSION

In the previous sections of this chapter we have presented a number of strands of evidence which all point to the importance of the global topic of discourse in helping to determine the significance of a sentence in a text. In common to all the arguments was the simple assumption that derivation of significance arises in the main from the resolution of referring expressions in the sentence. In some cases this resolution may be based upon a relatively straightforward representation of things mentioned in the prior text, but in others it seems to come about as a result of the establishment of substantial mental representations or *scenarios* which go well beyond what is explicitly stated. Nevertheless, in either case the content of the representation reflects the *currently* active global topic and all that has been brought into focus with it.

One of the key proposals which we have made is that reference resolution, and hence determination of significance, may come about directly so long as the solution to referential assignment is available within the currently focused representation or scenario. In other words, resolving definite reference even when there is no directly stated antecedent need not entail drawing complex bridging inferences as long as the reference is consistent with the current topic of discourse. This type of resolution was described as an example of what we termed 'primary processing'. But what exactly is intended by this term?

We would like to propose that primary processing reflects the decisions which a reader or listener is able to make at the time of initially parsing the sentence; decisions based on analysis of single syntactic units in the sentence such as a noun phrase, which may be made automatically without recourse to an extensive search of knowledge.

In order to give a more precise characterization of referential analysis at both the primary and secondary levels, it may be fruitful to consider the semantics of referring expressions within a procedural framework (see for instance Johnson-Laird, 1977). With this in view we will attempt to describe them as directives to the language processing system to search limited partitions of memory, in order to recover potential antecedents. In this way a more concrete description of what we have termed primary referential processing will emerge and a place will be found for the linguistic notion of topic within a psychological processing framework.

Reference resolution as memory search

From the point of view of modelling sequential semantic analysis, referring expressions may usefully be described as directives to the processing system to search memory for appropriate antecedents. In fact, Sanford and Garrod (1981) have outlined a framework for describing referential analysis in these terms. According to this framework, any such expression can be characterized as a processing directive to carry out a memory search with the following parameters:

(a) the memory domain to be searched;
(b) a given partial description of the information to be found;
(c) the type of information to be returned.

In fact it can be argued that any description of memory retrieval should incorporate at least three parameters, and a further discussion of this is given in Sanford and Garrod (1981). For the present let us concentrate on the first parameter, concerning the search domain, and its relation to the second which derives from the semantic content of the referring expression itself.

If any search arising from a definite nominal reference is to be successful (at least in the absence of time-consuming bridging inferences), then it must identify some unique element (or set of elements) in memory. In order to do this the search domain must be limited in some way. This is perhaps most evident in the case of resolution of pronominal reference. Let us assume that the parser has just encountered the pronoun 'she'. How then might this reference be resolved? In terms of the parameter (b) such an expression incorporates a very limited partial description of the sort 'singular, not male, (probably human) entity'. It would therefore not be very useful to search all memory for such an element, since a host of female singular entities would come to the fore. What is necessary is that the search domain be severely restricted to include only those entities which may be eligible for pronominal reference at that time. Such a set has been described by Chafe (1972) as the set of things which are currently 'foregrounded', or more recently by Grosz (1979) as the set of elements currently in 'explicit focus'. In terms of our own previous discussion this set may be identified as the set of *previously mentioned* entities which constitute the current global topic of discourse.[4]

Thus to describe resolution of pronominal reference according to a memory access framework, it will be necessary to postulate a partition of memory which contains representations of the limited set of explicitly mentioned entities still in 'focus'. This may seem to be a somewhat arbitrary assumption, but it does in fact have its analogue in psychological accounts of a wide range of cognitive tasks, where it is referred to as 'working memory' (Baddeley and Hitch, 1974; Baddeley, 1976). Working memory is conceived of as a mental workspace of limited capacity, this capacity being shared between the data being processed and the information-processing operations themselves. What we have suggested is that one of the rôles of such a workspace during language comprehension is to store representations of the limited set of explicitly mentioned items from the prior text which are still within the scope of the current topic. Furthermore, it is to this partition of memory that pronominal searches in the first instance, will be directed (see Sanford and Garrod, 1981).

Considerations of pronominal reference therefore point to the existence of a limited dynamic partition of memory which constitutes one search domain for reference resolution. Sanford and Garrod have also argued for another dynamic partition of working memory, which seems necessary to account for resolution of reference arising from definite noun phrases. The distinction between pronominal and nominal references in this respect can be illustrated with the following examples:

(16)   Mary was dressing the baby.

(16′)   *The clothes* ⎱ were made of pink wool.
          They   ⎰

While it is possible to make a direct interpretation of the direct reference to 'clothes' in (16′), substituting a pronoun produces a Daliesque interpretation at best. This simple example illustrates the fact that prominal and nominal reference will need to be handled quite differently in terms of memory search since it is only in the latter case that situational antecedents are acceptable. To accommodate this fact, Sanford and Garrod (1981) have argued for a second dynamic partition of memory which allows for privileged access to the scenario currently in focus. In this way, the primary search domain for nominal reference will correspond to both the explicit partition postulated for pronouns plus the extension made available through the currently focused scenario. Together these two dynamic partitions of memory constitute the current processing focus, and offer a psychological realization of the concept of discourse topic, at least in the sense in which it has been discussed in this chapter.

It is beyond the scope of this chapter to go into the details of the memory access framework for referential resolution in general (see Sanford and Garrod, 1981, for more details). The main point we would like to emphasize is how such a system could make it possible to resolve reference automatically and on the sole basis of information at the level of the unit being analysed, in the case where search through the domain associated with the linguistic unit (i.e. pronoun, noun phrase) successfully selects a unique antecedent. As suggested, this may in some cases be part of the implicit knowledge structure in the second partition of working memory, in others be explicitly represented in the smaller limited capacity partition. This automatic and limited form of resolution is what we would describe as primary referential processing.

Not all references in a sentence, however, may be resolved on the basis of primary-level automatic memory searches, and in these circumstances we would propose that a different secondary type of process is called for.

Failures to resolve reference at the primary level, and secondary processing

Perhaps the most obvious case where primary processing will fail according to the memory access framework is when there is *no* matching antecedent available in the dynamic focused partitions of memory. Just such an example was considered earlier in this chapter. When the reader encounters the reference to 'the snow' in sentence (17′), there presumably is no antecedent available in memory on the basis of interpreting the prior sentence (17):

   (17)   Harry fell several times.
   (17′)   The snow was cold and wet.

The reference cannot therefore be resolved at the primary level, so a different form of analysis is called for and it is this we referred to as secondary analysis. We would suggest along with Clark (1975), that in those instances where there is *no* recoverable antecedent from the dynamic partition of memory, relatively complex bridging inferences may be called for, and that these inferences must be based upon analysis either of a higher level of sentential unit than the phrase (i.e whole clause or even sentence), and/or call upon knowledge *not* available in the currently focused partition of memory. The former type of secondary analysis emerges in the interpretation of restrictive relative clauses, which also serve to exemplify in an interesting way how when primary referential resolution is possible, more extensive secondary analysis does seem to occur.

   Given a relative clause of the form 'The X, who. . . .,' exemplified in 'The man, who is the captain of the ship', this may be interpreted in two quite distinct ways, either in a nonrestrictive sense where the contents of the relative clause are taken as providing additional new information about the man in question, or in a restrictive sense, when the identity of the man is not known immediately, but is identified through the given information in the relative clause. In other words, were we to encounter this clause in a context where the phrase 'The man' is sufficient alone to identify an intecedent, the subsequent information would be treated as new and attributed to this man, but when we cannot identify a unique antecedent solely on the basis of the partitial description 'man', the clause is treated as identifying, given information. In this way, with the nonrestrictive usage, resolution of reference must occur at the *primary* level and be based simply on information within the noun phrase, whereas with the restrictive usage primary processing will fail and a larger unit of analysis (constituting the whole clause) will be needed for the secondary resolution of reference. An interesting outcome of such an analysis of relative clauses is that the *restrictive* usage is applicable only in cases where the antecedent noun phrase does not *itself* uniquely select reference (as with proper names for instance). 'Harry, who is the captain of the ship. . .' may not normally be interpreted in a restrictive sense. In other words the restrictive relative clause seems to be specific device in the language to accommodate secondary referential processing, and exemplifies the case where analysis of units larger than the noun phrase seem to be necessary.

   Thus secondary referential analysis may come about both through calls made upon knowledge not available in the focused memory partition associated with the current topic, as in the case where Clark's (1975) bridging inferences are called for, and through taking into account increasingly larger units of the sentence being analysed. In fact, in most cases where primary resolution fails one might expect both measures to be called upon. Nevertheless, whichever special measures are taken to resolve such references, secondary analysis must be seen as more complex and hence likely to impose a greater load on the processing system, with subsequent effects on overall comprehension time. As soon as the size of the unit of analysis goes up or the domain of memory search is de-restricted, some executive processing control must be necessary and it is no longer possible to carry out the sort of simple automatic search associated with what we have described as primary analysis. For these reasons, it seems sensible in psychological terms to identify a distinction between primary 'topic' based, analysis and secondary, 'general knowledge' based analysis of reference.

FINAL CONCLUSIONS

In the preceding section we have attempted to sketch out the elements of a processing system which goes some way towards accommodating two components of language which are arguably central for determining the significance of a sentence in its context of usage; namely discourse topic and reference. In order to appreciate the significance of a sentence, it is necessary to determine what the speaker or writer is talking about, and this constitutes the problem of reference. In processing terms it is suggested that reference resolution comes about through one of two types of on-line processing. The first, or primary mode of processing is seen as an automatic analysis which may occur concurrently with syntactic parsing, while the secondary mode is seen as requiring more extensive prior analysis of the sentence and is only called for when primary resolution fails for some reason. What makes the primary type of analysis possible within the scheme is that it is bounded within the constraints of the current topic of discourse, thus any knowledge access is limited to that which is already available in focus. In this way determination of significance may occur without having to search the broader reaches of one's knowledge.

In more general terms the interpretation of any reference within a sentence of text can be seen to result from the intersection of information from three possible sources. First, from the nature of the referring expression itself; secondly, from the nature of the representation of the current discourse topic; and thirdly, from any additional new information which may have to be incorporated into the extant representation of this topic in order to accommodate the reference. It is only when this third source of information is called for that time consuming secondary analyis need take place.

Under what circumstances therefore might such an apparently maladapted form of processing be of communicative value? Looked at in terms of the reader's assessment of discourse topic, secondary semantic analysis can be seen as a device for registering shifts in topic. For, whenever it is impossible to resolve a reference during primary processing, this must mean that the reference introduces in some way a new topic. The new information which is called for to form the bridge will then help to build up the new definition of topic.

NOTES

1. It should be pointed out that the literature on topic presents the reader with a terminological minefield, and we have simply elected to tread carefully rather than try and clear the field.
2. Garrod and Sanford (1980) have shown that very strict criteria of entailment are necessary for determining verb-based scenarios.
3. Anderson, Garrod, and Sandford (in press) have shown that such effects are obtainable when one controls the predictability of the scenario-dependent character.
4. We will ignore more problematic cases where a pronoun may be used to refer to a previously stated or implied event, although it is still possible in principle to treat them in much the same way.

ACKNOWLEDGEMENTS

This research was supported by a grant from the British Social Science Research Council.

REFERENCES

Baddeley, A. *The Psychology of Memory*. New York: Harper Row, 1976.
Baddeley, A., and Hitch, G. Working memory. In G. H. Bower (Ed.), *The Psychology of Learning and Motivation*, 1974, **8**, 47–90.
Bower, G. H., Black, J. B., and Turner, T. J. Scripts in memory for text. *Cognitive Psychology*, 1979, **11**, 177–220.
Chafe, W. Discourse structure and human knowledge. In J. B. Carroll and R. O. Freedle (Eds), *Language Comprehension and the Acquisition of Knowledge*. Washington D.C.: Winston, 1972.
Charniak, E. Towards a model of children's story comprehension. Tech. Report 266, Artificial Intelligence Laboratory, Massachusetts Institute of Technology. Cambridge, Mass., 1972.
Clark, H. H. Bridging. In R. Schank and B. Nash-Webber (Eds). *Theoretical Issues in Natural Language Processing*. Proceeding of the Conference at the Massachusetts Institute of Technology, June 1975.
Cutler, A. Beyond parsing and lexical look-up. An enriched description of auditory sentence comprehension. In R. J. Wales and E. Walker (Eds), *New Approaches to Language Mechanism*. Amsterdam: North-Holland, 1976.
Foss, D. J., and Hakes, D. T. *Psycholinguistics: An Introduction to the Psychology of Language*. Englewood Cliffs, N. J.: Prentice-Hall, 1978.
Garrod, S., and Sanford, A. J. Interpreting anaphoric relations: The integration of

semantic information while reading. *Journal of Verbal Learning and Verbal Behavior*, 1977, **16**, 77–90.

Garrod, S., and Sanford, A. J. Anaphora: A problem in text comprehension. In R. N. Campbell and P. T. Smith (Eds), *Recent Advances in the Psychology of Language*. New York: Plenum Press, 1978.

Garrod, S., and Sanford, A. J. Bridging inferences and the extended domain of reference. In J. Long and A. Baddeley (Eds), *Attention and Performance IX*. Hillsdale, N.J.: Lawrence Erlbaum Associates, 1981.

Grimes, J. E. *The Thread of Discourse*. The Hague: Mouton, 1975.

Grosz, B. The representation and use of focus is dialogue understanding. Technical Note 15, SRI International Artificial Intelligence Centre, 1977.

Halliday, M. A. K. Notes on transitivity and theme in English. Part 1. *Journal of Linguistics*, 1967, **3**, 199–214.

Haviland, S. E., and Clark, H. H. What's new? Acquiring new information as a process in comprehension. *Journal of Verbal Learning and Verbal Behavior*, 1974, **13**, 512–521.

Hirst, G. *Anaphora in Natural Language Understanding: A Survey*. Technical Report 79-2. Department of Computer Science, C.F. 1979.

Hockett, H. C. *A Course in Modern Linguistics*. New York: MacMillan, 1958.

Johnson-Laird, P. N. Psycholinguistics without linguistics. In N. S. Sutherland (Ed.), *Tutorial Essay in Psychology*, Vol. 1. Hillsdale, N.J.: Lawrence Erlbaum Associates, 1977.

Lyons, J. *Introduction to Theoretical Linguistics*. Cambridge: Cambridge University Press, 1968.

Marslen-Wilson, W. D. Sentence perception as an interactive parallel process. *Science*, 1975, **189**, 226–227.

Minsky, M. A framework for representing knowledge. In P. H. Winston (Ed.), *The Psychology of Computer Vision*. New York: Mc-Graw Hill, 1975.

Rumelhart, D. E. *Introduction to Human Information Processing*. New York: John Wiley, 1977.

Sanford, A. J., and Garrod, S. Memory and attention in text comprehension: The problem of reference. In R. Nickerson (Ed.), *Attention and Performance VII*. Hillsdale, N.J.: Lawrence Erlbaum Associates, 1981.

Sanford, A. J., and Garrod, S. *Understanding Written Language: Exploration of Comprehension beyond the Sentence*. Chichester: Wiley, 1981.

Sanford, A. J., Garrod, S., and Henderson, R. Topic shift as a variable in text cohesion: Experimental evidence from studies in reading time. Paper presented at the Meeting of the Experimental Psychology Society, Cambridge, July 1980.

Schank, R. C., and Abelson, R. *Scripts, Plans, Goals and Understanding: An Enquiry into Human Knowledge Structures*. Hillsdale, N.J.: Lawrence Erlbaum Associates, 1977.

Searle, J. R. A taxonomy of illocutionary acts. In K. Grunderson (Ed.), *Minnesota Studies in the Philosophy of Language*, Minneapolis, Minn.: University of Minnesota Press, 1975.

Winer, B. J. *Statistical Principles in Experimental Design*. New York: Wiley, 1971.

Winograd, T. *Understanding Natural Language*. New York: Academic Press, 1972.

The Process of Language Understanding
Edited by G. B. Flores d'Arcais. and R. J. Jarvella
© John Wiley & Sons Ltd.

9

Making Sense of Nonce Sense

HERBERT H. CLARK

Stanford University, U.S.A.

A 'parser' is a device, either human or mechanical, that is designed to analyse a person's utterances as a part of deciding what that person meant. Most mechanical parsers do this by breaking down, or 'parsing', each utterance into parts, selecting senses for each part, and combining these senses into a meaning for the whole utterance. How human parsers do this is a question in which researchers have invested much time and energy, and for good reason. It is hard to imagine a model of language understanding without a parser of one sort or another.

One of the main stumbling blocks for parsers is ambiguity. When a parser encounters the word *post*, it must decide whether it means 'pole', 'mail', or something else. When it meets the phrase *good king*, it must decide whether it means 'king who rules well', 'king who is a good person', or something else. When it meets the clause *that he knew* in *He whispered to the woman that he knew*, it must decide whether it modifies *the woman* or is a complement of *whisper*. Parsers so far have been outfitted with syntactic, semantic, and pragmatic strategies for resolving ambiguity. For each expression, they anticipate the right meaning, or a small set of meanings, and thereby avoid the expensive computation of unintended meanings. Or they select the right meanings after the fact, pragmatically.

At the heart of what I will call traditional parsers is the *sense-selection assumption*. The idea is this. Each parser is in possession of a lexicon, or dictionary, that lists the potential senses for each word (like *post*), each morpheme (like *pre-*), and each idiom (like *kick the bucket*). For *post*, let us say, the lexicon lists six distinct senses. When a parser encounters *post* in an utterance, it selects from among these six senses the one that the speaker must have intended on this occasion. When it encounters *good king*, it parses the phrase into *good* and *king*, combines the possible senses of the two separate words by appropriate rules of combination, and arrives at, say, twelve possible senses for the phrase. From among these twelve it selects the sense the speaker must have intended. The skill to parsing is in making these selections deftly, with the minimum fuss and computation. Still, the assumption that is virtually always made in traditional parsers is this: each constituent of an utterance has a finite number of possible senses, and people *select* the intended sense from among them.

The sense-selection assumption seems so natural, so obviously true, that it isn't even open to dispute. Yet in the last few years, more and more evidence has been brought to the fore suggesting that it is in fact false. The problem is this. Not only can expressions be ambiguous, but they can also be *semantically indeterminate*. Many expressions, contrary to the assumption, do not possess a finite number of senses that can be listed in the parser's lexicon. Nor can they be assigned their possible senses by any rule. Each expression of this sort, instead, has only a *nonce sense*, a sense 'for the nonce', for the occasion on which it is used. It would be hard enough for traditional parsers if there were *any* such expressions, but, as I will argue, they are ubiquitous. No parser can avoid them, yet when traditional parsers meet them, they break down.

In this chapter I have two main aims. The first is to describe two fundamental problems that nonce sense poses for traditional parsers. In doing this, I will demonstrate how natural and ubiquitous nonce sense is in daily usage. The second aim is to argue for a new view of parsing altogether. In this view, the goal is to infer the speaker's intentions in using each word and constituent that he used. The idea is to meet nonce sense head-on, to treat nonce sense as an intrinsic part of language, which it is.

TWO PARSING PROBLEMS

For examples that will stymie any traditional parser, we need look no further than the daily newspaper, which is replete with them. The passage I have selected is from a column in the *San Francisco Examiner* by satirist Erma Bombeck about her daughter's difficulties in finding a roommate. Bombeck is quoting her daughter:

> We thought we were onto a steam iron yesterday, but we were too late. Steam irons never have any trouble finding roommates. She could pick her own pad and not even have to share a bathroom. Stereos are a dime a dozen. Everyone's got their own systems. We've just had a streak of bad luck. First, our Mr. Coffee flunked out of school and went back home. When we replaced her, our electric typewriter got married and split, and we got stuck with a girl who said she was getting a leather coat, but she just said that to get the room.

As newspaper prose, this paragraph is unremarkable. Yet of the eight sentences, six will fail on the traditional parser. Why? Not because the six sentences sound odd, or use a peculiar vocabulary, or are in a strange dialect. It is only because they each contain a noun phrase used in a nonce sense—*a steam iron, steam irons, stereos, our Mr. Coffee*, and *our electric typewriter*. For *steam iron*, the parser will search its lexicon for the sense Bombeck intended for it—'a person who has a steam iron'. Since this sense won't be in the lexicon, it will search in vain. It will fail to deal with *steam iron*, just as it will fail on the other five instances of nonce sense. Clearly, Bombeck isn't at fault. The parsers are.

The difficulties that parsers run into in this passage are of two kinds—non-parsing and mis-parsing. Consider *Our electric typewriter got married*. A traditional parser would meet *electric typewriter* and then *got married* and would search among the listed or computed senses for the two expressions to find ones that fit together sensibly. Because it wouldn't find any—electric typewriters, not being humans, cannot marry—it would fail to come to any interpretation. It would mark the utterance as uninterpretable nonsense rather than as interpretable nonce sense. This is what I will call the *non-parsing problem*.

The problem posed by *Stereos are a dime a dozen* is superficially quite different. As a sentence, this one is quite unremarkable and, unlike *Our electric typewriter got married*, is not semantically anomalous on the face of it. The traditional parser would work its way through the sentence and arrive at roughly the interpretation, 'Phonographs are very common.' The trouble is, this isn't what Bombeck meant. She meant, 'People who possess phonographs are very common.' Since the traditional parser would never list in its lexicon the nonce sence 'person who possesses a phonograph' for *stereo*, it could never come up with Bombeck's intended sense. It would discover an interpretation it would be willing to accept, but it is the wrong interpretation. This is what I will call the *mis-parsing problem*.

The difficulties underlying these two examples, however, are identical: *Electric typewriter* and *stereo* are both being used with nonce senses. The lexicons of traditional parsers list only the conventional senses of words, morphemes, and idioms, and rightly so. They couldn't possibly list—or store in memory—all the possible nonce senses a word, morpheme, or idiom might be used with. As I will argue, there is no end to the nonce senses for words like *electric typewriter* or *stereo*; furthermore, these nonce senses cannot be enumerated by rule. As a consequence, these parsers will invariably fail to parse utterances like *Our typewriter got married* and will invariably mis-parse ones like *Stereos are a dime a dozen*.

THE UBIQUITY OF NONCE SENSE

For nonce sense like Bombeck's to pose a significant threat to traditional parsers, it must be more than a marginal part of language. I will argue both that nonce sense is ubiquitous and, more importantly, that it is a regular part of the language. When we encounter it, we perceive it to be natural and proper. We don't hear it as only partially acceptable or grammatical. Any parser that is to handle ordinary language must therefore be able to interpret nonce sense in the natural course of processing.

Contextual expressions

It is well known that while some expressions have a fixed reference, others have a shifting reference. Those with a fixed reference are proper names, like *George Washington, the Second World War*, and *France*, which rigidly designate certain individuals. Those with a shifting reference are indexical expressions, like *I, now*, and *the bachelor over there*, whose referents depend on the time, place, and circumstances in which they are uttered. It has been virtually unrecognized, however, that while some expressions have fixed senses, others have shifting senses. Those with fixed senses might be called 'purely intensional expressions', like *bachelor*, *blue*, and *colorful ball*, each of which has a small number of conventional senses known to almost everyone in a speech community. Those expressions with shifting senses—what I am concerned with here—are called *contextual expressions*. Their senses depend entirely on the time, place, and circumstances in which they are uttered (Clark and Clark, 1979). Thus, we have the following two analogies:

sense : reference : : purely intentional expression : proper name

: : contextual expression : indexical expression

And:

fixed : shifting : : proper name : indexical expression

: : purely intentional expression : contextual expression

These two analogies lead to the four-way classification given in Table 9.1.

For the main properties of contextual expressions, which have shifting *senses*, let us first look at indexical expressions, which have shifting *references*. One such indexical expression is *he*, which has two important characteristics. First, it has an indefinitely large number of potential referents, and these

Table 9.1   Classification of expressions

Aspect of meaning	Alterability of aspect of meaning	
	Fixed	Shifting
Sense	Purely intensional expression (e.g., *bachelor*)	Contextual expression (e.g., *to teapot*)
Reference	Proper name (e.g., *George Washington*)	Indexical expression (e.g., *he*)

referents are not denumerable. *He* can be used to refer to any of an indefinitely large number of males, past, present, and future, real and imaginary.
These males cannot be listed, even in theory, since someone can always
imagine another male and refer to it with *he*. Let me call this property *non-
denumerability*. Second, what *he* is actually used to refer to on a particular
occasion depends on who uttered it, where, what he was pointing at, who had
just been mentioned in the conversation, what his addressee knew and didn't
know, and many other points of coordination between the speaker and
addressee (see, e.g., Clark and Marshall, 1981). Let me call this dependence
on moment-to-moment coordination *contextuality*. These two properties—non-denumerability and contextuality—are characteristic of indexical
expressions but not of proper names.

   Non-denumerability and contexuality should also be characteristic of contextual expressions but not of purely intensional expressions. Imagine that Ed
and I have a mutal friend named Max, who has the odd occasional urge to
sneak up behind people and stroke the back of their legs with a teapot. One
day Ed tells me, *Well, this time Max has gone too far. He tried to teapot a
policeman.* Ed has used the noun *teapot* as a verb with a nonce sense, namely
'rub the back of the leg of with a teapot'. As for non-denumerability, note that
the verb *teapot* could have been preceded by an indefinitely large number of
introductory scenarios and could have possessed an indefinitely large number
of different meanings. Neither the distinct scenarios nor the distinct senses it
could possess are denumerable. As for contextuality, note that what *teapot*
means depends crucially on the time, place, and circumstances in which Ed
used it. He couldn't have meant just anything by it, and he could only have
intended it to mean 'rub the back of the leg of with a teapot' for addressees
who had just the right background knowledge. The verb *teapot*, then, is a
contextual expression, and so are innovative denominal verbs in general
(Clark and Clark, 1979).

Some types of contextual expressions

Most contextual expressions are word innovations that are formed from well
established words or morphemes. The verb *teapot* is a novel construction built
on the noun *teapot* plus a change in form class from noun to verb. This sort of
word formation is often called zero-derivation, as if the noun *teapot* is provided with a zero suffix to form the verb *teapot-Φ*. Not every innovation, however, is a contextual expression. Nouns formed from adjectives by adding
-*ness*, as in *fakeness* and *chartreuseness*, aren't contextual expressions, as I will
spell out later, whereas verbs formed from nouns by adding the zero suffix, as
in *to teapot* and *to apple*, are. It is an important empirical question which
constructions produce contextual expressions and which do not.

   To give an idea of the range of contextual expressions, I will list some construction types that I believe contain contextual expressions. Some of these types contain well-documented cases of contextual expressions. Others contain cases I only conjecture to be contextual expressions. My conjectures are based on examples that work like the verb *teapot* in exhibiting the properties of non-denumerability and contextuality. Since it would be impossible to give the whole range of such construction types, I will restrict myself to expressions formed from concrete nouns. I will list the categories of contextual expressions by the form class of the derived word—by whether it is a noun, adjective, or verb. There are undoubtedly many types of contextual expressions other than those listed here.[1]

1. *Indirect nouns*. The nouns in such expressions as *the horse, a car*, and *some water* appear to denote concrete things in an obvious way. Appearances, however, are deceiving. One way to ask for a glass of water in many contexts is to say *One water, please. Water*, of course, is a mass noun that denotes the substance water. To get it to denote a glass of water, one must take *one water* in the nonce sense 'one glass of water'. In other contexts, the same phrase could be used to denote one tub of water, one type of water, one drop of water, one teaspoon of water, one person who ordered water, and so on indefinitely. Other examples of indirect nouns include: *Last night they played a Beethoven; I saw a Henry Moore today; That ten minutes was too long for a commercial; Stereos are a dime a dozen*; and *Our electric typewriter got married*. These expressions have been studied under various names—beheaded noun phrases' (Borkin, 1970), 'shorthand expressions' (Clark, 1978), and 'deferred reference' (Nunberg, 1979). It is important to notice that on the surface they are often impossible to distinguish from purely intensional expressions. *The water* could be used in the conventional sense 'the substance called water' or in some nonce sense 'the glass, or pail, or drop, or the teaspoon, or . . ., of water'. One can only tell from context.

2. *Compound nouns*. In English, idiomatic compound nouns like *dog sled*, *tea garden*, and *apple pie* are common. Because they are idiomatic, their conventional senses are listed in the dictionary and, presumably, in most people's mental lexicons. Compound nouns with nonce senses, however, like *finger cup, apple-juice chair*, and *Ferrari woman*, are also common, and their meanings will not be found ready-made in the dictionary or in mental lexicons. Although Lees (1960), Levi (1978), and Li (1971) have all assumed that such compound nouns fall into a small number of paradigms, Downing (1977), Gleitman and Gleitman (1970), Jespersen (1942), Kay and Zimmer (1976), and Zimmer (1971, 1972) have argued that they do not. Both Downing, and Kay and Zimmer, have shown, in effect, that innovative compound nouns are contextual expressions since their possible meanings aren't denumerable and what they mean on any occasion depends on the close coordination of the speaker and addressee.

3. *Possessives*. We tend to think of the so-called possessive construction as

denoting possession and a small range of other things. *John's dog* means 'the dog John possesses'. Yet in the right contexts, *John's dog* could also mean 'the dog John is standing in front of', 'the dog John saw yesterday', 'the dog John always wanted', and any number of other things. The possibilities are in theory unlimited in number and cannot be enumerated, and what it is taken to mean on any occasion relies heavily on the coordination of the speaker and addressees. Possessives, in short, are contextual expressions.

4. *Denominal nouns.* Nouns like *Nixonite, bicycler*, and *saxophonist* are formed from concrete nouns like *Nixon, bicycle*, and *saxophone* by derivation. There is a plethora of idiomatic cases of this sort in English, but what innovative examples mean can vary enormously from one occasion to the next, depending on certain cooperative measures between the speaker and addressees. Each has an unlimited number of possible meanings, or so it appears. Denominal nouns, then, although they have stricter requirements than, say, possessives or compound nouns, are also contextual expressions.

5. *Denominal verbs.* It is easy to turn nouns into verbs, as in *to graphite the locks, to farewell the guests*, and *to Houdini one's way out of a locked closet*. Some denominal verbs are already well established in the language, but many are being invented all the time. Eve V. Clark and I (Clark and Clark, 1979) have argued in detail that innovative denominal verbs are contextual expressions. The denominal verb *teapot* has an unlimited set of potential senses, and what it means on each occasion depends on the coordination of speaker and addressees.

6. *Eponymous verbs.* In *The photographer asked me to do a Napoleon for the camera*, the expression *do a Napoleon* is being used innovatively. I will call this expression an eponymous verb—because it is built on the name of its eponym Napoleon—even though it consists of a pro-verb *do* and an indirect noun as direct object. Eponymous verbs can only be understood if the speaker and addressees coordinate their knowledge of the eponym, here Napoleon, so that the addressees can identify the act of the eponym that the speaker is alluding to. Since there are, in principle, an unlimited number of acts one could know and allude to about an eponym, there are also an unlimited number of senses that could be assigned to the verb. Eponymous verbs are never idiomatic. Each one we meet we are forced to treat as a contextual expression.

7. *Pro-act verbs.* In *Alice did the lawn, do* is what I will call a pro-act verb. It denotes an act like mowing, raking, fertilizing, or an unlistably large number of other things that one can do to lawns. Its senses are not denumerable, and what it is taken to mean depends critically on the time, place, and circumstances in which it is uttered. Pro-act verbs appear to be genuine contextual expressions.

8. *Denominal adjectives.* Adjectives derived from nouns, like *gamey, impish*, and *athletic*, from *game, imp*, and *athlete*, are common in English.

Although most such adjectives are idiomatic and have conventional senses, many of them can be innovative, with meanings dependent on the time, place, and circumstances of the utterance. *Churchillian*, for example, might mean 'with a face like Churchill', 'smoking a cigar like Churchill', 'with a speaking style like Churchill', or any number of other things. In principle, the list is unlimited; in practice, it is limited by what the speaker can assume the addressees know about Churchill and will be able to see that he is alluding to.

9. *Non-predicating adjectives.* Closely related to the first noun in noun compounds are the so-called non-predicating adjectives, like *atomic, manual*, and *marine* (Levi, 1978). These adjectives, formed from Latin and Greek roots, serve virtually the same purpose as the equivalent English nouns would serve in the same position. Just as there are *atomic bombs, manual labour*, and *marine life*, there are *atom bombs, hand labour*, and *sea life*. These adjectives are non-predicating in that one cannot say, with the same meaning as in *marine life*, that *life is marine*. For all these reasons, these adjectives share many properties with the first nouns of compound nouns and also with possessives (Levi, 1978). Innovative uses of non-predicating adjectives appear to possess both of the critical properties of contextual expressions—non-denumerability and contextuality. *Atomic*, for example, may indicate any of an indefinitely large set of unlistable relations between atoms and the things denoted by the noun that *atomic* modifies.

10. *Eponymous adjectives.* In examples like *She is very San Francisco* and *That is a very Picasso painting*, the adjectives are formed from the names of people or places—their eponyms—and allude to one of an indefinite number of unlistable properties of those eponyms, of San Francisco and Picasso. What the adjectives actually allude to depends on the time, place, and circumstances in which they are uttered. They too are contextual expressions.

Table 9.2   Ten types of contextual expressions

Category of derived word	Type of expression	Examples
Noun	Indirect nouns	*one water, a Henry Moore*
	Compound nouns	*finger cup, apple-juice chair*
	Possessives	*John's dog, my tree*
	Denominal nouns	*a waller, a cupper*
Verb	Denominal verbs	*to farewell, to Houdini*
	Eponymous verbs	*to do a Napoleon, to do a Nixon*
	Pro-act verbs	*to do the lawn, to do the porch*
Adjective	Denominal adjectives	*Churchillian, Shavian*
	Non-predicting adjectives	*atomic, manual*
	Eponymous adjectives	*very San Francisco, very Picasso*

The types of contextual expressions I have just laid out are summarized in Table 9.2.

Ubiquity and naturalness

With so many different types available, contextual expressions ought to be ubiquitous, and they are. They occur everywhere and generally without our being aware that their senses are nonce senses. Absolute numbers are difficult to estimate. One reason is that the line between contextual expressions and purely intensional expressions is difficult to draw (Clark and Clark, 1979). A sense may be conventional within one community, as among newspaper reporters or computer users, but it may be a nonce sense for the people being addressed. All I can do is give a feel for the numbers involved. As examples I will offer both deliberate uses by literary people trying for special effects and unpremeditated use by ordinary people trying to talk efficiently. Both types are common.

Many literary uses are designed for humour. When Bombeck has her daughter say, *We're looking for a size 10 with a steam iron*, meaning 'a person who wears dresses of size 10 and comes with a steam iron', she is making a point of her daughter's materialism. There is similar motivation behind the following examples (the obvious nonce uses in italics):

Subjected to the musical equivalent of 72 hours in a dentist's waiting room, Bradley was apparently in real danger of being the first tourist ever *Muzakked* to death. (*San Francisco Examiner*)

We've redone the entire living room in *Nelson Rockefeller* [alluding to Rockefeller's business of selling reproductions of art from his private collection]. (*New Yorker* cartoon)

I divide the world into two groups—the '*for me*'s and the '*against me*'s. (Mal cartoon)

The fire department capped the plug and the police department *jugged* the guest. (Herb Caen, *San Francisco Chronicle*)

J. W. Marriott Sr. and J. W. Jr. *Pan Am'd* out of here Sat. for Peking. (Herb Caen)

Tuesday is a good day for *noistalgics* who miss the daily noon siren sound from the Ferry Building. (Herb Caen)

Alexander Zinchuk, the USSR's consul General, inviting the local wretched *inkstains* to a reception May 3 in observance of—get set—'The Day of the Press'. (Herb Caen)

The bank's *buzzier guessips* tried to connect this odd coincidence with the Alvin Rice hoo-ha—Alvin being the former *No. 2* of B of A now being *grand-juried* for possible conflict in real estate loans—but at least two of the *Vanishing Bank of Americans* say coolly 'We resigned'. (Herb Caen)

Newspaper reporters and other writers rely on contextual expressions in everyday expository writing. This is illustrated in the following examples:

Gold plunges to new *lows*. [the price of gold, new low levels] (headline, *San Francisco Chronicle*)

I stopped in Perry's for a *quick crab*. [dish of crab meat that could be consumed quickly] (Herb Caen)

The initiative is aimed at preventing the *New Yorking* of the San Francisco skyline. (TV news)

Twenty-two nations and five international agencies agreed here yesterday to send a delegation to Cuba to urge Fidel Castro to ease the plight of thousands of his countrymen seeking to leave the island, and to regularize their departure. [Representatives from 22 nations and five international agencies] (*Los Angeles Times*)

I had a *teletype* on the situation half a hour ago. [a message sent by the teletype machine] (novel)

The *telephone* managed to get a word in. [The person on the other end of the telephone line] (novel)

Service for 8 includes dinner plates, *salads*, cups, saucers, *soup/cereals* plus oval platter, oval *vegetable*, *sugar* with lid, creamer. (advertisement)

Only a few of these examples stand out as innovations—the telephone and New Yorking examples, perhaps. The rest strike us as mundane and quite unremarkable.

You don't have to be a professional writer to come up with contextual expressions, as illustrated in these attested spontaneous examples:

In this program I could either *and* it or *or* it. [Use the computer language connectives '*and*' and '*or*'] (computational linguist)

(Can you tell a person by his car?) I'm a *Dodge Power Wagon*. That's what I've got. (*San Francisco Chronicle*, 'Question Man')

(What's good cheap entertainment?) Today I'm going *gallerying*. ('Question Man')

He's home today *jetlagging*. [Recovering from the effects of jetlag] (a friend)

Having *porpoised* my way through the arguments, I gave them my conclusion. (A well known psychologist)

I know that it's across from a quarry. That's the only way I can *landmark* it. [Person talking about finding a beach]

Once again, there is nothing particularly remarkable about most of these contextual expressions. We may identify many of them as novel, but we take them as a legitimate part of English.

Contextual expressions have to be legitimate in order to account for how new words come into English, which happens at an often alarming rate. Consider this example. In the *San Francisco Chronicle*, the 'Question Man' one day asked 'What's good cheap entertainment?' One woman replied, *Bouldering is great*. For readers like me, *bouldering* was an expression with no conventional meaning. In context, we took it to mean 'climbing on boulders'. Yet it was clear from the rest of the woman's answer that she took *bouldering* to be a conventional term for that activity—perhaps within the community of rock climbers. We understood her even though that conventional sense hadn't yet spread to the larger community of readers. For her convention to spread to the larger community, the rest of us must be able to interpret her term readily and as a matter of course. We must be willing to accept its Janus-like character for a while—as a conventional term for some of us and as an innovation for others. A good deal of the conventional vocabulary appears to have entered the language by just this route—from contextual expressions solidifying and petrifying into purely intensional expressions (see Clark and Clark, 1979).

TRADITIONAL PARSERS

Which parsers in the literature run into trouble with contextual expressions? Most of them, I will argue, or so it appears. The caveat 'or so it appears' is critical. For parsers in the psychological tradition, there have been few characterizations of the lexicon—of what lexical entries would look like and how they would organized. Yet these parsers proceed as if they were making the sense-selection assumption and don't appear able to handle contextual expressions. In the artificial intelligence tradition, more attention has been paid to the lexicon, but only a few of the parsers have been spelled out in any detail (e.g. Winograd, 1972). Yet these parsers also appear to follow the sense-selection assumption, and so they too will fall victim to the problems of nonce sense. To handle contextual expressions, both types of parsers will need to undergo major revisions. I will illustrate this point by considering several of the psychological parsers that have been proposed.

Heuristic parsers

Psychological approaches to parsing have followed two main traditions. The first, which I will call the *heuristic tradition*, has its roots in Miller and Chomsky (1963) and Fodor and Garrett (1966). But it is most clearly identified with Bever (1970), who set out a series of processing strategies, or heuristics, to account for the difficulties of people trying to understand complex sentences. Later, Kimball (1973, 1975) put these strategies into a systematic framework, and his is still the best description of this tradition. He proposed seven 'principles of surface structure parsing' and showed how they accounted for the phenomena Bever had identified and more. Frazier and Fodor (1978) have since offered a version of Kimball's parser, called the 'sausage machine', but it is like Kimball's parser in the ways that matter to the point I want to make.

For Kimball, parsing meant dividing an utterance into its constituents and labelling these constituents with the correct syntactic categories. His parser proceeded word by word through an utterance, deciding when to begin and end each constituent as it went. The main information it needed was the form class of each word from the lexicon, rules about the composition of surface constituents, and Kimball's seven heuristic principles. Take the utterance *George managed to read the newspaper yesterday*. When the parser reached the word *to*, it would look it up in the lexicon and find it to be either a preposition or an infinitive marker. So it would mark *to* as the beginning of a constituent—either a prepositional phrase or an infinitive complement. When it reached *read*, it would look up *read* in the lexicon, find it to be a verb, and then eliminate the prepositional phrase interpretation. And so on. The parser didn't deal directly with word or constituent meanings, although at critical times it made reference to these meanings in selecting between alternative parsings.

The first place where Kimball's parser would get into trouble is with words that aren't in the lexicon. Take *George managed to porch the newspaper yesterday*. *Porch*, though only a noun in the lexicon, is being used in this utterance as a verb. The parser would automatically classify *porch* as a noun and then not be able to parse the rest of the infinitive complement. The problem might be handled by outfitting the parser with lexical rules that change nouns into verbs, verbs into adjectives, verbs into nouns, and so on. This solution, however, won't work because of the mis-parsing problem. For *porch*, the parser, not being able to parse the noun *porch*, could be made to go to a lexical rule that changes nouns to verbs. Then it could identify *porch* as a verb and parse the other constituents correctly. But consider *George set out to Jesse Owens down the street* in circumstances in which *Jesse Owens* is intended to mean 'sprint', after Jesse Owens the Olympic sprinter. In parsing this sentence, there is nothing to force the parser to go to a lexical rule, since the sentence makes good sense with *Jesse Owens* as a noun. To get the analysis right, the parser would have to consult the speaker's intentions in using *Jesse Owens*, which it might only be able to infer from non-linguistic context. Kimball's parser is not designed to do this.

Kimball's parser will run into other difficulties too. Imagine that Bombeck had written *The neighbour swore at our electric typewriter who got married*. Ordinarily, Kimball (1973, p. 25) argued, the parser would try to attach the relative clause *who got married* to the nearest noun phrase, here *our electric typewriter*. If the parser couldn't do this for semantic reasons, it would attach it instead to some earlier noun phrase, here *the neighbour*, so that the utterances would mean 'the neighbour who got married swore at our electric typewriter'. Kimball's parser would be forced to take the second option. All it would have to go on would be the senses of *electric typewriter* listed in the lexicon. These wouldn't include 'person who has an electric typewriter' or any of the indefinitely large number of other nonce senses it could have. The parser, then, would misidentify the surface structure of this utterance and of all other utterances in which a nonce sense had to be consulted in order to get the right parse.

Augmented transition networks

The second main tradition in psychological approaches to parsing is the *augmented transition networks*, or ATNs. This tradition had its start with Woods (1970) and Kaplan (1972) and has since evolved in papers by Woods (1973), Kaplan (1973a, 1973b, 1975), Wanner and Maratsos (1978), and Kaplan and Bresnan (1982). ATNs consist of a set of interconnected operations. An ATN parses each utterance word by word, applying its operations in a well defined order and identifying the intended constituents and their functions as it goes along.

An ATN can be viewed, whimsically but pretty accurately, as a medieval game played by a king on the country roads around his castle. The object of the game is for the king to get from his castle to his rival's castle along these roads (called 'arcs') using only the words in the sentence to guide him. He must leave his castle by the road signposted with the first word in his sentence. That will take him to a nearby village (called a 'state') where he will take the road signposted with the second word, and so on, until he reaches his rival's castle. Often, he can't leave a village directly, since there isn't a signpost with the next word on it. Instead, he must take detours signposted with the category of the word he is looking for (say, 'noun') or with the category of a constituent that contains the category of the word he is looking for (say, 'noun phrase'). The king discovers the category of each word in his pocket lexicon. He can pass along the route signposted 'noun' only if the word he is looking for is listed in his lexicon as a noun.

ATNs run into the same two problems that heuristic parsers run into. The king will be stopped by *porch* in *George managed to porch the newspaper*. He will look for a road signposted 'porch' or 'noun' or 'noun phrase' or 'sentence' and find none. He will be condemned to remain in that wretched village forever. If he adds to his lexicon a set of lexical rules that change nouns into verbs, verbs into nouns, and so on, he will have a different problem with *George set out to Jesse Owens down the street* when *Jesse Owens* is intended to mean 'sprint'. Since *Jesse Owens* is in the lexicon as a noun, and since there is a noun-detour available, he will take it and not even try the verb-detour. The noun-detour will lead him to the wrong destination, which he will never realize. If, instead, he tries the lexical rule first and takes the verb-detour first whenever he encounters a noun, he will take many wrong roads that he will have to retrace before trying another route. And he will now get the *Jesse Owens* sentence wrong when *Owens* is intended as a noun. So because of contextual expressions, the king will get stranded, or finish at the wrong castle, or wander around needlessly before arriving at the right castle.

ATNs also base certain parsing decisions on meaning. The king is often forced to select routes based on what the current word means. For decisions about word meaning, he still has only his pocket lexicon, and it doesn't contain nonce senses for Bombeck's *electric typewriter* or *stereos*, or for any other contextual expression. Adding lexical rules won't help. As I will show later, there would have to be an indefinitely large number of lexical rules to account for the possible senses of contextual expressions. So when the king needs to make choices based on meaning, once again he can become stranded (as with *Our electric typewriter got married*), or be led to the wrong castle altogether (as with *The neighbour swore at our electric typewriter who got married*). The king's lexicon could never be large enough to parse nonce sense.

Lexical access

Aside form the heuristic and ATN traditions, there has been much experimental work on 'lexical access', the process by which people 'access' words in their mental lexicons in long-term memory. A significant problem for lexical access is ambiguity. Consider *The man was not surprised when he found several bugs in the corner of his room* (from Swinney, 1979). When a listener hears *bugs*, he has to access *bug* in his mental lexicon. There, it has been assumed, he will find, say, two senses—'insect' and 'listening device'. He must decide which of these two senses was intended on this occasion. In a long series of experiments, it has been shown that resolving ambiguities takes time and effort (for reviews, see Clark and Clark, 1977; Fodor, Bever and Garrett, 1974; Foss and Hakes, 1978).

Lexical access of ambiguous words has almost invariably been characterized in accordance with the sense-selection assumption. Fodor, Bever, and Garrett (1974) talked about listeners 'selecting among readings of ambiguities'. Foss and Hakes (1978) argued that the findings by Foss and Jenkins (1973) demonstrated 'that listeners always retrieve both interpretations of an ambiguous word from the mental lexicon and that the context then operates to help them decide among them'. Clark and Clark (1977) characterized the same findings in similar language: 'When listeners encounter an ambiguous construction, they compute multiple readings'; 'using the context, listeners then attempt to select the most plausible reading'.

These characterizations of lexical access ought to be inadequate for contextual expressions, and they are. Consider Swinney's (1979) 'post-decision model' of lexical access. As Swinney put it, his results 'support the existence of a postaccess decision process which acts to select a single meaning from those originally and momentarily accessed for involvement in further processings'. Listeners access all senses of *bug*, and only then do they use the context to select one from among them. Swinney argued against a 'prior decision model' in which listeners use the semantic context to guide lexical access—in which, for example, listeners use the prior context to access or activate only one sense of *bug*, the one appropriate to context.

Taken literally, the post-decision model has to fail on contextual expressions. When it encounters *porch* in *George managed to porch the newspaper yesterday*, it will have no lexical entries to access for the verb *porch* and hence no senses to select from. The model predicts that the verb *porch* cannot be understood. If lexical rules are added to derive the possible senses of the verb *porch* from the noun *porch*, the model has the opposite problem. The lexical rules, as I will show later, generate an indefinitely large number of possible senses for the verb *porch*. No model with a finite memory could access all of these senses, as the post-decision model requires, nor could any model select from among the possible senses in a finite amount of time.

With certain revisions, however, the post-decision model might be made to work. It would proceed roughly as follows. When it encountered the verb *porch*, it would access the senses for *porch* in the lexicon. These would consist entirely of *conventional* senses, such as the noun senses 'covered entrance to a house' and 'verandah'. The model would then select from among these senses the one on which it could create the intended verb sense. After all, the meanings of the verb *porch* are based on the meanings of the noun *porch*. How the model would decide which noun sense is the right one, and how it would create the intended verb sense from it, however, are matters that go beyond the assumptions of the post-decision model. They will be considered later. Yet with these emendations, the model could retain its most important property, the selection process that correctly predicts that ambiguous words should be difficult to understand.

Since virtually all current models of lexical access make the sense-selection assumption either explicitly or implicitly, they are open to the same criticisms as the post-decision model. These include the models of Cairns and Kamerman (1975), Forster (1976), Garrett (1978), MacKay (1970), Marslen-Wilson and Welsh (1978), Morton (1969, 1970), and Tanenhaus, Leiman, and Seidenberg (1979), to name just a few. Like the post-decision model, many of these models could perhaps be revised to handle contextual expressions. But these revisions would require a view of parsing that is rather different from the one on which all these models are based.

Sentence meanings

Most traditional parsers and models of lexical access are based on what I will call the *traditional view of sentences*, a view that has been held, explicitly or implicitly, by most investigators in these areas. According to this view, the grammar of English, including its lexicon of conventional senses for words, morphemes, and idioms, assigns readings to each string of words. If a string of words is assigned one or more senses that aren't semantically anomalous, as *Stereos are a dime a dozen* would be, it is adjudged to be a sentence of English. The readings assigned to it are called its *sentence meanings*. If a string of words can *not* be assigned any such readings, and *Our electric typewriter got married* could not be, it is adjudged *not* to be a sentence of English. In one terminology (e.g., Chomsky, 1965; Katz, 1964), it would be marked as 'ungrammatical'. In another terminology (e.g., Katz, 1972, 1977), it would be marked 'semantically anomalous'. For convenience, I will adopt the first terminology.

The traditional view of sentences, then, is this. What the speaker meant in uttering a string of words is identical to, or derivable from, one of its sentence meanings—one of the readings assigned to it by the grammar. What a speaker could mean by *Stereos are a dime a dozen* is derivable from its only sentence meaning 'Phonographs are very common'. And what a speaker could mean by *Our electric typewriter got married* is nothing, since this string of words yields no sentence meanings—since it isn't assigned any sensible readings by the grammar. (It might be treated as a 'semi-sentence', à la Katz (1964); I will discuss this possibility later.) This view of sentences fails to do justice to six of Bombeck's eight utterances. For those that are grammatical, what Bombeck meant is *not* derivable from any of the sentence meanings. For those that are not grammatical, Bombeck meant something that has no chance of being derived from a sentence meaning, since these strings don't *have* any sentence meanings.

Put in its strongest form, what a speaker means bears no direct relation to the sentence meanings assigned to it in the traditional view of sentences. Grammaticality as defined in this view bears no direct relation to ordinary language use. Consider these four types of utterances:

(1) A grammatical sentence used in one of its sentence meanings (like Bombeck's *We've just had a streak of bad luck*).
(2) A grammatical sentence used in something other than one of its sentence meanings (like her *Stereos are a dime a dozen*).
(3) An ungrammatical string used in one of the semantically anomalous readings assigned to it by the grammar (like *The rock cried*, meaning 'the stone wept', a made-up example).
(4) An ungrammatical string used in something other than one of the semantically anomalous readings assigned to it by the grammar (like Bombeck's *Our electric typewriter got married*).

According to the traditional view of sentences, speakers should only use sentences of type (1). These alone have sentence meanings from which one can derive the speaker's meaning. If a speaker used sentences of types (2), (3), or (4), they would be judged as mistakes. But as I argued earlier, cases

(2) and (4) are ubiquitous. Furthermore, they sound perfectly natural. They are as much a part of ordinary English as case (1) is.

So long as parsers and models of lexical access are based on the traditional view of sentences, they will be inadequate. They will miss every utterance that falls into cases (2) and (4), misparsing the first and failing to parse the second. They will fail to handle a significant portion of what ordinary people consider to be ordinary English.

TWO FALSE SOLUTIONS

Two mechanisms that have been proposed and at first appear able to handle contextual expressions are the lexical rule and the semi-sentence. Yet neither of these mechanisms offers any real solution. It is important to see why.

Lexical rules

The way a traditional parser would handle innovations is via *lexical rules* or via Miller's (1978) *construal rules* (which for present purposes are indistinguishable from lexical rules). Imagine that such a parser is confronted with the word *chartreuseness*, which is not in its lexicon. Nevertheless, the parser has in its lexicon the adjective *chartreuse*, the suffix *-ness*, and the following lexical rule:

X_{Adj} + *-ness*$_N$ has these and only these possible senses:

(a) state of being X
(b) quality of being X
(c) condition of being X
(d) instance of the state of being X
(e) instance of the quality of being X
(f) instance of the condition of being X

With this rule, the parser will generate six senses for *chartreuseness* and then select from among the readings just as it would for a word already in its lexicon. The difference between the listed senses and the senses generated by such a rule is that whereas the first are actual, the second are virtual. Otherwise, the two types of senses function in the same way.

For lexical rules to be sufficient, they must be capable of generating every sense of every innovation. For words like *chartreuseness*, which are assigned a fixed number of senses, lexical rules do a good job. But similar rules have been offered for other types of expressions. For denominal verbs, McCawley (1971) suggested a rule that would go like this (where Φ_V is the null verb-forming suffix of what is technically called 'zero-derivation'):

X_N + Φ_V has this (and other) possible senses:

(a) causes an X to hold onto

With this rule, *John nailed the note to the door* is interpreted as 'John caused a nail to hold the note onto the door.' The rule would also capture the sense of *to tack, to scotchtape, to glue*, and many other like verbs. Green (1974) suggested another lexical rule for denominal verbs to handle cases like *to hammer*:

(b) as by using X (on) in the usual manner, for the purpose for which it was designed

For denominal verbs like *to porch*, as in *George managed to porch the newspaper yesterday*, there would also be this rule:

(c) cause to be on an X

Rule (c) would also generate the right senses for *to bench a player, to beach the boat*, and *to shelve the books*.

The problem is that for contextual expressions, there would have to be an indefinitely large number of such rules (Clark and Clark, 1979). Take Ed's remark to me about Max, the man with the teapot compulsion: *He teapotted a policeman*. As a denominal verb, *teapot* would add still one more lexical rule to the list for $X_N + \Phi_V$, namely:

(d) rub the back of the leg of with an X

But since there are an unlimited number of other nonce senses that *teapot* (or any other novel denominal verb) could have had, there must also be an unlimited number of such rules for generating them. There would have to be rules like these:

(e) strike on the back of the leg of with an X

(f) rub on the back of the ankle of with an X

(g) scratch on the back of the neck of with an X

(h) turn into an X

And so on indefinitely. That is, since *teapot* can have a different nonce sense in each different situation, it would have to have associated with it a different lexical rule for each situation. This undermines the reason for having lexical rules in the first place.[2]

The same problem arises for all other contextual expressions. In the domain of compound nouns, Levi (1978) has proposed lexical rules too. She has argued that all the possible interpretations of novel noun–noun compounds like *horse chair* are captured in the following twelve rules:

$X_N + Y_N$ has these and only these possible senses:

(a) Y that causes X (as in *tear gas*, 'gas that causes tears')

(b) Y that is caused by X (as in *birth pains*, 'pains caused by a birth')

(c) Y that has X (as in *apple cake*, 'cake that has apples')

(d) Y that X has (an in *lemon peel*, 'peel that lemons have')

(e) Y that makes X (as in *honeybee*, 'bee that makes honey')

(f) Y that X makes (as in *daisy chains*, 'chains that daisies make')

(g) Y that uses X (as in *voice vote*, 'vote that uses voices')
(h) Y that is X (as in *soldier ant*, 'ant that is a soldier')
(i) Y that is in X (as in *field mouse*, 'mouse that is in a field')
(j) Y that is from X (as in *olive oil*, 'oil from olives')
(k) Y that is for X (as in *wine glass*, 'glass for wine')
(l) Y that is about X (as in *tax law*, 'law about taxes')

An important feature of these rules is that they rely on only nine different predicates—*cause, have, make, use, be, in, for, from,* and *about*—which appear to capture the major relations that hold in English compound nouns.

It is easy to see that these rules don't capture the *full* meanings of innovative compound nouns. Consider Downing's (1977) example of a friend being asked to sit at the *apple-juice seat*, meaning 'the seat in front of which a glass of apple-juice had been placed'. Levi would probably generate the meaning of this compound by Rule (i), giving it the analysis 'seat that is located with respect to apple juice'. This paraphrase, however, hardly does justice to the meaning that was intended. It may offer a broad category into which the nonce sense fits, but it doesn't explicate the nonce sense itself. The intended sense would require a lexical rule something like this:

(i') Y in front of which there had been X.

This rule would be a subrule of Levi's rule (i), and there would be other subrules as well. If Downing, and Kay and Zimmer (1976), are correct, novel compound nouns like this have an indefinitely large number of possible senses, and so there would be an indefinitely large number of such subrules. The problem with Levi's rules is that they are stated at an arbitrary level of abstraction; therefore, they capture an arbitrary amount of the sense of compound nouns like *apple-juice seat*. It is an illusion that there are only a small number of lexical rules. At the correct level, there would have to be an indefinitely large number of them (see also Carroll and Tanenhaus, 1975).[3]

For other categories of contextual expressions, the problem is just as serious. With eponymous verbs like *do a Napoleon*, there are a few broad categories of senses one might identify:

do a X_{PN} has these possible senses:

(a) do what X did (as in *I want you to do a Napoleon for the camera*)
(b) do what was done to X (as in *They did a Manhattan to downtown San Francisco*)
(c) do what happens in X (as in *The horse did a Pimlico*, or *a Derby, down the road*)

And so on. Yet the same problem arises as before. These categories are hardly fine enough to capture, for example, what a photographer meant in saying *I want you to do a Napoleon for the camera*. *Do a Napoleon* here doesn't mean 'do what Napoleon did' but 'pose with your hand inside the flap of your coat, as Napoleon did'. We would need a specific lexical rule to distinguish this meaning from other possible meanings of *do a Napoleon*, as in *The lawyer was asked to do a Napoleon for the legal system of Oahu, Hitler tried to avoid doing a Napoleon in attacking Russia in the winter*, and any number of other uses. Once again, the number of lexical rules is indefinitely large. No parser could manage that many.

Lexical rules, therefore, cannot solve the problems of nonce sense. Certain types of nonce sense, as in expressions like *chartreusness*, may be adequately captured with lexical rules, but other types are not. The types not captured are the contextual expressions. For them, there would have to be a new lexical rule for each new sense in which they were used. For them, lexical rules solve nothing at all.

Semi-sentences

Bombeck's utterance *Our electric typewriter got married* is an example *par excellence* of what in the traditional view of sentences would be called an 'ungrammatical string'. Yet Katz (1964) has argued, and many others have followed suit, that a string of words doesn't have to be grammatical to be comprehensible. For this purpose, Katz has proposed a theory of *semi-sentences*. *Our electric typewriter got married* would be such a semi-sentence in that it is a string of words that isn't grammatical but can nevertheless be understood. Katz seems to have intended his theory to account for utterances like Bombeck's, for he offered as examples of semi-sentences *It happened a grief ago, I have over-confidence in you*, and *He expressed a green thought*, all of which contain innovations, although they don't all sound as natural as Bombeck's utterance.

The basic idea of the theory is this. When a listener is confronted with a semi-sentence, he associates with it a set of fully grammatical sentences called the *comprehension set*. The members of the comprehension set, in effect, enumerate all the possible meanings the semi-sentence could have. For *Man bit dog*, the comprehension set would be as follows:

Man bit dog is associated with this comprehension set:

(a) The man bit the dog
(b) The man bit a dog
(c) A man bit the dog
(d) A man bit a dog

Sentences (a) through (d) each represent a possible reading of the semi-sentence *Man bit dog*. They are created by what Katz called *transfer rules*, although he offered only the sketchiest examples of what these rules might look like (see also Ziff, 1964). Katz's claim is that the listener's understanding of a semi-sentence is 'nothing other than his understanding of the sentences in the set with which the semi-sentence is associated' (p. 411), namely the comprehension set. The proposal is as ingenious as it is simple. It reduces the problem of understanding semi-sentences to the problem of understanding grammatical sentences, a problem that will presumably submit to the scientist's scalpel sooner or later.

For this scheme to work, the comprehension set associated with each semi-sentence must contain a finite number of sentences. As Katz put it (p. 411), 'the notion *sufficient structure to be understood* is analyzed as *structure that suffices to permit a semi-sentence to be associated with a finite number of sentences, each of which is a possible reading of the semi-sentence*' (all emphases are Katz's). This follows from Katz's general approach to semantics, which is to be able to enumerate for each sentence a finite number of readings. He wants to be able to do the same for each semi-sentence too. The requirement in this case has further value, according to Katz, since it distinguishes genuine semi-sentences like *Man bit dog*, which will have a finite comprehension set, from nonsense strings like *The saw cut his sincerity*, which will not.

Katz's theory of semi-sentences, however, cannot work for contextual expressions. The reason is simple. As I noted earlier, *Max teapotted a policeman* has an indefinitely large number of potential readings. It could mean 'rub the back leg of with a teapot', 'rub the back of the shoulder of with a teapot', 'rub both ankles and knees of with a teapot', and so on indefinitely. In the theory of semi-sentences, each of these readings would correspond to a grammatical sentence in the comprehension set associated with the ungrammatical string of words *Max teapotted a policeman*. Thus, the comprehension set for *Max teapotted a policeman* is not finite in size. But because the set isn't finite, the theory predicts that *Max teapotted a policeman* isn't comprehensible—that it doesn't have 'sufficient structure to be understood'. This prediction, of course, doesn't hold. For the same reasons, the theory also predicts as incomprehensible Bombeck's *Our electric typewriter got married*, Herb Caen's *I stopped in Perry's for a quick crab*, and *The photographer asked me to do a Napoleon for the camera*. These predictions obviously don't hold either.

The most glaring defect in this theory is that it requires each string of words to have a finite number of readings in order to be comprehensible. By definition, contextual expressions have an indefinitely large number of potential readings and, as we have seen, are taken to be a regular part of English. Conclusion: contextual expressions cannot be accounted for by the theory of semi-sentences.

A less obvious defect goes as follows. The basic assumption of the theory is that each meaning of a semi-sentence can be *precisely* and *completely* captured by at least one grammatical sentence of English. This assumption isn't really warranted. The *raison d'être* for the use of many contextual expressions is to say things that could not be said any other way. Consider *Harry managed to Richard Nixon the tape of his conversation with the chief of police.* Here *Richard Nixon* cannot be paraphrased by *erase*, or *erase with malice and conniving*, or *erase as Richard Nixon would have done*, without losing something of the original. The point of the utterance is to compare Harry's actions and motives, in all their complexity, with those of Nixon, and no paraphrase can do that comparison justice. If this is so, a theory that requires each reading of every sentence with a contextual expression to correspond exactly to a sentence of English is doomed to failure.

An additional complication for the theory of semi-sentences is that it would require two distinct accounts of contextual expressions—one for those found in 'ungrammatical strings', the true semi-sentences, and another for those found in 'grammatical sentences'. Let us return to Bombeck's *Stereos are a dime a dozen*, in which *stereos* is being used innovatively to mean 'people who have stereos'. The sentence itself is grammatical on Katz's criteria, but the meaning Bombeck intended is not one of those enumerated by Katz's rules of composition. *Stereo* is being used in something other than one of its conventional meanings. Since the theory of semi-sentences would not identify this utterance as a semi-sentence, it would need a new device to identify *stereo* as a contextual expression and to compute its possible meanings. It would interpret *electric typewriter* via the theory of semi-sentences and *stereos* via some other theory, when they ought to be handled by the same process. The underlying problem is that sentences that contain contextual expressions are sometimes grammatical and sometimes not. It was pure accident that *stereos* appeared in a grammatical sentence and *electric typewriter* didn't. As noted earlier, any theory that ties the interpretations of these expressions to grammaticality seems misdirected from the start.

In the end, the theory of semi-sentence fails for much the same reasons that lexical rules do. It is easy to see that Katz's transfer rules, which generate the comprehension sets for semi-sentences, have the same consequences as lexical rules. Both require the meanings of a sentence to be denumerable and to be definite in number. Both run afoul of contextual expressions, whose possible meanings are neither denumerable nor definite in number.

INDIRECT USES OF LANGUAGE

Contextual expressions, one could say, are ordinary words that are used indirectly for momentary purposes. Another type of expression that might be described this way are indirect illocutionary acts. When I use *It's raining out* to remind my wife to take her umbrella, or to request her to close the window, or to offer to bring her a raincoat, I am using an ordinary sentence indirectly for some momentary purpose. This analogy gives a clue to the approach I will take to parsing utterances with contextual expressions. I will argue for a general procedure for computing indirect uses of language. To see how the process might work, I will first review some characteristics of indirect illocutionary acts.

Indirect illocutionary acts

By now there is a good deal known about indirect illocutionary acts (Gordon and Lakoff, 1971; Sadock, 1974; Searle, 1975; Morgan, 1978; Bach and Harnish, 1979; Clark, 1979; Cohen and Perrault, 1979). There is even something known about how they are understood (Clark and Lucy, 1975; Clark, 1979; Clark and Schunk, 1980; Munro, 1977; Schweller, 1978; Gibbs, 1979). I will concentrate on five of their properties in order later to show a correspondence with contextual expressions. As my example, I will use the sentence *Do you know what time it is?*

1. *Simultaneous meanings.* In the right situation, I could use *Do you know what time it is?* to ask someone to give me the time. In this instance, I would mean two distinct things at once. I would mean 'I ask you whether or not you know the time', a yes/no question, which I will call the *direct meaning*. I would also mean 'I request you to tell me the time', a request, which I will call the *indirect meaning*. Genuine cases of indirect illocutionary acts all involve more than one meaning—a direct meaning and one or more indirect meanings.

2. *Logical priority.* In my use of *Do you know what time it is?*, the yes/no question is *logically prior* to the request. I perform the request by performing the question, and not vice versa. It is this that allows us to call the question the direct meaning and request the indirect meaning.

3. *Literalness of direct meaning.* The direct meaning of my utterance—the yes/no question—follows pretty directly, via conventions of language, from the literal meaning of the sentence *Do you know what time it is?* This is one reason that the speaker's direct meaning is often called the literal meaning. In the traditional view of sentences at least, one needs to know little more, often nothing more, than the sentence's literal meaning to know the speaker's direct meaning.

4. *Non-denumerability of indirect meanings.* Given the sentence *Do you know what time it is?*, there is no way to enumerate the possible indirect meanings a speaker could have in uttering it. In the right circumstances, I could use it to mean 'Please tell me the time', 'Don't forget your dentist appointment', 'You are late in getting home again', 'The party started an hour ago', and so on indefinitely. Whereas the direct meaning is pretty well determined by the literal meaning, if any, of the sentence uttered, the indirect meaning could be any number of things.

5. *Contextuality of indirect meanings.* What I mean indirectly in saying *Do you know what time it is?* is critically dependent on the circumstances in which I utter it. In particular, if I directed this utterance at my wife, I would expect

her to recognize that I was indirectly performing an illocutionary act that I had good reason to believe on this occasion she could readily compute uniquely on the basis of our mutual knowledge such that my direct meaning played some role. Thus, unlike my direct meaning, which is tied pretty closely to the literal meanings of the sentence I uttered, my indirect meaning is often completely dependent on my wife's recognition of my plans and goals in using that sentence on this occasion.

Indirect uses in contextual expressions

The five characteristics of indirect illocutionary acts bear a close, though not exact, resemblance to five corresponding characteristics of contextual expressions. I will illustrate these for the denominal verb in my earlier example *Max teapotted a policeman*.

1. *Simultaneous meanings*. In the circumstances I outlined earlier, Ed used the verb *teapot* to mean 'rub the back of the leg of with a teapot'. Without stretching things too much, we could say that Ed used the word *teapot* to do two things at the same time. He used it directly to denote teapots—those pots for brewing tea. He also used it indirectly to denote the act of rubbing someone's leg with a teapot. In other words, we can speak of a direct and an indirect meaning of the word *teapot*. These correspond, though are not exactly equivalent, to the direct and indirect meanings in my use of *Do you know what time it is?*

2. *Logical priority*. In uttering *teapot*, Ed denoted the rubbing of someone's leg with a teapot by denoting teapots themselves. That is, he performed the act of denoting the leg rubbing by performing the act of denoting teapots, and not vice versa. The direct use is logically prior to the indirect use, and this too corresponds to what happens in indirect illocutionary acts.

3. *Literalness of direct use*. Ed's direct use of *teapot*—his denoting of teapots—follows directly from one of the conventional meanings of the noun *teapot*. This is analogous to my direct meaning in uttering *Do you know what time it is?* which follows fairly directly from the literal meaning of this sentence. In both instances, the direct use of the expression is tied to the conventional meaning of the expression in the language.

4. *Non-denumerability of indirect uses*. There is no way of enumerating the possible indirect uses a speaker could have in using the noun *teapot* as a verb. This is a defining characteristic of contextual expressions: for something to be a contextual expression, its possible senses must be *non-denumerable*. Once again, there is a parallel with indirect illocutionary acts.

5. *Contextuality of indirect uses*. What Ed meant indirectly in using the word *teapot* is critically dependent on the circumstances in which he uttered it. Indeed, Eve V. Clark and I (Clark and Clark, 1979) have argued that there is a convention that governs how a speaker and addressee coordinate their use and understanding of innovative denominal verbs. The convention goes as follows:

The innovative denominal verb convention. In using an innovative denominal verb sincerely, the speaker means to denote:

(a) the kind of situation
(b) that he has good reason to believe
(c) that on this occasion the listener can readily compute
(d) uniquely
(e) on the basis of their mutual knowledge
(f) in such a way that the parent noun denotes one role in the situation, and the remaining surface arguments of the denominal verb denote other roles in the situation.

Here 'situation' is a cover term for states, events, and processes.

Once again, there is a striking parallel with indirect illocutionary acts, which also depend on a convention that refers to reasonableness in context, ready computability, uniqueness, and mutual knowledge of the speaker and addressee. The point at which indirect speech acts differ from denominal verbs is in condition (f). With denominal verbs, condition (f) makes reference to the conventional meaning of the parent noun (e.g., *teapot*) and the meanings of its surface arguments (e.g., *Max, a policeman*). With indirect illocutionary acts, condition (f) would make reference to the speaker's direct meaning, so that it perhaps would read 'in such a way that the speaker's direct meaning establishes a necessary condition for the speaker's indirect meanings'. In both cases, condition (f) makes reference to the direct use of the expression uttered, whether it is the whole sentence *Do you know what time it is?* or just the single noun *teapot*.

The parallels between indirect illocutionary acts and contextual expressions suggest that it ought to be possible to extrapolate from models of the understanding of indirect illocutionary acts to models of the understanding of contextual expressions. But how are indirect illocutionary acts understood? For an answer, we must consider the notion of *goal hierarchy*.

Goal hierarchies

In interpreting complete utterances, listeners ordinarily infer a hierarchy of goals they believe the speaker is trying to attain, and they interpret the speaker's current utterance as a step in the plan for attaining one or more of those goals. This is the conclusion of a number of studies of indirect illocutionary acts—studies of their formal properties (Gordon and Lakoff, 1971; Searle, 1975), studies of their understanding in natural settings (Clark, 1979; Merritt, 1976; Goffman, 1976), and studies of simulations in computer models (Cohen, 1978; Cohen and Perrault, 1979).

Consider an example from a study of my own on indirect requests for information (Clark, 1979, Experiment 5). I had an assistant call up restaurants in the Palo Alto, California, area and ask whether they accepted credit cards. Two of the questions she asked were these:

Do you accept American Express cards?

Do you accept credit cards?

(I will abbreviate these as *American Express cards?* and *Credit cards?*) My assistant would call up a restaurant and ask either *American Express cards?* or *Credit cards?*, listen to the restaurateur's reply, say *thank you*, and hang up. The interest was in the replies and what they implied about the restaurateur's interpretation of what my assistant had asked.

The restaurateurs apparently imputed my assistant with a different hierarchy of goals depending on which question she asked. For *American Express cards?*, the hierarchy was something like this:

(1) She wants to decide whether or not to patronize this restaurant.
(2) She wants to know how to pay for her meal.
(3) She wants to know if she can pay with the credit cards she owns, which consists (almost certainly) of just the one card, the American Express card.
(4) She wants to know if the restaurant accepts American Express cards.

The question *Do you accept American Express cards?* directly reflects the lowest subgoal, number (4), but an answer to it would also fulfil the next higher subgoal, (3). Hence the only thing the restaurateurs needed to do, if they did accept American Express cards, was say *Yes* or *Yes, we do*. Indeed, 100 per cent of the restaurateurs who were asked this question and were able to say *yes* gave this response. They interpreted the utterance as a direct question and nothing more.

For *Credit cards?*, the restaurateurs inferred a very different hierarchy of goals. It was something like this:

(1) She wants to decide whether or not to patronize this restaurant.
(2) She wants to know how to pay for her meal.
(3) She wants to know if she can pay with one of her credit cards, which (probably) include most or all of the major credit cards.
(4) She wants to know if any of the credit cards acceptable to the restaurant are among the cards she owns.
(5) She wants to know if the restaurant accepts credit cards.

The question *Do you accept credit cards?* directly reflects the lowest subgoal, number (5), and hence the restaurateurs should ordinarily answer that question. In fact, 84 per cent of those who could have answered in the affirmative did. However, the caller's reason for asking the question couldn't have been just to attain subgoal (5), since that isn't sufficient information for subgoal (4), the next goal up in her hierarchy. She must be indirectly requesting the restaurant's list of acceptable credit cards. In fact, 46 per cent of the restaurateurs inferred the next higher subgoal and gave the caller a list of the credit cards they accepted. They took *Credit cards?* to be both a direct question and an indirect request for the list of credit cards they accepted.

The contrast between *American Express cards?* and *Credit cards?* is striking, for the two questions are identical except for the object of the verbs. It was the content of those noun phrases that forced the restaurateurs to infer very different goals and to construe *American Express cards?* as merely a direct question while construing *Credit cards?* as both a direct question and an indirect request for a list of acceptable credit cards. Conclusion: it is the hierarchy of imputed goals that enables listeners to decide whether or not the speaker is performing an indirect speech act, and if so, what it is.

There are two main sources of evidence that listeners are intended to use in inferring the speaker's hierarchy of goals. The first is the utterance itself. It is pertinent whether or not a request is made via a conventional form like *Can you tell me the time?* or via a non-conventional form like *Do you happen to have a watch on you?*, whether or not a request is accompanied by *please*, and whether or not other 'linguistic' factors are present (Clark, 1979). The second source of information is the remainder of the knowledge, beliefs, and suppositions that the speaker and listener share—called their *common ground* (Clark and Carlson, 1981). It was pertinent in the experiment reported earlier that my assistant was telephoning the restaurateur at his restaurant and not at his home, that the restaurant's telephone number was public and intended to be used for enquiries about the restaurant's services, and that other such 'non-linguistic' factors were present (Cohen and Perrault, 1979). Listeners generally cannot, nor are they expected to, infer the speaker's hierarchy of goals accurately without consulting both the utterance and their common ground.

INTENTIONAL PARSERS

Parsing an utterance can itself be viewed as reconstructing a hierarchy of goals. When a friend tells me *Julia is a virologist*, I realize that he has specific goals. In making an assertion, he wants me to believe, and to recognize that he believes, some state of affairs. One of his subgoals is to specify that belief. However, he can't do this in one step. First, he designates the thing the belief is about, which he does via the word *Julia*. Next, he predicates what it is that he believes about that object, which he does with the words *is a virologist*. He makes this predication in two parts. He specifies that the predication is equative and that it holds at the time of utterance by using the word *is*. He specifies the predication proper with the words *a virologist*. This, too, is accomplished in two steps. He specifies the category of interest with the word *virologist*, and he indicates that he is predicting membership in that category with the word *a*.

Described this way, my friend is performing a series of acts, each of which accomplishes a subgoal along the path to getting me to believe that Julia is a virologist. Furthermore, he performs each of these acts by means of a constituent in the utterance. With the noun phrase *Julia*, he is performing the act of referring to Julia. With the verb phrase *is a virologist*, he is performing the act of predicating something about her. With the verb *is*, he is performing the act of designating the predication as one of equation and the time it holds as the present. With the noun phrase *a virologist*, he is designating the predication as membership of the category of virologists. With the noun *virologist*, he is designating the concept of virologist as the category being predicated. And with the article *a*, he is specifying that the predication is membership in the so-designated category. All I have done here is expand on Strawson's (1959) and Searle's (1969) notions of reference and predication as speech acts.

These acts, with their goals, form a hierarchy that corresponds to the hierarchy of constituents in the sentence. In uttering *a* and in uttering *virologist*, my friend has two separate goals. But these are subgoals in his uttering the construction that contains those two constituents, the noun phrase *a virologist*. Likewise, his goal in uttering *is* and his goal in uttering *a virologist* are both subgoals in his act of predicating with the construction of *is a virologist*. And finally, his goal in referring with *Julia* and his goal in predicating with *is a virologist* are subgoals of the 'propositional act' that he performs with the whole utterance (see Searle, 1969), the act in which he specifies the proposition to be believed, that Julia is a virologist. In general, the speaker's hierarchy of goals in uttering a sentence appears to have a many-to-one mapping onto the constituents of that sentence.

Parsing, therefore, can be viewed not simply as dividing a sentence into its parts—the traditional view—but as identifying the goals and subgoals the speaker had in uttering each part of the sentence, what I will call the *intentional view of parsing*. These two views might at first appear to be simple variants of one another—'notational variants' to use the jargon of the field—but they are not. In the traditional view, the aim of the parser is to yield one of the (traditional) sentence meanings, presumably the one the speaker intended. In the intentional view, the aim is to yield the speaker's intentions in uttering what he did. And for utterances such as Bombeck's *Our electric typewriter got married* and *Stereos are a dime a dozen*, the speaker's intentions are not derivable from any of the (traditional) sentence meanings.

These two views lead to different parsing implementations. Traditional parsers have been designed to rely totally, or almost totally, on the linguistic properties of the utterance. But recall that in order to understand indirect requests, listeners use *two* main sources of information. The first is the utterance itself, as in traditional parsers. The second is the speaker's and addressee's common ground. The speaker's intentions can be inferred only through the *joint* use of these two sources. What is missing in traditional parsers is any systematic reference to the common ground.

Even though common ground has not been welcomed at the front door of traditional parsers, it has sometimes been sneaked in through the servants' entrance. Many parsers have been designed to parse discourse and therefore to resolve anaphoric reference (see Charniak, 1972; Lockman and Klappholz, 1980). In the sequence *Ned went home for dinner; he got lost on the way*, such a parser would identify Ned as the referent of *he*, and the route Ned was taking home as the referent of *the way*. These two referents are resolved in the second utterance mostly by referring to that part of the reader's and writer's common ground that was established in the first utterance. Indeed, some utterances could not be parsed correctly without knowledge of such referents. In the sequence *Ned was introduced to a woman at the party; he whispered to the woman that he knew*, the phrase *that he knew* would be identified as the complement of *whispered*, since *the woman* presumably refers to the woman Ned just met, who couldn't possibly be 'a woman that he knew'. Here again, the first utterance establishes certain common ground that is used in parsing the second.

Yet in resolving reference, as in these two examples, traditional parsers exploit common ground only to a limited extent. A genuine intentional parser would need to consult the common ground systematically. Nowhere is this easier to demonstrate than in the parsing of contextual expressions.

Contextual expressions

With contextual expressions, reference to the speaker's and addressee's common ground is mandatory. When Bombeck wrote *Our electric typewriter got married*, she intended us readers to make use of the fact that she had just written about roommates and their possessions. She intended us to use this common ground in conjunction with the fact that she was uttering the phrase *our electric typewriter* and was predicating of its referent, that it got married. She intended us to use both sources of information in inferring her hierarchy of goals.

As an illustration of such a goal hierarchy, consider Ed's assertion to me *Max teapotted a policeman*. Ed's goal hierarchy in using *teapot* might be described as follows:

(1) Ed wants me to recognize that he is using *teapot* to denote 'rub the back of the leg with a teapot'.
(2) Ed wants me to recognize that what he is asserting Max did to a policeman is the kind of action that he has good reason to believe that on this occasion I can readily compute uniquely on the basis of our common ground in such a way that teapots play one role in the action, Max is the agent, and the policeman is the patient.
(3) Ed wants me to recognize that he is using *teapot* to denote teapots.

I am to infer the lowest subgoal, (3), from the fact that Ed is using the noun *teapot.* I am to infer the next subgoal up, (2), from the fact that he is using it as a verb too. And I am to infer the highest subgoal, (1) from the computations required in (2).

The main addition to traditional parsers is subgoal (2). For contextual expressions, the speaker always intends the addressees to compute the novel meaning on the spot. As subgoal (2) makes clear, this requires the listener to consult the speaker's and addressee's common ground. But when does this addition need to be made? If *teapot* were actually in the lexicon as a verb with the sense 'rub the back of the leg of with a teapot', then I wouldn't have needed any goals but (1). I wouldn't have had to go beyond the conventional meaning listed in the lexicon. In Ed's utterance, it was partly because the verb *teapot* wasn't in my lexicon that I was forced to infer Ed's subgoals (2) and (3).

It need not work this way. Subgoals such as (2) and (3) need not be forced by a semantic anomaly. In Bombeck's *Stereos are a dime a dozen*, the noun *stereos* has a proper noun lexical entry meaning 'phonographs' that makes perfectly good sense in the sentence Bombeck uttered. Nothing in Bombeck's sentence *per se* forces us to look for a non-conventional interpretation. So subgoals such as (2) and (3) must always be present—or almost always. Virtually every word can be used with a nonce sense in at least some situations. It is just that in conventional cases, the computation required to capture these goals is trivial.

To see how this would work, imagine Arlene telling Bill *Stereos are dime a dozen*, by which she means 'Phonographs are very common'. The goal hierarchy for *stereos* would look like this:

(1) Arlene wants Bill to recognize that she is using *stereos* to denote phonographs.
(2) Arlene wants Bill to recognize that what she is asserting are a dime a dozen are the kind of thing that she has good reason to believe that on this occasion he can readily compute uniquely on the basis of their common ground such that this kind of thing has something to do with phonographs.
(3) Arlene wants Bill to recognize that she is using *stereos* to denote phonographs.

The use of *stereos* by Bombeck, in contrast, would have this goal hierarchy:

(1′) Bombeck wants us to recognize that she is using *stereos* to denote people who possess phonographs.
(2′) Bombeck wants us to recognize that what she is asserting are a dime a dozen are the kind of thing that she has good reason to believe that on this occasion we can readily compute uniquely on the basis of our

common ground such that this kind of thing has something to do with phonographs.

(3′) Bombeck wants us to recognize that she is using *stereos* to denote phonographs.

The difference between Arlene's and Bombeck's uses of *stereos* lies entirely in goals (1) and (1′). For Arlene, the kind of object she intended to have something to do with phonographs are phonographs themselves. The relation to be computed in subgoal (2) is the identity relation. For Bombeck, the kind of object she intended to have something to do with phonographs are people who possess phonographs, a more complicated and indirect relation.

The point is that Bill, in parsing Arlene's utterance, can't ever be content with subgoal (1) alone. He can't ever know for certain, ahead of time, which words Arlene is using in their conventional senses, and which she is using in contextually innovative senses. How does he know she isn't using *stereos* to mean what Bombeck meant, or to mean something still different, as in *Nowadays monaural recordings are rare, but stereos are a dime a dozen*? Only by consulting his and her common ground can Bill recognize when *stereo* is to be construed as the identity relation and when as something else. Subgoals such as (2) and (3) are implicitly required wherever there is the possibility of a nonce sense.

Intentional parsers create senses and don't just select them from a predetermined list of senses. Subgoal (2) is an injunction to listeners to use the common ground, plus certain guidelines about rationality, to create the sense the speaker intended. The listeners need never have thought of the intended sense before, either as a sense of the word the speaker uttered or, for that matter, as a sense of any word they have ever heard before. When we first hear *The photographer asked me to do a Napoleon for the camera*, most of us have never before thought of 'tuck one's hand into one's vest' as the sense for any word, let alone for *do a Napoleon*. We create this sense for this occasion alone. It is truly a nonce sense.

How intentional parsers can be made to work, and how they create the speaker's intended senses, are questions for future research. The argument is that parsers need to take account of the speaker's intentions in every step they take. Their goal must be to create the speaker's hierarchy of intentions in uttering the words he uttered on that occasion.

CONCLUSION

Nonce sense is a genuine puzzle for traditional parsers, for they don't even recognize its existence. It exists all right. In everyday speech, it is ubiquitous, sometimes taking shapes that are easily recognized as innovative expressions, but other times sounding no different from anything else in language. Parsers can no longer pretend that nonce sense doesn't exist. They must make sense of nonce sense or fail.

The failure of traditional parsers to handle nonce sense, I have argued, reveals a fundamental problem in their design. Traditional parsers generally do their job without regard to who uttered the sentence or to whom. Any concern that they show for the interlocutors is indirect and limited, as when they identify referents from the surrounding discourse. Yet understanding ultimately requires listeners to decide what the speaker meant—to reconstruct the speaker's intentions, or goals, in uttering what he did. The traditional assumption is that parsers need to take account of these intentions only after they have parsed the sentence uttered. The existence of nonce sense makes this assumption untenable. Parsers must worry about the speaker's intentions at every turn.

The current conception of parsing needs revision. It ought to be thought of not as the analysis of the sentence uttered, but as the analysis of the speaker's intentions in uttering the sentence. All that counts in the end is the speaker's meaning, even if it is only for the nonce.

NOTES

1. Novel metaphors are one such type. They appear to pose the same problems for traditional parsers as do the contextual expressions I will discuss, and they appear to require the same new view of parsing that I will propose. In this paper, however, I will stick to expressions that are ordinarily considered non-metaphorical.
2. Lexical rules (a) through (c) may appear to be more general than rules (d) through (h), but this isn't really so. Rules (a) through (c) are incomplete. *To glue a stamp to an envelope* ordinarily means something more specific than rule (a)'s 'cause glue to hold a stamp to an envelope'. There are many extraordinary ways of causing glue to do this that wouldn't be called 'gluing'. Rule (a) is really a collapsing over a large set of related rules. This point is made later for the compound *apple-juice chair*. The broad types that do emerge in denominal verbs, and in other constructions, do so not because they reflect lexical rules, but because they reflect general categories of experience, of encyclopedic knowledge (see Clark and Clark, 1979, pp. 787–92).
3. Jespersen (1942, p. 137) said this about noun compounds: 'Compounds express a relation between two objects or notions, but say nothing of the way in which the relation is to be understood. That must be inferred from the context or otherwise. Theoretically, this leaves room for a large number of different interpretations of one and the same compound, but in practice ambiguity is as a rule avoided.'

ACKNOWLEDGEMENTS

The writing of this chapter was aided by Grant MH-20021 from the National Institute of Mental Health. I am indebted to Lawrence W. Barsalou, Eve V. Clark, and Robert Schreuder for comments on and discussion of several points in this paper.

REFERENCES

Bach, K., and Harnish, R. M. *Linguistic Communication and Speech Acts*. Cambridge, Mass.: M.I.T. Press, 1979.

Bever, T. G. The cognitive basis for linguistic structures. In J. R. Hayes (Ed.), *Cognition and the Development of Language*. New York: Wiley, 1970.

Borkin, A. Coreference and beheaded NPs. *Papers in Linguistics*, 1970, **5**, 28–45.

Cairns, H. S. and Kamerman, J. Lexical information processing during sentence comprehension. *Journal of Verbal Learning and Verbal Behavior*, 1975, **14**, 170–179.

Carroll, J. M., and Tanenhaus, M. K. Prolegomena to a functional theory of word information. In R. E. Grossman, L. J. San, and T. M. Vance (Eds), *Papers from the Parasession on Functionalism*. Chicago: Chicago Linguistics Society, 1975.

Charniak, E. Towards a model of children's story comprehension. *MIT Artficial Intelligence Laboratory TR-266*, 1972.

Chomsky, N. *Aspects of the Theory of Syntax*. Cambridge, Mass.: M.I.T. Press, 1965.

Clark, E. V., and Clark, H. H. When nouns surface as verbs. *Language*, 1979, **55**, 797–811.

Clark, H. H. Inferring what is meant. In W. J. M. Levelt and G. B. Flores d'Arcais (Eds), *Studies in the Perception of Language*. New York: Wiley, 1978.

Clark, H. H. Responding to indirect speech acts. *Cognitive Psychology*, 1979, **11**, 430–477.

Clark, H. H., and Carlson, T. B. Context for comprehension. In J. Long and A. Baddeley (Eds), *Attention and Performance IX*. Hillsdale, N.J.: Lawrence Erlbaum Associates, 1981.

Clark, H. H., and Clark, E. V. *Psychology and Language*. New York: Harcourt Brace Jovanovich, 1977.

Clark, H. H., and Lucy, P. Understanding what is meant from what is said: A study in conversationally conveyed requests. *Journal of Verbal Learning and Verbal Behavior*, 1975, **14**, 56–72.

Clark, H. H., and Marshall, C. R. Definite reference and mutal knowledge. In A. K. Joshi, B. Webber and I. Sag (Eds), *Elements of Discourse Understanding*. Cambridge: Cambridge University Press, 1981.

Clark, H. H., and Schunk, D. H. Polite responses to polite requests. *Cognition*, 1980, **8**, 111–143.

Cohen, P. R. *On knowing what to say: Planning speech acts*. Unpublished doctoral dissertation. University of Toronto, 1978.

Cohen, P. R., and Perrault, C. R. Elements of a plan-based theory of speech acts. *Cognitive Science*, 1979, **3**, 177–212.

Downing, P. A. On the creation and use of English compound nouns. *Language*, 1977, **53**, 810–842.

Fodor, J. A., Bever, T. G., and Garrett, M. F. *The Psychology of Language: An Introduction to Psycholinguistics and Generative Grammar*. New York: McGraw-Hill, 1974.

Fodor, J. A., and Garrett, M. F. Some reflections on competence and performance. In J. Lyons and R. J. Wales (Eds), *Psycholinguistics Papers*. Edinburgh: Edinburgh University Press, 1966.

Forster, K. I. Accessing the mental lexicon. In R. J. Wales and E. Walker (Eds), *New Approaches to Language Mechanisms*. Amsterdam: North-Holland, 1976.

Foss, D. J., and Hakes, D. T. *Psycholinguistics: An Introduction to the Psychology of Language*. Englewood Cliffs, N.J.: Prentice-Hall, 1978.

Foss, D. J., and Jenkins, C. M. Some effects of context on the comprehension of ambiguous sentences. *Journal of Verbal Learning and Verbal Behavior*, 1973, **12**, 577–589.

Frazier, L., and Fodor, J. D. The sausage machine: A new two-stage parsing model. *Cognition*, 1978, **6**, 291–325.

Garrett, M. F. Word and sentence perception. In R. Held, H. W. Liebowitz, and H. L. Teuber (Eds), *Handbook of Sensory Physiology*, Vol. 8: *Perception*. Berlin: Springer-Verlag, 1978.

Gibbs, jr. R. W. Contextual effects in understanding indirect requests. *Discourse Processes*, 1979, **2**, 1–10.

Gleitman, L. R., and Gleitman, H. *Phrase and Paraphrase: Some Innovative Uses of Language*. New York: W. W. Norton, 1970.

Goffman, E. Replies and responses. *Language in Society*, 1976, **5**, 257–313.

Gordon, D., and Lakoff, G. Conversational postulates. In *Papers from the Seventh Regional Meeting, Chicago Linguistic Society*, 1971.

Green, G. M. *Semantics and Syntactic Regularity*. Boomington: Indiana University Press, 1974.

Jesperson, O. *A Modern English Grammar on Historical Principles,* Vol. 7: *Morphology*. Copenhagen: Ejnar Munksgaard, 1942.

Kaplan, R. Augmented transition networks as psychological models of sentence comprehension. *Artificial Intelligence*, 1972, **3**, 77–100.

Kaplan, R. A general syntactic processor. In R. Rustin (Ed.), *Natural Language Processing*. Englewood Cliffs, N.J.: Prentice-Hall, 1973(a).

Kaplan, R. A multi-processing approach to natural language. In *Proceedings of the First National Computer Conference*. Montvale, N.J.: AFIPS Press, 1973(b).

Kaplan, R. *Transient processing load in sentence comprehension*. Unpublished doctoral dissertation. Harvard University, 1975.

Kaplan, R., and Bresnan, J. W. Lexical-functional grammar: A formal system for grammatical representation. In J. W. Bresnan (Ed.), *The Mental Representation of Grammatical Relations*. Cambridge, Mass.: M.I.T. Press, 1982.

Katz, J. J. Semi-sentences. In J. A. Fodor and J. J. Katz (Eds), *The Structure of Language: Readings in the Philosophy of Language*. Englewood Cliffs, N.J.: Prentice-Hall, 1964.

Katz, J. J. *Semantic Theory*. New York: Harper and Row, 1972.

Katz, J. J. *Propositional Structure and Illocutionary Forces*. New York: Crowell, 1977.

Kay, P., and Zimmer, K. *On the semantics of compounds and genitives in English*. Paper presented at the Sixth Annual Meeting of the California Linguistics Association, San Diego, California, May 1976.

Kimball, J. Seven principles of surface structure parsing in natural language. *Cognition*, 1973, **2**, 15–47.

Kimball, J. Predictive analysis and over-the-top parsing. In J. Kimball (Ed.), *Syntax and Semantics*, Vol. 4. New York: Academic Press, 1975.

Lees, R. B. The grammar of English nominalizations. *International Journal of American Linguistics*, 1960, **26**, Publication 12.

Levi, J. N. *The Syntax and Semantics of Complex Nominals*. New York: Academic Press, 1978.

Li, C. N. *Semantics and the structure of compounds in Chinese*. Unpublished doctoral dissertation. University of California, Berkeley, 1971.

Lockman, A., and Klappholz, A. D. Toward a procedural model of contextual reference resolution. *Discourse Processes*, 1980, **3**, 25–71.

McCawley, J. M. Prelexical syntax. In R. J. O'Brien (Ed.), *Linguistic Developments of the Sixties—Viewpoints for the Seventies. Monograph Series on Languages and Linguistics*. Georgetown University, 1971, **24**, 19–33.

MacKay, D. G. Mental diplopia: Towards a model of speech perception. In G. B. Flores d'Arcais and W. J. M. Levelt (Eds), *Advances in Psycholinguistics*. Amsterdam: North-Holland, 1970.

Marslen-Wilson, W. D., and Welsh, A. Processing interactions and lexical access during word-recognition in continuous speech. *Cognitive Psychology*, 1978, **10**, 29–63.

Merritt, M. W. On questions following questions (in service encounters). *Language in Society*, 1976, **5**, 315–357.

Miller, G. A. Semantic relations among words. In M. Halle, J. Bresnan, and G. A. Miller (Eds), *Linguistic Theory and Psychological Reality*. Cambridge, Mass.: M.I.T. Press, 1978.

Miller, G. A., and Chomsky, N. Finitary models of language users. In R. D. Luce, R. R. Bush, and E. Galanter (Eds), *Handbook of Mathematical Psychology*, Vol. 1. New York: Wiley, 1963.

Morgan, J. L. Two types of convention in indirect speech acts. In P. Cole (Ed.), *Syntax and Semantics*, Vol. 9: *Pragmatics*. New York: Academic Press, 1978. 261–280.

Morton, J. The interaction of information in word recognition. *Psychological Review*, 1969, **76**, 165–178.

Morton, J. A functional model for memory. In D. A. Norman (Ed.), *Models of Human Memory*. New York: Academic Press, 1970.

Munro, A. *Speech act understanding in context*. Unpublished doctoral dissertation. University of California at San Diego, 1977.

Nunberg, G. The non-uniqueness of semantic solutions: Polysemy. *Linguistics and Philosophy*, 1979, **3**, 143–184.

Sadock, J. M. *Towards a Linguistic Theory of Speech Acts*. New York: Academic Press, 1974.

Schweller, K. G. *The role of expectation in the comprehension and recall of direct and indirect requests*. Unpublished doctoral dissertation. University of Illinois, Champaign-Urbana, 1978.

Searle, J. R. *Speech Acts*. Cambridge: Cambridge University Press, 1969.

Searle, J. R. Indirect speech acts. In P. Cole and J. L. Morgan (Eds), *Syntax and Semantics*, Vol. 3: *Speech Acts*. New York: Academic Press, 1975.

Strawson, P. F. *Individuals*. London: Methuen, 1959.

Swinney, D. A. Lexical access during sentence comprehension: (Re)consideration of context effects. *Journal of Verbal Learning and Verbal Behavior*, 1979, **18**, 645–659.

Tanenhaus, M. K., Leiman, J. M., and Seidenberg, M. S. Evidence for multiple stages in the processing of ambiguous words in syntactic contexts. *Journal of Verbal Learning and Verbal Behavior*, 1979, **18**, 427–440.

Wanner, E., and Maratsos, M. An ATN approach to comprehension. In M. Halle, J. Bresnan, and G. A. Miller (Eds), *Linguistic Theory and Psychological Reality*. Cambridge, Mass.: M.I.T. Press, 1978.

Winograd, T. *Understanding Natural Language*. New York: Academic Press, 1972.

Woods, W. A. Transition network grammars for natural language analysis. *Communications of the A.C.M.*, 1970, **13**, 591–606.

Woods, W. A. An experimental parsing system for transition network grammars. In R. Rustin (Ed.), *Natural Language Processing*. Englewood Cliffs, N.J.: Prentice-Hall, 1973.

Ziff, P. On understanding 'understanding utterances'. In J. A. Fodor and J. J. Katz (Eds), *The Structure of Language: Readings in the Philosophy of Language*. Englewood Cliffs, N.J.: 1964.

Zimmer, K. E. Some general observations about nominal compounds. *Working papers on language universals*, Stanford University, 1971, **5**, C1–C21.

Zimmer, K. E. Appropriateness conditions for nominal compounds. *Working papers on language universals*, Stanford University, 1972, **8**, 3–20.

Subject Index

Access files, 26
  of the mental lexicon, 171
Active and passive sentences, 251
  comprehension, 5
Adjectives, effect on noun phrase
    processing, 178
Algorithms and heuristics in processing
    language, 3
Allomorphs, 82
Ambiguity,
  lexical, 310
  structural, 297
    in language comprehension, 193
  systematic, 65–67
Analytic philosophy, 228
Anaphora, 275
Anaphoric reference, 329
Aphasia, 144
Artificial intelligence, 3
  approach to language, 115
  models of language comprehension, 3,
    273
Attentional component in lexical access,
    172
Augmented Transition Networks (ATN),
    21, 160, 165, 309
Automatic processing
  in language understanding, 122
  of sentences, 122
  of syntactic information, 78
Autonomy
  hypothesis of language understanding,
    171
  of grammar, 138
  of syntax, 3, 4 ff
  position in language comprehension
    processes, 4 ff

Base word lexical entry, 65
Beheaded noun phrases, 302

Binding, 126, 146
  and coindexing, 159
Bottom-up processing of language, 193 ff
Bridging inferences, 275, 293–294

Cascade model, 195
Categorical grammar, 128
Category monitoring technique, 17
Causal chain and story structure, 35
Causative verbs, 53–54
Clausal hypothesis, 14, 15, 159, 214
  strong and weak form of, 16, 18
Clause
  boundaries effects on lexical access,
    214
  boundary and sentence
    comprehension, 214
  functional, 16
  segmentation, 14
  structural, 16
  subordinate and main, 117
Cleft
  and pseudo-cleft sentences, 255
  sentences, 243, 253
Clefting as a focusing device, 256
Clicks, 14–15
  studies, 12
Cohort model of word recognition, 27,
    28, 88, 104, 163, 213
Comment, 273
Competence and performance, 158
Complementizing verbs, 72
Completeness, high *vs.* low *c.* sentences,
    17
Complex sentences, strategies for
    understanding, 307
Componential analysis of meaning, 160
Compositionality principle in Frege, 162
Compound nouns, 302–314
Comprehension

333

difficulty for sentences, 288
set, 316
strategies, 196
time for sentences, 287
Consciousness and presupposition, 246
Conceptual domain, 31
Constancy hypothesis in language
    comprehension, 4 ff
Context
    adjectives as context to noun, 178–179
    effects in lexical decision, 30
    expression, 300 ff, 306
    facilitation in lexical access, 172
    facilitation of, in word recognition, 27
    focus, 261–262
    indirect uses of contextual expression,
        320
    use of, in word recognition, 11, 197
    interpretation, 119, 164
Contrast and focus, 241 ff
Cross-modal priming paradigm, 66

Deep
    and surface linguistic structure, 2, 460
    sentoids, 14
    structure in segmentation, 14
Deferred reference, 302
Definite and indefinite articles, 230
Definiteness and indefiniteness, 228
Denominal
    adjectives, 303
    nouns, 303
    verbs, 303, 314
Denotation (of nouns), 302
Derivational
    complexity of nouns, 61
    suffixes, 61–63
    theory of complexity, 2, 136, 162
Derived verbs, 43 ff
Dichotic presentation of speech, 29
Direct
    and indirect meaning, 319
    meaning, 22, 319
    requests, 23 ff
Discourse
    comprehension, 32 ff, 203 ff
    connected, 277
    processing, 1
    topic, 273 ff
        and reference resolution, 279
    understanding, 215
Disruptions in oral reading, 200

Domain of reference, extended, 282

Ear location shift technique, 13, 17
Eponymous
    adjectives, 304
    verbs, 303, 315
Eye fixation
    recording during sentence
        comprehension, 7–8
    text comprehension and, 215
Eye-voice span, 202 ff

Factitivity, 48–49
Factive
    presupposition, 45
    verbs and adjectives, 48–49
Filters, 125
Fluent
    oral reading, deviations from, 205
    restoration, 11
    speech, 203
    speech restoration, 213
Focus
    and clefting, effects of on language
        comprehension, 255
    and presuppositions in declarative
        sentences, 242
    and reference, 283
    presupposition and contrastiveness,
        241 ff
    shift and topic, 284
Freezes, 24
Frequency effect in lexical access, 57, 171
Frozen idiomatic phrases, 68 ff

Garden path, 10
Germanic, verb forms in, 91–93
Gestalt psychology, 21
Given-new, 225–228, 274
    and lexicon, 228
    and prosodic information, 228
    and sentence understanding, 236–237
    and syntactic information, 228
Goal hierarchy
    in parsing, 326 ff
    in understanding indirect illocutionary
        acts, 321
Grammar, 136
    and processing, 136 ff
Grammatical
    rules, application of, 164
    ungrammatical word order and, 107
Grammaticality, 312

Homographs, 29
Homophones, 29

Idiomatic
  meaning, 24
  phrases, 67
    in context, 68
Idioms, 22, 67 ff
  literal interpretation of, 68 ff
Implicature, conventional, 161
Indefinite
  and definite articles and sentences
      perception, 254
  reference, 229
Indexical expressions, 300
Indirect
  illocutionary acts, 318 ff
  meaning, 23 ff, 319
  nouns, 302
  requests, 23
  uses in contextual expressions, 320
Inferences
  and deduction, 161
  in story comprehension, 35
Infinitive complement, 308
Inflection, 59
  and word perception, 84–85
  and word representation, 83 ff
  use of, in lexical access, 214
Information
  sources in comprehension, 294
  use of in reading, 200 ff
Inner speech, 232
Innovative
  denominal verbs, 301
  donominal verb convention, 321
Integration hypothesis, 178
  of context effect, 181 ff
  of lexical activation, 173
Intentional expressions, 300 ff
Intentional parsers, 323 ff
Interactive models
  of language comprehension, 6 ff, 197,
      273
  of language processing, 4, 134 ff, 213
  properties of, 9, 195 ff
Intonation, 118
Intrinsic meaning, 45

Knowledge
  sources, use of in reading, 206 ff
  use of in processing, 275

Language
  comprehension as an interactive
      process, 9 ff
  perception, 225 ff
    and language comprehension, 117
  production, 225 ff
  understanding, 135
Left-to-right processing, 83
Lemmas in the mental lexicon, 105
Levels
  of language understanding, 115
  of processing, interaction among, 195
  of understanding, 149
Lexical
  activation, 31–32, 172
  ambiguity, 29, 45, 159
  ambiguity and lexical access, 46
  complexity, 43 ff, 72–75
    and memory performance, 55
  decision, 44, 85, 170
    cross modal, 30
    phoneme triggered, 170
    variables affecting time of, 44
  decomposition, 84–86, 130
  entries for suffixed and prefixed words,
      61–62
  complex, 44
  negatives, 50–53
  processing, 170
  representation, 82–83
    of ambiguous words, 43 ff
    of idiomatic expressions, 43 ff
    of morphologically complex words,
        73–75
  retrieval, 27
  rules, 213 ff
  simplicity, 44
  stress errors, 62
  violations, effect of, on reading, 201 ff
Lexical access, 26 ff, 81–82, 105 ff, 171,
    310
  activation models of, 26 ff
  file of, 171
  inhibition in, 172
  interaction of bottom-up and top-down
      information in, 213
  models, 310–311
  post-lexical decision and, 30
  search models of, 26 ff
  stems and, 86 ff
  time course of, 188–189
  use of inflection in, 214

use of semantic information for, 212
Lexicon, mental, 297
  organization of, 104 ff
Limited capacity assumption, 13
Linear
  ordering of a structure, 125, 154–155
  structure of language, 135
Linguistic
  categories, 228 ff
  communication, 226 ff
  context, 169 ff
  pragmatic features, 244
Literal and idiomatic interpretation,
    68–69
  meaning, 319
    extraction of, 279
    of sentences, 25, 272, 273
Localization of speech, 15
Location shift model, 171
Locus of context effects, 103, 109
Logical
  form of sentences, 120
  form of an utterance, 115 ff
  priority in contextual expressions, 320
    in indirect illocutionary acts, 319
Logogen model, 27, 28

Macro
  -rules in story comprehension, 34
  -structure and discourse
    understanding, 215
    of stories and reading, 209
    of texts, 34
Meaning
  integration and text comprehension,
    215
  multiple access to, 29
  selective access to, 29
Memory
  and language processing, 146
  load and sentence processing, 215
  search, 290 ff, 294
  for sentences, 12
Mental
  lexicon, 43, 81
    organization of, 170
  representation of sentences, 133
    of speech, 133 ff
    of words, 44
Message
  processing, 7
  processor, 171

Metaphor, 22, 24 ff, 328
  comprehension in sentence
    understanding, 201
  two stages processing of, 24–25
Minimal attachment principle, 20
Mispronunciation detection, 11
Misunderstanding of language, 117
Model theoretic semantics, 132
Modularity of components in language
    processing, 138
Monitor
  category, 17
  ear shift, 13
  latencies for phonemes, 11
  phoneme, 12, 27, 29
  rhyme, 17
  tasks, 17
  word, 10
Montague grammar, 159, 160
Morpheme
  pre-morphological analysis, 89
  theories about, 82
Morphological
  complexity, 56–65
  decomposition, 43, 62
    in word recognition, 107
  judgements, errors in, 98–101, 103,
    104
    speed of, 96–104
  rules, 125
  same–different judgements, 96–104
Morphology, verb, 89–92
Multiple meanings, 54
Multi-word units, 67

Naming and lexical access, 28
Natural language processing, 282
Negation and processing difficultiy, 50
Negative
  implications, 45
  sentence, processing of, 50 ff
Negatives
  explicit, implicit and affixed, 51
  explicit *vs.* implicit, verbs and
    adjectives, 51–52
Neuroliguistics, 165
Non-denumerability, 301
  of direct use in contextual expressions,
    320
  of indirect uses in contextual
    expressions, 320
Non-linear representation, 144

Non-literal meaning, 22 ff
Non-predicting adjectives, 304
Non-words processing, 210

Obligatory *vs.* optional processing of
 syntax in language comprehension, 7
On-line
 measures of story comprehension, 215
 processing, 3, 145
 vs. off-line models, 3
Oral
 production, 200
 reading, 193 ff, 200
 reading performance, 200 ff

Parallel processing, 139
 of language, 123
 of linguistic information, 195
Parser, 20–22, 162
 heuristic, 307
 sausage machine, 165
 traditional, 307 ff
Parsing, 19, 273, 297 ff
 computation in, 326
 constituents in, 308
 of contextual expressions, 325 ff
 traditional *vs.* intentional, 324 ff
Passive sentences comprehension, 5
Passivization in English, 236
Past participles, 90–91, 108
Perceptual
 errors in sentence comprehension, 261
 information and lexical access, 197
 salience and sentence understanding,
  258
 segmentation, 14
 strategies, 19
  in language comprehension, 3
 unit of language comprehension, 14
Peripheral word list, 107–108
Phoneme monitor, 29
 monitoring, 44
  effect of verb structure, 71
  following idiomatic phrases, 69
  latencies, 176
  lexical ambiguity, 46
  task, 27, 170, 174
Phoneme restoration, 10–11
Phonetic
 attributes, 135
 features, 159
  matrix, 161

interpretation of speech, 156
prominence, 352
representation, 127
structure, assignment of, 118
 of an utterance, 115
Phonological
 rules, 125
 structures, 162
 theory of Chomsky and Halle,
  126–127
Phrase, preliminary phrase packager,
 20
Picture inspection time, 257
Plausibility, conditions in sentence
 understanding, 261
Polish, oral reading in, 214
Polysemy, 29
 and lexical access, 46 ff
Possessiveness, 302–303
Post-access decisions, 69
Post-decision model of lexical access,
 310–311
Pragmatic
 analysis in language comprehension,
  271, 273
 information in sentence
  comprehension, 9
 plausibility in sentence comprehension,
  6
 presuppositions, 134
Pragmatics, 225 ff
 and psycholinguistics, 262
Pre- and post-lexical decision processes,
 310–311
Prefixed words, 56–59
 and lexical access, 85
Prefixes and word recognition, 84
Pre-morphological analysis, 108
Presuppositions, 228
Primary processing, 290
Prime
 effect in lexical access, 176
 word, relation to target, 186
Procedural semantics, 290
Processing
 automatic, 196
 during language understanding, 12
 load, 275
 memory and semantic facilitation, 183
 skills, 196
 stages in language understanding, 137
  ff

Production times of words in sentences, 210 ff
Productive morphology, 63–65
Propositional
    content of a sentence, 119
    phrases, 308
    structure, 308
        of stories, 33–35
Prosodic information, 126
Prosody in utterances, 240–241
Pseudo-cleft sentences, 243, 253
Psychological
    predicate, 232
    reality of linguistic constructs, 2
    subject, 231

Quantifiers, 133

Rapid serial visual presentation
    technique, 6
Reading
    comprehension during, 193 ff
    disruptions, 213
    time, 276
    times for stories, 215
Real-time processing, 2, 138
Reference,
    definite nominal, 291
    denotion and, 133
    domain, 286
    extended domain of, 279
    fixed vs. shifting, 300
    meaning and, 273
    memory search and, 290
    nominal, 291, 292, 298
    pronominal, 291
    resolution, 273, 276, 290, 293
Referential
    analysis, secondary, 293
    coherence and reading, 215–216
Representation
    of episodes, 282
    of phonetic attributes, 123
Restorations, fluent, during reading, 201
Restrictive verbs and adjectives, 50
Reversible
    passives, 5
    sentences, 5
Rewrite rules, 34
Rhyme monitoring technique, 17
Russian folktales, 32

Sausage machine, 20

Scenario and mental representation, 281
Scheme for interpretation in language
    comprehension, 194
Scope
    determination, 143 ff
    of quantifiers, 151
    syntactic and semantic, 150
Scripts, 282
Search model of lexicon, 171
Selection restrictions, 49–50
    and meaning, 45
Semantic
    activation, 31
    ambiguity, 66
    anomaly in sentence, effects of, on
        reading, 202 ff
    complexity, 45 ff
    context and word recognition, 29
    cues in sentence comprehension, 8
    decomposition, 53–56
        and processing difficulty, 55
    distance, effect of, in sentence
        processing, 186
    facilitation, 169 ff, 177
        decay of, 183, 184 ff, 187
        duration of, 188
        effects in clause understanding, 18
        locus of, 188
        time course of, 182 ff, 187–188
        word recognition and, 169 ff
    indetermination, 298
    integration, 6
        in sentential context, 181
    interpretation, 173
    memory, 33
    network, 171
    priming, 28 ff, 135
    processing, 121
    relatedness among lexical items, effects
        of, 177
    representation, theories of, 161
    violations, effects of, on reading, 200 ff
Semantically complex words, processing
    of, 48
Semi-sentences, 312, 313 ff, 316 ff
Senses
    conventional, 302
    fixed and shifting, 300 ff
    idiomatic, 302
    selection assumption, 307
    shifting vs. fixed, 300

Sentence
  comprehension, 1, 196 ff, 214
    and autonomy of processing, 212
    processing stages in, 271
    stage approach to, 271 ff
    time, 51
    two-stage models of 272
  meaning, 311
    construction of, 196
  picture verification and cleft and
      pseudo-cleft sentences, 257
  processing and pragmatic operations,
      273
  structure supervisor, 20
Set theoretical structures, 133 ff
Sequential processing, 139, 163
Shadowing, 170
Shorthand expression, 302
Short-term memory for sentences, 17,
    146–147
Simultaneous meanings in contextual
    expression, 320
Slips of the ear, 155 ff
Spectrographic analysis of speech
    production, 204
Speech
  act, 272
  perception, 118
  repairs during shadowing, 13
  shadowing, 10, 13, 200
    and word restoration, 209
Spoken
  language understanding, 250
  word recognition model, 88
Spreading activation, 170
Stem
  and inflections, 83
  morphemes, priming of, 86–87
  -organized lexical representation,
      57–58
  -organized lexicon, 60, 104–110
Story
  grammars, 32
  understanding, 215
  Strategies, processing, 307
Stress
  and syntactic boundaries within idioms,
      69–70
  contrastive, 238, 240
  final, 239
  initial of speech signal, 124
Stroop task, 46, 195

Structural representations of language,
    123
Structure of texts and comprehension, 35
Subject and predicate, 274
Subordinate clause, 17
  in Dutch, 95, 109
Suffixed words, 59–63
Superstrategy, parsing, 21
Suprasegmental features, 118
Surface structure, 124
  in parsing, 307–309
SVO sentences, 249
Syntactic
  ambiguity, 66
  and semantic information, use of, in
      lexical access, 206
  category, 125
  complexity, 65–72, 116
  computation during language
      comprehension, 4 ff
  formatives, 135
  structure, 120
    of an utterance, 117
  violations, effects of, on reading, 200 ff

Temporal
  order of processing, 144
  ordering, 139
Text
  analysis, 32
  base, 34
  linguistics, 32
  processing, 183
  structure, 261
Theme of a sentence, 233
Theme–rheme, 233, 235
Time compressed speech, 47
Top-down
  and bottom-up information in language
      comprehension, 9, 157, 193
  effects in language comprehension,
      194
Topics, 273 ff
  and comment, 235, 273
  and mental representation, 280
  effects in language processing, 271 ff
  global vs. local, 274
  shift, 286
Topicalization, 234, 236
Trace theory of movement rules, 160
Transfer rules, 316
Transformational grammar, 2 ff

Transitional error probabilities, 14
Translation programs in A.I., 7
Two-factor of context effects, 172

Ubiquity, 305
Understanding
  of indirect illocutionary acts, 321
  partial, 118
Ungrammatical and grammatical strings,
  318
  strings, 312, 316

Vague reference, 193
Verb
  and object, semantic relation between,
    181
  morphology, 89–92
    in Germanic languages, 92
  subcategorization, 71–72
Verbal prefixes, 91–107
Verbs, strong and weak, 91–93, 106
Violation of factual information, effects
  of, on reading, 201

Word-by-word
  hypothesis of sentences processing,
    214–215
  processing, 163
Word
  and constituent order, 231
  formation errors, 62
  innovation, 301
  naming, 30
  order, 248–249
    and sentence information, 233
  probe techniques, 15
  production latency, 204 ff
  recognition, 1, 169 ff, 193
    and context, 195
    point, 64
    recognition point, 88
  restoration during reading, 209
  roots and word recognition, 88
  superiority effect, 193
Working memory, 16, 291
  and clause processing, 18
  during sentence processing, 146
  for stories, 34